Economic Scenes

Economic Scenes

Theory in Today's World

Fifth Edition

Stanley L. Brue

Professor of Economics
Pacific Lutheran University

Donald R. Wentworth

Professor of Economics
Pacific Lutheran University

Prentice Hall, Englewood Cliffs, New Jersey 07632

Library of Congress Cataloging-in-Publication Data

Brue, Stanley L. (date)
   Economic scenes : theory in today's world / Stanley L. Brue,
Donald R. Wentworth. — 5th ed.
     p. cm.
   Includes index.
   ISBN 0-13-223934-5
   1. Economics. I. Wentworth, Donald R. II. Title.
HB171.5.B75 1992
330—dc20   91-20650
                                      CIP

Acquisitions editor: Whitney Blake
Editorial/production supervision and
   interior design: Colby Stong
Copy editor: Peter Reinhart
Cover design: Patricia Kelly
Prepress buyer: Trudy Pisciotti
Manufacturing buyer: Robert Anderson

Printed in the United States of America
10 9 8 7 6 5 4 3 2 1

ISBN 0-13-223934-5

Prentice-Hall International (UK) Limited, *London*
Prentice-Hall of Australia Pty. Limited, *Sydney*
Prentice-Hall Canada Inc., *Toronto*
Prentice-Hall Hispanoamericana, S.A., *Mexico*
Prentice-Hall of India Private Limited, *New Delhi*
Prentice-Hall of Japan, Inc., *Tokyo*
Simon & Schuster Asia Pte. Ltd., *Singapore*
Editora Prentice-Hall do Brasil, Ltda., *Rio de Janeiro*

CONTENTS

PART IV: MACROECONOMICS

PART V: INTERNATIONAL ECONOMICS

PREFACE

The purpose of this book is to help people understand major economic concepts and relationships. To accomplish that goal, we have built *Economic Scenes* on a foundation consisting of several premises. First, we believe that if the goal is to help people understand *major* economic principles and relationships, then the text should be confined to a *limited* number of economic concepts. These major ideas should be explained, not simply stated.

In keeping with this premise, we have written 22 chapters, each spotlighting a predetermined set of interrelated micro- or macroeconomic concepts and terms. The economic concepts are listed at the beginning of the chapter in which they are covered, enabling the reader to know what to look for as the chapter unravels. The spotlight on the selected concepts is bright and remains fixed for some time—long enough, we hope, to allow the reader to reach and surpass the critical threshold level of understanding before being swept on to new ideas.

Our second premise is that economic concepts and relationships cannot be fully understood and appreciated when they are divorced from the multitude of human activity from which they are derived. Economics is the study of the actions and interactions of millions of individual people trying to achieve their diverse objectives.

Each chapter is a window into a scene involving individual and group behavior. We have abandoned the typical approach, which is to present abstract economic models *and then* provide a few applications. Instead, we focus on the behavior, case situation, or issue as a *means of formulating* the abstract principles that the situations exemplify. The "economic scenes" contain the stuff of which economic principles are made.

A third supposition underlying the text is that variety has pedagogical value. The chapters form a collage of presentations — each somewhat unorthodox, but all sharing the basic characteristics described in the preceding paragraphs.

A fourth premise is that people who take their subjects too seriously are often simply taking *themselves* too seriously. We have tried to maintain a sense of perspective in that regard. Occasional humor and comic relief prove to be useful tools to hold students' attention in class lectures and discussion. We believe that they can perform a similar function in a textbook.

Our final premise is that texts should be flexible. The past editions of *Economic Scenes* were used in a variety of courses in several differing ways. Many instructors employed the book as a core text in one-term courses for noneconomics majors. Others used *Scenes* as a supplement to standard hardbounds in major or nonmajor courses and in one- or two-term classes. Still others combined the book with one or more paperbacks. It is apparent from this pattern that those who found the book useful were able to find a good fit for it in their courses.

This edition of *Economic Scenes* is thoroughly revised and updated. Some of the more important changes are as follows:

- Chapter 22, which is new to this edition, addresses the economics of exchange rates and international finance. The focus of Chapter 21 is now limited to comparative advantage and a new discussion of tariffs, quotas, and nontariff trade barriers.
- The formal macroeconomic analysis has been bolstered in several ways. First, greater discussion is given to the measurement of gross national product and the price level in Chapter 16. Second, the aggregate demand–aggregate supply model in that chapter is developed more systematically and completely, including discussion of factors that shift the curves. Third, exchange rate and net export considerations are now discussed in relationship to fiscal policy (Chapter 16) and monetary policy (Chapter 18). Finally, the new classical perspective on macroeconomics is given more attention than in the previous edition (Chapters 16 and 18).
- International economics is incorporated throughout this edition, both in the micro- and macroeconomics. Just a few of the many global topics in *Economic Scenes* include diamond and oil cartels, import competition, the U.S.-Canadian Free Trade Agreement, strategic trade policy, budget deficits and trade deficits, and intervention by central banks in the international currency market.
- An appendix on graphs has been added to Chapter 1 to help students get off to a good start in the course.
- The discussion of public choice theory in Chapter 11 has been expanded.
- In Chapter 7 the implicit costs of Harvey and Pop Cornwell's caramel corn business are pointed out and explained.
- Numerous quantitative problems have been added to the end-of-chapter questions. These "workbook-style" problems require students to manipulate data, and this process should help them gain a better understanding of the basic economic principles.

Numerous other modifications, deletions, and additions are scattered throughout this edition. In making all these changes, we have endeavored to maintain the style and accessibility that has set *Economic Scenes* apart from standard textbooks.

Several individuals have aided us over the years in writing and revising

Economic Scenes. Specifically, we wish to thank the following people who have offered criticisms, suggestions for improvement, or encouragement. These individuals, none of whom should be held accountable for the final outcome, are Ernest Ankrim, Pacific Lutheran University; James Aylsworth, Lakeland Community College; John Bockino, Suffolk County Community College; M. Neil Browne, Bowling Green State University; Lester O. Bumas, Polytechnic University, New York; Thomas F. Cargill, University of Nevada–Reno; Kenneth W. Clarkson, University of Miami; Charles Frodigh, Hudson Valley Community College; Roger Goldberg, Ohio Northern University; Douglas A. Greenly, Moorhead State University; Louis H. Henry, Old Dominion University; Bill Huerter, Northwest Technical Institute, Iowa; Robert Jensen, Pacific Lutheran University; Phillip Larsen, North Central Technical Institute, Wisconsin; Ken Leonard, Seattle Pacific University; Keith Lumsden, Heriot-Watt University, Scotland; W. R. Massey, Santa Rosa Junior College; Campbell R. McConnell, University of Nebraska–Lincoln; Richard F. Measell, Saint Mary's College, Indiana; Emil Meuer, Xavier University of Louisiana; Marlen Miller, Pacific Lutheran University; James M. Rigterink, Polk Community College; Stephen L. Shapiro, University of North Florida; David Vinje, Pacific Lutheran University; James N. Wetzel, Virginia Commonwealth University; and Klaus H. Wolf, Middlebury College.

We also wish to thank the people and corporations listed on the credits pages for their permission to reproduce photos and cartoons. Finally, we desire to thank the many instructors throughout the country who have used this book in their classes over the past 16 years. Their decisions to adopt the book account for its continued success.

CREDITS

1

TEN-THREE COMBINATION ONCE TO THE SIDE

Economic Reasoning

Concepts and Terms Examined in This Chapter

1. Economic Terminology
2. Fallacy of Composition
3. Cause-and-Effect Fallacy
4. Bias and Preconception, Oversimplification
5. The Economic Perspective

As you pursue the study of economics, you will discover that there are two requirements for engaging in sound economic analysis. First, you must be able to think logically and systematically, carefully avoiding common errors in economic reasoning. Second, you must employ an economic perspective in your thinking process. This perspective will alert you to aspects of everyday actions that provide clues for accurate economic analysis.

The story that follows is a blend of the ridiculous and the real. It illustrates several common reasoning problems in economics and provides examples that we use to discuss the economic way of thinking.

ECONOMIC NONSENSE

"Take a look at these data, Bob! We have real problems!"

Bob Miner quickly glanced over the computer printout. Miner, unlike his colleague, Dan Anderson, was a calm, reflective person. A tall handsome sort with a master's degree in business administration from Harvard, Miner had proved himself to be a brilliant, cool, and capable manager in his six-year tenure as chief executive of the Men's Hairpiece division of Hair Up There, Inc. The company had witnessed phenomenal success since its inception in 1980, the big break coming in 1982, when it was acquired by ICU Corporation. Since then, it had operated as a wholly owned subsidiary of ICU, a well-known conglomerate that began as a manufacturer of binoculars, telescopes, and door security peepholes and later acquired such giants as Buddummer Breweries, Honeypoor, Inc., and Worst Eastern Motels.

Dan Anderson, a diminutive, ruddy-faced man of 52, had worked his way up through the ranks of Hair Up There. Joining the firm in 1980, he worked as a model for a before-and-after advertisement and then recently advanced to his present position as sales promotion manager. "Dan Anderson," states ICU's promotional literature, "is what Hair Up There and ICU are all about. We are people helping people."

Now, back to Miner's and Anderson's crisis.

"Are you sure these figures are accurate?" asked Miner.

"Yes, Bob, they've been double-checked! Jim Farris down in Data Processing assured me that this is not a computer error!" Anderson continued, "Do you realize that this represents a 62 percent decline in sales compared to the same month last year? *Sixty-two percent!* I figured we'd be down a bit, but this is terrible."

"It's a 54 percent decline over last month's sales!" interrupted Miner, as he finished dividing figures on the printout.

"Terrrible, terrible!" repeated the distraught Anderson. "What do you make of it, Bob?"

"I'm inclined to think that the economy is in a severe downturn," responded Miner. "Our hairpiece sales have been growing faster than the economy in general. I think that our sales decline indicates that the economy is in a tailspin—a certain depression, and maybe even a recession."

"That makes sense," mourned Anderson. "You know, the way the unions have been increasing wage rates these last two years, you could just about figure that an economy-wide depression was right around the corner. Plain ol' economics—you've got to pay the price sooner or later."

"Well, this is sobering news, but let's not allow it to depress us," said Miner. "We can't really do much about it. In fact, I suggest that we get our minds off this and go to Harry's for a beer."

Anderson, suddenly coming back to life, concurred. "Great idea! I sure could use a beer."

As Miner and Anderson entered Harry's Bar and Grill, they were greeted by Joe Shipley, the amiable bartender.

"No Miners allowed, Bob," Shipley chortled. Anderson and Miner laughed heartily.

"Two beers, Joe."

"Coming right up. I suppose you want Buddummer Heavy," replied Shipley.

"You bet," stated Miner. "It has 800 percent more calories than the regular Buddummer. You can't beat that for value."

"Speaking of percentages," Anderson interjected, "I just can't get my mind off those declines in our hairpiece sales. I simply can't understand why—"

"Dan," interrupted Miner, "we agreed we wouldn't worry about those figures!" Miner then turned to the bartender, who was busy at the far end of the bar.

"By the way, Joe, how have your beer sales been this past month?"

"They're up considerably," replied Shipley.

"Up considerably," echoed Anderson softly. "How does that square with our notion of an economic depression, Bob?"

"Well, I think it's entirely consistent with it. Expectations are important in economics. Intuitively, people nationwide apparently realize that a depression is coming, and they are instinctively spending more time drinking."

"That makes sense," responded Anderson.

As Miner and Anderson ordered their second Buddummers, a challenge was issued from the vicinity of the pool table.

"Are you two guys interested in a game of pool?"

Anderson leaned toward Miner and whispered, "Let's play them. They don't know which end of the cue is up."

Miner nodded in agreement.

"Sure, we'll play," answered Anderson. "What's the game?"

"How about call shot to 25?" asked the more talkative of the two opponents, a big heavyset man named Ron Hurley, who looked as if he could maul a grizzly bear.

"Sounds good to me. OK with you, Bob?"

"Sounds fine. What are we playing for? A pitcher of beer?" Affirmative nods followed.

"Let's lag to see who breaks, gentlemen," said Anderson.

The game was much closer than Anderson and Miner had figured, even though Miner was shooting reasonably well. He ran a nice shot down the rail, making the score 15 to 14.

As Miner set up a new rack, Anderson hurried over to the candy machine. After examining the selection and angrily pulling the lever, he exclaimed. "Seventy-five cents for a candy bar!" He returned to the table, muttering, "Damn inflation."

Ron Hurley picked up the complaint. "I absolutely refuse to pay 75 cents for a candy bar. Isn't this economy in a mess?"

"Sure is," concurred Anderson.

Miner shot and missed. As Hurley glanced over the potential shots, he continued, "You know, the sad state of the economy all goes back to the big increase in imports from Japan. These imports caused a large deficit in the federal budget, which in turn caused higher prices. Furthermore, Japanese imports have increased homelessness. If you want proof of all this, just compare the size of the budget deficit, the price level, and the homeless population now with what they were before the increase in Japanese imports."

Miner glanced quickly at Anderson and snickered slightly, as if to say, "Catch this. This guy has it figured."

After making a rather difficult bank shot, Hurley continued, "You know, it amazes me that the economists and politicians don't know how to stop inflation. The logic is simple. Inflation is caused by rising prices—it isn't all that complex. If you stop prices from rising, inflation won't continue long. We ought to pass a law making it illegal to raise prices."

"Now, that is absolute nonsense," Anderson interjected. "Things aren't that simple. You can't just legislate inflation away. Nor can you legislate away discrimination, unemployment, and homelessness. These are very complex economic and social problems. However, if you insist on placing blame for inflation and unemployment, you needn't look any further than the labor unions. Now, there is something we *can* and *should* legislate away."

Hurley, noticeably angered, reacted violently. "You are a real bozo, fella! You keep talking like that and you're going to have the number 17 on this pool cue indented in your forehead! I happen to be a union officer!"

Miner quickly intervened. "Hey, cool it, you two. You're acting like a couple of kids."

After several shots and a long period of silence, Miner attempted to reorient the conversation. "Dan Anderson and I are executives for Hair Up There, Inc., and our jobs require a solid understanding of economics. For example, just today we discovered that our sales are way down. The economy is in a depression—in fact, it's clear that it has already begun. The general public just isn't aware of it yet."

"What does that have to do with unions?" Hurley challenged.

"I'll tell you what," butted in Anderson. "Unions have raised wage rates in each of the last two years, forcing prices up. As a direct result of these higher prices, sales are down. Firms will have to lay off workers. And what's the cause? *Labor unions*—like those at Hair Up There. They've caused higher prices and greater unemployment."

"You're asking for it again, buddy! Why don't you just shoot the ball and shut up!" Hurley countered.

Anderson, satisfied that he had made his case, addressed the cue ball and declared boldly, "This one will win it, gentlemen. Three-ten combination once to the side."

The cue ball smacked the ten, the ten sliced the three perfectly. The three ball hit the side cushion and banked directly into the pocket on the opposite side. Just as it had been called! The cue ball scratched.

Anderson looked up at Miner, shook his head, smiled faintly, and spoke softly. "It's just one of those days, Bob—just one of those days."

PROBLEMS IN ECONOMIC REASONING

The dialogue among Dan Anderson, Bob Miner, and Ron Hurley at Hair Up There and Harry's Bar provides a wealth of examples of problems in economic reasoning.

Terminology

One reason why individuals fail to understand economics is the problem posed by economic terminology. The language problem is particularly difficult for most beginning students. Be persistent and attempt to learn economic terms; they are a necessary feature of precise communication. Think back to the fictitious dialogue at Harry's Bar and Grill. If you are a pool player, the terms *cue, cue ball, scratch, lag, cushion, combination, pocket,* and *rail* conveyed clear, precise meanings to you. The comment "Ten-three combination once to the side" predicted a definite and precise behavior. If you don't play pool, the same statement probably left you completely confused and unable to anticipate the action that was to follow. The need to understand terminology in economics is just as instrumental as it is in pool. Economic terms allow precise communication of ideas or concepts that enable one to understand economic behavior. To be a successful student of economics, *you must learn the meaning of economic terms.* To aid you, we have provided a glossary at the end of this text.

The lack of a clear understanding of the meaning of economic terms often results in economic nonsense. Recall the dialogue between Hurley, Anderson, and Miner in which Hurley stated that "inflation is caused by rising prices." This is an example of economic illogic. Economists define inflation as an overall increase in the level of prices in the economy. Thus, inflation *is* rising prices. Hurley's conclusion that "if you stop prices from rising, inflation won't continue long" is a truism, to be sure, but it tells us nothing about how to stop inflation. Hurley could just as well have said that inflation is inflation and to stop inflation you have to stop inflation. Brilliant!

Confusion over economic terms is also apparent in Miner's appraisal that "the economy is in a tailspin—a certain depression, and maybe even a recession." His statement falsely implies that a recession is a more severe decline in national sales and output than a depression. In fact, the opposite is true. A recession is a relatively mild downturn in national output; a depression is a dramatic and long-lasting fall in economic activity and output.

The Fallacy of Composition

The fictional dialogue contains other reasoning problems. One particular type of reasoning error is so common that it has been given a special name: the *fallacy of composition.* This fallacy occurs when a person erroneously concludes that things that are true for the part must necessarily be true for the whole. You should be able to discover several places within the dialogue where the characters commit this reasoning error. For example, Bob Miner concluded that the decline in Hair Up There sales indicated an economy-wide depression. He jumped from the part, Hair Up There's sales, to the whole, the state of the economy. But the decline in men's wig sales at Hair Up There was probably caused by something unrelated to the overall health of the economy. Perhaps changes in tastes had made Hair Up There's wigs unfashionable. Perhaps a competitor marketed a higher-quality, lower-priced wig. Any one of a number of possible occurrences might have reduced hairpiece sales. Economic nonsense can result when the entire economy is judged on the basis of activity in one of its component parts.

The Cause-and-Effect Fallacy

Another reasoning error in the dialogue is evident in Ron Hurley's views on the cause of the large federal budget deficit. He noted that the rise in the budget deficit occurred *after* the surge in imports from Japan. He erroneously concluded, therefore, that the imports *caused* the budget deficit. From there he falsely concluded that the budget deficit caused higher prices, greater unemployment, and more homelessness. This form of erroneous reasoning is called the *post hoc, ergo propter hoc* (after this, therefore because of this) or *cause-and-effect fallacy.* People often falsely assume that events that follow previous events were caused by the prior events. In reality, events that follow others may have nothing whatsoever to do with the previous events.

Dan Anderson's contention that union wage increases over the preceding two years had caused higher prices, smaller sales, and unemployment is another example of the cause-and-effect problem. Anderson concluded that wage rates had risen prior to the price rises and, therefore, the wage increases must have caused them. But price increases can be caused by many factors, as we shall see later in the text. It is entirely possible that the wage gains referred to by Anderson were not responsible for the price rises to which he was referring.

Bias and Oversimplification

Two final types of reasoning problems need to be explored: *bias and preconception* and *oversimplification.* Both problems occur in the story. Dan Anderson was strongly biased against labor unions. He appeared to hold preconceived ideas that unions are the cause of all economic ills, including the sales decline at Hair Up There, inflation, unemployment, and recessions.

We all carry biases into our inquiries and analyses, but rigid ideas and overtly prejudicial attitudes impede reasoned, logical discussions of economic issues. Beware of views that are based upon biased self-interest—including your own! On the other hand, don't apologize for giving priority to particular viewpoints that are based on sound reasoning, careful study, and strong evidence. Some views are indeed correct, others are patently wrong; the task is to sort through the positions to determine which are supported by evidence.

Oversimplification is also evident in the dialogue. Ron Hurley stated that inflation is a simple problem with an equally simple solution. His proposal was to pass a law outlawing price rises. Dan Anderson made the point that "things aren't that simple." He correctly asserted that problems such as inflation, shortages, unemployment, and homelessness are complex phenomena.

Alfred Marshall, one of the most influential economists of the 1800s, once wrote, "All short statements about economics are misleading." But even Marshall could not leave well enough alone. He added, in parentheses, "with the possible exception of my present one." The truth is that most economic issues and problems are complex, and simple statements seldom explain complex phenomena.

THE ECONOMIC PERSPECTIVE

In addition to avoiding the reasoning errors discussed, sound economic analysis requires observation of specific aspects of ordinary human behavior and events. Those trained in economics do not think in a special way; they analyze events from a special perspective. This perspective contains important assumptions about human behavior that guide economic analysis. These assumptions are listed here, and they are discussed and applied throughout this book.

1. *People make choices from alternatives; therefore, all actions entail costs.* Wants exceed the capacity of people's resources to satisfy them. Because people are unable to obtain all that they desire, they must *economize*; they must choose from among alternatives and give up some things to obtain others. For every choice, something is gained and something else is sacrificed. That sacrifice, or cost, is the loss of the alternative not chosen. Hence, all actions involve costs. For example, Buddummer Brewery's decision to use selected resources to produce beer meant that it could not use those resources in such alternative ways as making ale, rubbing alcohol, or soft drinks. The choice made by Bob Miner and Dan Anderson to play a game of pool meant that they could not use that time to analyze their firm's monthly sales data. Economists view people's actions as the outcomes of choices and focus on the costs and benefits of those choices.

2. *People engage in purposeful behavior.* Economists look for purpose in behavior, even when the conduct appears to be random and chaotic. Economists assume that people pursue their interests in order to increase their well-being. This assumption does not suggest that people pursue only narrow, selfish goals but, rather, that whatever their interests — money, prestige, security, helping others — people pursue them purposefully through deliberate choices.

Dan Anderson acted purposely when he decided to buy a candy bar at Harry's. Although he complained bitterly about the price, he compared that price with the satisfaction or pleasure to be gained from consuming the bar and decided that the purchase was in his best interest. Hair Up There's decision to produce wigs was not made randomly, either. The company management felt the company would earn profits by producing wigs. Even Dan Anderson's behavior of lining up the final shot of the pool game reflected purposefulness. He made numerous instantaneous calculations in deciding what shot was optimal, how much force to use in striking the cue ball, and what "cut" was proper for making the shot. The fact that Anderson's calculations or execution failed to produce the desired outcome — recall that the cue ball scratched — does not negate the reality that purposefulness characterized the action.

A second aspect to notice in this purposefulness is its *future orientation*. All choices are made on the basis of *predicted* outcomes. Dan predicted a well executed shot without a "scratch" and Hair Up There predicted excellent sales. Neither would make the same choices if they knew the actual outcomes in advance. Risk is an important component of all economic events. People do not possess perfect knowledge of how things will turn out; consequences lie in the future.

3. *People respond to incentives and disincentives.* Because people act purposefully, costs are a disincentive (discouragement) and benefits an incentive (encouragement) to act in particular ways. When incentives and disincentives change, people adjust their behavior. For example, if the men's wig sales and profits at Hair Up There continue to slide, the company will respond by reformulating their product, increasing advertising, or shifting resources to the production of an alternative product. Likewise, Ron Hurley refused to buy a candy bar because the higher price represented a strong disincentive. Economists believe that people respond in a rather consistent way to changes in prices, costs, profits, taxes, subsidies, and other forms of incentives and disincentives. They also believe that people display great adaptability in redefining and pursuing their interests in response to changing incentives.

4. *People hold different personal values and value things differently (economists included).* Ah, the infinite variety of human beings. Not only are their shapes and sizes different, but their personalities and desires vary widely. For example, some people gain satisfaction from listening to sacred music; others enjoy driving sports cars; still others like playing pool; and some place a high value on maintaining close family relationships, bargaining for a higher wage, reducing poverty, expanding freedom, eating Twinkies, or riding a dirt bike. Others attach no or little value to such things. Economists tend to accept these differences in tastes, and to study people as they are, not as some wish them to be. Economists examine the costs of obtaining valued things (no matter why we may desire them) and analyze the social relationships necessary to allow as many people as possible to fulfill their various wants. Returning to an earlier point, economists also remind us that individuals and society cannot gain *all* the things they value; therefore, they make choices based upon expected costs and benefits.

5. *Production and exchange create income and wealth.* Producing things for which people are willing to pay generates income—wages, salaries, rent, interest, and profits—for the participants in the production process. Voluntary exchange (for example, the use of land exchanged for rental payments, labor services exchanged for wages, or products or services exchanged for money) is a vital feature of the entire goods-producing and income-generating process in the economy. *When an exchange takes place, both parties expect benefits greater than sacrifices; otherwise, the exchange would not occur.*

Dan Anderson, Bob Miner, Ron Hurley, and Joe Shipley (the bartender) all earned income for themselves by producing products or services purchased by others. For example, Anderson and Miner provided their skill and effort at managing the production and sale of men's wigs in exchange for salaries.

Those at the bar used part of their income to buy beer. Apparently, they believed that the beer provided more satisfaction to them than the money paid to buy it. On the other hand, Harry's Bar preferred the money to the beer. In turn, those who produced the beer and served it received income for their efforts. Voluntary exchange increases satisfaction and is the basis for most economic behavior in a market economy.

6. *Economic actions often produce secondary effects.* The process of voluntary exchange weaves people together into an intimate economic web. According to economists, "You cannot do just one thing." Choices made by one person influence

many other people. These people may be your neighbors next door, people scattered throughout the country, or even individuals living in foreign lands.

The simple decision by Dan Anderson and Bob Miner to drink beer influenced the lives of the tavern owner, the Buddummer Brewery workers, hops farmers, and assorted other people. Analyzing the initial actions of individuals (beer purchasers) and then ascertaining the secondary effects (tavern profits, hops prices, brewery workers' wages) is essential to clear economic analysis. Furthermore, initial actions can produce unintended secondary outcomes. Ron Hurley's policy suggestion that the government pass legislation to outlaw price increases as a way to stop inflation is a case in point. As we will learn later, the consequences of such a law might well be severe shortages of goods and services that people desire to buy.

SUMMARY

Sound economic thinking is much like all clear thinking. It involves the use of logic and the avoidance of such common reasoning errors as misusing terms, committing the fallacy of composition, engaging in post hoc, propter hoc reasoning, and allowing preconception and bias to distort one's vision. *But economic thinking also involves learning what to think about.* Economists employ a special perspective when analyzing ordinary day-to-day behavior and activity. That perspective assumes that people make choices between alternatives; all actions entail costs; people behave purposefully; people differ in their personal values; production and exchange create income and satisfaction; and actions often have secondary effects. These elements of the "economic perspective" are used throughout this book to explain individual behavior and economic outcomes.

STUDY QUESTIONS

1. What reasoning problem is involved in each of the following statements?
   a. "The stock market crash of 1929 caused the Great Depression."
   b. "People can see better if they stand up at basketball games."
   c. "The cause of all our economic problems is too much government spending."
   d. "The cause of unemployment is people out of work."
2. What factors besides a national recession might explain the tremendous decline in men's wig sales by Hair Up There?
3. Are wealthy people forced to choose between alternatives? Cite examples.
4. If a tire dealer advertises that a *free* tire will be given to the purchaser of three tires, is the *cost* of the fourth tire zero?
5. Explain what is meant by the statement, "People behave purposefully." Cite several economic examples of purposeful economic behavior.
6. Explain how voluntary exchange can increase the level of satisfaction for the participants in the transaction.

7. Miner felt that the increase in beer sales at Harry's Bar and Grill occurred because people were drinking more in anticipation of an economic recession. Can you cite a more plausible explanation?

8. According to the economic perspective, people respond to incentives and disincentives. Yet people attend college, which is expensive and time-consuming and requires much effort. Does this contradict the economist's perspective of human behavior? Explain.

9. Economists are fond of saying, "There is no such thing as a free lunch." Explain this statement.

10. People usually agree that food, clothing, and shelter are *necessities*; people have "no choice" but to purchase these products. Does this analysis contradict the economic perspective, with its emphasis on choices made among alternatives? Hint: Which of the following items are necessities: Dairigold milk—one-gallon container; Nike athletic shoes; Coleman tent; McDonald's hamburger; Holiday Inn motel room; Levi's 501 jeans?

APPENDIX: GRAPHFEETY (A PRIMER ON GRAPHS)

As indicated on the accompanying street map (Figure 1-1), Hair Up There, Inc., is located at the intersection of Zero Street and Zero Avenue in the town of Wigsville, Rug Island. Two of the firm's executives—Bob Miner and Dan Anderson—decided to leave their offices to walk to Harry's Bar and Grill, located at the corner of Third Street North and Second Avenue East in Wigsville. Thus we see

Figure 1-1 Street Map of Downtown Wigsville
This grid map shows the distances of a location (Harry's) from a point of origin.

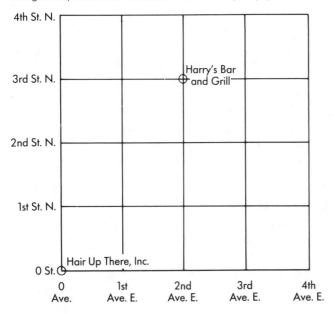

from the map that Miner and Anderson must walk 3 blocks north and 2 blocks east to get to Harry's.

A specific location on a grid map like Figure 1-1 tells us the two distances we are away from a point of origin. So it is with points on graphs. Observe from Figures 1-2, parts A and B, that the "origins" or the graphs, labeled zero, are the places where the variables measured on the vertical and horizontal axes are both zero. That is, the origins are located at the far southwestern corners of the two grids. A point such as Z in Figure 1-2A measures two variables, one shown on the vertical axis and the other on the horizontal axis. These variables are not "streets" and "avenues," as is the case with our map, but rather "prices of hairpieces" and "quantity of hairpieces bought." Point Z on the "curve" tells us that consumers collectively desire to buy 200,000 wigs when the price of hairpieces is $300. Similarly, the other points on the curve show additional specific levels of prices and hairpiece sales.

Observe that the particular line in Figure 1-2A is downsloping, meaning that the relationship between the two variables is *inverse*, or *negative*. When one of the variables increases, the other variable declines. In this case, higher prices for hairpieces result in fewer hairpieces purchased. Figure 1-2B, on the other hand, shows an upsloping curve, indicating a *direct*, or *positive* relationship between the two variables shown. Specifically, this curve tells us that people buy more beer when the average daily temperature rises. Conversely, lower average daily temperatures are associated with fewer purchases of beer.

Graphs are useful in economic reasoning because they enable us to visualize the relationships between two variables, holding all other variables constant. When you observe the many graphs in this textbook, always remember that each point on a curve shows *two* variables, one measured vertically and the other horizontally.

Figure 1-2 Inverse and Direct Relationships Between Variables

As shown in graph *A,* an *inverse* relationship exists between the price of hairpieces and the number sold. When the price of hairpieces goes down, the number sold goes up. Graph *B* depicts a *direct* relationship; more bottles of beer are consumed as the temperature rises.

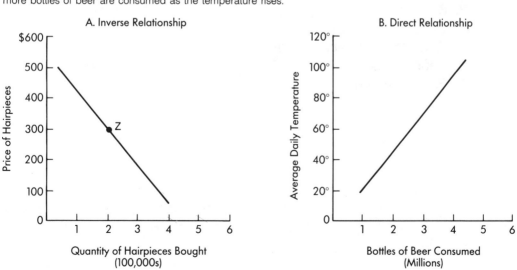

2

LAND OF OPPORTUNITY (COSTS)

The Economics of Scarcity
and Production Possibilities

Concepts and Terms Examined in This Chapter

1. Economics
2. Resources (Land, Labor, Capital, Entrepreneurial Ability)
3. Scarcity
4. Opportunity Costs
5. Production Possibilities Curve
6. Capital versus Consumer Goods
7. Economic Growth

Firms Bid Away Faculty from Universities—
Is Industry Eating Its Seed Corn?

Battle Rages over the Colorado River!

Declining Federal Aid Forces More Students
to Combine Work and Study

U.S. Capital Expansion Lags Behind Japan and Germany—Economic Growth at Stake?

Crisis in the Persian Gulf

Lumber, Natural Gas, and Mining Interests Oppose Expansion of Wilderness Areas—Claim Resources Are Being Locked Away

Newspapers are filled with headlines such as these. Each story involves economics—the study of how society chooses to allocate scarce resources, produce goods and services, and distribute the latter items to members of society. The economic content of each story may not be obvious to most readers, but careful examination reveals three common themes introduced in Chapter 1 as part of the economic perspective: *scarce resources, choice,* and *opportunity costs.* This chapter pursues those themes through the newspaper stories and reaches two conclusions. First, economic choices touch nearly all aspects of human behavior, and, second, individuals, businesses, and nations need to analyze the opportunity costs of alternatives in order to make optimal decisions.

SCARCE RESOURCES

Economic resources are people or things that possess the ability to help produce commodities and services that people value. These "productive agents" or "factors of production" are broadly classified as land, labor, capital, and entrepreneurial ability.

Land, as an economic resource, includes sites for manufacturing firms, tree farms, shopping centers, fish hatcheries, cattle ranches, schools, and other enterprises used to produce goods and services. Land also embraces the productive items on or under the earth's surface, such as water, oil, lumber, iron ore, sand, coal, and natural gas. Such natural resources become economic resources when they are used for the production of valuable goods and services.

All productive people and their efforts to produce goods and services are classified as *labor*. Examples include carpenters, dentists, assembly-line workers, computer programmers, senators, police officers, nurses, and corporate managers.

The third category of resources — *capital* — includes all human-made items used to produce goods and services. This category includes all tools, machines, factories, and transportation vehicles used to make or deliver consumer products and services. Interestingly, it does not include money. Money is a commodity used to facilitate the exchange of resources and other items, but it is not productive itself (unless you burn $100 bills to heat your factory).

Entrepreneurial ability is the fourth resource category. The entrepreneur is the driving force in the market economy. He or she takes the initiative in combining the other resources — land, labor, and capital — in producing goods and services. The entrepreneur is the innovator and the risk bearer who attempts to anticipate the wants of consumers.

Because people want more goods and services than available resources can provide, economists contend that all economic resources are *scarce*. Meeting all human wants appears to be an impossible goal because people expand their wants faster than the economy increases its ability to produce desirable goods and services. This relative scarcity is a theme common to all the news items described in the opening headlines. Available land conducive for use for wilderness or for lumber, for example, is scarce relative to the amount that people wish to have. The same situation is true regarding the labor and capital resources needed to design and build machinery and factories. Even water is scarce. Water?

As we well know, water is plentiful in an absolute sense. Four trillion gallons of rain fall to the earth in the United States on the average day, and in most places water is cheaper than dirt. A dollar, or so, will get a ton of it delivered to your house in most urban areas (assuming that you are hooked up to a water system). Just turn on your faucet. Yet water is a scarce resource; the desired uses for it exceed its availability. This is dramatically seen in the controversy described by the headline "Battle Rages over the Colorado River!"

The Colorado River begins as a trickle in the Rockies and ends its 1,450-mile journey exactly the same way as it enters the Gulf of California in Mexico. In between, people use it both as a resource and as a direct consumer good. The water irrigates more than 3 million acres of desert, provides drinking water to several rapidly growing Sunbelt cities, and furnishes extensive recreational opportunities.

Who decides how this scarce resource is used? At present, the choices are made through a complex array of state laws, interstate compacts, federal laws, treaties, and court decisions. The allocation problem, however, is far from being solved. Once fully operational, the Central Arizona Project will pump 90 tons of water per second from the Colorado across 310 miles to Phoenix and Tucson. Increased demand for irrigation on the Indian reservations in the Southwest will add to the problem. In Tucson, the city has begun buying up farmland to divert irrigation water to city needs. San Diego has shown a willingness to pay as much as $200 an acre-foot for water (enough to cover an acre of land one foot deep), although many farmers in California's Central Valley are charged less than $20 an acre-foot for irrigation water. Discrepancies such as this have led some economists to suggest that a market-allocation system be implemented to replace the existing administrative system as a way to handle this scarcity problem. Under the market plan, water would be priced at its cost and people would be allowed to buy and sell their water rights. Whatever the mechanism used, it must deal with the fact of scarcity.

Scarcity is also the central element described in the headline "Firms Bid Away Faculty from Universities—Is Industry Eating Its Seed Corn?" The computer and biotechnical revolutions have increased the corporate demand for people holding PhD degrees in these areas. High salaries and excellent working conditions offered by many corporations attract professors away from university employment. The problem, of course, is that corporations depend on the universities to train the skilled people they need. If college students fail to get adequate preparation because of understaffed college programs, bidding away the best and the brightest faculty may create an even greater scarcity of skilled engineers and scientists in the future.

CHOICE

A second major theme woven among the headlined news items is the existence of alternatives and the consequent need to make choices. In each situation, resources are limited and the alternative uses abundant. As indicated in the discussion of the economic perspective in Chapter 1, scarcity forces people to choose. Choices must be made on how best to use scarce resources.

Should Colorado River water quench city thirst or irrigate more desert land? Should universities increase salaries to retain their science and engineering faculty, or should they tighten enrollment limits and force the private sector to train people for their own needs? Should wilderness areas be opened for natural gas exploration, mining, and lumbering? Should society allocate more or fewer labor resources to the military? Should you, as a student, take a part-time job or concentrate all your effort on studying? Should the United States spend less on consumer goods and more on capital goods? Decisions, decisions, decisions.

How are these decisions made? Individuals and companies responding to competitive market forces make most choices in the United States. They compare expected costs and benefits and bid against one another to obtain scarce resources, the highest bidder securing the property right to the resource (or, in the case of labor, the use of the worker's time). The owner (employer) is then entitled to decide how the scarce resource is used. In most cases, competitive forces in the market require them to use the resource in a manner that yields the greatest societal satisfaction. The specific manner in which markets work is analyzed in Chapters 4 through 10.

The government also makes decisions on how resources are to be used. For example, elected representatives decide how many and what types of the nation's resources are allocated for national defense. Likewise, government representatives decide whether public lands should be set aside as wilderness, made available for logging, or leased to oil and natural gas producers. Presumably, if the majority of the voting public does not like the decisions, it will vote for new representatives. The government's extensive economic role is discussed in Chapters 11, 12, and 13.

To summarize, scarcity and choice are closely related. Society must choose because it lacks unlimited resources for producing goods and services. Because wants exceed means, decisions must be made on which wants to fulfill and which to leave unfulfilled. *Recognizing this reality is an important element of the economic perspective.*

OPPORTUNITY COSTS

Opportunity cost is the third important thread in the headlines. An opportunity cost, or alternative cost, *is the value of the benefit sacrificed by choosing one alternative rather than another; it is the gain forgone.* All decisions concerning the use of scarce resources entail opportunity costs when one use of the resource forecloses another valuable use. For instance, the use of PhDs who have skills in electronics to design computers precludes the use of that labor resource to teach engineering students at a university. The loss of the second use is then the opportunity cost of the first. The opportunity cost of using Colorado River water to irrigate more land is the value of that substance as drinking water. The opportunity cost of the 1991 war in the Persian Gulf was the goods and services that the involved nations could have obtained by using these same labor and capital resources in a different manner.

The headline "Declining Federal Aid Forces More Students to Combine Work and Study" contains a multiple set of opportunity costs. First, consider the decision by government to provide financial aid to college students. The opportunity cost of that decision is the loss of the benefits that those funds could create elsewhere—for instance, aid to home buyers, aid to the poor, reduced taxes, or crime prevention. But not providing student aid also creates opportunity costs. It may mean that fewer people will have access to higher education, which may reduce the future quantity of skilled labor resources in the nation.

Students encounter a different set of opportunity costs as they respond to the decline in federal aid. A part-time job will help to replace funds, but then less time is available for studying. That change might result in less comprehension and lower grades. Students might also consider dropping out of school, attending school part-time, or reducing their social activities; but each alternative, if chosen, carries with it an opportunity cost. People need to assess these costs and weigh them against the expected benefits as they consider their choices.

Two important points bear mentioning. First, notice that opportunity costs are not always the same as monetary costs. A movie may only cost $5.00, but that $5.00 may not measure the opportunity cost involved. If the moviegoer passed up an important reading assignment covered on the next morning's final exam, the actual opportunity cost might exceed $5.00.

Second, all choices involve opportunity costs. Because it is impossible to avoid opportunity costs, the best strategy is to minimize them and maximize the benefits associated with a decision. Identifying opportunity costs and examining the consequences of alternative choices are major tasks in the study of economics.

THE PRODUCTION POSSIBILITIES CURVE

Economists employ a visual aid called the *production possibilities curve* to illustrate scarcity, choice, and opportunity costs. The production possibilities curve reveals all the possible combinations of total output of any two products that could be produced by using a fixed amount of productive resources. This graphical tool is helpful in analyzing the trade-offs involved in all economic choices. The remainder of the chapter will focus on production possibility analysis by discussing two issues: wilderness use and economic growth.

Case One: Lumber versus Wilderness

The headline "Lumber, Natural Gas, and Mining Interests Oppose Expansion of Wilderness Areas" identifies several alternative uses of U.S. Forest Service land—two of which are lumber production and wilderness. To limit the scope of the inquiry and focus the analysis on key relationships, three assumptions are necessary:

1. A *fixed* amount of roadless, heavily timbered national forest land is involved in a debate over whether or not it should be classified as wilderness.
2. Technology, the technique of combining resources to produce useful items, does not change.
3. All the land area will be employed as wilderness, for logging, or for some combination of each use.

Figure 2-1 is a production possibilities curve illustrating all possible combinations of wilderness and lumber production obtainable using the limited area of land. Each point on the curve depicts a particular combination of wilderness use and lumber production. All points on the curve, such as points A, B, C, and D, are obtainable combinations, whereas those points beyond the curve, such as E, are unreachable.

Figure 2-1 Production Possibility Curve: Lumber versus Wilderness

Each point on the production possibilities curve represents maximum combinations of wilderness and lumber production, assuming fixed resources and technology. Points on or within the curve are obtainable; points beyond the curve are not. Two specific combinations are shown: $W_L L_S$ (large wilderness, small lumber production) and $W_S L_L$ (small wilderness, large lumber production).

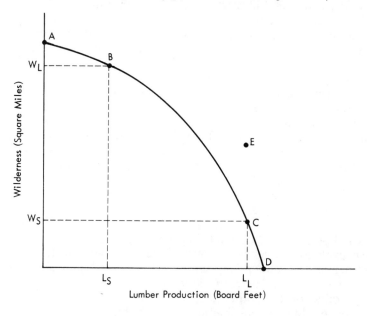

Lumber Production (Board Feet)

Three general options are available to decision makers. First, the government could choose point A and declare the entire area as "wilderness." A classification of "wilderness" means that the region is designated by Congress as "an area where the earth and the community of life are untrampled, where people themselves are visitors who do not remain." Logging and road building are not permitted in these areas. A second option, shown by point D, is to use all the land as a tree farm, where the lumber can be intensively harvested and renewed. The third alternative is to designate a portion of the region as wilderness and the remainder for timber production (points such as B and C).

Two of the many possible combinations of wilderness and lumber are spotlighted in Figure 2-1. Option B is a "large wilderness, small lumber production" choice. A second choice, point C, is a "small wilderness, large lumber" alternative. Several additional options are possible, because each point on the curve depicts a feasible combination of wilderness and lumber. For purposes of this example, however, suppose that options B and C are being debated.

Each concept mentioned earlier is illustrated by comparing the two alternatives. Scarcity exists; the availability area is limited relative to the possible uses for it. This scarcity forces people to choose. Congress must make a decision between the "large wilderness, small lumber production" possibility and the "small wilderness, large lumber production" one. Opportunity costs are present with either alternative. Increased use of the land as wilderness requires that less land can be used for lumber production. In the same manner, lumber production cannot be increased without reducing the amount of wilderness land. The "wilderness-timber" land-use choice is controversial because, as indicated in our discussion of the economic perspective, people have different values and value things differently. A logger views a stand of old, large trees as a wasted opportunity for production and income while an environmentalist sees it as something of scenic beauty.

The shape of the curve in Figure 2-1 shows that society must give up lumber to get more wilderness; it also illustrates the amount of lumber that must be forgone to get additional square miles of wilderness. The curve is concave to the origin because extra, or marginal, opportunity costs increase as additional square miles are used for wilderness. In a similar manner, marginal opportunity costs increase as more of the area is used for lumber production.

Why is this the case? Some portions of the land area in question—high mountain ridges, alpine meadows, and scenic rivers—are well suited for wilderness enjoyment; other areas—accessible, dense forest regions—are highly useful for timber production. Designating as wilderness the high mountain terrain, which supports few trees and is difficult to log, would entail a lower opportunity cost in terms of lost lumber output. As more total area is classified as wilderness, however, the opportunity costs per additional square mile rise because land increasingly more suitable for timber production is lost. As one moves from the bottom of the production possibilities curve (no wilderness) in Figure 2-1 to the top (all wilderness), the extra opportunity costs increase. The same situation occurs as timber production increases; land with increasing suitability for wilderness use is lost. Resources are usually not perfectly substitutable in producing specific products or services. This analysis explains the concave shape of the curve and illustrates a general economic principle: *the law of increasing costs*. To achieve successive increases in the production of a good, increasing amounts of scarce resources must be diverted from the production of another good.

In terms of the production possibilities curve in Figure 2-1, decision makers must attempt to discover the single combination of wilderness and lumber production from this area that best conforms to society's preferences—that is, produces the least opportunity cost. This combination is an optimal choice.

Case Two: Consumer versus Capital Goods

"U.S. Capital Expansion Lags Behind Japan and Germany—Economic Growth at Stake?" This headline provides an opportunity to use the production possibilities curve in a more complex manner. Again, three initial assumptions are necessary: fixed resources, constant technology, and full employment of all resources. In the lumber versus wilderness case, these assumptions remained in place to maintain simplicity, but in this example, two will be released later to expand the analysis.

All commodities produced in a society can be broadly classified as either capital or consumer goods. Recall that capital consists of human-made items produced solely to serve as resources in producing goods and services. Being human-made, capital is a resource that people can consciously decide to increase or decrease. Fewer scarce resources can be used to produce consumer goods, such as automobiles, hamburgers, furniture, personal recreation, haircuts, child care, houseplants, milk, newspapers, and the like, leaving more resources for the production of capital goods such as irrigation systems, factories, commercial trucks, industrial computers, warehouses, and retail establishments.

Figure 2-2 illustrates the production choices that exist in this example. Capital goods (new capital resources) are measured on the vertical axis and consumer goods (things that provide direct satisfaction) are shown on the horizontal axis. The analysis in Figure 2-2 is identical to that of the previous case. All points—

Figure 2-2 Production Possibilities Curve: Consumer versus Capital Goods

Assuming fixed resources and technology, a society must sacrifice consumer goods to obtain more capital, and vice versa. Over the past two decades, Japan and Germany have selected capital-consumption combinations represented by point B, whereas the United States has chosen a combination illustrated by point C.

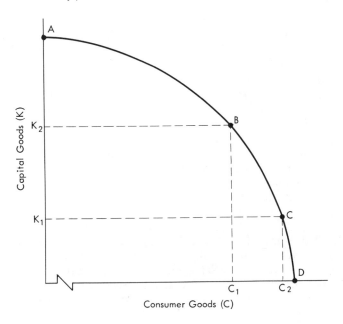

A, B, C, and D and any other locations on the production possibility curve—are possible production levels. People must choose how much present consumption to forgo to produce capital goods. As indicated in the headline, Japan and Germany historically have selected points such as B on their production possibilities curves, and the United States has chosen points represented by C. That is, Japan and Germany have had higher rates of savings (nonconsumption) and capital production than has the United States. Notice that at point B, the capital-to-consumption ratio, K_2/C_1, is higher than at C, K_1/C_2.

For the United States to achieve the same capital formation rate as Japan and Germany, consumer goods must be sacrificed by an amount shown by the distance from C_2 to C_1. These lost consumer goods represent the opportunity cost of producing at point B on the curve rather than at C. This curve illustrates that scarce resources require choice, and choice produces opportunity costs. Any change in the level of production represents a gain in production of one item at the cost of forgone production of another item.

Why might people choose to sacrifice present consumer goods to produce more capital resources? What are the consequences of the rather low capital-consumer good ration in this country? Why has there been an attempt to use public policy in the United States to increase savings (reduce consumption) to increase the production of capital resources? Figure 2-3 will help to answer these questions.

Figure 2-3 shows the original production possibility curve ABCD, but it also shows a new curve, EFGH, which lies to its right. The outward movement from curve ABCD to EFGH depicts economic growth. The second curve presents an improved trade-off between the production of capital and consumption goods. To test your understanding of this, compare points C and G on the graph. Originally, society could produce K_1 capital and C_2 consumer goods (point C), but economic growth has enabled society to maintain the same level of capital formation, K_1, and obtain an increase in consumption goods by an amount shown by distance C_2 to C_3. Alternatively, society could continue to have C_2 consumption goods and increase its capital goods to K_2.

Economic growth is possible in our model only if we release the initial assumptions that resources and technology are fixed. At a specific time there is a production possibilities curve such as ABCD in Figure 2-3, but over time a country can improve its technology and increase its resources to permit greater production. This expanded capacity is depicted in the second curve.

A nation's economic growth partly depends on the degree to which it chooses to forgo present consumer goods to produce more capital. Hence, we are back to the headline "U.S. Capital Expansion Lags ... Economic Growth at Stake?" This nation's decision to devote a smaller fraction of its resources to producing capital resources than Japan and Germany over the past several decades has resulted in our rate of economic growth being lower than theirs. Our decision to consume relatively more than Japan and Germany has come at the opportunity cost of experiencing a lower percentage increase in output.

Another insight surfaces by releasing the assumption that all resources are fully employed. If society should find itself at, say point U in Figure 2-3, it is experiencing unemployment of some of its available land, labor, and capital resources. Rather than achieving the potential output, such as points B and C on curve ABCD, it is producing below that potential level. In this case, if a means can be found to achieve full employment of the resources, society need not sacrifice

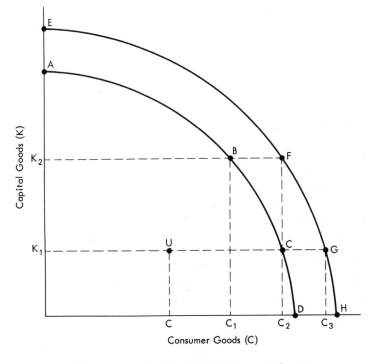

Figure 2-3   Production Possibilities Analysis: Economic Growth

Economic growth is shown by the movement of the production possibilities curve from ABCD to EFGH. Such growth improves the trade-off between capital and consumer goods; for example, society can produce K_2 capital and C_2 consumer goods rather than K_2 capital and C_1 consumer goods. The extent to which a nation's production possibilities curve shifts outward from year to year depends partly on the degree to which it chooses to forgo present consumer goods to produce more capital resources.

consumer goods to obtain more capital ones, or vice versa. Unemployment of resources is discussed in Chapters 14 through 18.

SUMMARY

Economic resources are limited, but human wants are virtually unlimited. That relative scarcity dictates that choices must be made on how to allocate resources, what products to produce, what methods of production to use, and how to distribute the goods and services to members of society. The production possibilities model illustrates these choices and uses the interrelated concepts of scarce resources, opportunity costs, increasing marginal opportunity costs, and trade-offs to depict the consequences of each choice. It demonstrates the impact of additional resources on economic growth and shows (but does not explain) unemployment.

Because individuals and society are forced to make choices, and because choices involve opportunity costs, it makes sense to identify and measure these costs and compare them with expected benefits. This is the process of economizing, which is the subject matter of economics. Economists identify actions and policies that will produce the maximum benefits for people and society at the least possible costs.

STUDY QUESTIONS

1. Define the term *resource*. Why is capital considered to be a resource?
2. Which of the following decisions would have the greatest opportunity costs? Why?
   a. A decision to use an undeveloped square block in the center of the Chicago financial district for a used-car lot.
   b. A decision to use a square mile of the southwestern desert for a used-car display area.
3. "From an economic perspective, few things are actually free. Even wilderness is not really *free*." What does the author of this quotation mean? Isn't wilderness provided free by Mother Nature?
4. Did it cost you anything to read this chapter? Explain.
5. Would drafting people into the military at low pay, rather than enticing them through higher pay, reduce the opportunity cost of the military to society?
6. Use the information in the accompanying production possibilities table to answer the questions that follow.

Product or Use	Production Alternatives				
	A	B	C	D	E
Sweatshirts	10	9	7	4	0
Dresses	0	1	2	3	4

   a. What is the extra, or *marginal,* opportunity cost of obtaining the third dress? The fourth dress?
   b. What is the *total* opportunity cost of obtaining three dresses? Four dresses?
   c. If the economy characterized by this production possibilities curve were producing two dresses and five sweatshirts, what could you conclude about its use of its available resources?
7. Explain how a society's decision as to where to locate on a consumer versus capital goods production possibilities curve affects the extent to which the curve moves outward from one year to the next.
8. If each extra square mile of the land in the wilderness-lumber example were *equally* well suited for lumber production and for wilderness, *constant* opportunity costs, rather than increasing ones, would exist. Draw a production possibilities curve that illustrates constant marginal opportunity costs.
9. Why isn't money considered to be a capital resource?

10. Relate the following quotation concerning federally owned land in the western United States to the subject matter of this chapter: "There are no unused lands. Every acre has uses, every acre has rules. The questions are: what uses, and what rules?" (Senator James McClure of Idaho).

11. Whale oil and wood were important resources used to provide light and heat during the 1800–1870 period in the United States. Both resources are still available today, but little used relative to other energy sources. Using the economic perspective, explain why this is the case.

3

IT'S ALTOGETHER FITTING

The Features of the American Economy

Concepts and Terms Examined in This Chapter

1. Private Property
2. Profit Motive
3. Consumer Sovereignty
4. Demand
5. Competition
6. Specialization
7. Product and Resource Markets
8. Circular Flow Model
9. Capitalism
10. Socialism

Nearly everyone is familiar with blue jeans. Those of you who own these durable denims may not know that they contain 60 threads to the inch or other such details, but you certainly understand their basic features. People are also familiar with the American economy. They participate in it when they purchase a product, work for a wage, or sell something. Yet studies show that many Americans do not actually understand how the economy operates, why it changes, and what guides its activities. Many people are like backpackers deep in a forest. They see, sense, and react to the stimuli surrounding them, but they lack the perspective necessary to see the forest itself.

This chapter is a modest beginning in the process of describing and explaining the operations of the total economy. It is an overview that identifies the most prominent features of the economic landscape below. Specifically, the chapter analyzes the following features of the economy: private property, self-interest behavior, consumer sovereignty, competition, specialization, government participation, and the circular flow of money, products, and resources.

Levi Strauss & Co. is used to identify the characteristics and dynamics of the economy. This company was selected for a simple reason: its main product is the nearest thing to an international uniform for the young, the not-so-young, and the old (and we figured that you would fit into one of those categories). In fact, a pair of Levi's blue jeans is enshrined in the Smithsonian Institution in Washington, D.C. It therefore seems "altogether fitting" to use the history, structure, performance, products, and success of Levi Strauss & Co., "the pant maker of the world and the world's largest producer of blue jeans," to develop insights into the operation of the economy itself.

In 1850, Levi Strauss decided to follow the gold rush to California. At that time he lived in Louisville, Kentucky, having emigrated there from Bavaria at age 14. Strauss reasoned that he could successfully mine money from the pockets of California miners by selling them supplies. His brothers, Jonas and Louis, operated a merchandising business in New York and offered to grubstake him for this West Coast venture.

Levi left New York for San Francisco armed with silk and broadcloth, fine dress clothes, and canvas material for tents and Conestoga wagons. The trip around Cape Horn was long—too long. By the time he reached San Francisco the only supplies remaining were the canvas material. The silk, broadcloth, and clothes had been sold along the way for room, board, and passage.

In San Francisco, prospectors were less than enthusiastic about buying his canvas material because their tents and wagons covers rarely wore out. What they really needed were pants. One dusty old prospector reportedly told Levi, "Pants don't wear worth a hoot up in the diggin's, and you can't get a pair strong enough to last no time."

Strauss took the cue. He hired a tailor to convert his canvas into pants and began selling them to the local miners. The durable garments quickly became popular, and Levi's business prospered. Strauss's two brothers arrived in California in 1853, and with Levi, they established Levi Strauss & Co. In a short time, the company began making the pants from a heavyweight fabric called denim. They dyed the material indigo blue, and a durable fashion tradition for work clothes had begun.

Not everyone was impressed with these pants. One old prospector, named Alkali Ike, had a habit of stuffing his pockets with mining tools when he went to pan for gold. Invariably, the heavy tools would rip the pocket corners and render the pockets useless. Old Alkali was prospecting in the Virginia City, Nevada, area and did most of his complaining to a local tailor named Jacob W. Davis.

Weary of listening to Alkali, Davis played a joke on him. He took a pair of Ike's pants to a local harness maker and had the pocket corners riveted with copper. Several weeks later, much to Davis's surprise, the prospector returned to town with his pockets intact and nothing but praise for Jacob W. Davis. Davis shared this experience with Strauss, and soon copper rivets were a feature of all Strauss's blue jeans, known by then as "Levi's."

Levi Strauss died in 1902, but his company continued its role as a jeans manufacturer and Western-clothing wholesaler under the direction of his nephews. After World War II, the company began to concentrate exclusively on manufacturing pants and selling them under its own label. It continued to target its product toward working people and Western customers but began to place heavy emphasis on the youth market. Today, more than 100 years and a billion pairs of pants later, the Levi's blue jean remains the most important garment in the Levi Strauss line. The company is the world's largest manufacturer of branded apparel. Although pants remain the company's major focus, it also sells jackets, shirts, and skirts. It has 75 plants and distribution centers in North and South America, Europe, Asia, and Australia. Its major divisions are Levi Strauss International, Men's Jeans, Womenswear, Youthwear, Menswear, and Britannia. Jointly, these divisions employ about 30,000 people worldwide.

Interesting—but what do Levi Strauss, canvas pants, Alkali Ike, copper rivets, womenswear, and youthwear have to do with the American economy? Answer: many of the major characteristics of the economic system are featured in the activities of Levi Strauss & Co. These characteristics are the threads of a garment that has proved to be rugged and durable—the American economy.

PRIVATE PROPERTY

Individuals have the right to own, buy, and sell property in the American economy. This property includes millions of things—land, clothing, houses, machinery, tools, furniture, frisbees—all of which can be used and exchanged as desired.

The economic system in which Levi Strauss & Co. has operated has an obvious and important feature—the private ownership of the means of production. Young Strauss established a business, acquired capital (tools), purchased property (canvas material), and secured labor services (a tailor's time and talent) to produce a different kind of private property—pants. He sold these pants to miners in exchange for gold, still another type of property. It is this ownership and exchange of private property, both personal property and the means of production, that is the most visible and important element in the American economy. Private property underlies the market mechanism that distributes the products, services, and resources among the participants in the system. Restated, it enables production and exchange, which create income and wealth in the society.

Today, Levi Strauss & Co. has facilities spread throughout the world. The property that the company owns is the land and capital that it uses to produce, distribute, and market its products. Because the company owns these resources, its stockholders and management can decide how best to combine them with the labor they hire to make products that will satisfy customers and produce a profit for the enterprise. This is a unique feature of a capitalistic economy. Individuals and firms have the right to own and direct the use of land and capital for private benefit. The terms _free enterprise system_ and _capitalism_ are often used interchangeably to describe the private sector of the economy in the United States. Capitalism is an economic system predicated on the _private_ ownership of capital, or the means of production. Socialism, on the other hand, is a system in which the means of production are owned by the government.

The accumulation of property in the form of production, distribution, and marketing facilities, coupled with the strong demand for the firm's product, has enabled Levi Strauss & Co. to expand its sales and earnings over the years. The _motive_ behind the firm's behavior and growth was not, and is not, the desire to help clothe citizens, even though that is the outcome. Basically, the Strauss brothers desired to make money and to share in the economic wealth of the country. They acted from self-interest and, by producing something that people wanted, served society at large. Self-interested behavior is a second important feature of the American market economy.

SELF-INTERESTED BEHAVIOR

Levi Strauss went to California at age 20 to sell supplies to the gold miners. The problem was that the San Francisco customers didn't want the supplies he had to offer. He could have been stubborn and followed his original plans to make tents and repair Conestoga wagons, but he preferred to produce something for which people were willing to pay dearly. He desired to earn revenue by an amount over and above his costs; he was interested in making a _profit_. Levi recognized the demand for pants, concluded that miners would pay high prices for them, and immediately went into business.

The profit motive is evident in the entire history of the firm's activities. In 1968, the corporation formed its womenswear division. The motivation?—an opportunity to expand profits, in view of the increasing place of blue jeans in the wardrobes of young females. Likewise, it developed its Sta-Prest no-iron pants, its preshrunk denim, its "stretch-to-fit" Actionslacks for men, its vast Levi Strauss International Division, its popular "501" line, and its cotton Dockers. The motive in each case was profit. The desire for profit is the driving force that motivates enterprises in the capitalistic economic system. The pursuit of profit leads to the production of goods or services that fulfill people's wants. This is not to suggest that firms look only to short-term profitability. Many firms recognize that corporate giving and responsibility create community goodwill that enhances their firm's potential for long-run profitability. For example, Levi Strauss & Co. is noted for its strong financial support, through a corporate foundation, for social programs for the elderly, minorities, and victims of family violence.

Purposeful economic behavior is not confined to business firms in the American market system. Workers and consumers are also looking for the "best deal available." Workers try to find jobs with the highest pay, best working conditions, most job satisfaction, and best location. Consumers shop for the lowest price for the most durable and useful product they can find. The early California gold panners did not buy Levi's durable, copper-riveted blue jeans because they wanted to make Levi wealthy. They bought these pants because, in their personal judgment, the gold spent on Levi's pants yielded more value than similar expenditures on other available products.

Today, people who purchase Levi's make the same decision. They have a choice of several brands of blue jeans and other pants. Consumers spend their money in ways that give them as much satisfaction as possible. If they perceive that a purchase of Levi's jeans is worth more to them than spending that money elsewhere, they buy the jeans. Consumers operate from the same self-interest motivation that firms do. Both pursue their own interests, and both benefit from exchange.

This pursuit of economic self-interest should not be confused with selfishness. Business owners are human beings, with human emotions, who often direct their managers to donate corporate funds to worthy causes. In addition, the owners may use part of their dividend income (distributed profits) to help churches and charities, to buy presents for others, or to leave bequests to their children. Similarly, consumers need not be buying goods simply for themselves. For example, a church official may be buying new pews for the church. In so doing, the official will compare price and quality among alternative brands.

CONSUMER SOVEREIGNTY

In a capitalistic economy, consumers direct the production of products and allocation of resources. Consumers have the final authority to determine economic production because they are the ones who buy the goods and services produced. Consumers possess this sovereign power because they have the ability and desire to purchase products. Through their spending, consumers signal what they deem to be valuable economic production. Their expenditures are dollar ballots which elect products for continued production and guide the allocation of resources among various production possibilities in the economy.

The ability and willingness of consumers to purchase a product is classified as *demand,* which is discussed in detail in Chapter 4. The California miners had a demand for durable pants that would wear well in the gold mines and stream beds. They possessed income and were willing to spend part of it on denim pants if, in their estimation, the price was reasonable.

Levi Strauss originally intended to produce strong, durable canvas tents and wagon covers. He changed his mind because he recognized consumer demand, potential revenue, and the opportunity for profits. Ultimately, consumers, not Levi Strauss, determined that blue denim pants should be produced and that denim, labor, thread, and buttons should be channeled to this use. Levi Strauss physically produced blue jeans, but it was consumers' "dollar voting ability" that motivated the firm and kept it going. It remains consumer demand that proclaims the message "Produce blue jeans."

The potential revenue available from the sale of demanded products provides a strong incentive for firms to discover and provide goods that consumers desire. In the early days, Levi Strauss heard of consumers' wants by word of mouth. When miners desired pockets that could carry gold and mining tools without ripping, Strauss responded with copper rivets. Today, the company has a market planning department and a product development department that systematically attempt to discover and implement changes in the products that will appeal to consumers and attract their dollars. The activities of these departments are one reason why the firm has introduced preshrunk denim pants, Sta-Prest fabrics, "501" jeans, prefaded fabrics, Dura Plus denim for boys' jeans, Bendover women's slacks, and acid-washed blue jeans.

"Dollar votes" buy elections in the market economy. Consumers elect the products that they desire, and producers respond by gathering resources and producing the desired items. But consumers are fickle voters; although their preference for clothing in general is stable, they often desire fashion changes. Companies such as Levi Strauss are aware of this and respond accordingly. Case in point: The demand for men's blue jeans has fallen considerably in the past several years, mainly because aging baby boomers with expanding waists have opted for more flattering looks. Levi Strauss has successfully responded to this change in tastes by creating Dockers, baggy cotton twill pants with pleats. Sales of Dockers for men jumped from $35 million in 1986 to more than $500 million in 1990. Flush with this success, Levi Strauss has now extended the Docker line to women's pants and men's shirts. A key executive of Levi Strauss & Co. once stated, "We have a pretty good antenna and we follow what the consumers ask for. We don't try to force our ideas of fashion on them. If they want to wear kilts, then we'll make kilts."

COMPETITION

Competition is a fourth important characteristic of the economy. *Competition, formally defined, is the effort of two or more parties, acting independently, to secure the business of a third party by offering the most favorable terms.* This competition is essential to the correct operation of the economy, and answers an important question, "What controls the self-interest behavior and channels it toward economically and socially acceptable outcomes?"

Football announcers sometimes accompany the replay of a fumble with the remark "It sure draws a crowd." Large profits have the same magnetism. Whenever consumers spend heavily on a particular product, a crowd of competing producers soon develops. This crowd is annoying to the original producer, but it is vital to the proper operation of a market economy.

Strauss's success in California did not go unnoticed. Other tailors soon began to produce blue denim work pants. Those people who could not afford tailors began to make their own denim pants. Levi survived that competition and continued to sell large numbers of pants. Today, the company has a popular product and a well-known brand name, but it has much competition. VF Corporation, with its Wranglers, Lee, and Rustler brands, has a larger American market share than Levi Strauss. In addition, many department stores, designer jeans firms, and discount outlets sell blue jeans under their own labels. Société Jacques Jaunet competes strongly with Levi Strauss & Co. in Europe and has subsidiaries in Germany, England, and New York City. Several Japanese companies compete with Levi Strauss International in Japan. In the United States, Levi's market share for jeans is about 22 percent. Lee brand has 10 percent, Rustler 9.5 percent, and Wrangler 5.5 percent. Farah and Haggar compete vigorously with Levi's men's slacks.

In a market economy, competition transforms self-interested behavior into socially desirable ends. It constrains, or limits, the self-interest of companies and ensures that groups or individuals do not obtain the power to promote their own interests *at the expense of other people.* Consumers *direct* the market system, self-interest *motivates* people to act, and competition *regulates* their behavior.

Competition benefits the public in the following ways. First, it encourages firms to increase production in those areas where product demand is strong. If people desire more blue jeans, Levi Strauss & Co. must expand its capacity. If it doesn't, competitors who do expand their facilities will gain a larger market share at Levi's expense. Second, competition leads to lower prices and profits as firms compete for the consumer dollar. If Levi Strauss prices its products higher than comparable-quality ones offered by competitors, consumers will shift purchases away from Levi Strauss's products. If the Levi company's profits are extremely high, new firms will enter the industry and "compete away" some of Levi's sales and profits. Third, competition forces producers to improve the quality of their products. Levi Strauss & Co., whose slogan is "Quality never goes out of style," spends more than a million dollars annually to monitor the quality of its garments. If customers were to become disgruntled with the quality of Levi-labeled products, they would spend their incomes on products offered by competitors. Finally, competition forces firms to reduce their costs and combine their resources efficiently. As an example, Levi Strauss & Co. has developed cost-saving machinery such as the Servo Sewer, which sews a pocket and facing together into a pair of pants in less than a second. Another example is a machine that allows a single operator to produce 23,000 blue-jean pockets in an eight-hour day. In addition, Levi Strauss has developed a state-of-the-art computerized inventory system that lets the company keep track of the inventories (unsold goods) held by itself and its customers. This system enables Levi's to respond immediately to changes in consumer demand and to keep its own costly inventories at a bare minimum.

To summarize, firms such as Levi Strauss, which *help others* by providing customers with reasonably priced, high-quality products, *help themselves* to a profit. The extent of that profit is restrained by competition. Competition channels profit-motivated behavior toward the important social goal of achieving the most efficient allocation of limited economic resources.

SPECIALIZATION

Specialization is a fifth basic feature of the U.S. economy. Companies specialize in producing certain products. For example, Levi Strauss & Co. confines its activity to making clothing, as opposed to producing oil, building automobiles, or growing wheat. In making this decision, managers of the company continually assess the opportunity costs of using resources for this purpose rather than for some other one. Individuals who work for the corporation also specialize; some market the products, others stitch and sew, and still others clean the premises after normal work hours. Furthermore, the capital within the plant is also highly specialized. Some machines cut fabric, for example, and others preshrink denim and ship pants to retail outlets.

Specialization of labor and capital in the economy occurs because people recognize that it adds to productivity and therefore increases wages and profits. This specialization necessitates exchange. The buying and selling process that is so characteristic of the economy is the way in which people exchange things they have much of for things they want more of. For example, the owners of Levi Strauss own more blue jeans (annual production) than they personally wish to use. They have an incentive to sell blue jeans to get money, which they then can use for buying other products that yield greater satisfaction.

To summarize, just as the economic perspective in Chapter 1 suggested, specialization increases production (output) and leads to greater exchange. As a result, income and wealth are increased.

ACTIVE GOVERNMENT INVOLVEMENT

Government (federal, state, and local) is an active participant in the U.S. economic system. In a *pure* market or capitalistic economy, governmental involvement would be minimal. On the other hand, in a totally government-planned and -controlled economy, the private sector would be largely nonexistent. The U.S. economy lies between these two extremes; it is a *mixed economy* that has a large private sector supplemented by active government involvement.

The economic functions of government are analyzed in Chapters 11, 12, and 13. Although there is no elaboration on these functions in this chapter, "active government involvement" is definitely a major feature of the mixed economy in the United States. The role of government must be understood to gain an accurate view of the economy's operation.

CIRCULAR FLOW IN THE MIXED ECONOMY

In a mixed economy, the roles of private property, private enterprise, self-interest behavior, consumer sovereignty, competition, specialization, and government all merge and interact to establish the total pattern of economic activity. This activity is summarized in Figure 3–1.

The diagram shows three basic sectors of the economy: households, government, and business firms. First, note the top half of the diagram and the arrows that flow through the circled area labeled "Product Market." *The product market is a composite of all the individual markets where buyers and sellers interact to exchange products and services.* Business firms such as Levi Strauss produce products and offer them for sale. The products flow to the households and government (depicted by the solid arrows in the upper portion of the diagram).

In return for these products, the households and government pay money to the firms. This monetary flow is shown as the broken lines in the top portion of Figure 3–1. Note that money flows in the opposite direction to the product flow. From buyers' perspectives, this spending is a cost, but from the firms' view, it is revenue necessary to make a profit.

Next, turn your attention to the flows in the lower half of Figure 3–1. Business firms cannot create their products from thin air. They must purchase land, labor, and capital in the *resource market. This is the composite of the individual markets where economic resources are exchanged.* Levi Strauss, for instance, has hired 30,000 workers through the resource market. Note that the government also needs to buy or hire resources to provide public goods and services to households and businesses. The resources, such as labor, are provided by resource owners. The flow of resources to business and government through the resource market is shown as the solid arrows in the bottom portion of the diagram.

The business firms and government pay for the resources with money, represented by the broken lines. This spending is a cost to the companies and to government, but it is income to the households and resource owners. *The income*

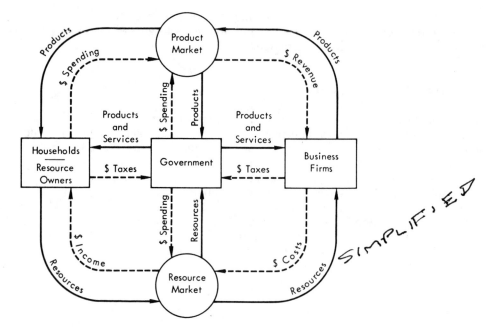

Figure 3-1 The Circular Flow of Products, Resources, and Money in the American Economy
Households and resource suppliers, business firms, and government are linked through the product and resource markets. The solid lines show real, or physical, flows of products, services, and resources. The broken lines show money flows that move in the opposite direction.

that people receive gives them the ability to buy products in the product market. So the circle is complete, and the interdependence of producers and consumers is demonstrated. This flow and interaction must continue or the economy will sputter to a halt.

Carefully consider the role of the government as it is depicted in the diagram. The government buys land, labor, and capital from the business firms and resource suppliers through the resource market and purchases products from the product market. Government spends money on these items so that it can provide products and services to the nation. This flow of services is shown by the solid horizontal lines connecting the government sector to the household and business sectors. Government must receive revenue to pay for these services, and so it levies taxes on the households and businesses. Taxes, a monetary flow, are shown by the broken lines connecting the households and resource owners and businesses with the government sector.

In diagrammatic form, then, Figure 3–1 represents the entire economy and depicts the circular flow of money, resources, and products. This diagram provides a concise picture of the American economy and the relationships embodied within it. The features of the economy—private property, self-interested behavior, consumer sovereignty, competition, specialization, and government participation—all interact within this circular flow diagram. Check your understanding of each feature by asking yourself how each can be explained within the context of the overall circular flow. It *is* altogether fitting—just like a three-year-old, faded pair of Levi's blue jeans.

STUDY QUESTIONS

1. Define the terms *capitalism* and *socialism*. Why is the U.S. economic system termed a *mixed economy?*
2. What is the role of profit in the American economy?
3. Many large American corporations donate money to cultural and charitable institutions. Is this consistent with the position that firms act out of self-interest and attempt to maximize profits?
4. Explain the idea of consumer sovereignty. Are all consumers equally sovereign?
5. How do producers know what consumers wish to buy? Does the fact that some products fail to sell as much as producers expected invalidate the proposition that producers act purposefully, or rationally?
6. How does competition serve to promote efficiency?
7. What is the role of money in the circular flow of the economy?
8. Distinguish between the resource and product markets in a capitalist economy.
9. Explain the difference between the economic roles played by government and private for-profit corporations in the U.S. economy.
10. Describe how specialization and exchange increase output and income.

APPENDIX: A SKEPTIC'S VIEW

The preceding chapter presented a standard description of the major characteristics of the economy. The features discussed — private property, self-interested behavior, consumer sovereignty, competition, specialization, and government participation — are those that most conventional economists would cite. A few economists, however, would declare the discussion inadequate in several areas. In an attempt to identify the areas of dispute, free rebuttal time has been given to a fictitious, purposely provocative, economist named Robert N. Scott. He will critique the chapter, and explain an alternative view of how the economy operates.

*   *   *

Robert N. Scott: Brue and Wentworth do a credible job of defining the characteristics of a well-functioning, competitive, market economy. Unfortunately, that is precisely the problem. The reader is being misled to think that the features of an *ideal* economy are those of the *real* American economy. Not so! The discussion contains many inappropriate assumptions and conclusions. Permit me to cite some examples.

1. *References to the profit motive and profit-maximizing behavior.* The main motivation of large American firms such as Levi Strauss is *not* profit, and most corporations do *not* base their behavior on attempting to maximize it. After all, the owners of the corporation are faceless stockholders who have little to say about the daily operations and decisions made by the professional managers. Why should these managers maximize the interests of those they don't even know? To

be sure, the managers must ensure that their firms make a decent return to *satisfy* stockholders, but once that is accomplished, they are motivated by other factors in their behavior. They are motivated by the need to maintain their own jobs, by the desire to expand their own incomes and their own status and prestige, and by a host of other factors that are unrelated to profits. Corporate executives and middle managers have discovered that the best way to meet the needs of security and increased income and prestige is through rapid, vigorous growth of their firms. *Growth,* not profits, is the major force that motivates large American enterprises. Levi Strauss & Co.'s expansion into new product lines and new countries, its 1979 acquisition of Koracorp Industries, and its enormous pride in the number-one sales position of its Levi brand jeans are all examples of the dominance of the growth motive in Levi's operations. Growth has not meant more profits per dollar of investment, but it has meant more power, prestige, and security for executives and workers.

2. *References to consumer sovereignty.* The idea that the consumer is completely sovereign in the American economy is ridiculous, and I am surprised that it still finds its way into textbooks. American capitalism is characterized by *producer sovereignty,* not consumer sovereignty. The economy is dominated by gigantic corporations that spend massive sums on advertising. This advertising is designed to shape and even create demand for products. Consumers do not decide what gets produced; producers do, and, once they decide what to produce, they use advertising to ensure that people will buy the product. Levi Strauss's men's slacks line is a good example. Do you think consumers decide that pants should be narrow-legged one year, flared the next, and cuffed the next; or that pockets should be straight across one year and down the side the following year? Levi Strauss changes styles and then *creates* a demand for the "new look" through massive advertising. It creates demand by making consumers feel that their old pants are obsolete and downright funny looking.

3. *References to the role of competition.* Competition *is* a vital force in a *pure* market economy, but the authors leave the incorrect impression that the American economy is vigorously competitive. Just the opposite is true! Most of our products are produced by industries in which three or four firms dominate and control supply in the market. Rivalry exists, but not the type of competition that lowers prices and benefits consumers. Competition takes the form of expensive advertising and product changes, which influence the consumer's decisions but do not reduce prices.

This isn't the way competitive firms and industries are supposed to work. How can one conclude that the present structure of the American economy is highly competitive and therefore produces a socially desirable allocation of resources?

*   *   *

We know Dr. Scott, and *his* pants are "downright funny looking." Even though we think that Dr. Scott's views are rebuttable by theory and evidence, we agree that the questions he raises and the assumptions he challenges merit further discussion. Competition, monopoly, advertising, market concentration, and related topics are analyzed more completely in several chapters in the Microeconomics section of the text. Also, an appendix at the end of Chapter 9 directly counters Dr. Scott's comments.

4

FIRST AND TEN,
ECONOMICS AGAIN

The Basic Elements of Supply and Demand

Concepts and Terms Examined in This Chapter

1. Demand
2. Supply
3. Determinants of Demand
4. Determinants of Supply
5. Market
6. Equilibrium Price (Market-Clearing Price)
7. Fixed Prices
8. Shortages and Surpluses
9. Income and Substitution Effects

Football has become one of America's most popular and exciting spectator sports. Throughout the fall, *Homo sapiens* in its infinite variety jams into concrete structures in every section of the nation to watch groups of colorfully uniformed men knock each other around in an attempt to advance a leather object to pay dirt. Upon completion of this feat, the gathered multitudes go wild.

Football is a fascinating phenomenon that has been analyzed by sportswriters, social columnists, sociologists, and psychologists. The subject may also be approached from an economic perspective. Although an analysis of the overall economics of football—revenues, costs, profits, and losses—would be interesting, space constraints dictate the examination of more limited aspects of the football scene. Specifically, this chapter explores the market for the main focus of football fever—the football itself—and then continues toward its goal by examining the market for tickets to two specific college games.

The market in which footballs are bought and sold demonstrates the typical situation where supply and demand interact to establish a *market-clearing price*. The two examples involving the supply and demand for football tickets show why shortages or surpluses occur in circumstances where prices are not free to move to the market-clearing level. Combined, the examples and scenes illustrate how markets function to motivate buyers and sellers and serve to facilitate exchange.

This chapter is designed to provide a *basic* understanding of supply, demand, and market equilibrium. Chapter 5 extends the analysis through a discussion of elasticity of supply and demand and changes in supply, demand, and prices.

THE MARKET FOR FOOTBALLS

People use the word *market* in various ways. For example, a shopper might speak of "going to the market"; an advertising executive, "increasing the market"; an exporter, "moving into the Asian market"; and a real estate agent, "placing a house on the market." For an economist, a market is not an open-air store, or a volume of sales, or a region of the world, or an offer to sell; rather it is *a grouping of buyers and sellers exchanging products or services in some geographical area.*

The market for footballs in the United States involves a product (footballs), buyers (individuals, schools, and professional teams), sellers (manufacturers, wholesalers, and retailers), and exchange (money for footballs, footballs for money). Who decides how many footballs should be produced? Who or what determines their price? What keeps producers from manufacturing too few footballs and too many soccer balls? How can the desire by producers for high prices and profits be reconciled with the concern by consumers for low prices? To answer these questions, economists find it useful to separate markets into two parts: demand, which reflects the behavior of buyers, and supply, which involves the conduct of sellers.

Demand

Demand is a relationship showing the specific quantities of a product or service that buyers are willing and able to purchase at each price in a set of prices. Note the key relationship between quantity and price implied by the definition. As price changes, people's willingness and ability to purchase a product change (quantity changes). Table 4-1 shows a hypothetical market demand schedule for footballs and demonstrates the price-quantity relationship.

The table shows that, other things being constant, the higher the price for footballs, the fewer footballs the buyers will purchase. For example, notice that consumers desire 500,000 footballs annually at a $50 price but they wish to buy 1,900,000 at $10. This demand schedule for footballs is typical of schedules for other products and services; it reflects an *inverse*, or *negative*, relationship between price and quantity. This price-quantity relationship is called the *law of demand*.

The information in Table 4-1 is plotted graphically in Figure 4-1. Notice that the curve shows the quantity of footballs demanded at each price in the range of prices, $50 through $10. The downward slope of the demand curve depicts the prospective behavior of buyers: they desire to purchase more items at lower than at higher prices.

Why does the typical demand curve slope downward and to the right? In other words, why do buyers purchase more of something when its price falls and less when its price rises? The answer comes directly from the definition of demand itself.

Recall that demand reflects the quantities of a product that buyers are *willing* and *able* to purchase at each price in a set of prices. When the price of a product falls, people are *willing* to buy more of that product and less of other items whose prices have remained unchanged. For example, if the price of a football declines from $50 to $10, a football becomes a "better buy" relative to such other goods and services as basketballs, hamburgers, books, motion picture tickets, and gasoline. People will be enticed to buy more footballs; they will substitute footballs for other purchases. The increase in purchases resulting from an increased *willingness* to buy more of an item when its price falls is called a *substitution effect*.

A second reason why individuals buy more footballs when the price falls is also apparent from the definition of demand: people are *able* to buy more. The lower price, for example, $10 rather than $50, means that consumers experience an increase in their *real income*, or purchasing power. People's real income depends on their money, or nominal, income and the prices of the products they buy. When the price of a product falls, their real income rises; consumers are *able* to buy more footballs. For example, a high school team that has a $200 budget to buy footballs can buy 20 at $10 as opposed to only 4 at the previous $50 price. The increase in purchases resulting from the greater ability to buy more of a product whose price has fallen is called an *income effect*. To repeat, the demand curve slopes downward

**Table 4-1   Hypothetical Market
Demand for Footballs**

Price (P)	Quantity (Q) (100,000s)
$50	5
40	8
30	10
20	13
10	19

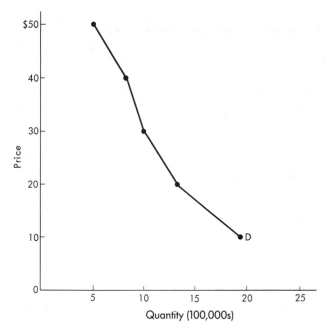

Figure 4-1 The Demand for Footballs

The demand curve reflects an inverse relationship between price and quantity demanded. At a price of $50, consumers will buy 5 units of footballs (500,000); at $10, they will purchase 19 units (1,900,0000).

and to the right because lower prices create an increased willingness and ability to purchase more of a product or service.

An important distinction, discussed in more detail in Chapter 5, should be noted here. "Demand" and "quantity demanded" are two different concepts. As the price of footballs increases from $10 to $30, the quantity demanded falls from 19 units (1.9 million) to 10 units (1 million). Nevertheless, demand stays the same because it includes all the possible price-quantity combinations shown by the curve. Demand is the entire schedule and curve shown in Table 4-1 and Figure 4-1, and quantity demanded is determined by assuming one specific price in the range of prices.

One final point about demand needs to be made. The demand curve in Figure 4-1 reflects a price-quantity relationship, *other things constant.* What are those things being held constant? What happens if they change? The factors assumed to be constant for purposes of isolating a demand curve are called *determinants of demand.* They include (1) tastes, (2) population, (3) income, (4) prices of related products, and (5) expected future prices. These determinants are discussed in Chapter 5. For now, be aware that changes in one or more of the determinants of demand shift the demand curve rightward or leftward. A rightward shift is an increase in demand, for it means that more of the product is desired at each price in the set of prices. For example, an increase in population in the United States would shift the demand curve for footballs to the right, assuming that the other determinants remained unchanged. On the other hand, if tastes changed dramatically so that soccer replaced football in high school and college sports programs, the demand for footballs would shift inward, indicating that the quantity of footballs desired would be less at each price in the range of prices.

Supply

Now let's turn to the seller side of the market for footballs. Supply depicts the behavior of sellers or products or services and can be depicted by a schedule or curve such as shown in Table 4-2 and Figure 4-2. *Supply shows the specific quantities of a product or service that sellers are willing to offer for sale at each price in a range of prices.*

Table 4-2 shows a typical supply schedule, in this case, the hypothetical supply of footballs, Figure 4-2 plots the data in the table to show a supply curve. Higher prices, measured on the vertical axis, entice sellers to offer a greater quantity of an item for sale. For example, if the price of footballs in the market rose from $10 to $50 in Table 4-2 and Figure 4-2, sellers would increase their offers from 2 units (200,000) to 20 units (2,000,000). A price decline from $50 to $10 would produce the opposite result. Thus supply is a *direct*, or *positive*, relationship between price and quantity, other things constant. This relationship is called the *law of supply.*

Higher prices increase the profit incentive to produce more; therefore, sellers offer more for sale when the price they receive rises. Lower prices, conversely, cause sellers to reduce their production. Suppliers, as do all economic agents, behave purposefully by adjusting their actions to changes in economic incentives.

The distinction between "demand" and "quantity demanded" discussed earlier has its counterpart here. Supply is the entire curve shown in Figure 4-2, whereas quantity supplied is measured on the horizontal axis by first selecting a specific price. As the price of footballs changes from $10 to $30, the *quantity supplied* increases from 2 units (200,000) to 10 units (1,000,000), but supply remains unchanged because it is the full range of price-quantity relationships depicted by the curve.

Can supply itself ever change? The answer is "of course," but to do so, one of the "other things constant" must change. These *determinants of supply* include (1) number of sellers, (2) cost of production, (3) prices of other products, and (4) expectations about future prices. If one of these factors changes, the entire supply curve shifts. For example, if the price of cowhide increases, then the cost of producing footballs will also rise, and the supply curve in Figure 4-2 will shift

Table 4-2   Hypothetical Market Supply for Footballs

Price (P)	Quantity (Q) (100,000s)
$50	20
40	15
30	10
20	5
10	2

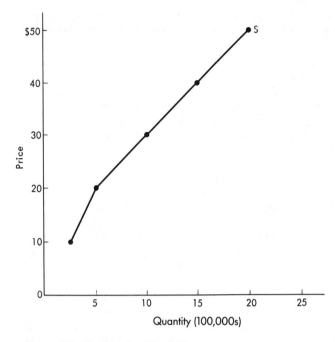

Figure 4-2   The Supply of Footballs

The supply curve reflects a direct, positive relationship between price and quantity supplied. At a price of $10, producers will offer to sell 2 units of footballs (200,00); at $50, they will offer 20 units (2,000,000). The curve slopes upward and to the right, because higher prices generate profit incentives to offer more footballs for sale.

leftward. If, on the other hand, foreign producers enter the U.S. market, the supply curve will shift outward, reflecting the fact that producers collectively will then be willing to offer more footballs for sale at each price. The determinants of supply and changes in supply are discussed more thoroughly in the following chapter.

Equilibrium Price and Quantity

Demand and supply analysis is a useful and powerful model to explain how markets function. Table 4-3 incorporates the demand and supply data from the previous discussion.

Close inspection of the information in Table 4-3 allows us to determine the equilibrium price and quantity. *Equilibrium price is the price that equates the quantity demanded by buyers with the quantity supplied by sellers.* Thus the equilibrium price is the *market-clearing price*. It is a price that will prevail unless one of the determinants of demand or supply changes, causing entirely new demand or supply schedules. The equilibrium price in Table 4-3 is $30, because at that price, buyers desire 10 units of footballs and sellers wish to sell 10 units. The $30 price clears the market, leaving neither a shortage nor a surplus of footballs. Contrast the market-clearing price to other prices in the table. At a price of $50, buyers desire to purchase 5 units, but sellers want to sell 20 units. The resulting surplus of footballs on the market (15 units) will drive the price down until the market clears at $30 and

Table 4-3   Hypothetical Market for Footballs

Q (demanded)	P	Q (supplied) (100,000s)
5	$50	20
8	40	15
10	30	10
13	20	5
19	10	2

10 units. On the other hand, if the price in this market is $10, a shortage of 17 units will develop (19 − 2) and that shortage will increase the price to $30.

Figure 4-3 shows the market information graphically. The demand curve shows the predictable behavior of buyers; the supply curve, the behavior of sellers. The $30 price is the only one that will clear the market. That price, and the equilibrium quantity of 10 units, will remain until either the supply or the demand curves shift. Those shifts can only occur if one or more of the determinants of supply and demand changes.

The market for footballs is typical of most markets in that the price is free to seek a market-clearing level. But what if a specific price is frozen or fixed by the

Figure 4-3   The Market for Footballs

The equilibrium price and quantity of footballs are determined by the intersection of supply and demand. The equilibrium price, $30, equates the quantity demanded and supplied, 10 units, so that the market clears. Hence, the equilibrium price is also the market-clearing price.

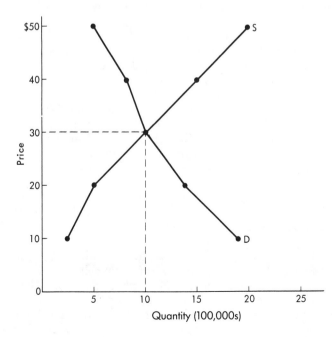

government or the seller? Will the market then clear? The answer is "no, not necessarily" and is explained by examining a second market, the one for college football tickets.

THE MARKET FOR FOOTBALL TICKETS

The market for football tickets, as opposed to footballs, is somewhat unusual. Officials set ticket prices far in advance of game day. The fixed prices are set roughly on the basis of the anticipated supply and demand for the typical game on the schedule, but once set, these prices remain stable regardless of changes in demand. The fixed prices may not be equal to equilibrium prices for each game, and they do not ensure that the quantity of tickets desired will equal the number of tickets available. Because price does not effectively ration the tickets, a "first-come, first-served" method of rationing is required.

One of two outcomes is likely under a "first-come, first-served" rationing procedure. First, a surplus of tickets may occur, because not all tickets may be sold at the fixed ticket price. Second, a shortage may result; that is, the number of fans desiring tickets at the stated price may exceed the stadium capacity. The two scenes that follow formalize those outcomes.

Scene One—The University of Minnesota Gophers

The appeal of the University of Minnesota Gophers at the box office has experienced wide swings over the last several decades.

In 1960 university football fever was a way of life in Minneapolis–St. Paul, as the Minnesota Gophers marched to a national championship. But University of Minnesota football fortunes, particularly at the box office, fell on difficult times during the 1970s and early 1980s. As the Minnesota win-loss record fell, Gopher ticket sales plummeted. Memorial Stadium, with its 60,000 seats, was half empty on some Saturday afternoons.

The Twin City fans' lack of interest in Gopher football was partially the result of an unexciting win-loss record, but that was not the only factor. In 1960, the Minnesota Vikings professional football team was formed. By the 1970s, while the Gophers were being defeated by Michigan and Ohio State on Saturdays, the Minnesota Vikings were defeating such teams as the Los Angeles Rams and the Green Bay Packers on Sundays. As the Vikings emerged as a National Football League power, many fans transferred their loyalties and ticket demand from the Gophers to the Superbowl-contending Vikings. In economic terminology, the quality of a close *substitute good* increased, resulting in a decline in the demand for Gopher tickets. *Substitutes are products that are interchangeable in satisfying consumer wants.*

In the mid-1980s, the situation began to improve. The Vikings fell to the bottom of the standings, while the Gophers, under the leadership of head coach Lou Holtz, made it to a bowl game. Interest in the Gophers picked up dramatically. After only one season at Minnesota, Holtz left for Notre Dame, but Gopher hopefuls believed the program's appeal would continue to grow. That did not happen. The Gopher win-loss record and local fan support again fell.

Full houses may once again become the rule at Gopher games, but that remains for the future to reveal. The more typical situation over the past decade has been that shown in Figure 4-4, which depicts ticket supply and demand for a

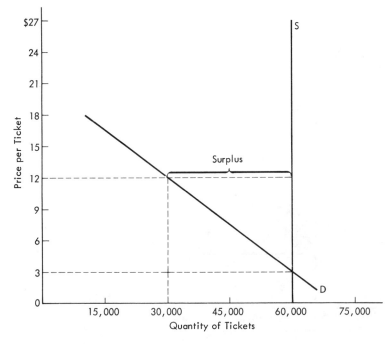

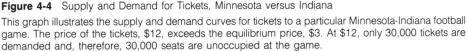

Figure 4-4   Supply and Demand for Tickets, Minnesota versus Indiana

This graph illustrates the supply and demand curves for tickets to a particular Minnesota-Indiana football game. The price of the tickets, $12, exceeds the equilibrium price, $3. At $12, only 30,000 tickets are demanded and, therefore, 30,000 seats are unoccupied at the game.

specific Minnesota contest. The demand for tickets to this Minnesota versus Indiana game is typical; it is an inverse relationship between quantity and price. For example, if the price per ticket is $12, people will demand 30,000 tickets, but if the price falls to $3, they will wish to buy 60,000 tickets. The supply curve in Figure 4-4 is *not* typical, however. Football stadiums are expensive to build, and once in place, have fixed capacities. True, people can be squeezed closer together or temporary bleachers can be added at the bottom of the end zone, but in general, the available number of seats, and therefore tickets, is *fixed* by the stadium capacity. Only by expanding the structure via new construction can the quantity of seats supplied be increased substantially, and this type of expansion *requires considerable time*.

Because capacity is fixed, the price charged per ticket is of no consequence in determining the quantity of tickets the university will offer. Figure 4-4 depicts a supply schedule for a 60,000-seat stadium. The university will try to sell all its 60,000 tickets, whether the price is $6, $12, or $21.*

Notice that, at the ticket price of $12, the demand curve indicates that only 30,000 fans desire to buy tickets, although the available supply is 60,000.

*Once the university sets the price of its tickets, say at $12, the supply curve becomes a horizontal line that extends from that ticket price on the vertical axis rightward to the stadium's capacity (60,000 tickets in Figure 4-4). At the stadium's capacity, the supply curve becomes vertical, as shown in Figures 4-4 and 4-5. For simplicity we are assuming that all seats are identical and interchangeable and therefore that all tickets command the same price.

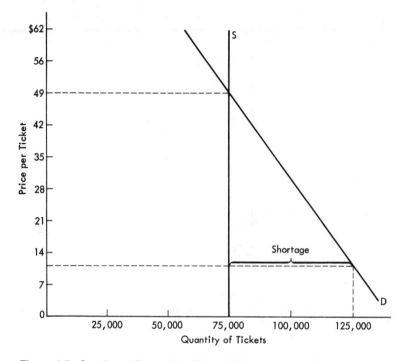

Figure 4-5   Supply and Demand for Tickets, Nebraska versus Oklahoma
The demand and supply curves for a particular Nebraska-Oklahoma game produce an equilibrium price of $49. At the lower price printed on the tickets, $12, the quantity demanded is 125,000, producing a shortage of 50,000 tickets. This shortage gives rise to scalping activity.

Clearly, a surplus of tickets exists. Since the price per ticket is fixed by the university, the price cannot fluctuate and thereby ration the available seats. Rather, the tickets are distributed on a "first-come, first-served" basis, and the result is a stadium only half full. If people who had purchased tickets in advance wished to sell them at game time, they may have hoped for $12, but they probably received something less. The equilibrium price in the diagram appears to be approximately $3, for at that price, the quantity of tickets desired just equals the available supply. A general conclusion may be drawn from this example: *when the price of a product is fixed at a level higher than the equilibrium price, a surplus will occur.*

Scene Two—The University of Nebraska Cornhuskers

The football scene at Lincoln, Nebraska, home of the Big Eight Conference Cornhuskers, stood in contrast to that at Minnesota during the last decade. Nebraska's win-loss record over this period was one of the best in the nation; they consistently ranked in the top ten teams nationally; and they appeared in numerous postseason bowl games. Furthermore, unlike Minnesota, the Cornhuskers had little competition for the sports entertainment dollar. For example, the state of Nebraska had no major professional football, baseball, or hockey teams.

As a result of these factors, fans flocked from all corners of the state to jam Memorial Stadium on game day. The stadium has a seating capacity of approximately 75,000. Since the quantity of tickets demanded was great relative to the supply at the existing price, those who had tickets became a social elite. Residents of Wahoo, Beatrice, Geneva, and Surprise proudly proclaimed to their friends and neighbors that they managed to get tickets to the next game.

Because tickets were sold out months in advance at the University of Nebraska, in contrast to Minnesota, no ticket lines were to be seen at the stadium box office prior to the game. Yet enterprising fans could and did obtain tickets just outside the stadium. Loiterers with tickets could be observed there on game days, just prior to the kickoff. They made no attempt to enter the stadium, but waited for people to approach and begin conversations. Market transactions occurred as money was exchanged for tickets. The amounts transferred were anywhere from $20 to $100 a ticket, depending on the competition and the location of the seat. Figure 4-5 describes the supply and demand for a specific Nebraska football game.

In the Minnesota example, a surplus of tickets was observed, but just the opposite case is evidenced in Figure 4-5. At the printed ticket price of $12, the number of tickets demanded is 125,000, whereas the number supplied is 75,000. The result is a *shortage* of 50,000 tickets. In this case, the "first-come, first-served" rationing method ensures a full stadium, but it also produces a substantial shortage.

Notice that the price that will clear the market, or equate the quantity demanded with the quantity supplied, is approximately $49. This suggests that many people who are unable to get tickets are willing to pay considerably more than the $12 price. The conditions shown give rise to a *second market* for tickets. Before further examining that market, however, let's pause to state another general conclusion. *When the price of a product is lower than the equilibrium price, a shortage will occur.* If the product price is freely determined, the shortage will drive up the price and the shortage will thereby be eliminated. But, if the price is fixed, the shortage will remain and a second market will mostly likely form.

The behavior of selling tickets for an amount higher than the printed price is called "scalping." The Nebraska situation lends itself to this human activity, because a shortage of tickets occurs and numerous people are willing to pay inflated prices. The transactions in front of the stadium on game day are duplicated everywhere in the state—in taverns, executive office buildings, the university student union, and even the state capitol building.

This second market is highly unorganized. The buyers and sellers transact their business individually and do not have full knowledge about other prices being charged. Nevertheless, a "going rate" or equilibrium price tends to become established. This price varies considerably from game to game, depending upon the supply and demand conditions.

Second markets may be either legal or illegal, depending upon the law. If scalping were legal in the case represented by Figure 4-5, the market price would be $49 per ticket (equilibrium price) because all ticket holders and prospective buyers would feel free to participate. In many states, however, scalping is a misdemeanor, and sellers are prosecuted. As a result, many ticket holders choose not to participate in the illegal market, even though they would otherwise be willing to sell their tickets for an inflated price. The consequence is that ticket supply in the illegal market is reduced markedly, and the going price may exceed $49. As a general proposition, the larger the penalty imposed on scalpers and the greater the risk of being caught, the higher the price in the illegal market.

SUMMARY AND CONCLUSIONS

Markets and prices play a crucial role in the American economy: they motivate economic participants, facilitate exchange, and help to allocate scarce resources to their highest-valued uses. They accomplish these things by providing incentives and information to market participants, which in turn encourage buyers to assess opportunity costs in making purchasing decisions and sellers to employ scarce resources in least-cost ways.

The market price rations scarce resources and goods to those willing and able to pay the price. Markets clear—that is, quantity demanded equals quantity supplied—when prices are free to adjust to the supply and demand conditions present. When the price is fixed by government or a seller, and that price is above or below the equilibrium price, shortages or surpluses occur.

Supply and demand analysis is a powerful tool for analyzing markets. The model developed in this chapter is applicable to a wide range of markets in the economy and will be used throughout the textbook to explain the processes of production and exchange.

STUDY QUESTIONS

1. Define the term *equilibrium price*. Why is it also called a *market-clearing price?*

2. Suppose that the demand for footballs increases such that the number of footballs demanded rises by 7 units (700,000) at each price listed in Table 4-3. That is, 12 units are now demanded at $50, rather than 5 units; 15 units are now demanded at $40, not 8 units; and so forth.
   a. Determine the new equilibrium price and quantity.
   b. Suppose that government sets a legal maximum price of $30 on football tickets. Determine the size of the shortage or surplus that would result from this legal maximum, given the new demand schedule.
   c. Suppose that government sets a legal minimum price of $50 on football tickets. Determine the size of the shortage or surplus that would result from this legal minimum price, given the new demand schedule.

3. If a university lowered its ticket price to a game, would you expect an increase in *demand* for tickets or an increase in the quantity of *tickets demanded?* What's the difference between these two terms?

4. Why does a typical demand curve slope downward and to the right?

5. Assume that government set a minimum price of an item such as grain at its equilibrium level, and then the supply of the product increased markedly. Diagram this situation. What would be the result?

6. Scalping laws usually penalize only the seller. Do you think the illegal second market price of a ticket would be higher or lower if the laws were changed so that the buyer was subject to a fine or imprisonment, as well as the seller? Why?

7. Explain: "Prices help ration limited goods and services by allocating them to those willing and able to pay the market price."

8. If the supply schedule changed in Table 4-3 so that sellers offered 8 more units of footballs at each price, what would be the new equilibrium price? Explain.

9. Why are shortages and surpluses of products the exception and not the rule in the American economy? Can you think of a reason why shortages and surpluses are more prevalent in centrally planned economies than in market economies?

10. One aspect of the economic perspective is the idea that people respond to incentives and disincentives. Use this idea to explain demand and supply curves.

5

GALLSTONES, 747s, FISH, AND CALCULATORS

The Economics of Utility, Elasticity, and Changes in Supply and Demand

Concepts and Terms Explained in This Chapter

1. Supply and Demand
2. Equilibrium Price
3. Elasticity
4. Determinants of Supply and Demand
5. Changes in Supply and Demand
6. Change in Equilibrium Price
7. Zero-Priced Commodities
8. Utility
9. Diminishing Marginal Utility
10. Substitutes and Complements
11. Total Revenue Test

This chapter extends the analysis of Chapter 4 by explaining concepts such as elasticity, determinants of demand and supply, zero-priced commodities, and changes in supply, demand, and equilibrium price. Four economic scenes—involving gallstones, 747s, fish, and calculators—are used to introduce and explain the new concepts. Each scene emphasizes different aspects of supply and demand.

SCENE ONE—GALLSTONES

You have a pain in your side—dull at times, excruciating at others. You see a physician who asks several questions: "Have you had the pain before?" "Do you eat high-fat foods?"

X-rays are taken. Gallstones are spotted. Surgery occurs. The physician and hospital bills arrive. Ouch! Welcome to the world of modern medicine.

The gallbladder is a pear-shaped organ that rests below the liver and above the small intestines. Its main function is to store and concentrate the bile salts and cholesterol from the liver. The gallbladder sends bile into the small intestines where it helps to absorb and digest the fats. Occasionally, the bile in the gallbladder becomes supersaturated with cholesterol and something triggers a formation of cholesterol crystals that mass into stones. When the stones work their way through the system, intense pain occurs.

Fortunately, the gallbladder can be completely removed without impairing the overall functioning of the body. And that is where economics comes in. Each gallbladder removal costs as much as $8,000, depending upon the location of the hospital where it is performed. Physicians in the United States remove approximately 500,000 gallbladders annually. This is an activity that involves over a billion dollars of expenditure and revenue each year.

In some respects, gallbladder surgery is a unique economic activity; in other regards, it is similar to all market situations. The ideas of utility, demand, and elasticity help to identify both the uniqueness and representativeness of this economic action.

Utility and Consumer Behavior

The demand for all products and services is based on the idea of utility. *Utility* is a personal, subjective, difficult-to-measure value that influences the buying behavior of all consumers. Economists define utility as "want-satisfying power" or "satisfaction." People purchase an automobile, a painting, skis, a hot dog, or a textbook because such products and services offer utility. They yield satisfaction or satisfy wants.

Anticipated satisfaction (utility) is the incentive influencing consumer behavior. Consumers, no matter what they purchase, are trying to increase their level of satisfaction. This behavior is an example of the purposeful, nonrandom, actions of people referred to in that latter part of Chapter 1.

Notice the subjective nature of utility. A particular painting may provide you with substantial utility, but the aesthetic qualities that you see in it may not be evident to someone else. You may think the painting is terrific; a friend may think it is worthless. Translated into economics, this painting may have high utility for you and low utility for your friend.

A consumer's demand for any product depends on the degree of utility that the person expects to receive from using it. If no utility is expected, no demand will be present. But, when substantial utility is foreseen, strong demand will be evident. Different people, with different tastes, incomes, and perceptions, will have different demands for products and services.

People with normal, healthy gallbladders do not have a demand for gallbladder surgery because they anticipate no utility from an operation. A healthy, rational person would not undertake this surgery, even if it were priced at zero. But, for people with gallstones, the utility is high, because the surgery eliminates long-run suffering and removes the risks of jaundice, liver damage, and infection. The anticipated utility of a successful operation and recovery far outweighs the discomfort and medical costs of the operation.

The decision to remove the gallbladder is made at the margin by the rational consumer. He or she compares the *marginal utility* of the operation to its price, or cost. "Marginal," in economics, means "extra" or "added," so *marginal utility is the extra satisfaction, or benefit, received by consuming one more unit of a product or service*. As a person consumes more of a product, marginal utility falls. This phenomenon is called the *law of diminishing marginal utility*. For example, the first fast-food hamburger consumed may yield much utility, but the second, third, fourth, fifth, . . ., eighteenth yield reduced *extra* satisfaction (at one meal). Likewise, the first successful gallbladder operation might yield substantial marginal utility, but an unnecessary second, third, and fourth would not.

If the *marginal* utility (MU) of an item is less than its price (P), a consumer will conclude that "the item just isn't worth buying." If marginal utility of the product exceeds the price, then a person will strongly consider buying it. If the MU/P ratio exceeds that of ratios for other possible products, and the consumer has sufficient income, then the person will buy the product. This is a theory of rational consumer behavior or rational choice. Stated succinctly, the rational consumer should compare the ratios of MU to P for affordable products and allocate money income so that the last dollar spent for each product or service will yield the same amount of marginal utility. In other words, the consumer maximizes total utility when the MU/P ratios of all products purchased are equal. For if one product has a MU/P ratio that is higher than that for other products, the consumer can increase total utility by purchasing more of it and less of the other products. As one consumes more of the product with the high MU/P ratio, MU falls due to diminishing marginal utility. Hence, the ratio falls until the consumer is in equilibrium in which

$$\frac{MU_x}{P_x} = \frac{MU_y}{P_y} = \frac{MU_n}{P_n} \qquad (5\text{-}1)$$

The theory of consumer behavior can be applied to the gallstone situation. Consider two cases, the first "elective" surgery and the second "emergency" surgery. In the elective situation, suppose that a person has been informed that the cause of mild discomfort is gallstones, and the decision to undergo surgery is left to the patient. A patient who assesses that the marginal utility of the operation will be less than its price will rule out surgery. A person who expects the marginal utility of the operation to be large, relative to the price and to other uses for income, will elect to have a physician perform the operation. A person's budget and insurance are also important to the consideration. To check your understanding of the analysis, ask yourself what the effect of complete insurance coverage would have on the decision to have elective surgery.

In the second case, emergency surgery, the patient does not have much of a decision to make. The extra utility—preservation of one's life—is so great relative to the price of the surgery that the operation is routinely undertaken.

Demand

Having established the utility underpinning of demand, we can extend the analysis by graphically depicting the market demand and supply curves. Recall that demand reflects the predictable behavior of buyers and can be illustrated by plotting the quantities demanded at each price in a series of prices. The market demand curve in Figure 5-1 shows the quantity of gallbladder operations, elective and emergency combined, that people desire to purchase at each of the prices shown on the vertical axis.

Supply, also shown in Figure 5-1, reflects the predictable behavior of sellers and depicts the number of gallbladder operations that doctors will perform at different price levels.

The equilibrium price is $6,000, and the quantity of operations demanded and supplied at that price is 500,000. Carefully note the demand curve D. This curve depicts an inverse relationship between price and quantity and shows the *entire range* of intended behavior of surgery buyers at different prices. Demand is the entire line in the graph. It is *all* the price and quantity combinations repre-

Figure 5-1   The Market for Gallbladder Surgery

The market for gallbladder surgery produces an equilibrium price of $6,000 at which the quantity of operations demanded and supplied is 500,000. The demand curve is inelastic over the $6,000 to $10,000 price range. A 50 percent change in price will change quantity by only 22 percent.

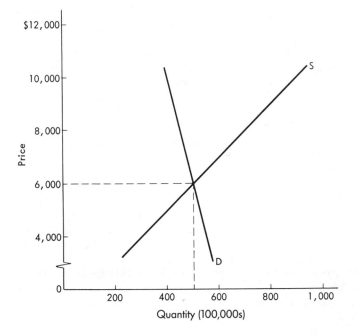

sented by the curve. Thus, it is *incorrect* to say that a decline in the price of surgery would increase *demand*. Demand is the entire curve, and it does not change when price falls. Rather, it is the *quantity demanded* that increases. Using our marginal utility concept, we can say that as price falls, people's MU/P ratios rise, and, consequently, more people elect to have the surgery. Be careful not to confuse this "change in quantity demanded"—a movement along the horizontal axis—with a "change in demand"—a complete rightward or leftward shift in the demand curve. An example of change in demand would be a decline in the demand for gallbladder surgery associated with a decrease in the price of a close substitute, such as medication that dissolves stones or laser devices that crush them. Changes in demand are caused by a change in one of the determinants of demand.

Elasticity of Demand

The demand curve for gallbladder surgery in Figure 5-1 has a particular shape, reflecting its *elasticity*. Elasticity of demand is the measure of buyer responsiveness to price changes. As suggested previously, the demand curve indicates that consumers will reduce their purchases as the price increases and will increase their buying as the price falls. Elasticity measures the *extent* of the consumers' change in purchases, given a particular price change. Think of quantity demanded as a rubber band. In some cases, a small decline in the price of a product entices consumers to increase their purchases dramatically. The quantity demanded increases or s-t-r-e-t-c-h-e-s substantially; demand is said to be *elastic*. In other instances, consumers are less responsive to declines in product price, and the quantity demanded stretches only slightly; demand is termed *inelastic*.

The *midpoint formula* for determining elasticity is given as

$$E_d = \frac{Q_1 - Q_2}{(Q_1 + Q_2)/2} \div \frac{P_1 - P_2}{(P_1 + P_2)/2} \tag{5-2}$$

This equation expresses the percentage change in quantity divided by the percentage change in price. The need to compute the coefficient by using the $(Q_1 + Q_2)/2$ and $(P_1 + P_2)/2$ denominators arises from a problem of comparing percentage increases and decreases. For example, a price increase from $1 to $2 is 100 percent change ($1/$1), using the conventional procedure, but a decline in price from $2 to $1 is only a 50 percent change ($1/$2). Equation 5-2 solves the problem by computing the percentage change using the midpoint of the two prices. In this example, the percentage change in price is 67 percent, that is, $1/[($1 + $2)/2] whether the price rises or falls.

Demand is elastic when the change in quantity, in percentage terms, exceeds the change in price ($E_d > 1$). Demand is inelastic when the percentage change in quantity is less than the percentage change in price ($E_d < 1$). Economists disregard the negative sign attached to the elasticity of demand coefficient. Therefore, if $E_d > 1$, demand is elastic, and if $E_d < 1$, it is inelastic.

The demand curve in Figure 5-1 indicates that patients would reduce their purchases only slightly if prices rose. If the price of the operation increased from $6,000 to $10,000, the quantity demanded would decline from 500,000 to 400,000. Using the special formula just given, this means that a 50 percent change in price would produce only a 22 percent change in purchases, which implies that demand is inelastic over this range of the curve.

Factors Affecting Elasticity of Demand

What factors influence the elasticity of demand? Why do consumers substantially change the amount purchased when the price changes on one product, whereas a price change on another product has little influence on the amount purchased?

One important factor is how necessary a consumer considers a product or service. Some things such as a gallbladder operation, drinking water, and electricity are considered necessities; therefore, consumers are less responsive to changes in price. As the price rises, only small cutbacks are made, and, when the price falls, consumers increase their purchases only moderately because they are already buying the "necessary" amount. Other products are considered luxuries, and people respond significantly to price changes.

A second factor determining elasticity is the number and quality of close substitutes that are available. *Substitutes are products or services that can be used interchangeably to satisfy consumer wants.* Consumers can substitute beef for fish in satisfying their hunger. For example, if the price of fish doubles, people will greatly reduce their consumption of fish and will substitute beef. Hence, the demand for fish is elastic. But what can a patient substitute for a needed gallbladder operation, even if the price doubles? A number of substitutes for surgery have proved disappointing. For example, physicians have discovered that lithotripsy, a procedure using ultrasonic waves to pulverize gallstones, works best on a single small stone. Consequently, multiple subsequent treatments of this procedure are often required. Removal of the gallbladder, on the other hand, permanently ends the patient's gallstone problem. Similarly, experimental procedures whereby physicians pump drugs through the gallbladder to dissolve existing stones often do not permanently end the patient's gallstone problem.

As a general proposition, if an item is considered to be a necessity and has few close substitutes, its demand will be inelastic. If an item is considered to be a luxury and has many close substitutes, its demand will be elastic.

If the "necessity" and "close substitute" criteria were the only determinants of elasticity, the demand for gallbladder operations would be even more inelastic than shown in Figure 5-1. But another important factor also determines elasticity. *Other things being equal, the greater the price of a product or service relative to buyers' budgets, the more elastic (less inelastic) the demand.* Think in terms of two items, products A and B. Assume that both products have the same degree of close substitutes and are viewed with the same degree of necessity. Now let the price of both items increase by the same relative amount—from 1 cent to 2 cents for A and $10,000 to $20,000 for B. In which of the two cases would you expect the greatest percentage decrease in quantity demanded? Budget constraints may force consumers to forgo product B, but people are likely to continue purchasing product A.

A gallbladder operation is expensive relative to the budgets of most people. That factor alone would tend to make demand elastic. But, in this particular case, the "necessity" and "no close substitutes" factors overwhelm the "price-as-a-percentage-of-budget" determinant, and demand in the market is inelastic. The existence of health insurance also plays a role here. If patients are insured, the personal cost to them as a percentage of their budget may be quite small.

In summary, this gallbladder "scene" provides an example of utility, marginal utility, demand, and elasticity. It emphasizes several important points that deserve repeating:

1. Demand is based on utility.
2. Consumer behavior may be explained in terms of marginal utility and price comparisons.
3. A change in quantity demanded is measured along the horizontal axis; a change in demand is a complete shift in the demand curve.
4. Elasticity of demand is a measure of consumer responsiveness to price changes.
5. Elasticity varies depending on the extent to which a product or service is deemed to be a necessity, the number and quality of substitutes, and the price relative to people's budgets.

SCENE TWO—747S

You are flying high now—in a wide-bodied Boeing 747. The aircraft is winging its way between two U.S. cities, and it is completely packed. The normal fare on this route is $200. Today, because of a special fare, the price is $125.

"Not a bad price," you state to the passenger beside you.

"Not a bad price for what?" he replies.

"For this airfare," you respond. "Furthermore, I understand that the airline's total revenue is higher than it would be at the normal fare."

Suddenly, several people in the plane spring to their feet. They look amazingly familiar. You quickly recognize one as Vanna White, another as Sonny Bono, a third as Arsenio Hall. Right behind you stands Tony the Tiger. In the rear of the craft stands Bo Jackson, holding a smelly sneaker. In unison, all these people shout, "Elastic demand curve!"

What a trip! If you can't trust people like Tony the Tiger for the truth, who can you trust? They are right. Airlines find that, by offering sharp fare discounts during special periods of slack demand, they can increase their traffic in percentage terms more than the percentage decline in fares. That is, demand is elastic during some periods. Contrast this situation to the demand for gallbladder surgery. A big discount on such surgery during a particular period will not result in a more-than-offsetting increase in new customers. In other words, the demand for gallbladder surgery is inelastic.

The demand curve indicates that at the price of $200, the number of passengers will be 100. At the lower price of $125, 250 people will buy tickets. Based on the midpoint elasticity formula (equation 5-2), the percentage change in quantity is 86 percent, $\frac{100 - 250}{(100 + 250)/2}$; the percentage change in price is 46 percent, $\frac{200 - 125}{(200 + 125)/2}$. Hence the elasticity coefficient over this range of the curve is 1.9, and, because it is greater than 1, we know that demand is elastic. Remember, economists ignore the negative sign attached to the elasticity coefficient.

The Total Revenue Test

By using the *total revenue test,* the elasticity of demand can be determined without computing the elasticity coefficient. If price declines and the total revenue to the seller increases, the demand is elastic. If price declines and total revenue falls, demand is inelastic. Total revenue is determined by multiplying the price of the product by the number of units purchased (P × Q).

Note in Figure 5-2 that, when the price is $200, quantity demanded is 100. Total revenue is $20,000. But, when the price falls to $125, quantity increases to 250 passengers and total revenue rises to $31,250. Demand is elastic because total revenue rises when price falls.

This 747 "scene" illustrates an elastic demand curve and describes the relationship among price changes, total revenue changes, and elasticity. In this airline example, a drop in price is more than offset by an increase in ticket purchases, and total revenue rises. This case illuminates the general proposition that, if price and total revenue move in *opposite* directions, demand is elastic. In the previous gallbladder "scene," demand was inelastic. When such is the case, price and revenue change in the *same* direction. A price reduction on gallbladder operations will reduce the surgeon's total revenue.

SCENE THREE—FISH

You are half asleep. The boat is swaying in the Pacific Ocean—or is it Lake Erie, or Lake Shasta, or Lake Anna, or Dale Hollow? The location isn't important. The point is that you are fishing.

Figure 5-2 The Demand for Airline Tickets

The demand for airline tickets proved to be elastic over the $200 to $125 range. This can be determined by using the total revenue test. At price $200, quantity is 100 and total revenue is $20,000. At a price of $125, the number of passengers increases to 250 and total revenue rises to $31,250. When price falls and total revenue rises, demand is elastic.

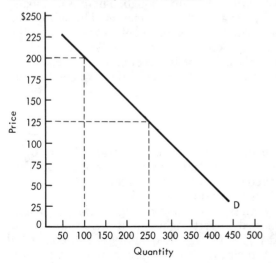

"How are they biting?" you asked on arrival.

"Mainly with their mouths," responded the resort owner.

"Nobody likes one of those types," you thought to yourself.

The scene is a fishing trip, and everyone but you is catching a limit. Ah—that's the word we were fishing for—"limit." For economists, that word produces thoughts of communal property rights, supply and demand, and nonprice rationing.

Markets for products or resources exist in most supply and demand situations to facilitate exchange between sellers and buyers. To sell something, someone must possess property rights to it. *Private property rights are the legally defined prerogatives to possess resources and products and to exclude people from using them.*

Any typical market involves the use of private property rights and the relationship between exchange and price. Consider the example of a fishing tackle business. Owners of the store possess the right to use their legally owned fishing rods and to exclude people from entering the store, taking the poles, and driving away without paying. The market becomes the mechanism for exchange. There is a demand for fishing tackle, the sporting goods stores provide the supply, and payment at an agreed-on price enables the private property rights to be transferred from sellers to buyers. Price rations the fishing tackle to those who are willing and able to pay, and the price excludes those who are unwilling or unable to do so. If there is a surplus of fishing tackle, price falls; if there is a shortage, price rises. At the equilibrium price, neither a shortage nor a surplus occurs and the market "clears."

People, corporate entities, or other institutions own the property rights to fishing tackle. But who owns the property rights to fish? Excluding private fishing ponds, all people in the society collectively own uncaught fish. No one has the right to exclude anyone else from their use, for the uncaught fish are communal goods. Apart from a fishing license fee, no price is established for the right to pursue game fish, and no market exists. Only when sport fish are caught do they become private property, and, even then, people cannot legally sell them.

There is an interesting twist to this situation, though. There is a demand for fish and a supply of uncaught fish, just as in a private market. The supply and demand factors reflect and influence the behavior of people, even though the behavior is not channeled through the market mechanism. This situation will be examined to illustrate the general applicability of the economic perspective, to discuss the special problems of using zero-priced resources, and to explain determinants of demand.

Sportfishing: 1900

In 1900 the supply of game fish in rural areas was large relative to the demand for them. The communal property rights posed no rationing problem because the availability of fish exceeded the quantity of fish demanded, even at the price of zero. This surplus situation is shown in Figure 5-3.

The demand curve is downward sloping and to the right. Even though no price is allowed because of the communal property rights, an "if-there-were-a-price" situation can be conceptualized. At higher prices, the quantity of fish demanded would be less than at lower prices. Actually, there is an indirect price on the fish. The inconvenience and cost of getting to a good fishing location were high for

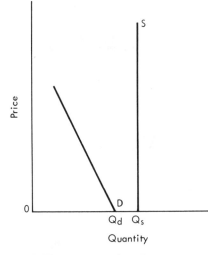

Figure 5-3 Sportfishing: 1900

At the price of zero, in 1900, the quantity of sport fish available (Q_s) exceeded the quantity demanded (Q_d). Because of the surplus, $Q_s - Q_d$, there was no need to set fishing limits or seasons.

most people in 1900. Only those living near the fishing area found this indirect price low enough to engage in the activity. The supply curve in Figure 5-3 is perfectly inelastic, because the quantity of fish is completely unresponsive to changes in price.

At a price of zero—the price of communally owned products and resources—the quantity of sport fish available Q_s exceeds the quantity of fish demanded Q_d. Therefore, in 1900, no limits were needed to ration the fish, for they were abundant relative to the fishing pressure.

Determinants of Demand

The demand for fishing and fish has increased rapidly since 1900. The main determinants of demand are listed as follows. When any one of the determinants of demand changes, the entire demand curve shifts positions.

1. *Population.* The size and the age composition of the population is an important determinant of the demand for products and services. When population increases, the number of potential buyers rises. Assuming that the other determinants of demand remain unchanged, a larger number of buyers will increase demand. In the fishing scene, population growth has been a significant factor in shifting the demand curve rightward. More people are fishing because there are many more people.

2. *Tastes.* Tastes, or preferences, are influential in changing demand. These tastes determine what products or services provide utility to consumers. When new tastes emerge rapidly they are termed "fads." The demand for pet rocks, Star Wars toys, and E. T. dolls shifted rapidly to the right and then either slowly or quickly declined. But fads are the exception, not the rule. Normally, tastes change gradually, as new circumstances, products, and ideas emerge.

The demand for fishing, along with other types of recreation, has increased partially because of changes in tastes. Fishing is a leisure activity, and many people now value such activities more than in the past. They recognize that engaging in relaxing activities far from their complex and hectic work world enhances mental and physical health.

3. *Income.* Changes in income also influence demand. Even though sport fish do not have a market price, there are costs associated with equipment and transportation necessary to pursue the sport successfully. Higher income levels have enabled people to "buy" additional leisure and use more of their time for fishing. The higher income levels also have allowed more people to afford the equipment and transportation expenses involved in the sport. More people now are able to spend time fishing, compared with 1900, because they have more income and can afford more leisure.

4. *Price and quality of related products.* The price and quality of related products affect the demand for items. If the price or quality of the related products changes, the demand for the product in question changes.

Substitutes are one set of related products. *A substitute is a product that performs a similar function to another product.* In some sense, all recreational activities are somewhat substitutable for one another. The price (not cost) for fishing was zero in 1900 and is zero today. But the prices of many substitutes for fishing have increased substantially (e.g., golf, bowling, skiing, theater tickets). The result, though certainly a modest one, is an increased demand for zero-priced activities such as fishing. Also the prices of substitutes for sport-caught fish such as beef, pork, chicken, and store-bought fish have increased, therefore conceivably increasing the demand for fishing.

A second set of related products is *complements.* *A complementary product is one used in conjunction, or jointly, with another product.* Examples are shotguns and shotgun shells, skis and ski lift tickets, tuition and books, butter and bread. If the price of a complement rises, the demand for the related good falls. For example, if college tuition rose appreciably, the demand for college textbooks would likely fall.

Boats, motors, tackle, gasoline, bait, and fuel are all complements to fishing. Some of these products have increased in price relative to other prices in the economy since 1900, dampening the demand for fishing. But other determinants, particularly population and income, have more than offset the effect of the relative price increases of these complements.

5. *Expectations.* Consumer expectations about future prices influence present demand for products. If people expect the price of fishing boats to be substantially higher tomorrow, they demand more boats, at each price, today. So the location of any demand curve depends partly on price expectations. These expectations are powerful determinants of demand in many circumstances, but they do not play a significant role in determining the demand for sport fish.

Sportfishing: Present

The present sportfishing situation is depicted in Figure 5-4. The shift from D_1 to D_2 in the figure represents the increase in demand for fish, 1900 to the present. At each supposed price, the quantity demanded at present exceeds the demand of 1900. The supply of fish remains where it was in 1900. This is a reasonable approximation of the reality of supply because two opposite actions

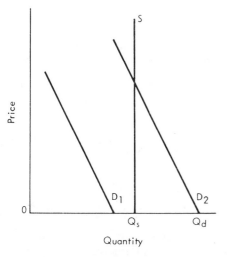

Figure 5-4 Sportfishing: Present

The rightward shift in the demand for sport fish from D_1 to D_2 illustrates an increase in demand during the period 1900 to the present. The shift occurred because of changes in several of the determinants of demand, including increased population, increased income, and changed tastes. At a price of zero, the new quantity demanded (Q_d) exceeds the availability of fish (Q_s). Because no price mechanism exists to ration the fish, government is forced to allocate them via limits and seasons.

have offset each other. First, water pollution and past overfishing have reduced supply, but, second, stocking activity by fishery departments has increased supply. For simplicity, assume that there are approximately the same number of fish available now as in 1900.

The graph shows that a shortage of sport fish now exists. At a price of zero on the graph, the quantity demanded Q_d is greater than the amount of fish available Q_s. No price mechanism exists to ration the fish among the many enthusiasts. The situation forces governments, as representatives of the public owners, to allocate fish to the many potential fishermen. The government restricts fishing to certain seasons and places limits on the number of fish that may be caught per day. This rationing system operates as an alternative to a market to allocate communal property such as sport fish. Without some system of rationing, zero-priced communal resources may be overused.

This scene is definitely a fish story, but the economic concepts—property rights, determinants of demand, changes in demand, substitutes, and complements—help to explain both market and nonmarket economic behavior in the economy.

SCENE FOUR—CALCULATORS

You are an automobile salesperson in St. Louis close to making a sale. The customer wants to know the exact amount of the cost, net of the value of the trade-in. You press the buttons on your pocket calculator, and it flashes the "best deal" you have ever offered. Or so you claim, anyway.

You are using an auxiliary brain that is now a commonplace consumer good in the society. The pocket calculator moved from nonexistence to market saturation in less than 20 years. What was the secret to this product's success? How do calculators relate to concepts of supply, determinants of supply, and equilibrium price?

Pocket calculators are consumer hand-me-downs from the space program. Sharp Electronics introduced the first version in 1970 and priced the unit at $395. Bowmar Instruments of Fort Wayne, Indiana, became the first firm to aim its pocket calculators squarely at the general noncommercial market. It produced a model priced at $239 in late 1971. Today, many firms produce electronic calculators, and units are priced as low as $5.

The decline in prices of pocket calculators has been remarkable, particularly when one considers that the prices of numerous goods have risen dramatically since 1970. Between 1970 and 1990, the Consumer Price Index rose by about 225 percent while the price of calculators fell by nearly 100 percent! In 1970, for example, a McDonald's hamburger was 18 cents, a gallon of gasoline cost about 32 cents, a bottle of Coke sold for a dime, and new Volkswagen Beetles were priced at less than $2,000.

Why did the price of pocket calculators decline so drastically? The answer is that supply increased at a rapid pace relative to demand. Figure 5-5 shows this circumstance graphically. The rapid rightward movement of the supply curve from S_1 to S_2 clearly outpaced the increase in demand. The result? Price fell from P_1 to P_2 and the equilibrium quantity jumped from Q_1 to Q_2.

Several factors caused the substantial increase in supply. Each is discussed under the broad category *determinants of supply*. Determinants of supply are the "other things" assumed to be constant when economists isolate the relationship between price and the quantity that sellers supply. When the determinants change, the entire supply curve shifts either leftward or rightward. Another way of

Figure 5-5   The Calculator Market

The supply of pocket calculators increased rapidly after their introduction in 1970. This increase, illustrated by the shift from S_1 to S_2, occurred because of changes in determinants of supply, specifically, an increase in the number of producers, lower resource prices, mass production, and improved technology. Demand also increased—from D_1 to D_2—but not so dramatically as supply. The result? A decline in price from P_1 to P_2 and an increase in sales from Q_1 to Q_2.

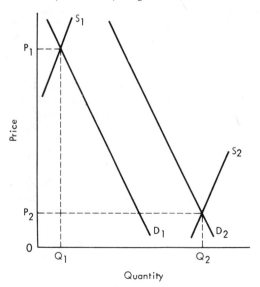

saying this is that the quantity supplied is either smaller or larger at each price than it was previously.

Determinants of Supply

1. *The number of sellers.* Numerous companies invaded the calculator industry during its period of rapid ascendancy. At first, only two or three firms produced calculators; then other producers entered the industry. At one time, more than 40 firms manufactured the devices. This increase in the number of sellers shifted the supply curve rightward. At each price, more calculators were available for sale. Existing firms continued or increased their production, and the new entering firms added to the available supply.

The industry has now greatly consolidated, but the existing producers have huge production facilities capable of turning out more calculators than the sum total for the smaller, although more numerous, producers that operated during the early years of the industry.

2. *The costs of production.* Several factors determine a firm's cost of producing a product. Of particular importance are the *prices of the resources* used in the production process and the *technology* used to produce the product. Other factors influencing costs of production are excise taxes, subsidies, and government regulations.

Two general propositions are relevant here: first, changes in resource costs tend to change supply in the opposite direction. For example, a decline in the price of a component increases the supply of a final good. Second, improvements in technology increase supply in most cases. Both of these propositions help explain the rapid supply increase in the pocket calculator industry. Manufacturers learned to make MOS chips, the calculator's brain, smaller, less costly, and better than before. In 1970, a MOS chip cost more than $20; today, more complex chips than the originals cost less than $1. Time-saving mass-production techniques and the new answer-display technology produced other cost reductions. The assembly time for a minicalculator was 30 minutes in 1972; today, it is less than 5 minutes. It cost approximately $1 a digit to produce the lighted answer-display component in 1973; just two years later, it cost 30 cents a digit. Little wonder that pocket calculator producers became increasingly willing and able to supply more units at any given price.

3. *Prices of other products.* A third determinant of supply—one that is of only minor consequence in the calculator situation—is the price of other products. Sometimes firms can shift their production process to products other than what they are offering. If the price of one of these other products rises in the market, the firm may curtail its output of the product it is making and turn its attention to the more profitable one. An increase in the price and profitability of home computers, for instance, might cause a reduction in the supply of pocket calculators.

4. *Price expectations.* Sellers who expect to receive higher prices in the future may curtail their supply today. If they foresee lower prices in the future, they may offer more of the product for sale today. Although not a major factor in our calculator "scene," this can be an important determinant of supply in some cases. For example, farmers sometimes withhold their grain from the market in anticipation of a higher market price in the future.

Returning to the calculator example, one can see how the determinants of supply influenced the supply and the market price. The rapid increase in supply was caused by reduced costs of production, new technology, and the entry of new firms into the industry. As supply increased faster than demand, price fell from $395 to less than $10.

One idea still remains. That is the elasticity of supply. Producers respond to price changes, just as consumers do. The response, though, is opposite to that of consumers. Higher prices entice producers to offer more for sale. Elasticity of supply is the measure of the degree of response by producers to price changes. If an increase in price prompts producers to increase their production by a greater percentage than the price rise, then supply is elastic. If the price increase does not cause much producer response, supply is inelastic.

The major factor determining the supply elasticity of most products is *time*. The longer the period producers have to adjust their production plans, the more elastic the supply curve. In the short run, calculator producers have inelastic supply curves because production plans are set and adjusting the plans is difficult, but, given enough time, producers can and do respond to higher prices by offering more of a product for sale. The longer the period considered, the more elastic are supply curves.

So there you have it—gallstones, 747s, fish, and calculators. Each scene emphasizes one or more special aspects of supply and demand analysis. If you understand these aspects *and can combine them,* you will possess the ability to analyze numerous market situations. You also will be able to predict how changing behavior of consumers and producers will affect the prices of various products and services in the economy.

STUDY QUESTIONS

1. Do you think that demand for electricity is elastic or inelastic? Explain.
2. The airlines often use dual rates. People who make reservations far in advance and stay at a destination over a Saturday night pay less than business travelers. Why might business travelers have an inelastic demand and vacationing travelers have an elastic demand for airplane travel?
3. Can the quantity demanded of a product decline even though demand does not change? Explain.
4. What is wrong with the following statement? "When demand increases, price increases. But when price rises, demand falls. So price never changes."
5. Some of the new technology in medical care increases costs while improving the quality of care (for example, CT scanners). Use the supply-and-demand graphics to show the impact of such technology on the price of medical care.
6. What effect would a decline in feed costs have on the supply of beef? On the quantity of beef demanded?
7. Use a supply-and-demand graph to diagram the effects of a very large

seizure of heroin by the New York City police force. How might these changes affect behavior of heroin addicts in the city?

8. Which statement correctly uses the terms involved? Explain.
   a. Supply was greater than demand today at the original price, and therefore the price fell.
   b. The quantity supplied today was greater than the quantity demanded at the original price, and therefore the price fell.

9. If the price of a product increased and the total revenue to the sellers declined, would the demand be elastic or inelastic? Explain.

10. Answer the following questions by referring to Table 4-3 in the previous chapter. Substitute the following supply schedule for the one listed in the table: $P = \$50$, $Q_s = 42$; $P = \$40$, $Q_s = 31$; $P = \$30$, $Q_s = 18$; $P = \$20$, $Q_s = 13$; $P = \$10$, $Q_s = 5$.
    a. In what direction has supply changed? What might have caused this change?
    b. What is the new equilibrium price and quantity?
    c. Did demand change? How about quantity demanded?
    d. In what respect did the price change in this example serve as an incentive for consumers to change their buying behavior? Explain in terms of comparisons between marginal utility and price.

11. Use the midpoint formula (Equation 5-2) to determine whether demand is elastic or inelastic over the $50 to $40 price range of the demand schedule in Table 4-1 in the previous chapter. Double-check your answer using the total revenue test for elasticity.

12. How will each of the following changes in demand, supply, or both affect equilibrium price in, say, the market for fishing worms? In each case cite a factor that might *cause* the indicated change in demand or supply.
    a. Demand increases and supply is constant.
    b. Supply declines and demand is constant.
    c. Demand declines and supply increases.
    d. Demand increases substantially and supply increases only slightly.

6

A CORNY STORY WITH
A KERNEL OF TRUTH

The Economics of Production Costs

Concepts and Terms Examined in This Chapter

1. Increasing Marginal Returns
2. Diminishing Marginal Returns
3. Fixed Cost
4. Variable Cost
5. Total Cost
6. Average Cost
7. Marginal Cost
8. Marginal and Total Product
9. Short Run
10. Long Run

The previous chapter contained the assertion that, if all else is equal, firms have an incentive to offer more of a product for sale when the market price of that output rises. Conversely, firms tend to reduce their output when the market price falls. In the present chapter and the one that follows, we explore this supply behavior of competitive firms in greater detail. The vehicle for our discussion is a tongue-in-cheek exercise that concretely develops and explains several important economic concepts. The fictitious characters discover kernels of economic truth that confront nearly all firms in the economy. Study the tables and graphs, and share economic insights with the Cornwells.

Harvey Cornwell had always had a talent for making money. He operated a lemonade stand when he was 6, sold cinnamon-flavored toothpicks at 8, developed a system of converting low-handlebar bicycles into high risers at age 12, and operated the most profitable newspaper route in the country during junior high.

It was this newspaper route that gave Harvey's money-making talents the best opportunity to exhibit themselves. He hired younger children in the neighborhood to deliver his papers for him and paid them only a portion of the difference between his cost of the papers and his receipts from their sale. Harvey's success in the newspaper business made a lasting impression upon him, and the youngster began to entertain thoughts of withdrawing from school and establishing a business enterprise.

Harvey finally hit upon what he felt was the right idea during his senior year of high school. He would drop out of school, start a caramel corn manufacturing plant and sell the product in local department stores and at all area sporting events. The idea had one drawback. Who would finance the start-up costs? It was clear that his parents would not help, because they were irate that he had withdrawn from school. He could not get a business loan from the bank because of his age and inexperience. Young Cornwell's only hope was his grandfather, a retired English teacher who was considered to be the family eccentric.

"Well, what do you think?" Harvey asked, as he finished his pitch to the oldster.

"Frankly, I think you're crazy. Harvey—that's what I think," Richard Cornwell replied. "Your chances of making a success of this are very poor. But—I also think that you will attempt this scheme no matter what—so I'll make you a deal. I'll finance the initial costs of the operation on two conditions."

"Oh, no, here it comes," Harvey thought to himself. "He probably wants discount prices for senior citizens."

"The first condition is that I want a piece of the action. It's a 50–50 partnership or no deal," stated Cornwell. "And the second condition is that you immediately return to school. You can work on the caramel corn operation in the late afternoons and during the weekends. After all, as a partner, I can run things during the day."

Harvey's reactions were mixed. He was elated that his grandfather was willing to finance the company and that it could, therefore, become a reality. Yet he was less than enthusiastic about returning to school and was skeptical about working with an eccentric old man.

"But I don't have any choice," he thought to himself. He hesitated a few more seconds and then reached for his grandfather's hand, shook it, and declared, "You've made yourself a deal."

The grandfather smiled. "This might be fun," he mused, as his mind momentarily pictured a scene of a bustling caramel corn factory. He quickly snapped back to reality, however, and the smile faded.

"Now look, Harvey. Don't expect miracles. We could write what we know about running a business on the back of a postcard. We'll have to use trial-and-error methods, and we might lose our shirts."

"We'll manage," responded the optimistic youngster. "And we'll make money—I'm sure of it."

"Well, if nothing else," punned the older man, "we'll have a Jolly Time."

And so it began! Harvey Cornwell, age 17, and Richard Cornwell, age 68, became partners in the caramel corn business. The nickname "Pop" stuck with the older partner, and the pair decided to use it in the company name—the Harvey and Pop Cornwell Company.

"After all," quipped Harvey, "How can we possibly fail in the caramel corn business when one of the owners is named Pop Cornwell?"

The firm began small. The pair purchased three used movie theater popcorn poppers and rented a small abandoned barbershop. Then they purchased corn, bought the ingredients for the caramel solution, and made arrangements for a distributing firm to buy and market their product.

"Now, we'll need a work force," said Harvey brightly. "The more workers we hire, the better off we'll be. Let's begin with 15."

"I don't think we'll need *that* many," Pop interjected. "But let's figure it out scientifically. I suggest that we add one worker at a time and keep track of our caramel corn output at each level of employment."

"Come on, Pop," Harvey replied impatiently. "This isn't an intellectual exercise—we need to get moving. I'm sure we'll need at least 15 workers. I don't intend to waste time adding one worker at a time!"

"Now hold on, Harvey," Pop responded in a raised voice. "Remember who is bankrolling this operation—and besides, didn't we agree we were going to learn along the way? If we ever do make money on this deal, we want to know *why* we are making it."

Harvey shook his head, muttered unintelligibly, and walked away.

The first worker was hired at $6 per hour, and production began. It soon became clear that the single worker could not efficiently handle the numerous tasks. He was always behind on some part of the job, as he attempted to juggle the use of his time among making the caramel solution, popping the corn, soaking the popcorn, and packaging the finished product. As a result, he was able to produce only 80 bags of caramel corn in an eight-hour day. Pop carefully recorded this amount on a piece of paper in a column entitled "Bags per Day—Total Production (TP)." Meanwhile, Harvey impatiently pestered Pop to approve the hiring of more workers.

Finally, Pop gave Harvey the OK. A second employee was hired and, as expected, production increased. Pop recorded the new daily output total in his table. Then a third employee was hired and, a few days later, a fourth. The retired English teacher continued to absorb himself in carefully recording the daily production totals.

Harvey's impatience with the slow hiring pace finally gave rise to outright anger. He approached his grandfather, who was busy studying his data sheet, and proclaimed in disgust, "This is ridiculous! Are we in this business to make money, or to see how much we can lose? You know we don't have enough workers!"

"Hey—cool down," Pop replied calmly. "You're going to get ulcers. We've only been in this business for two weeks. Besides, I have some interesting information here. Our total product, or output, was 80 bags per day when we had just one worker; it jumped to 250 bags with two, 500 bags when we had three, and now we are producing 800 bags per day with our four employees. We are getting increases in caramel corn output, just as we expected, but notice the nature of these increases. Total output is *increasing at an increasing rate*. Each new worker added more output than the preceding one."

"Would you run that by me again?" asked his somewhat confused partner.

Pop reached for his pencil. "Here, I'll add another column to the table (Table 6-1) and label it, 'Marginal Product,' because it shows the *extra* or *additional* production that we obtained when we hired each new worker."

"See what happened? Look at this third column. The marginal product increased as we added more workers. The hiring of the second worker added 170 bags, but the addition of the third added 250, and the fourth, 300. We are getting *increasing marginal returns* by hiring more workers."

"That's interesting, Pop, but it doesn't surprise me. I told you that we had to hire more employees to get production rolling."

Pop seemed to tune out Harvey's remarks. He continued, "Apparently, what has happened is that we are using our equipment and space more efficiently than when we just had one or two workers. We now have two men on the poppers, one woman ordering supplies and preparing the caramel syrup, and another woman specializing in packaging.

"Increasing returns," Pop repeated to no one in particular. "We're learning, Harvey—we're learning."

"Well, *you* may be learning, but all I know is that we need to keep hiring more workers—we're selling corn faster than we make it," Harvey replied.

The hiring process started anew, but Pop insisted on the "one-more-at-a-time" pace so that he could compile his production table. A fifth worker was hired, then a sixth, and so on, until the firm had 13 employees. As the hiring progressed, the small room became increasingly crowded. Workers began to bump into one another, popcorn spilled all over the floor, and people were forced to stand around waiting for the three poppers to complete new batches of popcorn.

"We've got problems!" Harvey complained to Pop. "There are too many people in this place! The popper operators are threatening to quit because the syrup people are hassling them to speed up the popping, some of the workers are disgruntled because of the crowded working conditions, and others are complaining that they don't have anything to contribute."

Table 6-1   Production Data, Harvey and Pop Cornwell Company

Number of Workers	Bags of Caramel Corn, Total Product (TP)	Additional Bags of Caramel Corn, Marginal Product (MP)
0	0	0
1	80	80
2	250	170
3	500	250
4	800	300

"Maybe we could solve things by hiring a few more workers," Pop suggested sarcastically.

"OK, OK—I get your point," responded Harvey sheepishly.

"But I agree," offered Pop, "we do have problems, and they are reflected in these production data. He handed a copy of his table to Harvey. "Look at these figures" (Table 6-2).

"Our total production increased as we added more workers, but not in the same manner as previously. We are no longer getting increasing returns. The addition of the fifth worker increased total production by 130 bags of caramel corn; the addition of the sixth, 80 bags; the seventh, 50 bags; the eighth worker, only 40. Note the MP column in the table. Whereas before, we were experiencing increasing returns, now we have been getting *diminishing marginal returns*. And look what occurred when we added the last two workers—our total production actually declined!"

"No doubt about it!" said a puzzled Harvey. "Maybe the last few workers we hired are goofing off. Let's fire them and hire some productive people."

"No, no—you're missing the point," Pop responded. "This is a rather normal occurrence for any firm; it's not the workers' fault. We are cramming more and more people into a limited space, and they are just getting in one another's way. Also, they don't have enough equipment—we still have only three poppers. We've hired far too many workers."

"Maybe you're right," Harvey admitted, with a bit of uncharacteristic humility. He glanced at the graph attached to the data sheet and asked Pop what it was for (Figure 6-1).

"I simply made a graph that shows the relationship between our caramel corn production, shown on the vertical axis, and the number of workers, shown on the horizontal axis. I plotted the total product and marginal product data from the table against the various sizes of our work force. I then connected the points so that we could have a visual picture of this relationship.

"Notice that total product (TP) first increased at an increasing rate as

Table 6-2   Production Data, Harvey and Pop Cornwell Company

Number of Workers	Bags of Caramel Corn, Total Product (TP)	Additional Bags of Caramel Corn, Marginal Product (MP)	
0	0	0	
1	80	80	Increasing returns
2	250	170	
3	500	250	
4	800	300	
5	930	130	
6	1,010	80	
7	1,060	50	Diminishing returns
8	1,100	40	
9	1,130	30	
10	1,140	10	
11	1,140	0	
12	1,130	−10	Negative returns
13	1,070	−60	

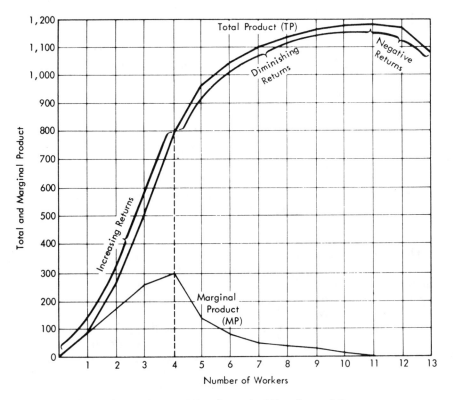

Figure 6-1   Total and Marginal Products, Harvey and Pop Cornwell Company

As the Cornwells hired more workers, total product (TP) first increased at an increasing rate, then increased at a diminishing rate, and finally, declined. Alternatively, marginal product (MP) increased as the first four workers were hired and then declined as diminishing returns set in.

marginal product (MP) rose. When we hired the fifth worker, however, the total product began to increase at a diminishing rate and marginal product declined. At this point, the diminishing returns business set in. See how MP peaks at four workers?"

Pop Cornwell was obviously enveloped in the excitement of his discovery, but Harvey reminded him that they still didn't know a thing about their production costs.

"Isn't that what you said you were ultimately trying to determine?" he remarked. "This is a nice diagram, Pop, but it isn't going to help us make money."

"This is the first step," Pop replied. "We're learning. Now that we know something about the relationship between our production and the number of workers, we can figure costs. I'll go to work on it right away."

"Well, don't take too long—I think we're going broke."

Pop began to gather all the data on the firm's *fixed costs*—those that did not change with increases or decreases in production. These costs included the rent for the small building, the cost of the three popcorn poppers, the insurance premiums, and the monthly utility bills. Having established these costs, he turned to those that changed as production increased. Among these *variable costs* were the workers' wages and the costs of the corn, syrup, brown sugar, cellophane, and other materials. These costs were higher at higher levels of production than at lower ones.*

Pop discovered that the total fixed costs averaged $12 per day. Total daily variable costs were computed for each level of caramel corn production. Labor costs were $6 an hour or $48 a day for each worker, and the costs of materials such as corn, brown sugar, syrup, and cellophane were 30 cents per bag. Thus, Pop determined the firm's variable costs by summing the labor costs and the material costs. For example, the variable cost of 1,140 bags of caramel corn was $480 of labor cost (10 workers at $48 per day) plus $342 of material costs (30 cents per bag times 1,140 bags), for a total variable cost of $822. Cornwell then simply added the variable costs to the $12 fixed costs to get the *total costs* for each level of caramel corn production.

"Well, here it is—our complete cost-of-production record," Pop proudly proclaimed as he handed the teenager an elaborate cost table. "Sit down and I'll explain it to you" (Table 6-3).†

Harvey was skeptical, yet he was also becoming curious about what Pop's complex tables would show this time.

"OK, Harvey—this is the situation. I determined our *fixed costs* on a daily basis (column 3). These include things such as rent, which we must pay regardless of our production level. It costs us $12 a day for these things whether we produce zero bags or 1,140 bags daily.

"Column 4 shows our *variable costs* at each production level. These include labor costs and material costs. Our labor costs are $48 per person per day, and our material costs are 30 cents per bag. I arrived at the *total costs* by adding the fixed costs (column 3) and the variable costs (column 4). Once I knew the *total costs*, I just divided the total in each row by the number of bags of caramel corn to get the *average cost* per bag, or the per unit cost (column 6). These average cost data are important to us."

"That's strange," said Harvey, noticing that the average costs fell from $1.05 to 56 cents as production increased, but then began to rise considerably as production was expanded beyond the 800-bag-per-day level. "Our average costs declined, bottomed out, and then rose. What's the deal?"

"The same thing occurred in the last column, *marginal cost*," Pop noted. "The marginal cost—the cost of an additional bag—in the 0 to 80 range was 90 cents, then fell to 58 cents for those in the 80 to 250 range, and so forth. The lowest marginal cost was 46 cents, but then it increased to 66 cents, 90 cents, $1.26, $1.50, and $1.90, respectively, as diminishing returns set in."

Pop paused briefly, then handed Harvey two pieces of paper, Figures 6-2 and 6-3, and continued his presentation.

"You can really see what happened to our costs in these graphs," he

---

*In the *long run*, all costs are variable, because the firm can discontinue insurance payments or purchase more insurance, sell or expand its plant and equipment, and so on. But in the *short run*, some costs must be paid regardless of the level of production—they are fixed—while other costs, such as labor and materials, are variable. In fact, economists define the *short run* as a period of time in which some costs are *fixed* and the *long run* as a period in which all costs are *variable*.

†Pop fails to include all the costs in his appraisal. In economic terms, he should include the forgone wage income that he and Harvey could have earned by doing something else and the profit they could receive by employing their funds in some other way. These are indeed costs! But Pop is a retired English teacher, not an economist, so bear with him. So-called implicit costs, including the idea of a normal profit as an economic cost, are discussed in the following chapter.

Table 6-3   Daily Production Costs, Harvey and Pop Cornwell Company (Short Run)*

(1) Number of Workers	(2) Bags of Caramel Corn	(3) Fixed Costs	(4) Variable Costs	(5) (3) + (4) Total Costs	(6) (5) ÷ (2) Average Costs	(7) Change in (5) ÷ Change in (2) Marginal Costs
0	0	$12.00	$ 0	$ 12.00	—	—
1	80	12.00	72.00	84.00	$1.05	$ .90
2	250	12.00	171.00	183.00	.73	.58
3	500	12.00	294.00	306.00	.61	.50
4	800	12.00	432.00	444.00	.56	.46
5	930	12.00	519.00	531.00	.57	.66
6	1,010	12.00	591.00	603.00	.60	.90
7	1,060	12.00	654.00	666.00	.63	1.26
8	1,100	12.00	714.00	726.00	.66	1.50
9	1,130	12.00	771.00	783.00	.69	1.90
10	1,140	12.00	822.00	834.00	.73	5.10
11	1,140	12.00	870.00	882.00	.77	—
12	1,130	12.00	915.00	927.00	.82	—
13	1,070	12.00	945.00	957.00	.89	—

*The reader is reminded that the short run is a period of time when the size of the plant and the amount of equipment are fixed, that is, when some costs are fixed. Also, all average and marginal cost figures in the table are "rounded."

declared. "I plotted the total cost data in Figure 6-2 and the average and marginal cost information in Figure 6-3."

"You are really taking this seriously!" Harvey interrupted in near disbelief.

"Well, it's nice to be able to actually see a *picture* of what has been happening—and that's what these graphs give us."

"Look at Figure 6-2, the total cost graph, first, Harvey. Total costs increased as production increased—that is, as we moved rightward on the horizontal axis—but they increased at an uneven rate. Now, observe Figure 6-3, the second graph, which shows average and marginal cost.

"I have given this graph considerable thought," Pop continued. "First, notice the marginal cost curve. Marginal cost fell initially because when we added the first few workers, we experienced rapidly increasing marginal returns. Remember our experiment of adding additional workers one at a time? We had three poppers and as we added more labor we greatly increased our output by assigning our workers to specialized tasks. Eventually, these increasing marginal returns gave way to diminishing marginal returns. Thus we see that the marginal cost curve in the graph began to rise. The marginal cost curve has a reverse shape to that of the marginal product curve we drew earlier. Next, look at the average cost curve. It, too, is U-shaped. When the marginal cost is below the average cost, the average necessarily falls. It's like a batting average in baseball: if your average is .333 and you have a game in which you go 1 for 4 (= .250), your average gets pulled down. Similarly, over the zero-to-about-800 range of output, our marginal cost was below our average cost, thus pulling the average down. Once the marginal cost rose above the average cost, the average naturally increased. The point here is that the marginal and average cost curves are U-shaped because of increasing and diminishing marginal returns."

Harvey, forgetting his initial skepticism and finally beginning to see the

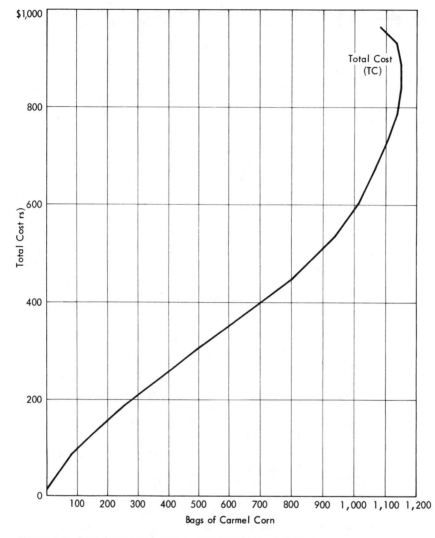

Figure 6-2 Total Cost (Daily), Harvey and Pop Cornwell Company

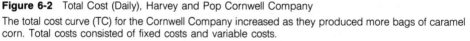

The total cost curve (TC) for the Cornwell Company increased as they produced more bags of caramel corn. Total costs consisted of fixed costs and variable costs.

logic underlying the cost curves, added, "Yes, I remember that after we hired the fourth worker we started to have diminishing returns. We added five or six more workers, but our output increased from 800 to only 1,100 or so. It's easy to see why the marginal and average cost per bag increased—we had to pay increased labor costs, and we didn't get much additional output from these workers."

"That's correct," responded Pop. He thought to himself, "Maybe this kid is finally beginning to realize the value of all this analysis—as opposed to running off in all directions without knowing where he's been." Pop chuckled, 'I'm going to make a cost expert out of you yet, Harvey old boy! Look—we've learned something interesting. The shape of these marginal and average cost curves is the result of the

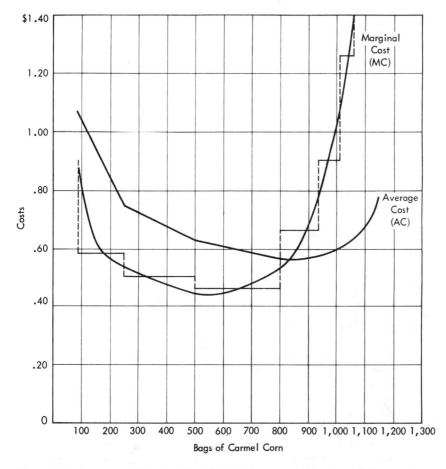

Figure 6-3   Average and Marginal Cost (Daily), Harvey and Pop Cornwell Company

The Cornwells' average cost (AC) and marginal cost (MC) curves are U-shaped. These are typically shaped cost curves for business firms in the short run. The stepped MC curve is the actual MC curve, because the firm hired one additional worker at a time. The MC of *each* unit of the *new* output was constant. If the firm had increased labor by smaller units at a time, for example, an hour of added labor, then the MC curve would have approximated the smooth MC curve in the graph.

basic relationships between the additional inputs—labor, in our case—and additional output. The cost curves decline because of increasing returns and rise because of diminishing returns. I'm certain that the **U** shape of these curves is typical of cost curves faced by all firms that have a fixed amount of capital."

"OK, OK, professor!" needled Harvey. "I get your point, and I'll have to admit that I've learned something."

"Right!" responded Pop. "We're learning economics the hard way—but we're learning."

"But we still don't know *what* level of caramel corn production is *best* for us," Harvey reminded, as he reverted to his skepticism and impatience. "I suppose it's where our average cost is lowest—800 bags per day? We'd better immediately cut back to four workers."

"I'm not too sure about that," Pop quickly cautioned. "We need to do some more serious thinking about that question. We're closer to being able to determine our most profitable level of production than we were a couple of weeks ago—that's for sure—but we still need to analyze the *revenue* side of the picture. Let's sit down and do some thinking. Besides, we need a break. We've learned a lot of economics in a short time."

THE END
(To Be Continued)

Will Harvey and Pop be able to determine the most profitable level of caramel corn production? Will the Harvey and Pop Cornwell Company go broke while Pop draws graphs? Will the company diversify into corncob pipes and cornflakes? Will Harvey graduate from high school? Will the dynamic duo continue to learn basic economic concepts through trial and error? Does anyone really care?

Tune in to the next chapter for a continuation of this explosive adventure.

STUDY QUESTIONS

1. Suppose that Harvey and Pop attended a management seminar where they learned how to organize their workers and equipment better. The new organization of the Cornwell production line was a complete success and resulted in more output per worker—20 more bags of caramel for each worker employed. In Table 6-2, then, the total product associated with the first worker would be 100 bags of caramel corn, not 80 bags; the total product of two workers would be 290, not 250 (each of the two workers adds 20 more bags); and so forth.

   Determine the new values for total product and then determine the new values for marginal product. What effect do you think these changes in total product and marginal product will have on the Cornwells' average and marginal costs curves? Explain your reasoning.

2. Would a decline in the demand for caramel corn have any *immediate* impact on the location of the firm's average cost curve? Explain.

3. What effect might a drought in the Corn Belt have on the firm's cost curves? Explain.

4. Why are diminishing returns a common reality for manufacturing firms in the *short run* (a length of time too short to add capital or build larger plants)?

5. Explain why a marginal cost curve always intersects a U-shaped average cost curve at the latter's lowest point.

6. The average cost curve in the graph is based upon the Cornwell Company's existing plant size and level of equipment. Speculate as to why this curve might shift downward and rightward if the company expanded into a larger building and purchased modern commercial popping equipment?

7. (For mathematically minded students) What is the mathematical relationship between the total product curve (equation) and the marginal product curve (equation) in Figure 6-1?

8. Cite some examples of economic factors of production used by the Cornwells in their business.

9. Use the information in Table 6-3 to determine the Cornwell Company's *average* fixed cost (fixed cost divided by output) of 80, 250, and 500 bags of caramel corn. How does average fixed cost change when the level of output increases, decreases? Explain this relationship.

7

ALL IS NOT WELL THAT ENDS WELL

The Economics of Pure Competition

Concepts and Terms Examined in This Chapter

1. Total Revenue
2. Marginal Revenue
3. Average Revenue
4. Profit Maximization
5. Economies and Diseconomies of Scale
6. Explicit Costs
7. Implicit Costs
8. Normal Profit
9. Economic Profit
10. Short Run
11. Long Run
12. Pure Competition
13. Efficient Allocation of Resources

In the last Harvey and Pop Cornwell episode, the two men created a caramel corn firm that had 13 employees crammed into a small room. The two tycoons had a bagful of problems. They knew little about their financial situation except that their average and marginal cost curves were U-shaped on graph paper. Pop had hypothesized that this shape was caused by increasing and diminishing returns. In his more cynical moments, Harvey was willing to bet that the shapes of the curves were caused by Pop's inability to draw a straight line.

We return to the pair and find them once again immersed in economic analysis. Reason through the tables and graphs with the Cornwells, and share their insights as they continue their corny adventure.

"Well, Pop, your inability to make fast decisions has finally caught up with us," Harvey Cornwell declared disgustedly. "Three of our 13 workers just quit! They said they were fed up with the overcrowded working conditions, and I'm afraid we will lose our entire work force unless we take some immediate action."

Pop Cornwell did not share Harvey's concern. "It won't be as crowded with 10 as it was with 13," he reminded his teenaged partner. "We would have had to lay off workers anyway. Besides, you were the one who insisted that we needed at least 15 workers—remember? So don't blame me for the crowded conditions!"

"I remember—but that's syrup down the drain. Now, I think we should cut back to 4 workers—that's where our average cost is the lowest," Harvey offered. After all, a reduction in the number of employees was desirable, according to Pop's cost figures.

"Well, I don't think a work force of 4 workers is the most profitable size either," Pop stated. "I have additional data that suggest otherwise. Do you have time to look at them?"

Harvey nodded and the pair walked to Pop's desk. The retired English teacher handed the boy a copy of Table 7-1 and an accompanying graph, Figure 7-1.

Table 7-1 Daily Revenue, Harvey and Pop Cornwell Company

(1) Number of Workers	(2) Bags of Caramel Corn	(3) Total Revenue	(4) Average Revenue	(5) Marginal Revenue
0	0	$ 0	—	—
1	80	72.00	$.90	$.90
2	250	225.00	.90	.90
3	500	450.00	.90	.90
4	800	720.00	.90	.90
5	930	837.00	.90	.90
6	1,010	909.00	.90	.90
7	1,060	954.00	.90	.90
8	1,100	990.00	.90	.90
9	1,130	1,017.00	.90	.90
10	1,140	1,026.00	.90	.90
11	1,140	1,026.00	.90	.90
12	1,130	1,017.00	.90	.90
13	1,070	963.00	.90	.90

Product price = $.90

"Here we go again," thought Harvey.

"I compiled some information about the money we are receiving from sales," Pop said. "We are selling caramel corn for 90 cents a bag. I multiplied 90 times the number of bags to get *total revenue* (column 3) and then divided this by the number of bags to get our *average revenue* (column 4). Notice that average revenue is always equal to the price—90 cents. Marginal revenue (column 5) is the *extra* revenue that we get when we sell one more bag. Naturally, it too is 90 cents.

"That seems simple enough," said Harvey. "Apparently, we have exactly the right size work force—10 workers—since this gives us the greatest revenue, $1,026, and maximum production, 1,140 bags."

Pop was obviously disappointed in Harvey's logic. "Wait a minute, Harvey! A while ago you argued that we should have only 4 workers and produce 800 bags per day, because that was where our average costs were the lowest. Now you want to switch to 10 workers. Don't be in such a hurry to draw conclusions. Think! We have to consider *both* revenues *and* cost to determine our best level of production."

Pop's criticism angered Harvey, and the youngster replied, "Then let's quit playing games and do it! I've just about had it with all of these mental gymnastics."

"Now we *can* compare costs and revenues—that's the point. We need all this information and we need to understand it. Calm down and take a look at this graph. I plotted the average and marginal revenue data from the table, along with our cost curves."

Harvey reluctantly studied Figure 7-1.

Pop continued, "The horizontal line, $.90, is marginal revenue and average revenue, both of which are equal to the price. The cost curves are those we developed previously. It's all there, Harvey—everything we need to select our most profitable output."

Figure 7-1   Profit-Maximizing Output (Price $.90), Harvey and Pop Cornwell Company

The Cornwell Company maximized its profit by producing all bags of caramel corn for which marginal revenues (MR) exceeded marginal cost (MC). The profit-maximizing output (MR = MC) was 1,010 bags of corn. At that output, total revenue exceeded total cost by approximately $306 per day.

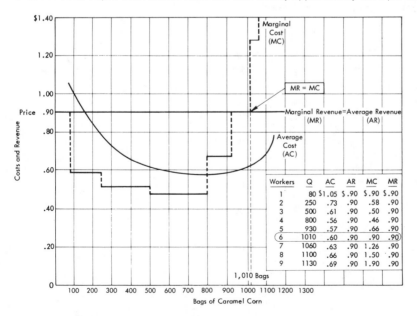

Workers	Q	AC	AR	MC	MR
1	80	$1.05	$.90	$.90	$.90
2	250	.73	.90	.58	.90
3	500	.61	.90	.50	.90
4	800	.56	.90	.46	.90
5	930	.57	.90	.66	.90
6	1010	.60	.90	.90	.90
7	1060	.63	.90	1.26	.90
8	1100	.66	.90	1.50	.90
9	1130	.69	.90	1.90	.90

"It looks like hieroglyphics to me," stated his unenthusiastic partner.

"It's really quite simple. What are we trying to accomplish in this business?" Pop asked.

"Well, *I'm* trying to make as much money as possible, but I'm not sure what *you're* trying to accomplish," answered Harvey, sarcastically.

"I'm interested in *maximizing profit* as much as you are," Pop responded, "and this graph helps us accomplish that. Let me ask you two hypothetical questions, and you'll see my point. What if we discovered that the marginal cost of producing one more bag of caramel corn *exceeded* our marginal revenue from selling it?"

"It wouldn't make sense to produce it," Harvey answered.

"OK—remember that. Here's the second question. What if we discovered that the marginal or extra revenue—90 cents, in this case—*was more than* the marginal cost of producing an additional bag?"

"If we gain more revenue from producing and selling a bag than it costs to make it, we should do so. One doesn't have to be a genius to recognize that fact. What are you getting at?"

"You've just discovered how we can determine our most profitable production level!" Pop declared. "If marginal revenue exceeds marginal cost, produce more, but if marginal revenue is less than marginal cost, produce less. *We can maximize our profit by producing until marginal revenue equals marginal cost.*"

Harvey had to admit that this decision rule made sense. The MC = MR condition applied only to the last bag of caramel corn produced. For all the prior bags, the additional revenue would be greater than the marginal cost.

"*Look carefully at Figure 7-1,*" Pop continued, "We want to compare MR and MC, so we need to focus on these curves. At all production levels up to and including 930 bags, marginal revenue (90 cents) exceeds marginal cost; notice that the MC curve lies below the MR line. So, through 930, we would definitely add to profits by producing more corn."

"I see that," Harvey interjected. He was not as enthusiastic about the analysis as his grandfather was. "*Above* the 1,010 level, the marginal cost curve (MC) lies above the marginal revenue curve (MR), so we would be stupid to produce more than 1,010 bags a day. I have to hand it to you, Pop—our best level of production is between 931 and 1,010 bags per day, because at these levels, MR = MC."

"We might as well produce 1,010 bags per day rather than somewhere else in the 931 to 1,010 range, even though any of these outputs would maximize our profit. That way we won't have to lay off as many workers," Pop added. "We know that we need six people to produce 1,010 bags a day."

Pleased with the discovery, but impatient as usual, Harvey switched to another subject.

"Will we be making a profit?" he queried, as the dollar signs appeared in his eyeballs again.

"Well, of course, Harvey—that's what we're in business for, aren't we?" Pop boastfully proclaimed. "Here's how I have it figured." He began calculating on a scratch pad.

Production level = 1,010 bags per day
Revenue per bag (average revenue) = $.90

$$\begin{array}{r} 1{,}010 \\ \times\ \$.90 \\ \hline \$909.00 \end{array} = \textit{Total revenue}$$

"What is our average cost per bag at the 1,010 production level?" Pop asked.

"It looks as though it's approximately 60 cents on the graph," Harvey answered.

Pop nodded in agreement and continued figuring.

$$Product\ level\ =\ 1,010$$
$$Average\ cost\ =\ \$.60$$

$$
\begin{array}{r}
1,010 \\
\times\ \$.60 \\
\hline
\$606.00
\end{array}
\ =\ Total\ cost^*
$$

Pop then subtracted total cost from total revenue to get total daily profit.

$$
\begin{array}{r}
TR\ =\ \$909.00 \\
TC\ =\ \$606.00 \\
\hline
\$303.00
\end{array}
\ =\ Total\ profit\ per\ day
$$

"Three hundred bucks a day!" Harvey exclaimed. "That's a profit of over $1,500 for a five-day week!"

"Or about $75,000 a year!" Pop added.

Harvey literally jumped three feet in the air in excitement. Pop smiled.

The number of workers at the company was reduced to six, and the company produced the profit-maximizing 1,010 bags of caramel corn daily. It continued to sell its product to the distributing firm for 90 cents a bag, and profits accumulated rapidly. Harvey was graduated from high school and devoted his full time to the prosperous enterprise. The company was a grand success.

But then, after nearly a year, events suddenly took a turn for the worse. Word of the company's profits had spread through the local community. Several small enterprises similar to the Harvey and Pop Cornwell Company sprang into existence in the area, and two larger, statewide firms entered the local market. The results were a substantial increase in the number of caramel corn competitors vying for business and a sizable increase in the supply of caramel corn being offered for sale in the local area. Naturally, the price of caramel corn began to fall.

Harvey brought the latest bad news to Pop.

"Our distributors called and informed us that as of tomorrow, they will pay us only 66 cents per bag!" he said. "They claim that the retail price has fallen so low that if they pay us more than that, they'll go broke."

Pop anticipated the price decline, but the actual amount was a shock. His immediate reaction was to suggest that they sell and distribute the caramel corn themselves, but, upon further reflection, he concluded that that wouldn't help. "After all," he thought, "the distributor *has* to lower its purchase price, because the retail price has fallen." Pop shook his head, turned to Harvey, and stated that they would just have to make the best of it.

"We'll need to make some production adjustments," he offered, as he pondered his cost-and-revenue graph once again.

---

*The actual total cost for 1,010 units is $603.00. See the cost table in the preceding chapter. The discrepancy arises because of "rounding." The actual profit per day is $306.00.

"I realize that, but what kind of adjustments should we make?" asked Harvey.

"Let's check our data. The marginal cost of our production on each bag in the 931 to 1,010 range is 90 cents. If our revenue will only be 66 cents, it sure doesn't pay to produce these bags." Pop drew a new line on the graph to show the new price and marginal revenue (Figure 7-2).

"At the new price of 66 cents, we should produce a maximum of 930 bags per day, according to our MR = MC decision rule," Pop declared.

Harvey agreed. "So we'll need to lay off a worker. We can produce 930 bags with five people, according to your production table."

"Right."

"The price decline cuts sharply into our profits," Harvey declared as he began figuring. "Our total revenue now will be

Number of bags = 930
Average revenue (AR) = $.66

$$\begin{array}{r} 930 \\ \times\ \$.66 \\ \hline \$613.80 \end{array} = \textit{Total revenue}$$

Figure 7-2 Profit-Maximizing Output (Price $.66), Harvey and Pop Cornwell Company

The price per bag of caramel corn, set by market forces, changed from $.90 to $.66 as more firms entered the industry. At $.66, the marginal cost of producing the 931st to 1,010th bag of caramel corn exceeded the new marginal revenue. Therefore, the Cornwells reduced their output to 930 bags; MR = MC at that point. The lower price substantially reduced the Cornwells' daily profit.

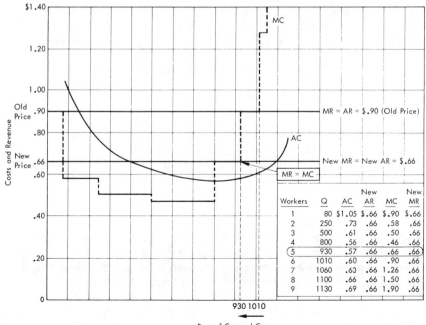

Workers	Q	AC	New AR	MC	New MR
1	80	$1.05	$.66	$.90	$.66
2	250	.73	.66	.58	.66
3	500	.61	.66	.50	.66
4	800	.56	.66	.46	.66
5	930	.57	.66	.66	.66
6	1010	.60	.66	.90	.66
7	1060	.63	.66	1.26	.66
8	1100	.66	.66	1.50	.66
9	1130	.69	.66	1.90	.66

Bags of Caramel Corn

"And our total cost is approximately

Number of bags = 930
Average cost (AC) = $.57

$$\begin{array}{r} 930 \\ \times\ \$.57 \\ \hline \$530.10 \end{array} = \textit{Total cost}$$

"So our daily profit is about $84. That's less than $25,000 a year!" Harvey complained as he glared at his figures. "We could make that much selling canoe rides to Hawaii."

Pop Cornwell chuckled and thought, "Ah, he's already planning his next business venture." Then he said, "We just had it too good last year. Those profits of ours stood out like a lighthouse beacon to everyone trying to make a quick buck. They just rushed in to compete with us. But that—"

"I'm afraid that the increased supply will reduce the price even lower," Harvey interrupted.

"I don't doubt it," Pop agreed.

"What do we do now?" Harvey asked.

"We don't quit at this stage," Pop quickly responded. "We're still making a small profit, and maybe we can become more efficient and reduce our costs. Or perhaps we can achieve lower average costs by expanding our production facilities and equipment. We will still face U-shaped average and marginal cost curves, but they may be lower because of *economies of scale*. Economies of scale are cost reductions resulting from an increase in the size of a firm."

Harvey kicked the wastebasket by Pop's small desk.

"Well, I'm willing to go along with this for a while," he declared, "But I've been doing some thinking lately. You know, I'll bet we could really make it big producing caramel corn necklaces, bracelets, and belts. Let's give it some thought."

Pop glanced at Harvey to see whether he was joking. He concluded that he was not.

"Is the world ready for Harvey Cornwell?" Pop wondered.

THE END

The Harvey and Pop Cornwell story is tongue-in-cheek fiction, but the economic principles therein are not. The story illuminates a variety of important economic concepts and human behaviors that deserve review and elaboration.

IMPLICIT AND EXPLICIT COSTS

The Cornwells did an excellent job of identifying their *explicit (or monetary) costs* of producing caramel corn. These costs included such things as the cost of the corn poppers, corn, syrup, and labor. Then, using standard accounting procedures, Pop and Harvey compared these explicit costs to their total revenue to determine their profits.

The Cornwells, however, failed to consider the opportunity costs of doing business. Pop and Harvey had to forgo other valuable uses of their time to manage their caramel corn enterprise. For example, Harvey might have worked in a fast-food restaurant, and Pop might have tutored students in reading. The wages that Harvey and Pop sacrificed are an implicit cost: *the money payments that resources can garner in their best alternative employments.* Likewise, the awesome twosome might have used the money they paid to lease the room and buy the popcorn poppers to establish some other business. The amount of profit they could have made in the next best business opportunity is an implicit cost of producing caramel corn. Whatever activity Harvey and Pop had as their next best alternative is the opportunity cost (implicit cost) of being in the caramel corn business.

Conclusion: From an economic perspective, Pop and Harvey need sufficient revenue to cover their explicit costs *and* their implicit costs (opportunity cost of the owners' labor and the opportunity cost of capital). If they do not cover these economic costs, they will eventually choose to do something else.

When a firm's total revenue equals its total cost (explicit cost plus implicit cost), it is making a normal profit. A *normal profit is the smallest accounting profit that owners of a firm will accept in the long run and still continue in business. Viewed this way, a normal profit is a cost of doing business because it is an opportunity cost of that particular activity.* If a firm does not earn a normal profit, it eventually will close down so that its owners can earn greater returns in an alternative line of business. Of course, if a firm's total revenue exceeds its total costs (explicit and implicit costs), it is making more than a normal profit. A profit in excess of a normal profit is called an *economic profit.*

Because neither Pop nor Harvey is an economist, we can perhaps forgive them for failing to incorporate all costs into their analysis. Hereafter, it will be convenient to assume that Pop and Harvey's cost data and graphs include all economic costs, both implicit and explicit. This assumption means that the profits evidenced in Figures 7-1 and 7-2 are *economic* profits.

MARGINAL ANALYSIS

Pop and Harvey discovered one of the key decision rules in economics. The rule involves *comparing benefits and costs at the margin.* They found that they could continue to increase their profits by expanding production if the additional income from that output exceeded the additional cost. As owners interested in maximizing their profits, they exploited all such production opportunities. They learned that a firm maximizes its profits at a level of production where MR = MC. This profit-maximizing decision rule applies to all firms in the economy, regardless of their size or the number of competitors.

Notice that this analysis focuses on the cost of one more unit of output, not on the average cost of that unit. Average cost includes fixed costs that must be paid irrespective of the level of production. Fixed costs are "sunk"; they represent past decisions. The only cost that is relevant, and subject to present control, is marginal cost. The firm's choice to produce or refrain from producing an extra unit depends upon the *marginal* cost and revenue. Only "at the margin" do choices and opportunities remain.

Decision making at the margin is an important part of the economic perspective, and it is used by all decision makers, be they consumers, workers, government officials, or business executives. Persons making decisions ask, "What are the added benefits of this prospective action, compared with the added costs?"

If the new benefits are less than the new costs, the decision is negative. If the benefits exceed the marginal costs, the action adds a net gain, be it utility or profits, and is undertaken. These decisions are not always made formally, with the person listing costs and benefits. Nor does the decision maker usually have complete information. Still, the decisions are based on expected costs and benefits and are thought to be optimal at the time they are made.

An example may be helpful here. When people enter a fast-food restaurant, they immediately decide which line to enter. Why do they choose the shortest line? Apparently, they assess the expected marginal costs and benefits associated with each of the alternatives. Because they value their time, they select the shortest line. If all the lines were extraordinarily long, they might even decide to go elsewhere. When they are in a long line and observe that a new register is open, they often scramble over to it.

But information is imperfect. Sometimes others beat them to the new register. At other times, people get into the shortest line only to discover that the person in front of them is ordering hamburgers, fries, and shakes for twenty members of a construction crew. The decision to enter the line was optimal at the time it was made in the absence of complete information. So why don't people conduct a survey of each person in line to see what they are ordering, as well as bring along stopwatches to check the speed of individual order takers to make sure all factors are being considered? The obvious answer is that people judge the marginal cost of obtaining that information to be too great relative to the marginal utility gained from the extra time (if any) saved. Again, a decision at the margin!

The Cornwell story illustrates marginal analysis used to maximize profits. This procedure involves estimating (either formally or intuitively) costs and revenues at the margin, given the information at hand. The optimal level of production occurs where marginal revenue equals marginal cost.

Other examples of benefit (revenue, utility) and cost (price) comparisons may be cited. Recall from Chapter 5 that a rational consumer uses this procedure to decide which products to buy and in what amounts. Similarly, a worker confronted with a decision to accept or reject overtime work compares the additional revenue (income) with the marginal cost (loss of leisure time). The income must be worth the loss of time, or the work opportunity will be rejected. Likewise, a government agency attempting to maximize the well-being of those served should compare the additional costs of a project with the additional benefits. The decision to fund a project will be a wise one only if the benefits exceed the costs. Formal "cost-benefit" studies are often an important ingredient in government decisions.

CHARACTERISTICS OF PURE COMPETITION

The Cornwell Company's experience demonstrates a second important economic concept, the notion of a purely competitive industry or market. Economists have developed a model termed *pure competition* that represents an ideal pattern of business behavior in a market economy. A purely competitive industry is characterized by (1) a large number of buyers and sellers, (2) a standardized product, (3) no control over the market price, and (4) freedom to enter or leave the industry.

Pop and Harvey found themselves in a market environment similar to pure competition. Eventually, there were many small firms; the product was standard in quality and appearance, regardless of who made it; the Cornwells were "price takers," not "price makers," for their firm was so small that it had to accept the going market price; and, finally, firms easily entered and left the industry.

In fact, this last characteristic—ease of entry—became a serious problem for the Cornwells. The enterprise was earning high profits in the short run, but those profits became signals to other profit-motivated people to enter the industry. As the new firms entered, the supply of the product increased and the price of the product fell. The lower price resulted in smaller profits for the existing firms in the industry.

NARROW VERSUS BROAD ECONOMIC PERSPECTIVE

The Cornwells' decline in profits and their reaction to it illustrate an interesting paradox in economics. *Often, that which is an undesirable occurrence from one's personal or business perspective may be a desirable outcome from an economic and social viewpoint.* This is exactly the situation in the story. All ends well in competitive industries (broad perspective), but all is *not* well (firm's perspective). Harvey and Pop were dismayed when other firms began to compete with them. This competition increased supply, reduced the price of caramel corn, and diminished the firm's profits. Under these circumstances, Harvey and Pop's self-interest might lead them to complain vigorously to all who would listen and to call for government actions to eliminate some of the competition. Such behavior is common in competitive industries and often results in demands that government limit the number of competitors or guarantee a higher than competitive price.

Economists view the situation from a *broad economic perspective*, however, and the entrance of new firms in the industry is judged favorably. High prices and economic profits in an industry mean that consumer demand for the product is great, relative to supply. Economic profits signal other potential and existing producers to shift their resources from other, less profitable uses to the one with the high return. This is the way that a market system efficiently allocates scarce resources to their most desired uses. Economic profits, in essence, declare "Profit opportunity here—more resources needed," whereas economic losses proclaim the opposite message. Harvey and Pop may not appreciate competition, but the market economy relies exactly upon the forces operating in the story to function efficiently.

EFFICIENT ALLOCATION OF RESOURCES

The Cornwell story illustrates the complex forces that lead to an *efficient allocation of resources* in a market economy. Resources are efficiently allocated when they are being used in such a way that opportunity costs are held to a minimum. The use of resources—land, labor, capital—for producing a product precludes using the resources in alternative ways. Thus society's interests are best realized when the resources are employed where they provide the largest benefit possible, given the wishes of consumers.

Competition and the desire for profit are the forces that produce an efficient allocation of resources in the pure competition model. In the short run—a period when some costs are fixed—a firm may earn an economic profit, break even (make a normal profit), or incur a loss. In the long run—where all costs are variable—new firms will enter industries where there are economic profits and leave industries where there are economic losses. As firms enter profitable industries, market supply will increase, product price will fall, and economic profits will erode, until there is a long-run equilibrium. Once this equilibrium is reached, there are no further incentives for firms to enter the industry because existing firms are earning only a normal profit. Moreover, no further shuffling of society's resources can improve upon society's well-being. That is, at this point society's resources are efficiently allocated. This long-run outcome of pure competition is shown graphically in Figure 7-3.

In Figure 7-3B, competition has reduced the market price to P_0. The individual firm, shown in Figure 7-3A, must accept the market price if it wishes to sell its product. The P_0 line is also the MR and AR lines, since both the marginal revenue from selling one more unit and the average revenue per unit are equal to the market price. The $P = MR = AR$ line is the demand curve as seen by the individual firm, because the firm knows that it can sell as many units as it desires at the market price P_0.

The most profitable output for this firm is Q_f, at which marginal revenue equals marginal cost. At all quantities less than Q_f, marginal revenue exceeds marginal cost, and thus added production will increase profits. At all outputs greater than Q_f, marginal cost is greater than marginal revenue, and hence profits can be enhanced by reducing output.

At the most profitable output Q_f, this firm is earning only a normal profit. We know this because the firm's total revenue, found by multiplying P_0 by Q_f, equals its total cost, found by multiplying AC by Q_f. Recall that a normal profit is included as a cost in the cost curves. Thus, when total revenue equals total cost, this firm is covering all of its costs, including a normal profit. This profit is just

Figure 7-3 Efficient Allocation of Resources; Long-Run Equilibrium in Pure Competition

Graphs A and B depict the long-run price, output, and profit outcomes in a purely competitive industry. The market (graph B) adjusts through the entry or exit of firms until the equilibrium price (P_0) equals the individual firm's (graph A) marginal cost. The firm maximizes its profit at Q_f because $P_0 = MR = MC$. At P_0 and Q_f the firm earns only a normal profit and resources are efficiently allocated.

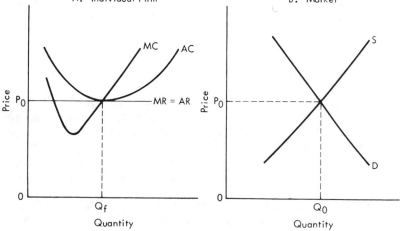

sufficient to keep the firm in business in the long run. In the short run, the firm might decide to operate at a loss, but it will not do so in the long run.

The long-run outcome in the pure competition model has special social significance; it represents an *efficient allocation of resources. The price of the product is just equal to the marginal cost of producing it, including a normal profit to the owner, and the firm is operating at its lowest average-cost level* (P = MC = lowest AC). Economic profits disappear; firms earn a normal return; resources are used in their lowest-cost, most efficient manner; and consumers are provided the product at the lowest reasonable price.

Long-run allocative efficiency may never be reached in the "real world" of competitive business. Nevertheless, competitive forces create a tendency toward this outcome in industries characterized by many firms, standard products, price-taking behavior, and freedom of entry. Self-interest and competition are powerful forces that tend to allocate resources to their most desirable uses.

ECONOMIES OF SCALE

Competition forces firms to use their existing plant and equipment efficiently and dictates that they discover their *optimal size.* At the end of the Cornwell dialogue, Pop suggested that perhaps they could lower their marginal and average cost curves by expanding the size of their firm. In the short run, plant and equipment levels are fixed, but in the long run, businesses can change the size of their firms. If an increase in firm size leads to lower minimum average costs, economies of scale are said to be achieved. Such gains in efficiency may come from increased specialization of labor and capital; greater ability to use large, more efficient units of capital; improved ability to use production by-products; or greater ability to attract high-quality labor or low-cost financing.

For example, the Cornwell's lowest average cost was 56 cents, which they achieved by employing four workers and producing 800 bags of caramel corn daily ($444 of total cost). Suppose that the Cornwells doubled the size of their operation (a room twice as large, six rather than three popping machines, and eight rather than four workers) and discovered that increased specialization and a more efficient work flow enabled the company to produce 2,000 bags a day. Their average cost would drop from 56 cents ($444 of total cost divided by 800 bags) to 44 cents ($888 of total cost divided by 2,000). Total cost rises, but because output rises proportionately more, average and marginal cost fall.

If an increase in the size of the firm causes the minimum average cost to rise, then diseconomies of scale are at work. The inefficiencies involved can arise from management and coordination problems that increase at a faster pace than firm size itself. For example, suppose that the doubling of the size of the Cornwell's firm caused coordination difficulties and output rose only from 800 to 1,000 bags daily. Average cost would rise from 56 cents ($444 of total cost divided by 800 bags) to 89 cents ($888 of total cost divided by 1,000 bags), and the firm would be experiencing diseconomies of scale.

Optimal firm sizes vary from industry to industry in the United States. Economies of scale are fully realized at a relatively small firm size in agriculture but dictate a large firm size for producing automobiles. Also, in many industries the range of output over which minimum average costs can be obtained is quite broad, enabling medium-sized firms to compete successfully with larger firms.

THE PURE COMPETITION MODEL AND REALITY

In an indirect manner, the Harvey and Pop Cornwell story reflects the difference between a model and reality. The story is fictitious and oversimplified, but it condenses complex economics into a framework that can be readily grasped. So it is with formal economic models. They abstract from the complex reality of the "real world," simplify, and condense key relationships into a manageable framework.

The pure competition model is useful for these very reasons. It reduces the complexity of reality into a manageable size, highlights the idea of an efficient allocation of resources, and shows the role of profits, prices, and competition in the market system.

The model closely resembles the actual workings of some industries in the economy. The production of beef is one such case. The firms are many, the product is standardized, the price is set on the basis of supply and demand in the market, and producers are free to enter and leave the industry. When economic profits on beef are high in one year, many producers switch the use of their resources to raising more cattle. This increases the supply of beef in the following year, beef prices fall, and profits in the production of beef return to normal.

Now a confession is necessary. All this attention on behavior in a purely competitive economy implies that our economy closely resembles this model. In reality, purely competitive industries are an endangered species. Their numbers are few and declining. This fact does not diminish the importance of the competitive model, however. It remains a useful yardstick against which real-world industry structures, resource allocation, prices, profits, competition, and firm behavior can be compared. The degree to which a particular industry departs from the outcomes of the purely competitive model is useful as a guide to public policy and corrective action. The pure competition model, then, like the Harvey and Pop Cornwell story itself, is a useful aid in understanding and evaluating individual and business behavior in a complex economy.

STUDY QUESTIONS

1. What effect would an increase in the demand for caramel corn have on the Cornwell Company's marginal revenue and short-run profits?
2. List the characteristics of pure competition.
3. "If marginal cost equals marginal revenue, a firm cannot be making a profit, because costs and revenues are equal." Do you agree? Why, or why not?
4. If economic losses are large in a *purely competitive* industry, what *long-run* effects would you predict as to
   a. the number of competitors
   b. the supply of the product produced
   c. the product price
   d. the industry profit picture
5. Explain why an efficient allocation of resources is said to occur when the product price equals the marginal cost and the lowest possible average cost.

6. If the price of cellophane packaging material increased, would the Cornwell Company reduce its production or increase it? Explain your answer on the basis of marginal cost = marginal revenue analysis.

7. Employ the concept of economies of scale to explain why the average size of a farm today is considerably larger than it was at the turn of the century.

8. Use the cost data given in Table 6-3, page 71, in answering this question. Assume that these data include a normal profit as a cost and that the market price of caramel corn is $1.60. Determine the Cornwell Company's
   a. marginal revenue
   b. most profitable level of output
   c. total revenue
   d. total cost
   e. level of economic profit

9. (Advanced analysis) "The short-run marginal cost curve for a purely competitive firm is its supply curve." Explain. (*Hint:* How does the firm make its decision on how much to produce? How will it adjust its output when the market price increases?)

10. Explain how the Cornwell story relates to each of the following elements of the economic perspective:
   a. People make choices from alternatives.
   b. Choices are made on the basis of available information and expected outcomes at the time of the decision.
   c. All actions entail costs.
   d. People have different values and value things differently.
   e. People respond to incentives and disincentives.
   f. Economic actions often produce secondary effects.

8

ALONE—AND LOVING IT

The Economics of Monopoly

Concepts and Terms Examined in This Chapter

1. Monopoly
2. Cartel
3. Monopoly Demand
4. Marginal Revenue, Marginal Cost
5. Monopoly Profit
6. Resource Misallocation
7. Monopoly or Market Power
8. Sherman Act (1890)
9. Natural Monopoly

This chapter consists of five sections, each relating to the economics of monopoly. The first three parts, entitled "The Making of an American Beauty Rose," "Sparkling Examples of Monopoly Behavior," and "Well, Well, Well—It's a Crude Cartel," provide examples of monopoly structure and conduct. The next segment explores the formal economic model of monopoly and relates the previous parts of the chapter to the model. The last section discusses public policies toward monopoly.

THE MAKING OF AN AMERICAN BEAUTY ROSE

> The American Beauty Rose can be produced in its splendor and fragrance only by sacrificing the early buds which grow up around it.
>
> John D. Rockefeller, Jr., in an address on trusts to the students at Brown University

The following excerpts are taken directly from the table of contents of Ida M. Tarbell's famous book, *The History of the Standard Oil Company*. This polemic, published in 1902, alerted the general public to the monopolization occurring in the oil industry. When combined, the excerpts form the skeleton of a dramatic story about the rise of the Standard Oil monopoly.

CHAPTER TWO
THE RISE OF THE STANDARD OIL COMPANY

John D. Rockefeller's First Connection with the Oil Business— ... —His First Partners—Organisation of the Standard Oil Company in June, 1870— ... First Plan for a Secret Combination—The South Improvement Company—Secret Contracts Made with the Railroads Providing Rebates and Drawbacks—Rockefeller and Associates Force Cleveland Refiners to Join the New Combination or Sell— . . . .

CHAPTER FIVE
LAYING THE FOUNDATION OF A TRUST

. . . —Rockefeller Now Secretly Plans Realisation of His Dream of Personal Control of the Refining of Oil—Organisation of the Central Association— ... — Rockefeller's Quiet and Successful Canvass for Alliances with Refiners—The Rebate His Weapon—Consolidation by Persuasion or Force—. . . .

CHAPTER TEN
CUTTING TO KILL

Rockefeller Now Plans to Organise Oil Marketing as He Had Already Organised Oil Transporting and Refining— ... —Reports of Competitors' Business Secured from Railway Agents—Competitors' Clerks Sometimes Secured as Allies— ... — This Information Is Used by Standard to Fight Competitors—Competitors Driven Out by Underselling—. . . .

CHAPTER FOURTEEN
THE BREAKING UP OF THE TRUST

. . . – Standard Investigated by New York State Senate – Rockefeller's Remarkable Testimony – Inquiry into the Nature of the Mysterious Standard Oil Trust – Original Standard Oil Trust Agreement Revealed – Investigation of the Standard by Congress in 1888 – . . . .

SPARKLING EXAMPLES OF MONOPOLY BEHAVIOR

De Beers Consolidated Mines Ltd. is one of the world's strongest monopolies. It produces a sizable portion of all rough diamonds in the world from its own mines and buys a large portion of the diamonds produced by other mines. The South African company then markets the combined world output of rough stones through its wholly owned Central Selling Organization (CSO), based in London. Smaller producers of diamonds willingly sell their gemstones to De Beers because a competitive price war would ruin them, and De Beers pays a top price.

De Beers can afford to pay a high price for rough stones, because it receives even higher prices when it sells them to buyers who cut and finish them into gemstones. Through the CSO, De Beers maintains high prices for rough diamonds by controlling the number of stones placed on the market. When demand is increasing rapidly, the company releases the surplus diamonds in its stockpile. This supply juggling is not a simple activity, for there are more than 2,000 varieties of diamonds.

De Beers's strategy is to control the supply of diamonds so that prices rise, slowly, yet steadily. The firm desires to market its stones, and those of its producer-clients in an orderly, controlled, and profitable manner. But several major occurrences in past decades threatened the price structure of diamonds and De Beers's orderly market control. The way in which the firm responded to each threat provides a lesson in monopoly behavior.

The first major problem threatening De Beers occurred in the first half of the 1970s. Recall that De Beers maintains its monopoly position by agreeing to purchase the uncut diamonds from mines around the world and then marketing the stones through its single CSO. This working arrangement operated smoothly until the world's mines began producing an increasing number of *small* stones (those less than 0.25 carats). That placed De Beers in the position of buying more small stones per year than it could sell at its current prices. If it placed the surplus stones on the market, the price of the small diamonds would fall, and this decline in prices might produce unfortunate ramifications for the prices of diamonds in general.

De Beers's solution to this threat was to reduce the flow of small diamonds to the market. This left De Beers with a large inventory of small stones. De Beers's executives then devised a strategy to increase the demand for small diamonds, so that the surplus stones could be eased onto the market without reducing their price. De Beers began a campaign to get the public to "think small." An advertising campaign was used to entice the public to buy small diamonds clustered into brooches, pendants, rings, and other jewelry. Figure 8-1 shows one such full-page advertisement. Other ads attempted to establish a new tradition similar to the

Figure 8-1

giving of engagement rings. The ads encouraged older married people to give their spouses an "eternity ring" as a symbol of continuing affection and appreciation. The eternity ring, to no surprise, consisted of a band containing many *small* diamonds. This campaign succeeded brilliantly and the price charged by De Beers for small sparklers rose throughout the 1970s.

Several interacting circumstances posed a far greater threat to the De Beers's diamond monopoly in the late 1970s and 1980s. First, a major recession in the United States and several other industrial nations in 1981 and 1982 reduced demand for polished diamonds and placed tremendous downward pressure on De Beers's price structure for uncut stones. Second, the Soviet Union began to offer many more *polished* diamonds for sale in the world market to gain foreign currency to buy needed grain and finance troops in Afghanistan. Third, investors and speculators in large diamonds reacted to the falling price of the polished stones by unloading their hoarded diamonds, hoping to get out of the market before prices dropped further. Fourth, lower inflation rates in the industrialized countries during the 1980s reduced the demand for commodities such as diamonds, which people earlier were buying as a way to maintain purchasing power. The price of a "one-carat D-flawless brilliant" investment diamond fell precipitously from $60,000 in 1980 to $6,000 in 1985! Fifth, De Beers's new Jwaneng mine in Botswana began production and added tremendously to De Beers's stock of large uncut diamonds. Sixth, Zaire, the world's biggest producer of diamonds, withdrew from the CSO and began marketing its rough stones directly. Finally, the gigantic Ashton Argyle mine in Western Australia began production, adding an estimated 40 percent to the world's diamond output in 1985.

De Beers's reactions to these events were swift and decisive. It negotiated an agreement with the Australians to market nearly all of the gemstone-quality rough diamonds produced from the new Ashton Argyle mine. It reduced production in its famed Premier mine in South Africa and laid off nearly 500 workers. It closed its Koffiefontein and Lesotho mines completely and cut 1982 production by more than 2 million carats. De Beers casually reminded its CSO cartel members that an Israeli attempt to break the CSO's grip in 1977 and 1978 nearly broke the Israeli diamond-cutting industry instead. It "enticed" Zaire back into the CSO. Zaire's output consisted mainly of low-priced, industrial-grade diamonds called *boart*. When Zaire left the cartel, De Beers "met the competition" by unloading boart from its large inventory. Boart prices fell 67 percent over a two-year period, and Zaire decided to rejoin the CSO. The company initiated a multimillion-dollar advertising campaign to promote large diamonds, hoping to prop up the demand for stones at the top end of the price structure. Finally, in 1990 De Beers negotiated a five-year deal to sell $5 billion worth of the Soviet Union's stockpile of rough diamonds.

De Beers did not reduce its prices on rough-cut stones! To maintain its carefully constructed monopoly and its price structure, it stockpiled vast quantities of stones. For example, in 1981 alone it withheld $1.3 billion in diamonds from the market. In that year, sales from its CSO fell nearly 50 percent and profits declined by nearly the same amount, but the CSO and its price structure were still intact. De Beers's rate of return on equity in this "bad" year was 20 percent.

In "good" years, De Beers's profits equal 60 percent of revenues and rates of return on equity are above 30 percent. Competitive firms would be pleased to duplicate De Beers's bad years. De Beers is a "price maker," through its control over supply, not a "price taker." Unlike the Cornwell situation in the previous chapter, it is nearly impossible for new firms to enter this industry in response to the economic profit being made. Yet De Beers is not immune from all economic and political threats. If the African nations opposed to South Africa's apartheid policies opt to withdraw from the CSO cartel, an increased supply of diamonds could overwhelm the monopoly price structure. History proves that few monopolies last forever, but at this time it seems premature to prepare to march in the De Beers funeral procession.

WELL, WELL, WELL—IT'S A CRUDE CARTEL

First Stop: Baghdad, Iraq, September 14, 1960

An important conference is about to end. Venezuela's minister of mining and hydrocarbons, Juan Pablo Perez Alfonzo, and his friend Sheik Abdullah Tariki, Saudi Arabia's oil minister, have been searching for ways in which to create a common front of oil producers. That search has ended. They, along with Iran, Kuwait, and other oil countries, have just signed an agreement establishing a new cartel called the Organization of Petroleum Exporting Countries (OPEC).

Perez Alfonzo and Tariki were aided by a move initiated by Standard Oil Company (New Jersey)—now Exxon—that resulted in a 4- to 14-cent-per-barrel price decline on Middle East crude oil just a few months before. This made Kuwait and Iran, two former important holdouts, angry enough to enter into the new organization.

Second Stop: Lincoln, Nebraska, September 1970

Ten years have elapsed since the formation of OPEC. A gas war is in progress in this state capitol city of 175,000 residents. This price war is nothing special; it is typical for those occurring sporadically in all cities of the country. "Get it while you can," drivers declare. "It's not going to stay at 21.9 for long." A day or two later, the price goes back to 31.9 cents per gallon. Everyone knew that 21.9 was too good to last, but 31.9 isn't that bad, either.

The supply of petroleum in the world has kept pace with increased demand over the decade of the 1960s. OPEC notwithstanding, the world price of oil at the wellhead is approximately the same as it had been in 1960.

Next Stop: Middle East, Late 1973

A war is raging on two fronts—the Sinai Desert and the Golan Heights. Egypt and Syria, supported by other Arab states, have attacked Israel in an attempt to regain territories lost in the 1967 Six Day War. Egypt and Syria are showing surprising military strength and unity.

An announcement flashes out to the world from the Middle East on October 16. OPEC is boosting its posted price of oil from $3.01 a barrel to $5.11. In January 1973, just nine months before, OPEC had raised its price from $2.48 to $2.59 a barrel, and on October 1 it had boosted the price to $3.01. These price hikes had caused minor concern, but nothing like this recent one. After all, this latest price rise—from $3.01 to $5.11 a barrel—is a 70 percent increase!

"They will never make it stick," most observers reason. "The cartel just does not have that kind of power; it is loosely knit and largely ineffective in actually fixing the market price for oil."

Three days later, opinions change. The Arabs announce that they are imposing an oil embargo on the United States, the Netherlands, and other nations that publicly support Israel. In addition, they declare that they intend to cut back production on a step-by-step schedule until a favorable settlement to the question of the occupied lands is obtained. The industrial world is thrown into economic confusion. Europe and Japan are dependent on OPEC crude, and the United States, prior to the complete embargo, depended on OPEC for nearly 30 percent of its oil. Arab production is the major part of all OPEC oil output.

On January 1, 1974, the military action over for more than a month, OPEC, led by Iran, announces that henceforth the posted price of oil will be $11.65 a barrel. This is a 100 percent increase over the previous price and a 400 percent increase over that of a year ago. The cartel is solidified; it is now an effective monopolist restricting production to ensure a monopoly price and monopoly profits to its members. The crude cartel of the 1960s is now a sophisticated crude (oil) cartel.

Third Stop: The United States, 1978

The oil embargo is long gone; the gasoline lines of the winter of 1973–1974 are now only a memory. The price of gasoline has stabilized in the 65- to 75-cents-a-gallon range. OPEC's pricing policy has moderated, its last price hike occurring on January 1, 1977.

But there is still uncertainty in the air. Iran is undergoing violent domestic upheaval. OPEC oil ministers will meet in December, but most observers are predicting a moderate 5 percent hike, from $12.70 to $13.34 a barrel.

In the United States, talk of the "energy crisis" has dwindled. But the reality is that the United States is importing a larger percentage of its total oil from OPEC than it did prior to the embargo five years ago. In that five-year period, OPEC has fundamentally altered the structure of world economic power. Its oil revenues have averaged well over $100 billion annually since 1974.

Fourth Stop: Vienna, Austria, March 1982

The OPEC oil ministers have just concluded an emergency meeting. The world is awash in an oil glut that is creating price cuts by non-OPEC oil producers and under-the-table discounts by OPEC countries. OPEC's dramatic price increase from $13.50 per barrel in 1978 to $30.00 in 1979 and $34.00 in 1980, combined with the impact of rapid conservation, expanded use of alternative energy sources, rising non-OPEC oil production, and recession-ridden industrial nations, has produced a 2- to 3-million-barrel-per-day surplus at the official $34.00 OPEC price.

The twelvefold increase in oil prices over the decade produced many behavior changes by consumers, producers, and governments. For example, in the United States, sales of small cars amounted to 35 percent of all new auto purchases in 1972; in 1981, they represented over 50 percent. The ratio of oil consumption to gross national product declined by over 25 percent in the industrial nations between 1973 and 1981. U.S. oil imports declined by 41 percent from 1977 to 1981 and 78,000 new natural gas and oil wells were drilled in 1981 in the United States alone. As a further example, from 1973 to 1980, Japan reduced the amount of oil to make a ton of steel by 68 percent.

Responding to the oil glut, the OPEC ministers reach a formal conclusion: the cartel, which already has cut production from 31 million barrels of oil per day to 21 million, must reduce output still further—to 18.5 million barrels per day.

Most oil analysts predict that the OPEC action is too little and too late and that the price of oil will slide to as low as $25 to $26 per barrel. OPEC is a crude cartel that appears to be coming apart at the seams.

Fifth Stop: The United States, June 1986

OPEC appears to have lost its control over the world price of oil. Saudi Arabia, which produces one-half of OPEC's output, has tired of reducing its production in an attempt to maintain the price of oil, particularly because other OPEC nations have been openly contracting for sales at prices far below the OPEC posted price. Saudi Arabia is presently engaged in a strategy to increase production to raise its oil revenues and allegedly to force the price of oil so low that some of the wells of non-OPEC producers will become unprofitable. This action conceivably could lead nations such as the United States, Norway, Great Britain, Mexico, and the Soviet Union to agree with OPEC countries to initiate production quotas. The price of oil in the open market has dropped dramatically to about $10 a barrel. Gasoline prices in the United States have fallen below $1 a gallon. Most observers believe that the alleged Saudi Arabian strategy has little chance of success. Put bluntly, the OPEC oil cartel appears to have been shattered by competitive forces; it no longer is the major player in the world oil market.

Sixth Stop: Kuwait, Spring 1991

The Gulf War is over! After weeks of bombardment and a 100-hour land battle, Iraq has effectively surrendered and agreed to the terms of the United Nations resolutions. In the fall of 1990 Iraq had invaded fellow OPEC cartel member Kuwait. Iraq's President Saddam Hussein had justified the invasion because Kuwait allegedly was pumping excessive oil from a jointly shared oil field and was cheating on OPEC oil quotas.

In response to the invasion, Saudi Arabia invited a United Nations military force, led by the United States, into the Arabian desert to deter a threatened Iraqi invasion of the Saudi Arabian oil fields. A naval blockade of Iraqi shipments of oil kept the combined output of Iraq and Kuwait—about 5 percent of the world's oil production—off the market. In response to this decline in output and the threat of further disruptions of the world's oil supply, speculators drove up the price of oil to about $40 a barrel. Gasoline prices in the United States increased to $1.50 a gallon.

These high prices did not last, however. Saudi Arabia and Venezuela, among other nations, expanded their oil production to make up for the world shortfall. The United States sold some oil from its strategic petroleum reserve. Following the decisive defeat of Iraq, the price of oil plummeted to $19 a barrel, a price roughly equal to what it was one year earlier. Gasoline prices at the pump fell to $1 a gallon. The world now faced a glut of oil, leaving a fractured OPEC once again relatively impotent as an effective cartel.

Final Stop: The United States, The Time
You Read This Chapter

What is the price of oil? Has OPEC regained its influence in the world oil market? What percentage of total world output is produced by the OPEC nations?

These are questions for you to answer, because the OPEC story deserves an update. This story reveals much about the nature of monopoly as well as the great difficulties of maintaining monopoly prices over long periods of time.

THE MONOPOLY MODEL

I was led to attach great importance to the fact that our observations of nature . . . relate not so much to aggregate quantities, as to increments of quantities, and that in particular the demand for a thing is a continuous function, of which the "marginal" increment is, in stable equilibrium, balanced against the corresponding increment of its costs of production. It is not easy to get a clear view of continuity in this respect without the aid . . . of diagrams.*

So spoke the Englishman Alfred Marshall, the grand synthesizer of the economic ideas of those who preceded him, whose *Principles of Economics*, in 1890, established him as the greatest economist of his day. Marshall participated in the "marginal revolution" in economics. These economists believed that decisions of firms and individuals were determined by comparisons of marginal benefits (revenue) and marginal costs.

Marshall was particularly interested in understanding the determination of price in a competitive market. He described this type of market as one in which there were numerous small firms, each having a small share of the total market and each selling nearly an identical product. According to Marshall, the price of the product was established by the interactions of sellers and buyers. He depicted this interrelationship graphically in the supply-and-demand diagram now familiar to anyone who has taken an introductory economics course.

Marginal analysis also lent itself to understanding monopoly, a situation in which there is a single seller, there are no close substitutes for the product, and new firms are blocked from entering the industry.

Figure 8-2 shows the pure monopoly model graphically. This diagram depicts either a single monopolist, such as De Beers, or a cartel, which is a group of producers, such as OPEC, that legally or illegally acts jointly as a monopolist.

First, notice the cost curves in the diagram. The curves have the same shape as those developed in previous chapters. The law of diminishing returns that gives rise to increasing average costs (AC) and marginal cost (MC) applies to monopolists as well as to other competitors.

The major difference between the monopoly model and the model of a firm operating in pure competition is on the demand side. Because the monopolist is the only firm in the industry, it *is*, in a sense, the industry itself. The monopolist faces a downward-sloping demand curve for its product. Given this demand curve, it cannot sell more diamonds, oil, or whatever the product, unless it lowers its price. Over time, of course, the demand for the monopolist's product may increase

*Alfred Marshall, quoted by William Breit and Roger L. Ranson, in *The Academic Scribblers* (Holt, Rinehart and Winston, 1971), p. 19.

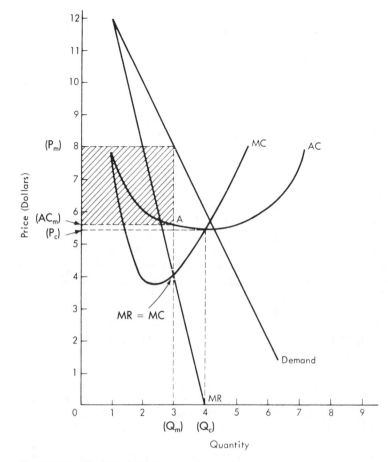

Figure 8-2 Monopoly Model

The pure monopolist restricts output to Q_m and charges price P_m. This price and quantity combination maximizes profits because MR = MC. The firm's total profit is represented by the shaded area in the graph.

because of increasing population, income, or other factors. This change in demand would mean that the monopolist could sell more units without reducing its price. But, at any point in time, higher output necessitates lower prices.

At first glance, the fact that a monopolist cannot sell more of its product without lowering its price seems to be a disadvantage. Recall that a purely competitive firm can sell as much as it chooses at the going price. Why would John D. Rockefeller or OPEC or De Beers go to so much trouble to establish a monopoly position when the outcome is a situation in which it cannot increase sales without lowering its price? The answer: while the downward demand curve may *seem* to be a disadvantage, it *actually* is an advantage to the monopolist. The monopolist can keep its price and profits high *by restricting production.* Because a monopoly can set prices or quantity, it can select a price-output combination that provides a higher than competitive profit.

Note the downward-sloping demand curve in Figure 8-2. Also note the curve labeled MR, which lies below it. This curve shows the marginal revenue that the firm receives when it sells *one more unit* of its product. The MR curve lies below the demand curve because the *additional* revenue resulting from the sale of another unit is *less than* the price charged for the product. To understand why this is true, look at the hypothetical data in Table 8-1.

Columns 1 and 2 show the relationship between price and quantity demanded that is depicted by the demand curve in Figure 8-2. The greater the quantity produced and sold, the lower the price that is charged. Column 3 shows total revenue, P × Q. It is greater at each successive quantity up to 3 units in the table. But notice that marginal revenue, column 4, *declines and is lower than price* at all but the first unit of output. This firm can sell 3 units at $8 per unit and take in $24, but it could sell 2 units at $10 per unit and make $20. The *additional* revenue, MR, that it makes by selling 3 rather than 2 units is only $4. In selling one more unit at $8, the firm gains $8, but it loses $2 per unit on 2 units that it *could have* sold for $10 each. The MR of the third unit, therefore, is $8 − $4 = $4. This is less than the price, $8. When the figures in the price and MR columns are represented graphically, they take the appearance of the D and MR curves in Figure 8-2. Both decline as output increases, and the MR curve lies below the demand curve.

It is important to note that the monopolist's motivation is identical to that of the ordinary competitor; each desires to make as much profit as possible. Each also employs the same decision rule—namely, "Expand production until MR = MC." The profit-maximizing quantity in Figure 8-2 is 3 units (Q_m), because at this output the marginal revenue just equals marginal cost (MR = 4, MC = 4).

Now, knowing that Q_m is the most profitable level of production, we can determine the price that this monopolist will charge. It is $8 ($P_m$) because the demand curve reflects the price that corresponds with each particular quantity—in this case 3 units. The firm's total revenue is easily determined, both numerically and geometrically. It is the rectangular area $P_m × Q_m$, which is $8 × 3 = $24. The monopolist's total cost is the average cost (AC_m) of 3 units, multiplied by 3, the number of units. Thus total cost is the rectangular area (OAC_mAQ_m) in the diagram.

Total economic profit, the shaded area of the diagram, is total revenue minus total cost. This particular monopolist is making more than a normal profit. *It is accomplishing this by restricting production below what would take place if there were pure competition (Q_m rather than Q_c) and charging a higher than competitive price (P_m rather than P_c).* Furthermore, this monopolist can retain the above-normal profit even in the long run, because competitors are blocked from entering the industry.

The advantage of being a monopolist is the ability to control output so as to set the best price and output level for one's product. A monopolist can select the best price-quantity combination, whereas the purely competitive firm has no

Table 8-1   Monopoly Demand and Revenue

(1) Quantity	(2) Price	(3) Total Revenue (TR)	(4) Marginal Revenue (MR)
1	$12	$12	$12
2	10	20	8
3	8	24	4
4	6	24	0
5	4	20	−4

control over the market price and cannot change it through any of its actions. Perfect monopolies are as rare as perfect competition, but the idea of monopoly power—the control over price—is essential to understanding many actual market situations. John D. Rockefeller demonstrated that he had a clear understanding of the benefits of monopolization when he drove to control the oil industry in the late 1800s. He desired and achieved high oil prices and profits. OPEC's movements toward strengthening the international oil cartel indicated a similar shrewdness. What was OPEC's means of achieving higher prices and profits? Answer: production cutbacks. Its behavior is identical to that which is predicted in Figure 8-2. Also recall that De Beers's monopoly position rested on restriction of output.

Not all firms or cartels possess the degree of monopoly power held by Rockefeller or De Beers, nor is monopoly always gained by design. There are many examples of "price makers" in the marketplace. For instance, the price of gasoline in the middle of the sagebrush country in Wyoming is high because few gasoline stations are around to provide competition. An existing single station in a small town along a lonely highway has natural monopoly power, and, as a consequence, the price of gasoline is higher there than in large city areas. Large convention hotels in our major cities charge very high prices for room service for the same reason: they have a degree of natural monopoly power. If you want breakfast without leaving your room on the 28th floor, what are your options? Competition is virtually nonexistent. You either order from the hotel's room-service menu, regardless of price, or go without. Did you ever wonder why a hot dog at a professional sporting event was priced so much higher than one downtown? Did you ever wonder why a hamburger at a ski lodge was priced so much higher than one at a corner café? Part of the reason is monopoly power.

In addition to collusion and inherent lack of competition, government regulation, economies of scale, and patent rights can produce monopolies. But, regardless of the cause, the short-run consequences of *unregulated* monopoly (assuming it has no cost advantage) are fourfold:

1. Monopoly produces higher prices for consumers than if there were competition.
2. Monopoly generates less production of a product than if competition existed. Fewer resources are devoted to this purpose, and resource allocation is inefficient.
3. Monopoly produces higher long-run profits for firms than if competition existed.
4. Monopoly transfers income from consumers to producers to a greater degree than under competitive conditions.

These consequences are evident in the examples in the first part of this chapter and in other situations where there is monopoly power. What should government do, if anything, to correct for this "market failure?" International cartels such as OPEC and foreign monopolies such as De Beers are largely immune from traditional U.S. antimonopoly policy, but three broad policy options exist for dealing with domestic monopolies: antitrust, public utility regulation, and *laissez-faire*.

PUBLIC POLICIES TOWARD MONOPOLY

The Sherman Act (1890) and the amended Clayton Act (1914) form the legal basis for the antitrust approach toward monopoly. Section 2 of the Sherman Act, in particular, addresses the monopoly problem by declaring monopolization and attempts to monopolize illegal. The Standard Oil Trust, for example, was found to have violated this provision in 1911 and was dissolved into several regional oil firms. More recently, IBM and AT&T were charged with violating Section 2 of the Sherman Act. In 1982, after more than a decade in the legal process, the federal government concluded that its case against IBM lacked sufficient merit and dropped the charge. In the same year, the government reached an out-of-court settlement with AT&T in which the giant telephone company agreed to divest itself of its regional Bell operating companies.

A second policy option for treating domestic monopoly is public utility regulation. In a few cases, for example, the local provision of electricity, natural gas, and telephone service, firms are natural monopolies. *A natural monopoly is one in which the economies of scale are so extensive that only a single firm can successfully achieve the lowest possible costs of providing the product or service.* In these rare cases, government chooses to allow the monopoly to exist, but then directly regulates the prices (rates) that the firm can charge.

A final approach to monopoly is *laissez-faire*, which translates into "let do" or "leave be." A conscious decision by government to "do nothing," after all, is a policy itself. This policy coexists with antitrust and regulation in the United States. Some unchallenged monopolies are the outcomes of patents; others involve products that have little total significance to the economy (Wham-O Frisbees); others occur because competitors leave the dying industry; and still others consist of new firms in emerging industries where the prospect for future competition looks bright.

Some economists recommend that this *laissez-faire* approach be broadened and that antitrust policy be focused on policing specific abusive conduct of firms, be they competitors or monopolists, rather than seek to break up monopolies. They point out that high monopolistic prices discourage people from buying monopolized products (oil, for example), encourage them to seek substitutes, and encourage other firms to discover new technologies and goods to compete with the monopolist. Supporters of a general *laissez-faire* approach view competition as a long-run, dynamic process, characterized by the rise and domination of some firms in some markets, inevitably followed by new competition based on new technology and products, and the eventual demise of the old monopoly. According to this view, the only way that monopolists can maintain their positions is by gaining protection from competition through government tariffs, regulations, licenses, or laws.

Mainstream critics of the *laissez-faire* approach counter that such nongovernmental entry barriers as economies of scale, entry-deterring pricing, and lack of access to raw materials can keep monopoly power entrenched for decades. They contend that antitrust is needed to enhance competition and reduce allocative inefficiency. Each of the three policy approaches to monopoly—antitrust, regulation, and *laissez-faire*—has at one time or the other been in great favor or disfavor. The debate over the appropriate way to treat monopoly power will surely continue. As you read about and participate in this debate, recall the basic monopoly model and remember that:

> Being alone is not necessarily being lonely.
> In fact, happiness is being alone (for monopolists).
> Lone producers create unhappiness (for consumers).
> Who cares?
> Monopolists and consumers, we suspect . . .

And economists . . .
And students of economics . . .
Perhaps. . . .

STUDY QUESTIONS

1. In Chapter 7, the Harvey and Pop Cornwell Company faced a demand curve that was perfectly horizontal (elastic). The demand curve facing a monopolist slopes downward and to the right. Why the difference?
2. Answer the accompanying questions on the basis of the following demand schedule for a monopolist:

Price	Quantity
$7	1
6	2
5	3
4	4
3	5

   a. What price can the firm charge for each of four units of output?
   b. What is the marginal revenue of the fourth unit of output? (Reminder: marginal revenue is the change in total revenue associated with one more unit of output.)
   c. Why is the marginal revenue of the fourth unit of output less than the product price received for that unit?
3. Does being a monopolist in the sale of a product guarantee profits? Explain.
4. A national investigation of hospital drug prices found that hospital patients are usually charged more for drugs given to them at the hospital than it would cost them to buy the same products at drugstores. How might this relate to the idea of monopoly power? Can you think of a rationale for hospitals' "overpricing" drugs?
5. Is the following statement true or false? "A monopoly charges the highest price it can get." Explain your answer, referring to Figure 8-2.
6. Define the term *cartel*. Cite an example of this type of organization.
7. Most industries in the United States are free to increase their prices if they feel it is in their best interest to do so. Why isn't the local telephone company free to increase telephone rates without getting special permission from state regulatory agencies?
8. Explain how De Beers's advertising of small diamonds might enable it to sell more diamonds without lowering the price.
9. Why is maintaining monopoly power so difficult in a capitalist economy? Relate your answer to the appropriate elements of the economic perspective.
10. What are the three broad policy options that society has for dealing with monopoly? Explain why a particular option may be the optimal policy in one situation but not in another.

9

WHAT'S BREWING IN THE BEER INDUSTRY?

The Economics of Oligopoly

Concepts and Terms Examined in This Chapter

1. Monopolistic Competition
2. Oligopoly
3. Economies of Scale
4. Product Differentiation
5. Differentiated Oligopolies
6. Homogeneous Oligopolies
7. Nonprice Competition
8. Advertising
9. Interdependent Pricing
10. Collusion and Price Leadership
11. Entry Barriers

Pure competition (Chapter 7) and pure monopoly (Chapter 8) represent the extremes in the continuum of degrees of competition in market models. In between these extremes lie markets in which there is competition, but individual firms exercise some degree of control over the price they charge. Economists have devised two market models to depict these situations. The first is termed *monopolistic competition*; the second is termed *oligopoly*.

Monopolistic competition is a market in which there are numerous firms, each selling a similar, but slightly differentiated product. Examples are restaurants, auto parts stores, furniture manufacturers, personal computer retailers, gasoline stations, and the like. Entry to these markets is relatively easy, and therefore economic profits tend to attract new sellers. The eventual outcomes are similar to those in the Cornwell story: price gravitates toward marginal cost, and there are only normal profits in the long run. Unlike the outcome in the pure competition model, price does not *equal* marginal cost, because each firm offers a product or service that is slightly distinct from those of its competitors. Thus each firm possesses some monopoly power, even though it is not sufficient to maintain long-run economic profits.

A second model of imperfect competition is *oligopoly*. Numerous industries can be classified as oligopolistic. Just a few examples of products produced in such industries are automobiles, home appliances, light bulbs, breakfast cereals, primary steel, aluminum, mainframe computers, records and tapes, and soft drinks. Another such product is malt beverages (beer), the focus of this chapter. We have selected this particular industry for analysis for three reasons: (1) Its product is well known and highly advertised; (2) it has increasingly become dominated by a few firms over the past two decades; and (3) it displays the typical characteristics of other oligopolistic industries that produce consumer goods.

As attested to by the following 1798 Massachusetts law, the American beer industry is as old as the United States itself.

AN ACT TO ENCOURAGE THE MANUFACTURE AND CONSUMPTION OF STRONG BEER, ALE AND OTHER MALT LIQUORS

[Passed by the Commonwealth of Massachusetts, 1798]

Whereas the manufacture of strong beer, ale and other malt liquors will promote the purposes of husbandry and commerce, by encouraging the growth of such materials as are peculiarly congenial to our soil and climate . . . and whereas the wholesale qualities of malt liquors greatly recommend them to general uses as an important means of preserving the health of the citizens of this Commonwealth, and of preventing the pernicious effects of spirituous liquors:

1. *Be it therefore enacted by the Senate and the House of Representatives in General Court Assembled, and by the authority of the same,* That all brewhouses, wherein shall be made and produced for sale annually, a quantity of strong beer or ale, not less than one hundred barrels of thirty-one and one half gallons each, beer measure. . . . The faculty of annual profit of such manufacture, shall be, and they hereby are exempted from all taxes and duties of every kind, for the term of five years next after the passing of this act.

2. *And be it further enacted,* That all brewers or others, who shall be owners or occupiers of such brewhouses, shall, as soon as may be after the passing of this act, and afterwards, at least once in every year, produce to the several assessors of the

towns and districts . . . satisfactory evidence of the quantities of beer and ale in their said houses respectively . . . in order that they may have the benefit of the exemption aforesaid.*

During the early years of the republic, every major settlement had brewhouses that manufactured and sold the frothy beverage that the Massachusetts lawmakers declared to be an aid in "preserving the health of the citizens of this Commonwealth." Most of these small, family-owned brewhouses were both producers of beer and retail sellers of the product.

This industry structure remained unchanged well into the twentieth century. Prohibition interrupted beer production in 1919, and for the next 14 years the only beer produced came from illegal "moonshining" operations. In the depths of the Great Depression, 1933, Congress abolished Prohibition, and 750 legal beer makers eagerly reopened their spigots. Economic activity soon returned to normal as the brewers rushed their product to the thirsty public. The brewing firms had no way of realizing that most of them would no longer be in business a few decades later. Breweries vanished like beer at a college keg party in the ensuing years, and the structure of the American brewing industry changed remarkably.

Of the 750 firms operating in 1934, only 250 still existed in 1955. By 1960, the number had dropped to 170, and at present fewer than 20 producers remain (excluding microbreweries). Today, two firms account for nearly 65 percent of total beer sales. As stated earlier, the present structure of the malt beverage, or beer, industry is described as an oligopoly.

Unlike pure competition, in which each firm has a negligible share of total sales, or monopolistic competition, in which numerous firms compete, or pure monopoly, in which a single firm controls the market, oligopoly describes an industry in which a small number of firms account for a large percentage of total sales. Oligopolistic industries are characterized by fewness. Other characteristics include interdependent pricing and entry barriers. Product differentiation is also a characteristic of many but not all oligopolistic industries. It will be instructive to examine these characteristics in detail.

CHARACTERISTICS OF OLIGOPOLY

Fewness

In 1990, Anheuser-Busch and Miller Brewing Company produced about 65 percent of all the beer sold in the United States. Anheuser-Busch's product line includes Budweiser, Bud Light, Busch, Busch Cold Filtered Draft, and Michelob. Miller Brewing Company is the maker of Miller High Life, Lite, Miller Genuine Draft, and Löwenbräu. Anheuser-Busch was the largest producer, with 42 percent of the market, followed by Miller with 22 percent. The third through fifth leading sellers were Stroh with 10 percent, Coors with 9 percent, and G. Heileman with 7

The Perpetual Laws of the Commonwealth of Massachusetts — from the Establishment of Its Constitution to the Second Session of the General Court, in 1798, 2 volumes, 1799. Quoted in Stanley Baron, *Brewed in America: A History of Beer and Ale in the United States* (Boston: Little, Brown, 1962), Appendix.

percent. Thus the top five brewers collectively accounted for 90 percent of all the beer sold in the United States.

What has led to "fewness" in the brewing industry? Why does a small number of firms dominate a market in which the demand for the product has consistently increased? Several reasons help to explain the historical trend toward fewness.

First, some brewers discovered that they could lower production costs for each barrel of beer by building larger breweries and using new production methods. Recall from Chapter 7 that reductions in cost resulting from larger firm size are termed *economies of scale*. Brewers who built larger facilities achieved these cost reductions and were able to produce beer at lower prices than could the small, local firms that continued to use old, smaller breweries. This competition caused many inefficient firms to shut down and concede their market to the more efficient regional and national firms.

The major areas where economies of scale are achieved in brewing are in packaging the beer and mechanization of warehousing and shipping. New large-scale plants have bottling-line speeds of 1,200 bottles per minute and canning-line speeds of 2,400 cans per minute. To keep this equipment fully used, a firm must have a sizable share of the total beer market.

The experience of Schlitz and Falstaff during the period 1965–1975 provides a good example of the importance of economies of scale. In 1965, Falstaff was the fourth best-selling brand of beer in the country and Schlitz was second. By 1975, however, Falstaff had fallen to a stale seventh, whereas Schlitz had retained its second-place position. Falstaff executives blamed their sales and profit decline on "cutthroat" pricing by Budweiser and Schlitz, but industry analysts suggested that the cause was Falstaff's high production costs. Schlitz constructed two highly automated breweries in that period, each producing over 4 million barrels of beer annually, with a combined work force of fewer than 500 production employees. Falstaff, on the other hand, had four breweries that *jointly* produced only 4 million barrels, an amount equal to a single new Schlitz plant; yet 1,800 workers were necessary to operate the four Falstaff plants. An industry expert estimated that Falstaff's cost per barrel in 1972 was $4.39, whereas Schlitz's cost per barrel in its two modern plants was only $1.08.

A second factor explaining the trend toward fewness in the brewing industry is mergers. Studies show that mergers, although numerous, explain only a small part of the increase in concentration in the industry between 1947 and 1972. In addition, mergers do not explain the growing market shares of Anheuser-Busch and Miller during the past two decades. But, since 1972, mergers *have* reshaped and consolidated the third through seventh positions in the industry. For example, G. Heileman climbed from thirty-ninth place in the industry to fourth by acquiring several regional breweries and their labels. Other mergers included Stroh's acquisition of Schlitz, Olympia's purchase of the Theodore Hamm Company and the Lone Star Brewing Company, and Pabst's merger with Olympia. Brewers attempted several other mergers, but the federal government enjoined them for violating Section 7 of the Clayton Act. That law declares that mergers between firms that produce similar products and sell them in the same geographical market are illegal when substantial reductions of competition will result.

The use of aggressive marketing tactics by the major producers is a third reason for fewer firms in the beer industry. These tactics are discussed in the next section.

Product Differentiation

Oligopolistic firms that sell consumer goods try to make their products appear to be distinct or different from those of their close competitors. This activity is termed *product differentiation,* and therefore these oligopolies are dubbed *differentiated oligopolies.*

Not all oligopolists engage in product differentiation. So-called *homogeneous oligopolies* that produce materials purchased by industries usually cannot differentiate their products because the products tend to be quite homogeneous, or standardized. Examples are producers of copper, iron ore, steel, gypsum, and crude oil. But oligopolists that sell products directly to consumers—for example, producers of autos, detergents, razor blades, tires, breakfast cereal, and beer—have an incentive to explain how their product is different from and better than those of other direct rivals. If a company can generate "brand loyalty" and convince the consumer that its brand is superior to all others, then it can increase sales, prices, and profits. In some instances, *product differentiation* is based upon physical differences in the product; in others, it is a fabrication of advertising and promotion. This *nonprice competition,* or *quality competition,* is common in the beer industry. Try watching television without seeing a beer commercial.

Beer advertisements do not say, "Buy our beer because it is priced lower than that of our competitors." Instead, they proclaim, "Buy our beer because it is distinct and better than those other brands." Advertising agencies are hired to develop slogans that, in effect, simply rephrase this statement. Familiar slogans include "It's the King of Beers," "This Bud's for You," "Nothing Beats a Bud," "It's from the Land of Sky Blue Water," "It's Brewed from Rocky Mountain Spring Water," "It Won a Blue Ribbon in 1844," "It's an Unexpected Pleasure," "Miller's Made the American Way," and "Give Me a Light—No, Bud Light."

Large national brewers maintain larger advertising budgets than do regional brewers, and the former are also able to use national media such as television for their advertising campaigns. More specifically, Anheuser-Busch spent $388 million on media ads in 1988; Miller Brewing Company, $189 million; and Adolph Coors, $125 million. These large advertising budgets have enhanced the long-standing "premium" images for the products of the dominant firms and are a very important reason for the demise of many small breweries.

Some taste differences do exist among beers, but most analysts in the industry doubt that actual taste preferences account for the growing market shares of the big brewers. Tests suggest that only 50 percent of beer drinkers can actually identify taste differences in beer. "Quality" is often unrelated to the process of brewing; instead, it is simply a matter of what the consumer perceives it to be. This explains the purpose of advertising. It accomplishes what actual taste differences do not—it clearly differentiates one brand of beer from another in the consumer's mind.

Miller Brewing Company used aggressive advertising and product differentiation to become the second largest producer. Upon acquiring Miller in 1969, Philip Morris, Inc., began a strategy of positioning Miller's brands where the potential sales were greatest. Sold previously as the "champagne of beers," Miller

High Life had attracted a disproportionate share of upper-income consumers and women who were only occasional beer drinkers. Miller's new advertisements attempted to change that image quickly. Advertising featuring young people and blue-collar workers (oil drillers, building demolition experts, tugboat operators, and lumber workers) were accompanied by a new slogan, "If you've got the time, we've got the beer." Miller's market share climbed dramatically!

Miller further increased its market share by introducing Lite, its low-calorie best seller. Large sums were spent on ads showing former athletes, and others, drinking Lite. This highly successful product-differentiation strategy spawned no fewer than 20 competitive brands of light beer, but Miller still dominates sales in this segment of the market.

Miller's successful strategy of differentiating its product from that of competitors also is evidenced in its introduction in 1985 of Genuine Draft. This "cold-filtered" beer is not pasteurized and therefore has the taste of beer from a keg. Genuine Draft pushed its way into the top ten sellers in 1990, prompting Anheuser-Busch to counter with its own cold-filtered beer.

Miller's drive to become number one, however, has fallen short of its goal. In the 1980s, Anheuser-Busch increased its market share, partly at Miller's expense. Because of the success of Lite, the name Miller's tended to get associated in people's minds with Lite instead of its flagship brand, Miller High Life. For this and other reasons, sales of Miller High Life declined dramatically. Meanwhile, sales of Budweiser continued to expand. In an attempt to recapture market share, Miller abandoned its old slogan, "Welcome to Miller Time." and stressed that "Miller's Made the American Way." It also changed its packaging to include an American eagle. But one analyst thinks Miller has a name problem: "High Life isn't a working-class name, it's upper class. I have yet to hear any beer drinkers say give me a High Life."[*] The largest segment of the beer market is composed of working-class customers.

In summary, much of the competition among the giants in brewing takes the form of product differentiation and nonprice rivalry. The fewness of major producers in the industry complicates price competition and leads to a third general characteristic of oligopoly.

Interdependent Pricing Decisions

A triple pricing system prevails in the brewing industry. The major producers usually have several brands. They price one brand low to compete with other "popularly priced" labels (Busch, Old Milwaukee, Keystone); they have their standard "premium"-priced beer (Budweiser, Miller High Life, Stroh); and they offer a "superpremium" brand at a higher price (Michelob, Löwenbräu). The major brewers charge similar prices for "popularly priced," "premium," and "super-premium" brands.

The pricing behavior of oligopolists differs from that of pure competitors and monopolists. Recall from previous chapters that pure competitors have no control over their product prices and are not directly affected by the decisions of other firms in their industries. Pure monopolists, on the other hand, have their

---

[*]Al Ries, chairman of Trout & Ries Advertising, Inc., as reported in "Miller Beer Ads Wave the Flag, But So Do Bud's," *Wall Street Journal*, February 11, 1985, p. 21.

markets to themselves and can seek the best price without regard to competitors. The price charged by an oligopolist is closely related to the prices charged by rival firms. In deciding to charge a price, the oligopolist must consider how rivals might react. This interdependence of pricing explains the nearly identical beer prices for similarly positioned brands in particular market areas.

There is considerable *price rigidity* (inflexibility of prices) among the major firms in oligopolistic industries. The following example should clarify why this is the case. Assume that Miller is considering a price change. If it increases its price, Budweiser, Stroh, and others might not follow with their own price increases. If these rivals do not raise their prices, Miller will lose business to them. Miller therefore rejects a unilateral price increase. What about a price reduction, to draw business away from competitors? This strategy might provoke Budweiser, Stroh, Coors, and others to reduce their prices to match Miller's reduction. This reduction would leave Miller worse off than before, because its sales would increase only slightly, but its revenue per bottle would decline appreciably. In view of the anticipated reactions of rivals, Miller might conclude that it is best to leave its price unchanged. Other brewers are in the same position. The nearly identical premium beer prices within market areas may be the result of this uncertainty of reactions to price changes.

Oligopolists are strongly tempted to remove pricing uncertainty by colluding and fixing a common monopoly price. Collusive price-fixing of this nature, however, is illegal under Section 1 of the Sherman Act. Hence, *price leadership* has emerged in many oligopolistic industries as an alternative to direct collusion. An "understanding" is established in the industry that when the price leader announces a price increase, the other major firms in the industry will follow. Price leadership provides a means through which price rigidity can be overcome and oligopoly prices can be increased when deemed desirable. Small firms are expected to match the price increases of the leader. If they fail to follow, they face the threat of retaliatory selective price reductions by the majors in the small firms' primary market areas. In brewing, Anheuser-Busch is viewed by other firms as a price leader, although a pattern of leadership is not nearly as clear as it is in some other oligopolistic industries. Anheuser-Busch did not match a price increase imposed by Miller in 1980. Miller suffered loss of sales, and since then has been content to allow Anheuser-Busch to announce price increases first.

The dominant firms in the brewing industry compete through product differentiation, advertising, and other marketing strategies. But, unlike many oligopolists, the major brewers have also shown a willingness to engage in price promotions to add to their market shares.

A typical price promotion works as follows. Anheuser-Busch, Miller, or another large producer gives a regional wholesaler a discount. The wholesaler then reduces its price to the retailer, and the retailer has a sale on that brand of beer. The regional and smaller national firms contend that these price promotions are used selectively to eliminate competition. They argue that the big firms reduce their price by as much as 20 percent for a few weeks in the price-promotion markets to entice customers to switch brands. Some converts to the national brand remain, even when the promotion terminates and prices rise once again. The firms that most often use price promotions simply reply that they are dispensing with their premium prices where competition dictates it.

The majors also compete with the lower-priced regional brands by packaging some of their beer under labels with popular prices. Anheuser-Busch prices its Busch beer, for instance, so that it will compete with local low-priced brands. Similarly, Miller has positioned its Meisterbrau and Milwaukee's Best in that market segment and Coors has marketed new low-priced brands called Keystone and Keystone Light.

Entry Barriers

A final characteristic of oligopoly is the existence of substantial barriers or obstacles to the entry of new firms. In oligopolistic industries, entry barriers take several forms, including patent rights, exclusive government grants, monopolization of key raw materials, and economies of scale. These types of obstacles to entry are less pronounced in brewing than in some oligopolies, but entry, nevertheless, is difficult. New national firms do not enter the brewing industry to challenge the profitable major producers because entry would require prohibitively large sums of money to finance the needed construction and equipment. A single new, efficient 5-million-barrel-capacity brewery costs about $250 million. The leaders in the industry themselves have difficulty justifying building new breweries, because the overall demand for beer has been rising slowly over the past several years.

Even if a new national firm could raise the necessary financial capital to enter the industry, survival might be difficult. Large advertising expenditures would be required indefinitely. Also, the major firms would fight vigorously to retain their market shares. They could be expected to use price-promotion activity and other weapons as a way of maintaining their positions and blocking the entry of a serious new rival. An individual or corporation may easily enter a competitive industry such as agriculture, where start-up costs are relatively low, but entry is extremely difficult when the industry is capital intensive and oligopolistic. Entry barriers are an important characteristic of oligopoly in general and the beer industry in particular.

It is important to note, however, that entry has occurred in a number of oligopolistic U.S. industries. In particular, foreign firms—themselves large enough to achieve economies of scale—have penetrated the American auto, steel, consumer electronics, electric razor, apparel, sporting equipment, and tire industries. In fact, many domestic oligopolists face their greatest competitive threats from foreign producers. This is not the case for American brewers. Although several brands of premium beers are imported, and Canadian firms have attempted to market their products in the United States, imports account for less than 5 percent of total U.S. beer sales.

The only entry of note in the brewing industry has been that of the so-called microbreweries. These small firms produce specialty beers that have appeal in local markets, but together they account for a minor share of total beer sales. No new firm—domestic or foreign—has obtained a significant market share in the American brewing industry since 1945.

In summary, then, the characteristics of oligopolies that produce consumer goods are fewness, product differentiation, interdependent pricing, and entry barriers. The next logical question is, "What are the economic outcomes of oligopolistic behavior?" The beer industry provides an example of the negative results of oligopoly as well as some positive ones.

OUTCOMES OF OLIGOPOLISTIC BEHAVIOR

In theory, oligopolistic structure and behavior lead to *higher product prices, lower production,* and *higher profit* than would occur if the industry were purely competitive. Several interrelated actions produce higher prices in oligopolistic industries. Most of these actions have already been discussed in conjunction with the brewing industry, but they merit restatement. First, price leadership and other joint-action behavior can give rise to higher prices. The price leader is able to set a price above the perfectly competitive level if a tacit agreement exists among other producers to follow the lead. This price leadership effectively eliminates price competition among the dominant firms. In a market economy, competition is responsible for reducing prices to the marginal cost of production. Any action that eliminates price competition is likely to lead to higher prices.

Product differentiation is a second behavior that may cause higher prices in oligopolies. For example, if all beer came in the same bottle, with a single label, "Beer," prices and the distribution of sales among the firms would be different from what they are today. Successful nonprice advertising differentiates the product in the beer drinker's mind, creates brand loyalty on the basis of nontaste factors, and enables the producer to charge higher prices. Product "uniqueness" created through advertising increases the demand for a particular brand of beer and may make the demand *less elastic* (the quantity demanded is less responsive to price changes). "Consumer loyalty" may permit the company to increase prices without experiencing as large a reduction in sales as would otherwise be the case.

Anheuser-Busch's pricing of its brands of beer is an interesting example of how product differentiation may lead to higher prices. Busch is aimed at people who buy the lowest-priced beer available. The demand curve for Busch is quite elastic; that is, a unilateral price increase would result in a considerable loss in sales to other low-priced brands. Thus, Anheuser-Busch prices Busch as a "popular-priced beer" and competes on this basis. Budweiser, on the other hand, is heavily advertised and has considerable brand loyalty. The demand for Bud is less elastic than is that for Busch. A price increase on Budweiser would not result in the same reduction in sales as it would in the case of Busch. Therefore, Anheuser-Busch charges premium prices for Budweiser. The company charges still higher prices for Michelob, which is, after all, "an unexpected pleasure." The cost difference of producing Busch, Budweiser, and Michelob is minimal. The "premium" prices charged for brands of beer such as Budweiser, Coors, and Miller and the "super-premium" prices charged for Löwenbräu and Michelob attest to the market power gained through product differentiation and market segmentation.

A final theoretical reason why oligopolistic prices may be higher than competitive ones is that oligopolists may find it in their best interest to restrict production below the level that would exist in a competitive industry. Oligopolists face a downward-sloping demand curve for their product. They must restrict their output somewhat if they wish to charge a higher price. Restriction of production, if it does occur, impedes the efficient allocation of resources in the economy, because too few resources are devoted to the production of the restricted product. The preceding chapter explained why restricting output may be in the best interest of a firm.

The higher prices in oligopolies produce higher profits than those achieved in purely competitive industries. Consistently large economic profits are a signal to all other firms and potential firms in the economy that money can be made by entering the profitable industry. This entry of new competitors might not take place in oligopolies, however, because the barriers to entry are substantial. New firms find it difficult to enter because of the large start-up costs and the pricing practices used by the dominant firms. Thus oligopolists may be able to maintain long-run economic profits.

The negative price and resource allocation aspects of oligopolies are of some concern to economists, especially since there is a trend toward even greater market concentration and oligopoly in some industries. Yet positive outcomes of oligopolies must also be mentioned. Oligopolies may result from economies of scale, technical innovation, or progressive management. Brewing firms, for example, must have large sales volumes to justify constructing gigantic breweries that utilize the latest cost-saving production and distribution techniques. Breweries must be large to be efficient—so large, in fact, that some degree of oligopoly may be inevitable in this industry. The fact that economies of scale underlie many oligopolistic structures, however, does not eliminate the problem of high prices. If price competition is lacking and entry barriers are high, there is little incentive to pass along to consumers the cost saving from the economies of scale.

A second benefit of oligopoly is that product differentiation enables consumers to select from a wide range of variations of the same general product. One element of the economic perspective is that people have widely differing tastes. Larry may like Keystone; Curley, Bud Light; and Moe, Miller Genuine Draft. Unlike the standardized product of pure competition, the product differentiation associated with oligopoly may better match with these diverse tastes.

A third potential benefit of oligopoly is that the large profits earned may enable these firms to engage in a greater amount of research and development than might occur in a more competitive, lower-profit industry. Some oligopolists use this advantage and are "progressive" in their attempts to discover and implement new technology. But data indicate that others do not spend as high a percentage of their revenue for research and development as does the average medium-sized firm in the economy. Large size and substantial profits are no guarantee that a firm will be efficient and innovative.

And, finally, competition may be "workable" even with a small number of competitors. The intense rivalry for market shares through expansion of capacity and occasional price discounting may counter the oligopolistic tendencies toward higher prices and may keep profits near normal levels. The beer industry supports this possibility. Compared with other manufacturing firms, the profits earned by the major brewers have not been excessive. Another factor that makes competition workable in many oligopolistic industries is foreign competition, mentioned earlier. Although only a few U.S. producers make some products, if profits are high, foreign firms have an incentive to enter the vast U.S. market. Some of the fiercest international competition is conducted by firms that have dominant market shares in their own economies, but see an opportunity to increase profits by selling abroad.

Oligopoly is a common market structure in the economy. It is a mixed blessing. The motives underlying the behavior of oligopolistic firms are identical to the motives of firms in more competitive industries—they wish to increase their profits. But the unique structure of oligopoly is such that this self-interest behavior may yield socially and economically undesirable outcomes. Policymakers must ensure that the behavior of large producers is consistent with the achievement of the economy's overall goals. Vigorous competition carries with it its own insurance in this respect, but substitutes may be needed when these competitive checks and balances are inadequate. These substitutes may involve government prosecution of specific abuses, divestiture of firms, prohibition of mergers, or government regulation. The task of shaping such policies is a vital one, and it will be in the forefront of public discussion for some time to come.

STUDY QUESTIONS

1. Distinguish between monopolistic competition and oligopoly.
2. How does oligopoly differ from pure competition in the following areas?
   a. Control over price
   b. Number of competitors
   c. Difficulty of entry into the industry
3. What purpose does nonprice advertising have in the beer industry?
4. What characteristics do nonadvertising oligopolists have in common?
5. Collusion can be a problem in oligopolistic industries. Why are collusion, price-fixing, and price leadership more likely to occur among oligopolistic firms than among firms in a purely competitive market?
6. The title of this chapter is a question, "What's Brewing in the Beer Industry?" Provide a concise answer.
7. In an example of price rigidity given in this chapter, Miller was concerned that it would lose sales and revenue if it increased price and rivals failed to follow. It also felt that it would lose revenue if it lowered its price and rivals matched this reduction. Miller perceived an unusual demand situation, which is reflected in the following kinked demand curve:

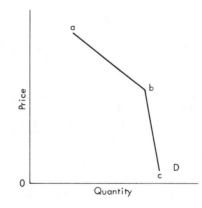

   a. Is segment *ab* of the curve less or more elastic than segment *bc?*
   b. What would be the "going price"?
   c. Why is the curve "kinked," or "bent"?

8. Some oligopolists do not advertise heavily to try to differentiate their products, while others do. Which of the following oligopolists represent the former group? The latter?
   a. Automobile manufacturers
   b. Copper refiners
   c. Toothpaste manufacturers
   d. Iron ore producers
   e. Gypsum producers

9. What is the role of foreign competition in maintaining competitive pricing among large U.S. oligopolistic firms? Cite an example.

10. Discuss: "An industry can be quite competitive and produce competitive market outcomes even if there are only a handful of firms in it."

APPENDIX: A REPLY TO THE SKEPTIC

Remember the skeptical Robert N. Scott who, in the appendix to Chapter 3, criticized the authors' analysis. Thus far no one has directly responded to his remarks. Scott clearly should not be permitted to have the last word, because this is not his book. Now that ideas such as the economic perspective, competition, monopoly, oligopoly, and advertising are more familiar, it is time to reconsider Scott's criticism.

Scott made three main points: (1) "The main motivation of large American firms ... is not profit, and most corporations do not try to maximize it." (2) Producers create demand through product advertising, and therefore the consumer is not sovereign. (3) Competition is not a vital force in oligopolistic industries. Each point deserves discussion.

1. *Motivation of the firm's managers.* According to Scott, because ownership and management are separated, large American firms emphasize growth at the expense of profits. Managers pursue their own interests, which are different from those of the faceless and powerless stockholders who own the corporations. Managers benefit by growth of sales, independently of higher profits. Although this is an interesting theory, the evidence does not support it! The general body of economic research indicates that profits are the major motive of firms in the economy. Managers *do* take actions to maximize the long-run profits of their firms. There are several reasons for this behavior. First, many executives are partial owners of the firms for which they work. Often some of their compensation takes the form of stock options. Therefore, executives can raise their own remuneration by increasing the profitability of their enterprises. In addition, many bonuses paid to executives are tied to the corporation's profitability. Finally, promotions often are based on contributions to the firm's profit goals.

A second reason that profits are pursued is defensive. Firms that emphasize growth at the expense of long-run profits have lower rates of return than do firms that maximize profits. As a result, the firm emphasizing growth will have lower stock prices relative to their profit-maximizing competitors. The profit-maximizing firms will be in a position to offer the stockholders of growth-maximizing firms a premium price for their stock. Corporate takeovers will take place, and the old managers will be replaced by executives who emphasize profits.

Much of Scott's confusion over profit maximization stems from his failure to distinguish between short-term and long-term goals. Corporate growth *is* important, because it normally is associated with greater total profits. Sometimes a firm's managers will sacrifice some short-term profit to increase sales as a strategy to increase the long-run flow of profits.

The day-to-day activity of firms, whether they are corner convenience stores or huge manufacturers, tends to be purposeful. The managers try to serve customers in a manner that allows the companies to maximize their profits over the long term.

2. *Consumer sovereignty.* Scott seems to think that consumers can be persuaded through advertising to buy anything at any price. Evidence does not support this view. New Coke is a relatively recent case of the inability to persuade the public to buy something it did not want. To no avail, Bill Cosby and a multimillion-dollar ad campaign extolled the virtues of New Coke. Consumers failed to buy it in adequate quantities, and therefore the Coca-Cola company had to admit its mistake and once again offer old Coke for sale (under the label "Classic Coke"). Advertising can *influence* consumer spending patterns, but it cannot *create* demand for products that consumers do not want.

If advertising were the only factor that determined product success, then no new product introduced with a good advertising campaign would fail. In reality, every year many new products fail to gain consumer acceptance and therefore do not produce sufficient revenue to continue their production.

Those firms whose managers think producers rather than consumers are sovereign are not long for successful existence.

3. *The role of competition.* Scott states that oligopolistic industries are uncompetitive. His problem is a too narrow definition of competition. He measures competition by the number of firms producing identical products. Therefore, in situations where only a handful of firms account for the majority of sales of a product, there is little competition. The discussion in the last three chapters, however, indicated that competition takes numerous forms. Even OPEC found it difficult to brace itself against new competition from new producers of petroleum and such petroleum substitutes as coal, natural gas, solar energy, synthetic fuels, and activities to conserve energy. When competition is absent in an industry, strong incentives exist for new producers to devise and offer substitute products that serve customers' wants at lower prices. This new competition may come from entirely different industries or from companies located in other countries. Consider the competition in automobiles and personal computers provided by Japan and South Korea. Competition may also come from small producers in the noncompetitive industry who gain market share through pricing closer to marginal cost than the majors.

The economic perspective suggests that competition, in one form or another, is quite pervasive. *People pursue opportunities for gain.* Consumers gain by searching for lower-priced ways to fulfill wants, and producers gain by finding less expensive or improved ways to fulfill consumer want.

In conclusion, mainstream economists reject Robert N. Scott's theories of the economy. Just as a highway map is not a perfect representation of the entire landscape traveled, the competitive model does not perfectly represent economic reality. But, unlike Scott's model, the competitive "roadmap" directs our economic inquiry in the right direction.

10

HELP WANTED, FOR HIRE

The Economics of the Labor Market

Concepts and Terms Examined in This Chapter

1. Labor Market
2. Labor Demand
3. Labor Supply
4. Human Capital
5. Derived Demand
6. Marginal Revenue Product
7. Marginal Wage Cost
8. Union Models
9. Monopsony
10. Collective Bargaining

Large variations in wages and salaries exist in the U.S. economy. For instance, outstanding defensive ends in the National Football League receive $1 million a year to demolish opposing quarterbacks, while nurses in charge of the quarterbacks' return to health earn $16,000 to $20,000 a year. Union plumbers make $25 an hour, but secretaries working in the plumbing firms' offices earn $5 an hour. Many professional management consultants are paid $75 per hour, but most babysitters receive $1.50 to $2.00 for an equal period of work. Who or what determines these wages and salaries? This chapter, consisting of three distinct "scenes," each followed by economic analysis, addresses this and related questions involving the market for labor services.

SCENE ONE: HERE'S HARVEY (AGAIN?)

Time flies. Harvey Cornwell, the caramel corn tycoon last discussed in Chapter 7, and his aging grandfather, Pop Cornwell, are now seven years older, and much wiser. Their caramel corn factory has been expanded to produce 10,000 bags of caramel corn per day.

"This is surely a different operation from when we started," Harvey reminisced to Pop as the two surveyed the efficient, highly automated process around them.

"That it is, Harvey, and you certainly are a different manager! Remember when you used to give me a bad time about all my numbers and graphs? Now you are the one who is really into that activity. Does that computer terminal in your office ever get shut off?"

"Not often," responded Harvey, "between my work here and the projects required in the MBA course I'm taking, it stays on most of the day."

"Are you learning anything from that course?" asked Pop.

"Quite a bit. The one I'm taking right now is Managerial Economics. Much of the material involves formal decision analysis."

"Such as?" asked Pop.

"Oh, for example, 'hiring theory.' Remember the decision rule that you developed for maximizing profits: produce until marginal revenue equals marginal costs?"

Pop laughed and stated, "Of course, that was one of my better insights. You wanted to hire every worker in the county and I convinced you that it might make sense to look at costs and revenues."

"Well, I've learned what economists term a *suboptimization rule*. The goal is profit maximization and that requires the MR = MC, but in achieving that outcome, you have to decide the optimum number of workers to hire."

"We were able to do that by working backward from our marginal cost data to the production information that related the number of workers to marginal product," replied Pop.

"Yes, but the decision on how many workers to hire can be made directly," stated Harvey.

"How?"

"It's quite simple once you understand it. The decision rule is to hire workers so long as marginal revenue product (MRP) exceeds marginal wage cost (MWC). *Marginal revenue product is the extra revenue generated when a firm hires one more worker.* For instance, if we add a worker and our hourly production increases by, say, 5 bags, and we sell the bags for $1 each, then the MRP is $5. *Marginal wage cost,* on the other hand, *is the added cost of hiring one more worker,* and in a competitive labor market, this amount is simply the wage rate. We are paying the market-clearing wage of $8 an hour right now, so marginal wage cost (MWC) is $8. Would it pay for us to hire a worker who adds $5 to revenue, but costs $8 to employ?

"Now you are the one asking questions," quipped Pop. "No, obviously it wouldn't pay to hire that worker. If we only gain $5 in revenue per hour and we have to pay the worker $8 for that hour of work, hiring him would reduce our total profit.

"Correct, Pop. I'm impressed. Come to my office and I'll show you how I decided to hire 53 workers rather than 52 or 54. It's all on my computer."

Harvey and Pop walked into Harvey's office. Harvey punched keys on the computer keyboard, and it quickly displayed Table 10-1.

"It's all there, Pop," stated Harvey proudly. "Look at Table 10-1. It is profitable to hire the fifty-first worker, for example, because she contributes an extra 10 bags of caramel corn to our output (MP), and at $1 per bag ($P_p$), that's $10 of extra revenue (MRP). We pay her the market wage, $8 (MWC), and add $2 to cover our nonwage costs and add to our profits. The same is true for the fifty-second worker. Hiring 53 workers is optimal because we then have maximized our profit; for each worker up to that point, marginal revenue product (MRP) exceeds marginal wage cost (MWC)."

Pop studied the table a moment and then stated, "And you wouldn't want to hire the fifty-fourth worker because the marginal revenue product (MRP) is only $7 while the wage we must pay is $8. And I wonder why marginal product (MP) and marginal revenue product (MRP) decline as we hire more workers?" asked Pop with a twinkle in his eyes.

Harvey smiled, remembering Pop's discovery of the concept of diminishing marginal returns some seven years earlier. "As successive units of a variable resource, such as labor, are added to a fixed resource (capital), eventually marginal output declines," stated Harvey. "You taught me that concept well and I'm now simply applying it to our demand for labor."

Pop beamed proudly, thinking to himself, "Harvey has come a long way."

Table 10-1 The Cornwell Company's Hiring Decision (Hourly Data)

Worker	TP	MP	P_p	MRP	MWC
	1,205				
51	1,215	10	$1	$10	$8
52	1,224	9	$1	9	8
53	1,232	8	$1	8	8
54	1,239	7	$1	7	8
55	1,245	6	$1	6	8
56	1,250	5	$1	5	8

ANALYSIS: A PURELY COMPETITIVE LABOR MARKET

Harvey and Pop Cornwell operate their firm in a competitive produce market and a competitive labor market. In a purely competitive labor market, wages and salaries are equal to the market-clearing price determined by the interaction of supply and demand. The market consists of many sellers and buyers of labor. No single worker can set his or her wage above the market-clearing wage *for fear of not being hired.* Similarly, each firm employing labor is so small compared with the total number of employers that it cannot set a wage rate below the market one *for fear of not attracting workers.* Employers are "wage takers"; power is dispersed throughout the market; and the equilibrium wage is determined by supply and demand.

Figure 10-1 shows the purely competitive labor market in which the Cornwell company participates.

The Supply of Labor

The labor supply curve is consistent with the general concept of supply discussed in Chapters 4 and 5. Hourly wages (prices of labor) are measured on the vertical axis, and the quantities of workers responding to each wage rate are shown

Figure 10-1   A Purely Competitive Labor Market

The labor supply curve (S) indicates that more workers are willing to supply their labor in this particular labor market as the wage rate rises. The demand for labor is a derived demand, and the demand curve (D) shows that employers are willing and able to hire more workers at lower wage rates than at higher ones. The equilibrium wage rate, $8, clears the labor market.

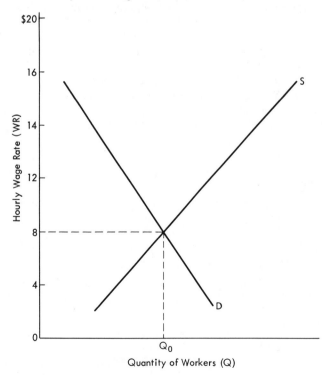

Quantity of Workers (Q)

on the horizontal axis. As shown in Figure 10-1, as wage rates rise, more workers are willing to supply their labor in a particular labor market. Higher wages attract workers from other occupations that require similar skills but where the wage rates have not increased.

The supply of less-skilled caramel corn workers is relatively large compared with the supply of more-skilled workers (plumbers, carpenters) and professionals (physicians, lawyers). The difference lies in the degree of human capital necessary to perform the required tasks. *Human capital consists of the skills, knowledge, experience, and know-how that enable a person to enter an occupation and be productive.* Only a small amount of human capital is required to be a production worker in a caramel corn factory. Therefore, many people are qualified and the supply of labor is large. On the other hand, much innate ability and long, costly training are required to be a professional such as a physician or lawyer, and the supply of labor to those occupations is smaller. Other things being equal (labor demand, in particular), the greater the supply of labor, the lower the wage rate. Conversely, the less the supply of labor, the higher the wage rate.

The Demand for Labor

The demand for labor also varies occupationally. The labor demand curve shown in Figure 10-1 is consistent with the general law of demand; it slopes downward and to the right. Employers are willing to hire more workers at a low wage than at a high one. Recall from Chapter 6 that, in the short run, hiring additional workers reduces the firm's marginal product. The Cornwell experience illustrates this point. At a wage rate of $8 per hour, the firm chooses to hire 53 workers (Table 10-1). But if the wage rate were to fall to $5 per hour, the firm would find it profitable to hire the fifty-fourth through fifty-sixth workers, even though those workers would have lower marginal products (MP) and marginal revenue products (MRP) resulting from diminishing returns. In fact, the Cornwell Company's demand curve for labor *is its marginal revenue product curve.* This curve shows the number of workers the firm will hire at each wage rate. Each firm in the caramel corn market has a demand for labor based on its marginal revenue product data, and summing those demand curves roughly provides the total demand for labor in the market for caramel corn workers.

Sounds complicated? It is! The important point is that a firm's demand for labor is based on the revenue generated by each worker's production, and a firm will hire people as long as the extra revenue generated covers the extra wage cost.

One further point about demand needs to be made: the demand for labor is a derived demand. *The willingness of an employer to hire workers is based on the consumer demand for the product that the workers help to produce.* Business firms do not hire workers for the sake of providing them income, no matter how pleasant, loyal, experienced, or creative they may be. Firms such as the Cornwell Company demand labor because consumers are willing and able to purchase caramel corn and other products. If there is no demand for caramel corn, there will be no demand for people who make caramel corn. On the other hand, if the demand for caramel corn soars, caramel corn prices will rise and producers will discover that each worker will contribute more to revenue (output times price) than previously. Hence, the demand for caramel corn workers will increase. This increase would be shown as a rightward shift of the labor demand curve in Figure 10-1.

Equilibrium Wage

The equilibrium wage in Figure 10-1 is $8 per hour. That wage rate clears the market; the quantity of workers demanded just equals the quantity of workers who are willing to supply labor services at that wage rate. A wage rate above $8 would create a surplus of people wishing to be employed as caramel corn workers and a wage rate below $8 would cause a shortage.

The labor supply and demand model helps to explain wage differences among occupational groups. In markets where labor supply is great relative to labor demand—such as the market for babysitters—wage rates are low. In labor markets where the supply of labor is limited and labor demand is great, wage rates are high. The latter situation characterizes such labor markets as those for professional athletes, computer experts, and corporate executives. In determining wages and salaries, the forces of supply and demand are cold and impersonal. They reflect the basic conditions of the market: (1) demand for the product, (2) productivity of labor, (3) demand for labor, derived from the first two conditions, and (4) the supply of labor.

The high salaries of some doctors, lawyers, accountants, dentists, engineers, actors, musicians, and professional athletes may not always conform to a person's sense of equity and justice, but they do conform to the realities of supply and demand in the marketplace.

SCENE TWO: JOHNNY LONGBOMB

During his senior year at college, Johnny Longbomb led the nation in total yardage via passing, highest percentage of passes completed, and most touchdown passes thrown. That splendid record was now about to pay big dividends, because it was draft day for the National Football League. On this day, the NFL teams select football players who have completed at least three years of their college eligibility. Once drafted by a specific team, the player is then able to sign a contract for labor services to be rendered.

Anxiously awaiting the beginning of the draft, Johnny left the television set on which a cable channel was scheduled to provide a live telecast of the draft, picked up the telephone, and called his agent.

"Any last minute speculation on who will draft me?" asked Longbomb.

"I just heard that the Cleveland Browns and Indianapolis Colts are interested," replied his agent. "The Browns select fourth on the first round and the Colts sixth. The word here at NFL draft headquarters is that you'll be the first quarterback taken."

"Great!" exclaimed the aspiring superstar. "Either of those teams would be fine. I'll admit, though, that I would prefer *not* to be drafted by several teams in the league."

"Well, if you want to play in the NFL, that's not one of your options," stated the agent.

"I realize that," replied Johnny.

"Here we go; the draft is beginning," the agent said. "I'll talk to you later."

Longbomb returned to his television set. The wait to see where he would work didn't take long. The New York Giants, the first team to select, announced that it was trading its first-round pick to the Indianapolis Colts for a second-team offensive guard (sorry, Giants fans). The Colts then used its newly acquired first-round pick to select Johnny Longbomb.

ANALYSIS: IMPERFECT COMPETITION — MONOPSONY

In a purely competitive labor market, individual employers are "wage takers" who must accept the market-determined wage rate and are powerless to set wages unilaterally. The market for caramel corn workers conforms to the competitive model in most respects, but several other labor markets do not.

In some markets, employers have the ability to "set" the wage rate that will maximize profits rather than "take" the market one. The wage rate selected is likely to be below the market wage. Under what circumstances is this possible? It is possible in circumstances described by economists as *monopsony*. A monopsony is a firm (or group of firms acting as one) that is the sole employer of a particular type of labor. Because it is the only employer, the monopsonist's supply curve is identical to the market supply curve (Figure 10-1). This means that it must pay higher wages if it wishes to attract and employ a greater number of workers. Furthermore, it has to pay these higher wages to all of its workers — including people it could have attracted at lower wages. The monopsonist therefore has a profit incentive to reduce the number of people it hires, so as not to drive up the wage it must pay. Hence, it hires fewer workers than would be employed in a competitive market and pays the workers less than the competitive wage. To reiterate: competition among employers for workers' services, other things equal, raises wage rates; without such competition, we can reasonably expect that wage rates will be lower.

Few examples of *pure* monopsony exist, but the National Football League illustrates the idea of monopsony power. The NFL draft, a system that assigns each potential player to a specific team, is an ingenious device used by nearly all sports leagues. Its value to team owners is enormous because it forces the player to negotiate only with the assigned team, and thereby eliminates competition for a player's services. By eliminating other teams from bidding for the player's services, the range of alternatives available to the player is reduced. Instead of playing for 1 of 28 football teams, the player can choose to play for the team that drafted him or not play in the NFL at all. The opportunity cost of deciding not to accept an owner's offer is greater under the draft than under free bidding, so a player may agree to a wage below what he could expect to receive under a free-bidding situation.

For example, assume that Johnny Longbomb is capable of starting on any team except the two top teams in the league. Through hiring Johnny, any team except those two could expect better won-lost records, more fans in the stadium, and additional television and playoff game revenue. Poor teams would benefit from his talent more than good teams would. His marginal revenue product would be greater there than at a top team that already wins its games and produces high revenues from television and playoff games. Teams with poor records would compete vigorously to hire him and bid whatever their demand schedules allowed. In a free-bidding situation, Johnny Longbomb would receive several large contract offers. The opportunity cost of turning one down would be small because he still could sign with other teams offering high wages. In this case, he could afford to wait for an offer that was acceptable to him.

Table 10-2   The Effect of Monopsony Power on Longbomb's Salary

Free Bidding		Draft	
Team	Salary Offers per Year	Occupation	Salary
Colts	$1,000,000	Colts quarterback	$800,000
Saints	1,200,000	High school coach	22,000
Vikings	900,000	Graduate student	8,000
Giants	800,000	Janitor	15,000
Seahawks	850,000	Insurance agent	25,000
Chargers	1,100,000		

What happens when he is drafted? One team makes an offer. If the offer is less than Johnny thinks he should receive for his services, and, if teams in the Canadian League cannot afford his salary demand, he must choose to play at the offered price or not play at all. Assuming that Johnny has no other occupation to turn to except a lower-paying job, the opportunity cost of refusing the offer is very high. Table 10-2 shows Mr. Longbomb's dilemma in numerical detail.

Under free bidding, it is clear the Indianapolis Colts would have to change their $800,000 offer to $1 million or lose Mr. Longbomb's services to another team. It is just as clear under the draft that the Colts will probably convince Johnny to play for them even if he thinks the offer is too low. His opportunity costs of refusing the contract are too great. Situations such as this are created in *monopsony* markets. Usually in such markets, employees are paid less than the competitive market wage.

Being the number-one selection in the first round of the NFL draft, the mythical Johnny Longbomb does not need our sympathy, for he possesses monopoly power of his own and will sign a long-term contract for millions of dollars. But can there be any doubt that he would receive even more if all the teams in the NFL were separate enterprises and could bid against each other for the rights to Longbomb's labor services?

Economists have found monopsony power in markets other than professional sports, including local markets for professional nurses, newspaper employees, public school teachers, and some workers in the building trades. However, monopsony is not widespread. Most workers have skills that are useful to a number of potential employers, particularly if workers are geographically mobile. Strong labor unions also counteract potential monopsony power in many industries.

SCENE 3: AND FINALLY THE CONTRACT WAS SIGNED

The television cameras were ready. The elevator opened and a tired-looking Joe Miller exited. The media thrust microphones forward and began to ask a barrage of questions.

"Mr. Miller, do you have a statement concerning the status of the negotiations? Has an agreement on a new contract been reached?"

"An official announcement will be forthcoming in the morning," Miller responded, as he walked through the lobby of the building.

"There are reports that agreement on a new contract has been reached. Can you confirm or deny those reports?"

"We have a contract, but it needs to be ratified by a vote of our members," stated Miller.

"Do you anticipate any problems on that?" asked a reporter.

"No. I'm sorry, people, but I'm very tired." Mr. Miller then reached into his briefcase, took out a piece of paper, handed it to one of the reporters, and stated, "This explains the process we used."

The reporters scrambled to get a look at this paper. It was a poem:

> We wheedled and threatened and blustered,
> We ranted and wrangled and roared;
> We chided and fretted, we scoffed and we petted,
> We snickered and wept and implored;
> We groveled and swore and demanded,
> We spurned and we fawned and we brayed,
> We trampled on data, we tossed ultimata,
> We grumped and we stamped and inveighed;
> We whimpered and simpered and shouted;
> Pretended, defended, and doubted;
> We smiled and we jested, reviled, and protested,
> Debated, orated, and shouted;
> We fumed and we sneered and we whined,
> We flattered, cajoled, and maligned,
> Consented, revoked, and declined . . .
> And finally the contract was signed!*

ANALYSIS: IMPERFECT COMPETITION—UNION POWER

Just as some employers have monopsony power because of their fewness, some workers possess monopoly power in the sale of labor, either because they have a monopoly on a special talent or because they are organized with fellow employees in a union. This power enables these workers to demand higher than competitive wage rates. Professional athletes, for example, possess a degree of personal monopoly power because of their unique talents. The superstars are the sole sellers of their special type of labor.

Few people possess a talent that is in such limited supply that little or no competition exists. But employees can unionize to establish power to demand higher wages. Unions give organized workers some degree of monopoly power. The union is able to say to the employer, in effect, "If you want any of us, you must negotiate with us on our wage demand. If you don't, you'll get none of us."

The difficult negotiation process described in the poem results where there is power on both sides of the labor market. The firms are "wage setters," not "wage takers," but they face strong offsetting, or countervailing, power in the form of labor unions. Supply and demand set the limits for the wage outcome. If wage rates are too high, one or more of the following consequences will occur. First, the firm may substitute capital for workers. Second, layoffs may be needed because the firm is losing sales to nonunionized domestic firms and international competitors. Third, the high wage may create such a large surplus of people desiring work in the occupation that the firm will be able to break a strike by hiring from the surplus

*Anonymous, quoted by Henry Mayer, "Should Politics Make Mediators Expendable?" *Labor Law Journal*, Vol. 4, No. 5 (Copyright May, 1953, by Commerce Clearing House, Inc.), p. 317.

pool. On the other hand, if wages are too low, the firm will be unable to attract a sufficient number of workers to produce the product at a profit-maximizing level. The range for collective bargaining is set by supply and demand, but the actual wage rate is the product of the collective bargaining itself. This situation is illustrated in Figure 10-2.

Figure 10-2 shows the supply and demand for labor in a market characterized by the combined existence of union and monopsony power. The competitive wage rate would be WR_c. Assume that the union desires to set the wage rate at WR_u and the monopsonist seeks the wage rate WR_m. The range between WR_u and WR_m is a range of collective bargaining, and the actual wage outcome from the negotiation will depend upon the relative strength and negotiating savvy of the union and the firm.

Unions can also raise wage rates in less dramatic ways. Figure 10-3 shows how unions might increase the wages of their employed members by restricting the supply of labor. Unions can shift the labor supply curve from S_1 to S_2 through restricting the number of workers in their occupation (requiring licenses, long apprenticeships, or other similar qualifications). They can also restrict labor supply by establishing rigid job requirements that discriminate against some potential workers. Informal *occupational segregation* — labeling some jobs as men's and others as women's, or some as white and others as black — often artificially reduces labor

Figure 10-2   The Range of Collective Bargaining

In markets characterized by the combined existence of union and monopsony power, supply and demand set the upper and lower limits for wage demands and offers, but the actual wage rate will depend on the relative strength and negotiating savvy of the union and firm. The distance between the union demand (WR_u) and the firm's offer (WR_m) represents a range of collective bargaining. In absence of the union and monopsony power, the wage rate would be competitively determined at WR_c.

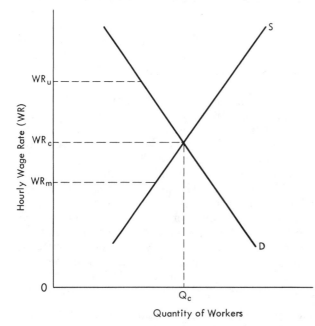

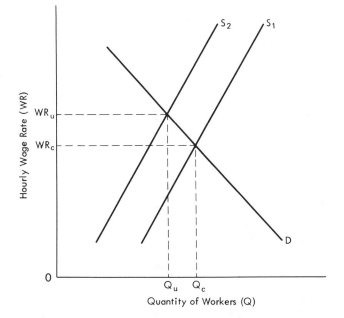

Figure 10-3 Union-Caused Supply Restriction in the Labor Market

Unions can increase the wage rate in a labor market from WR_c to WR_u by restricting labor supply from S_1 to S_2. Techniques for restricting labor supply include occupational licensure, long apprenticeship programs, and discrimination.

supply to some occupations and produces a wage rate such as WR_u compared with the competitive wage rate (WR_c) in Figure 10-3.

Finally, unions can increase wages by promoting increased demand for the product that they help to produce. This situation is illustrated in Figure 10-4 where an increase in the demand for labor from D_1 to D_2 would allow the union to negotiate a wage increase from WR_c to WR_u. The ability of unions to affect the firm's demand for labor is severely limited, but several examples of this union activity can be provided. The International Ladies' Garment Workers' Union, for example, advertises, "Look for the Union Label." If that advertising is effective, the demand for union-made garments will increase, and being a derived demand, so too will the labor demand for workers who make ladies' garments. A second example of this union activity is lobbying Congress and state legislatures for projects that require union labor. For instance, the construction trades unions often support proposals for new highways, plans to revitalize urban areas, and subsidies to buyers of new homes. Likewise, unions representing workers in the shipbuilding industry generally favor proposals to strengthen the navy by adding new vessels. Increases in the demand for government-purchased goods bolster the demand for the union labor that helps build them. The unions are therefore in an improved position to increase wage rates (WR_c to WR_u in Figure 10-4).

To summarize, unions exert power in the labor market and affect the actual wage rate by influencing or controlling labor supply and promoting increases in labor demand.

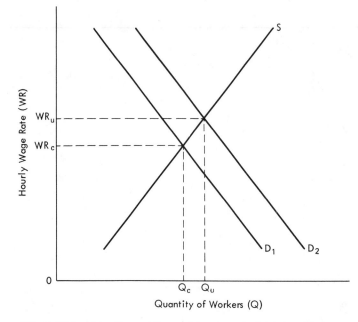

Figure 10-4 Union-Caused Demand Increases in the Labor Market

Unions can increase the wage rate from WR_c to WR_u by successfully initiating actions that increase the demand for the product that the union members help produce. The increase in the product demand will shift the derived demand for labor from D_1 to D_2.

Back to our original question, then. Who or what determines wages and salaries in the economy? The analysis in this chapter suggests that

1. Competitive market factors play an important role in determining wages and salaries. The demand for labor is derived from the demand for the product that the labor produces. The public's demand for products varies widely. In addition, the supply of labor varies considerably across occupations.

2. Power factors (monopsony, unions, discrimination, and government) shape many wages and salaries. When buyers and sellers have power in a labor market, wages and salaries, though constrained by supply and demand, are the outcomes of a bargaining process.

STUDY QUESTIONS

1. Assume that the labor market for fast-food workers is purely competitive. How would each of the following events influence the wage rate paid to these employees?
   a. Passage of a state law levying severe fines on people who fail to patronize a fast-food outlet at least once a day.
   b. A consumer boycott of fast-food establishments.
2. Explain the concept of derived demand and demonstrate how it helps to explain the difference in the amount earned by professional basketball players and college professors. What is the role of labor supply in this differential?

3. Assume that one clerk in a baseball card store can sell $60 worth of cards daily whereas two workers together can sell $69 worth of cards. What is the second worker's marginal revenue product? If the price per card sold is $3, what is the second worker's marginal product?

4. Answer the questions that follow on the basis of the information given in the accompanying table:

Quantity of Workers	Total Product	Product Price
0	0	$4
1	12	4
2	22	4
3	30	4
4	36	4
5	40	4
6	42	4

   a. What is the marginal product (MP) of the third worker? What is the marginal revenue product (MRP) of the third worker? Explain the difference between marginal product and marginal revenue product.

   b. Suppose this firm is hiring workers under competitive conditions at a wage rate of $15. How many workers will it employ? Why will it hire no more than this number of workers?

5. What is monopsony power? Why do employees working for monopsonists receive wage rates that are below those that would exist in a competitive market situation?

6. Imagine a large city where all city employees receive the same wage rate and choose their own work assignments. Which assignments will be most sought after? Which assignments will be least sought after? Relate this to the concept of labor supply to various occupations.

7. Using the information shown in Table 10-1, determine the impact that a government minimum wage of $10 per hour would have on the number of employees that the Cornwell Company would hire. Explain.

8. Many years ago, many states passed laws requiring public school teachers to attend college for a "fifth year" after graduation to retain their teaching certificate. What effect would this legislation have on the labor market? Teacher unions and professional associations actively lobbied in favor of these laws. Why would teachers find it to be in their economic self-interest to support such legislation?

9. Cite an example of how a union might suffer long-run consequences from short-run actions that force the wage rate upward.

10. Drawing on your knowledge of the difference between a change in demand for a product and a change in quantity demanded, cite a factor that would change the demand for labor. Cite a factor that would leave the demand for labor unchanged but change the quantity of labor demanded.

11. How high must the wage rate be to enable a particular employer to retain the services of a particular worker? Use the idea of opportunity cost in your answer.

11

A PICTURE IS WORTH . . . ?

The Public Sector:
Regulation, Public Goods, Externalities

Concepts and Terms Examined in This Chapter

1. Public Sector
2. Government Regulation
3. Public Goods and Services
4. Income Redistribution
5. Transfer Payments
6. Externalities
7. Taxes and Subsidies
8. Market Failure
9. Government Failure

If it is true that a picture is worth a thousand words, then 15 photographs should say something useful. The photos in this chapter show commonplace items, situations, or activities. Although they appear to be unrelated, they do posses a unifying feature: they relate to the economics of the public sector. Refer to the photos as they are mentioned in the text. This cross-referencing will reinforce your understanding of the subject.

THE PUBLIC SECTOR

As indicated by the flow diagram and discussion in Chapter 3, the United States has a "mixed economy." Although the bulk of the goods and services are produced and exchanged in the private sector, there also is a sizable and important public sector—the federal, state, and local governments. Governmental units influence the economy by establishing laws and rules of economic behavior, using resources to produce goods and services, and redistributing the pattern of private-sector income.

Table 11-1 provides useful information on the size and growth of the public sector in the United States. It reveals two measures of the size of the public sector: (1) total expenditures by federal, state, and local governments and (2) government expenditures as a percentage of the value of the nation's total annual output (GNP). The table indicates that between 1929 and 1990 federal, state, and local expenditures increased dramatically, with federal spending rising from $2.7 billion to $1,273.0 billion and state and local expenditures rising from $7.8 billion to $764.7 billion. Of even greater interest, the *relative* size of the public sector increased. This fact is show in the right-hand column, where we see that total government expenditures as a percentage of GNP grew from 9.9 percent in

**Table 11-1   Government Expenditures for Selected Years, 1929–1990
            (billions of dollars)**

Year	Federal	State and Local	Total*	Total as a Percentage of GNP
1929	$ 2.7	$ 7.8	$ 10.3	9.9
1933	4.0	7.2	10.7	19.1
1940	10.0	9.3	18.5	18.4
1945	84.7	9.0	92.9	43.5
1950	41.2	22.5	61.4	21.3
1955	68.6	32.9	98.5	24.3
1960	93.9	49.9	137.3	26.6
1965	125.3	75.5	189.6	26.9
1970	207.8	134.0	317.4	31.3
1975	364.2	235.2	544.9	34.1
1980	615.1	363.2	889.6	32.6
1985	985.6	516.7	1,402.6	34.9
1990	1,273.0	764.7	1,907.1	34.9

*Adjusted to eliminate double counting of federal funds provided to the state and local governments and spent by the latter.

Source: Economic Report of the President, 1991.

1929 to 18.4 percent in 1940. World War II jolted the figure to 43.5 percent, but the percentage fell back to 21.3 percent in 1950. Between 1950 and 1985, government expenditure as a percentage of GNP grew steadily, reaching 34.9 percent in 1985. Since 1985, the percentage has ranged between 34 and 35 percent.

The data in Table 11-1 are in current dollars with no adjustment for inflation. That adjustment would alter the expenditure numbers, but would not affect the percentage figures in the table. Other measures of the size of the public sector—taxes as a percentage of national income, per capita government spending, government employment as a percentage of total employment, and so forth—all confirm the conclusion that the public sector has grown in relative size and importance in the overall economy.

What explains this relative growth of government? A brief, but accurate, answer is that demand for public services has risen faster than the demand for private-sector goods and services. The United States is a different society from what it was in 1929. For example, it now spends massive amounts for national defense (Figure 11-1). As national income has risen, the demand for education, parks and recreational facilities, streets and highways, sanitation facilities, public health services, and police (Figure 11-2) and fire protection have increased rapidly. Furthermore, voters have asked—or at least permitted—government to expand its role in providing services such as food stamps (Figure 11-3), regulation of workplace safety, insurance against injury on the job, unemployment compensation, protection against fraudulent advertising and loan practices, medical care for the poor, and social security for those who have retired. All of these examples reflect a long-run relative shift of demand toward services provided by government.

Will the trend toward a larger public sector continue? The crystal ball is very cloudy! Tax reductions enacted at the federal level during the first half of the 1980s—and the large federal deficits that resulted—produced a growing pressure to halt the historical pace of the rise of federal expenditures. Similarly, "tax revolt" activity at the state and local levels placed limitations on the growth of state and local government. It remains to be determined if the sentiment to halt the relative growth of the public sector will translate into reduced government spending as a percentage of gross national product in the years ahead.

Figure 11-1

Figure 11-2

ECONOMIC FUNCTIONS OF GOVERNMENT

Government performs several functions in the mixed market economy. It sets and enforces rules (regulatory function), provides public goods and services, corrects for external effects of private actions, redistributes income, and attempts to stabilize the economy. The first three government roles are discussed in this chapter.

Figure 11-3

The controversial redistribution function of government is discussed in Chapter 13, and the government activities designed to stabilize the economy are examined in detail in several later chapters.

The Regulatory Function

A major role of government is to provide and maintain the overall legal foundation for the economic system. In the United States, the government, through the constitution, legislation, administrative action, and judicial decision, establishes general and specific rules, regulations, and protections that enable the private sector to operate. The government also enforces existing rules and occasionally intervenes with new ones.

In other words, the government's role is (1) *to set the rules* for economic activity, (2) to use its power *to enforce these rules*, and (3) to provide services *to facilitate economic activity*. Examples of these are sanctioning the right to hold private property (setting rules), prosecuting violators of the antitrust laws (enforcing rules), and providing money as legal tender (facilitating economic activity). Other examples of the regulatory role are license requirements (Figure 11-4), public utility regulations, antidiscrimination rules, environmental protection, occupational safety laws, minimum wage rules, "truth-in-lending" laws, and produce grading (Figure 11-5).

The important question is not "if government should regulate" but, rather, "what should it regulate and to what extent?" Nearly everyone agrees that government must use its regulatory power to establish and enforce the right to own and use property. Without this right, a market system could not exist. No one can be expected to produce or purchase products if others are free to steal and use the property without penalty. In this case, government regulation and enforcement are needed to prevent a state of anarchy. But should government establish rigid safety requirements for employees working in industry? Should it establish minimum

Figure 11-4

Figure 11-5

wages? Should it regulate advertising aimed at small children? Should it restrict the right of employers to fire workers "at will," that is, without apparent cause? These questions produce heated debate, among both economists and the general public.

Too much government regulation reduces society's economic well-being by diverting resources to uses that are less valuable than other alternatives. Also, critics point out that regulation often serves narrow interest groups at the expense of the broader public interest. The regulated groups, in a sense, "capture" the regulatory process and turn it to their own interests. They support regulation as a way to reduce business uncertainty and restrict competition. For example, many of the firms previously or currently regulated in the transportation industry favor government regulation.

Conversely, too little regulation would enable some groups to gain at the expense of others. For example, the firm that falsely advertises its product might at least temporarily gain sales and profits at the expense of honest sellers. Without appropriate regulation, local natural monopolies such as water companies, telephone companies, and electrical utilities would tend to restrict output and charge monopoly prices.

Government's task is to set an optimal level of regulation of economic behavior. To accomplish this task, it should use the economic perspective. Like all economic activity, regulation generates benefits and imposes costs. A "good" regulation would produce more benefits than costs. Cost-benefit analysis is a technique used to compare the marginal cost of regulation with the marginal benefit. Such analysis even considers the *secondary* effects of regulation. For example, suppose a city is planning to control rents charged by landlords. Among the costs and benefits analyzed, economists would consider such secondary effects as reduced incentives of landlords to maintain their buildings or to build new ones.

Public Goods and Services

A second economic function of government is to provide products and services that citizens desire but cannot purchase. The market fails to provide these products, or at least does not provide them in sufficient quantities, for special reasons that are discussed in the paragraphs that follow.

To finance the provision of public goods and services, governments tax and borrow from individuals and businesses, reducing the latters' ability to buy such private sector products as machinery, hamburgers, baby food, television sets, airline tickets, and health care. The purchasing power extracted from the private sector is used to acquire or command economic resources that are used to provide public goods such as highways, dams, education, police and fire protection, national defense, and courts. The result is a reallocation of limited economic resources in the economy. The government allocates resources to public use by taxing, borrowing, and spending. The private sector retains the use of the remaining resources. Thus the true cost of government is independent of the means government uses to finance its expenditures; the true cost is the opportunity costs of the resources absorbed by government.

Essentially, public goods are poor candidates for private production and sale because they cannot be marketed in a profitable way. In their *purest* form, public goods have two unique characteristics:

1. The consumption of a pure public good by one person does not prohibit others from also receiving the benefits.

A lighthouse (Figure 11-6) is a classic example. The benefits of the lighthouse are indivisible. One ship or 500 ships can benefit from its presence and the fact that one receives benefits does not interfere with others' receiving them, too. Notice the difference between the lighthouse and the product in Figure 11-5. If you consume a steak, someone else cannot. The benefits are divisible; they are yours alone.

2. No one can be excluded from receiving benefits of a pure public good or service.

Lighthouse services are desired by ocean transporters, commercial fisherman, and recreational boaters. So why don't corporations build lighthouses and solicit subscribers? That action would be unprofitable, because "free riders" could

Figure 11-6

not be excluded from receiving benefits. Free riders are people who gain but don't pay. Why pay for a product if it can be consumed legally without doing so? This characteristic justifies spreading the cost over a wide group and financing light-houses that way. A drive-in movie theater would have the same problem if there were not individual car speakers and a fence surrounding the grounds. Pure public products are not offered by private firms because there is no way to build a fence to exclude nonpayers from receiving the benefits.

Examples of *pure* public goods are rare. National defense, the court sys-tem, weather warning systems, and clean air and water are the closest available examples. Usually, publicly provided products and services are those with *high degrees* of indivisibility and *high costs* of exclusion, rather than the pure cases of *perfect* indivisibility and *complete* impossibility of exclusion.

Some products have an even mix of public and private good characteristics and are delivered in both the public and private sectors. The mix of public versus private provision is determined by historical precedence and social-political values rather than by inherent economic attributes. Campgrounds (Figure 11-7) and colleges (Figure 11-8) are examples of quasi-public goods. Both are offered through the public sector and by private entities.

Correcting for Externalities

In addition to providing public goods, the government sometimes corrects for a second failure of the market to provide an optimal level of production. In this case, either an over- or underproduction of a good or service occurs.

Before discussing this topic, however, some review is in order. Recall from the discussions of markets in previous chapters the (1) demand curves are utility or benefit curves (people demand products because the products yield utility or benefits to them) and (2) supply curves are cost curves (firm's experience increasing marginal cost is the short run and thus require higher prices to be induced into producing more output).

Figure 11-7

Figure 11-8

The graphical analysis in Figure 11-9 depicts the market for apples (Figure 11-10). This is a normal market, with typical supply and demand curves and an equilibrium price that equates the quantity supplied and demanded. *All the benefits and costs are internal.* That is to say, all costs and benefits touch only the lives of the buyers and the sellers. Buyers of the apples receive the benefits; nonbuyers do not. Those producing the product incur the costs for the land, labor, and capital required. No costs are transferred to nonproducers. The pursuit of self-interest by buyers and sellers leads to a socially desirable level of output Q_0. Because all benefits and costs are *internal* to the buyers and sellers, the equilibrium market price (P_0) and the quantity (Q_0) represents a "correct" outcome that allocates resources efficiently.

Negative Externalities: Analysis   Figure 11-11 shows a situation quite different from the one shown in Figure 11-10. The firm depicted is producing but is polluting the air in the process. It is incurring the costs of its plant and equipment, fuel, labor, and other private or internal expenses, but it is also imposing costs on people living in the surrounding community. These people experience reduced property values, higher health care costs, and generally reduced well-being. The firm is actually transferring part of its production costs to people other than the buyers of the product. This is an example of a negative

Figure 11-9   The Market for Apples

All benefits and costs are internal in the market for apples. Price (P_0) and quantity (Q_0) represent a "correct" outcome that allocates resources efficiently.

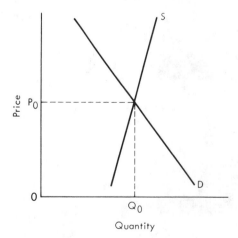

Figure 11-10

Figure 11-11

externality, social cost, or "economic bad." To repeat, *externalities are third-party effects. They are either the positive or the negative impacts that are transferred to nonparticipants in a particular market.*

Figure 11-12 shows the pollution situation graphically. Demand curve D_1, and supply curve S_1 reflect the internal benefits to buyers and the internal costs to the producers, respectively. Curve S_2, which lies above S_1 at all quantities of production, combines the internal costs to the producer and an estimate of the external pollution costs. Curve S_2 then is the supply curve that would exist *if* all costs were considered. Supply curve S_1 represents strictly the internal costs, and the vertical distance between S_2 and S_1 indicates the external costs.

Assuming no government intervention, the price of this product would be P_1 and the equilibrium quantity Q_1. The economic perspective suggests that buyers and sellers would base their respective behavior on their private benefits and costs shown in D_1 and S_1. The firm would have no direct economic incentive to reduce its pollution.

From the perspective of a socially efficient allocation of economic resources, however, the price of the product is too low, the quantity too great, and the pollution level too high. Price P_2 and quantity Q_2 maximize society's well-being. To test this, examine the P_1, Q_1 situation. At Q_1 the marginal social cost, shown by S_2, exceeds the marginal benefit, shown by D_1. This is true at all quantities greater than Q_2. It costs society more to produce each unit beyond Q_2 than the added benefits from that production. This leads to a major conclusion: *In unregulated markets where substantial negative externalities occur, production and consumption are too large to achieve an efficient allocation of resources.*

Other examples of negative externalities include traffic congestion (Figure 11-13), buildings that block views, noise pollution, and smog. You should attempt to relate each of these problems to the foregoing analysis.

Figure 11-12 Negative Externality: Pollution

Demand curve D_1 and supply curve S_1 reflect the internal benefits and costs, respectively, of producing a particular product. Pollution, however, transfers *external costs* to others. Curve S_2 combines both the internal and external (pollution) costs. The market price P_1 is too low for an efficient allocation of resources. Considering all costs, price should be P_2 and quantity should be reduced to Q_2.

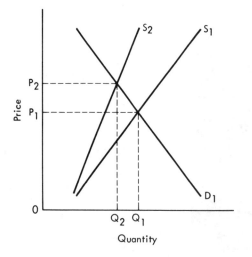

Figure 11-13

Negative Externalities: Remedies   Government can correct for negative externalities in several ways. First, it can clearly define and enforce property rights. In situations where property rights are clearly defined and enforced—for example, where a factory runs its sewer line to a privately owned pond—the negative externality is remedied by court action. No special government intervention other than legal protection is needed. In fact, the parties may decide to get together to eliminate the externality through out-of-court bargaining. For example, the company may offer the owner of the pond compensation for its use as a waste disposal site. Some economists contend that many existing negative externalities could be remedied simply by establishing clearly defined property rights.

Second, government can directly regulate the industry that is transferring costs. This response may be warranted in situations in which property rights are nonexistent and the externality affects the community at large. For example, government could force the polluter shown in Figure 11-11 to reduce its emissions as a condition of remaining in business. The firm would be forced to "internalize" the cost that it formerly transferred to third parties. The private cost curve S_1 would then approach the present S_2 curve, because the firm would have to buy, operate, and maintain pollution control equipment. The results: the market price would rise to P_2, the quantity bought and sold would decline to Q_2, the pollution would decline, and the economic resources would be allocated efficiently.

A third general remedy for negative externalities is to tax the polluter, subsidize the firm (to help defray pollution control costs), or subsidize the parties who incur the pollution costs. Consider each option: (1) If government taxed the firm on a per-unit-of-pollution basis, the firm would have to decide whether to pay the tax or incur the cost of cleaning up. In either case, the price of the product would rise toward P_2 in Figure 11-12, and the quantity of production, and pollution, would be reduced. (2) The government could subsidize the firm by paying for part of the pollution control costs. The reasons for doing so, though, are not compelling. The stockholders of the firm and those buying the firm's product should be assessed the cost of clean-up, not the general taxpayer. (3) Government could subsidize the third parties to compensate them for the pollution. This would be the option of choice only when the technology for pollution control was lacking or the costs of the equipment were prohibitively large. Ideally, the proceeds for these subsidies would come from "pollution taxes" levied on the firm.

Be careful not to forget the economic analysis on marginal costs and benefits mentioned in the government regulation section of this chapter. The marginal cost of cleaning up the *last* portion of pollution may be higher than the marginal benefits to the surrounding community. If so, a government policy that forced complete cleanup would be inefficient. Government officials must think in the "marginal benefit versus marginal cost" terms to find the type and amount of correction that is optimal.

Positive Externalities: Analysis   Externalities may be positive, just as they may be negative. In some situations, benefits from the production and use of products extend beyond the internal ones to the buyers.

Figure 11-14 provides a good example of a positive externality. The person being inoculated obtains a benefit from "consuming" the product. That benefit is a reduced probability of being struck by that disease. This is similar to the purchaser of the apples shown in Figure 11-9; the person obtains utility from consuming them. But, in the inoculation case, benefits flow to other people as well. Because the person pictured is less likely to get the disease, others who interact with that individual are also less likely to contract it. After the inoculation, there is one fewer potential carrier of germs.

The positive externality case is analyzed in Figure 11-15. Supply curve S_1 shows the costs of providing the inoculation. The demand curve D_1 is the actual demand, based on the private utility to the consumer. Because external benefits occur, D_1 fails to show the total benefits from each quantity of inoculations. Curve D_2 has been drawn to show the total benefits — both internal and external — at each quantity. To summarize: (1) D_1 shows the internal benefits, (2) D_2 depicts the total benefits, and (3) the vertical distance between D_2 and D_1 shows the extent of the positive externality associated with each level of output.

The analysis is similar to that in the negative externality graph, but the outcome is directly the opposite. The market, left free of interference, will generate price P_1 and quantity Q_1. But the socially optimal quantity, found by comparing marginal *social* benefits with marginal costs, would be Q_2. At the market price P_1, production and consumption of inoculations would be too low to achieve an

Figure 11-14

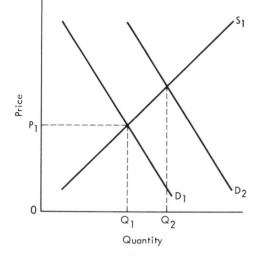

Figure 11-15 Positive Externality: Inoculations

Demand curve D_1 illustrates the internal benefits to people who get inoculated against disease; supply curve S_1 shows the internal, or private, costs to the producers. Some benefits, however, spill over to society. Curve D_2 includes these social benefits. The equilibrium quantity Q_1, based on the internal benefits and costs, is too low for an efficient allocation of resources. Actions that increase quantity to Q_2 improve the outcome, because at Q_2 the marginal social benefit equals the marginal cost.

efficient resource allocation. The marginal social benefits (D_2) of the units between Q_1 and Q_2 exceed the marginal costs, shown by the supply curve. *In unregulated markets where substantial positive externalities occur, production and consumption are too small to achieve an efficient allocation of resources.*

Two additional examples of positive externalities are bus systems (Figure 11-16) and education. If both were offered exclusively by nonsubsidized *private* firms, the quantity of the service purchased would probably be too low, for external benefits are large. For instance, benefits from bus ridership include reduced air pollution in urban areas and reduced traffic congestion. Examples of external benefits from education include improvements in the quality of political decisions, reduced crime, and enhanced productivity growth.

Positive Externalities: Remedies Government policies can correct for the underallocation that occurs when positive externalities exist by directly subsidizing either the buyer or the seller. For example, if the government directly paid people a part of the cost they incur in getting inoculated, people would increase their purchases. Alternatively, the government could subsidize those providing the inoculations. This subsidy would reduce their private costs and shift the supply curve outward from S_1, lowering the price to buyers. As the supply curve shifted rightward, and as the price fell, people would increase their purchases to Q_2, which is the socially desirable quantity. This is precisely the present rationale for government subsidies to private hospitals, clinics, and physicians for their vaccination programs.

A final alternative to the positive externality situation is to have the government take over and publicly provide products and services that have large social benefits. Through government provision, the desired quantity of the prod-

Figure 11-16

uct or service can be delivered. For example, the U.S. Public Health Service operates on this principle. In fact, recall that one major attribute of a public good is its indivisible benefits that spill over to numerous people.

Externalities, both positive and negative, provide a rationale for government intervention into the private sector. But keep in mind that in most markets, costs and benefits are largely internal, and therefore no government interference is required.

PUBLIC SECTOR FAILURE

Economic resources are limited, and economic wants are great. Hence, society rightfully is concerned about inefficiency in government. Much of this chapter, particularly the sections on public-good attributes and externalities, has examined "market failure" in the private sector. Previous chapters have addressed other private sector market failures such as monopoly. The private sector is clearly imperfect, but it has no monopoly on imperfection. Government does not operate with perfect efficiency either.

Many economists conclude that the incentives for efficiency in the public sector are weak. In the private sector, the incentives are in the form of a "carrot" and a "stick." The carrot is profits. Firms increase their profits by using resources in least-cost fashions. The stick is competition. Those firms that are unresponsive to consumers and do not use resources efficiently are driven out of business or acquired by the firms that do.

In the public sector, the profit incentive is nonexistent, and competition among government units is discouraged. The major incentives for efficiency in the public sector are the threat to elected officials of being voted out of office (Figure

11-17) and the ability of people to "vote with their feet" by moving away from government jurisdictions that are wasteful. Elected officials, however, can reduce the threat of being voted out of office by providing services that help the most politically powerful employer and employee interests within their jurisdictions. Elected officials in other jurisdictions do the same, and therefore it is difficult for people to reduce their personal taxes by moving to new areas. Furthermore, critics point out that government is inherently inefficient as an agent for achieving objectives that can be satisfied through private exchange. Government personnel seek their own objectives—for example, higher salaries or more power—and hence tend to divert a portion of the resources at their disposal to such ends. In the private sector, product-market competition and the competition for corporate control (takeovers) check such behavior, but not in the public sector.

Finally, there is no assurance that majority voting will result in the optimal types and levels of public goods. Consider, for example, a community consisting of three people, Adams, Brown, and Castro, who are considering voting to have government construct a community park. The park will cost $1,200, with equal $400 tax payments being levied on each of the three members of the community. Next assume that the park will generate $425 in personal utility for Adams, $425 for Brown, and $100 for Castro. How will the park proposal fare in a majority vote? The economic perspective tells us that both Adams and Brown will vote for the park because they value it more highly ($425) than their individual tax expense ($400). As a result, the community will get a park costing $1,200 that its members collectively value at only $950 ($425 + $425 + $100).

A counterexample can easily be constructed in which a park valued in excess of its costs would lose in a majority vote. The point is that majority voting does not always result in optimal economic decisions.

These examples point out that there are elements of *governmental failure*, just as there are types of *market failure*. The imperfections of both sectors of the economy must be recognized. It is misleading to compare a *concept* of a perfectly operating market system with that of the actual workings of the public sector. It is also misleading to compare a *concept* of a perfectly functioning public sector with that of the actual workings of the private economy. Both sectors must be compared in their actual operating forms if society is to achieve an optimal mix between

Figure 11-17

them. Citizens must identify and analyze the imperfections in both the public and private sectors, seek to remedy them, and be prepared to change the private-public mix when so doing increases society's well-being (Figure 11-18).

STUDY QUESTIONS

1. List the three economic functions of government discussed in this chapter. Give two examples of current government activity that could be classified under each function.
2. Discuss the major characteristics of a pure public good. Why would it be unprofitable for a private firm to produce and sell a product having these characteristics?
3. Have government expenditures increased more rapidly than GNP since 1929? How does your answer relate to Table 11-1?
4. Why will there occur an overallocation of society's scarce resources in those markets where substantial negative externalities exist?
5. Define the term *positive externality*. Provide a specific example and cite two ways in which government could correct the underproduction of the product or service.

Figure 11-18

6. Make a case for the following view: "The incentives for efficiency are not as great in the public sector as in the private sector." Can you think of ways this argument might be rebutted?

7. Government gets its revenues from taxing and borrowing from private individuals and corporations. Does it therefore follow that the government itself is inherently unproductive? Explain.

8. (Advanced analysis) In Figure 11-12, one solution to the negative externality is for government to impose a tax on the producer of the externality. Specify the exact per-unit tax, measured on the vertical axis, that it would have to charge to achieve the best output.

9. Following the example provided in the chapter, construct a three-person example in which a public good, collectively valued at more than its total cost, fails to win majority approval in an election.

12

PLUCKING THE GOOSE

The Public Sector: Taxation

Concepts and Terms Examined in This Chapter

1. Tax Incidence
2. Tax Shifting
3. Statuatory Marginal Tax Rates
4. Average Effective Tax Rates
5. Flat-Rate Taxes
6. Progressive Tax
7. Ability-to-Pay Principle
8. Tax Fairness
9. Value-Added Tax
10. Tax Trade-offs

As explained in Chapter 11, government performs several important tasks in the American economy. To accomplish them, it acquires land, purchases capital, hires labor, and buys goods and services produced in the private sector. The amount paid for these resources and commodities is the budgetary cost of government.

The federal government finances its expenditures through taxation and borrowing. The four most important sources of tax revenue for the federal government are the personal income tax, social security payroll tax, corporate income tax, and selected excise taxes. Over half of its tax revenue derives from the personal income tax. State and local governments, on the other hand, depend mainly on income, sales, and property taxes for their revenues.

Paying taxes is not a favorite American pastime. One reason is that taxation is coercive; an individual tax payment to the government is not voluntary. You may choose whether or not to buy a new video cassette recorder (VCR), but once government officials decide to provide a particular public service—for example, a community college—everyone in the governmental jurisdiction must help pay for it, regardless of personal benefits or political agreement. In addition, the benefits from taxes are often indirect and diffuse. It is difficult for the individual to assess the personal benefits received from government expenditures on such items as national defense, space exploration, research on crippling diseases, and public schools.

Taxation is both disliked and misunderstood. With respect to the former, Jean Baptiste Colbert, finance minister to King Louis XIV, stated:

> The art of taxation consists of so plucking the goose as to obtain the largest amount of feathers while promoting the least amount of hissing.

With respect to tax misunderstanding, the following statement is pertinent:

> To perform the art of taxation well, one must know much about the goose, for example, the feathers extracted most easily when pulled, those that must be retained by the fowl to survive, and the type of hissing that is normal as opposed to that indicating one is about to be bitten.

Stated more directly, the art of taxation requires an understanding of the economy and basic economic principles of taxation. The scenes that follow employ the economic perspective to develop some of these principles and to point out several common myths or misunderstandings about taxation.

SCENES 1A AND 1B: WHO PAYS?

Tax principle 1: Tax incidence
Myth 1: "People who pay the tax necessarily bear the full cost of the tax."

Bill Wilson and his fellow employees at Rudi's Sand and Gravel Company just received their monthly paychecks. Attached to his check was a note from the payroll department stating that the reduced take-home pay resulted from the recent rate increase in the social security tax. The *employee's* portion of the tax (7.65 percent in 1991) is subtracted from the gross pay each month, along with the personal income tax withholding, to determine the net pay. The statement also noted that the *employer's* portion of the social security tax (also 7.65 percent in 1991) was raised by an equal amount.

"I see that our take-home pay fell," stated Bill Wilson. "The social security tax went up. That tax bite is getting bigger every year."

"I agree," said Norris Manne. "Why don't they levy the whole thing on the employer rather than make us pay half of it? Employers can afford it better than we can, given our modest wages."

"I'll run right home and write to Capitol Hill," kidded Wilson, as he headed out the office door.

"Do that," stated Manne. "Be sure to credit me with the idea."

*   *   *

Congress recently had received a report by its budget experts that revenues from taxes were falling far short of those projected earlier. After rejecting the option of reducing government expenditures, several members of Congress met to map out a strategy for meeting the revenue shortfall.

"Of all the options, I favor the one to place excise taxes on the producers of extractive raw materials such as iron ore, gypsum, crude oil, copper, gold, silver, limestone, and the like," said Representative Roy Mintz. "These taxes could be set on a weight or volume basis and would yield considerable tax revenue."

Representative Smith, shaking his head, countered, "There is a major problem with that, Roy. The lobbyists for these industries will descend on us en masse. I'm not sure we could get it through the Senate or House. Nor am I sure the president would sign it if we did pass it."

"I don't buy that argument," Mintz retorted. "These groups don't pay the tax; they pass the entire tax through to their customers. I don't expect industry opposition to be that great."

Analysis

Many people erroneously conclude that persons against whom a specific tax is levied always bear the entire burden of the tax themselves. For example, Norris Manne, in proposing that employers be assessed the full amount of the social security tax, assumed that this change would shift the full burden of the tax from him to his employer. Other people mistakenly conclude that the entire burden of particular taxes *necessarily* gets shifted in full to parties other than those taxed. Representative Roy Mintz believed that the full burden of an excise tax levied against producers of raw materials would be passed forward to buyers of these resources. Therefore, the taxed industries would have little reason to object to the tax.

The economic perspective indicates that people who are assessed a tax will try to have someone else pay it, if possible, to minimize their personal cost. In some cases, they are unsuccessful; that is, they must bear the burden of the tax themselves. Examples would be the personal income tax and the employee portion of the social security tax. In other situations, the tax burden gets either partially or fully shifted to others. Restated, the party paying a particular tax to the government may not be the party that is actually bearing the burden of the tax. The art of taxation requires knowledge of *tax incidence* — the place of burden of the tax.

Who actually bears the cost of that portion of the social security tax paid by employers? What is the incidence of an excise tax levied on producers of raw materials? Each question merits careful economic analysis.

Suppose an employer was forced to pay all of the social security tax, just as Norris Manne suggested. Would the firm bear the full burden of this tax? The answer is no, because the tax would eventually reduce Manne's market wage below what it otherwise would have been in absence of the tax on the employer. Competitive employers pay market-determined wages (Chapter 10) based on the extra revenue they receive when they sell the output of the last worker it is profitable to employ. The greater the marginal revenue product of labor, the greater the demand for labor; the less the marginal revenue product of labor, the less the demand for labor.

From the employer's perspective, the social security payment to government on behalf of workers is part of the total salary package. When the tax increases, the firm's costs rise and the *net* revenue it gets when it hires each worker falls. The net revenue is the receipt from the sale of the product workers help make minus the tax payment on their behalf. By reducing the net gain from hiring workers, the tax in effect reduces the demand for sand gravel workers, and this decrease in demand eventually causes their market-determined wage to fall. Norris Manne's wage may not immediately fall, but over the long run it will not rise by as much as it would have in the absence of the employer tax. Therefore, Manne will bear part, if not all, of the burden of his employer's social security payroll tax through a lower market wage rate. In the long run, legislation of the type proposed by Manne is not likely to change his total compensation. Rather, it will mean a higher nonwage benefit (social security tax paid by the employer) and a lower direct wage payment.

Like Norris Manne, Representative Roy Mintz could use a lesson on tax incidence. He argued that the producers of raw materials would pass the *entire* amount of excise taxes through to consumers. However, basic supply and demand analysis indicates that *some* of the burden of the tax is likely to fall on the providers of the raw materials.

Supply curve S_1 and demand curve D_1 in Figure 12-1 show the before-tax supply and demand for iron ore. The equilibrium price and quantity in this market are $10 and 20 units, respectively. Now suppose that government levies an excise tax on iron ore of $4 per unit of output. From the producers' viewpoint, the excise tax increases the per-unit cost of production by $4, which reduces market supply to S_2. Recall that the market supply curve shifts leftward when costs of production rise. The vertical distance between supply curves S_2 and S_1 is the $4 per unit tax.

Notice that the tax increases the market price by $2 ($12 − $10) and reduces the equilibrium quantity by 4 units (20 − 16). The producers of iron ore receive an extra $2 per unit of sales because of the price increase, but must pay the extra $4 per unit tax. Clearly, the producers bear $2 of the tax burden themselves ($4 − $2), and their consumers bear the other $2 ($12 − $10) of the burden. Representative Mintz is wrong. The producers of the taxed products will indeed mount strong opposition to his tax proposal. So, too, will the firms that buy the taxed products. As has been demonstrated in other places in the book, economic actions often have secondary effects. In this case, the imposition of the tax increases the product price, which in turn changes consumer buying behavior.

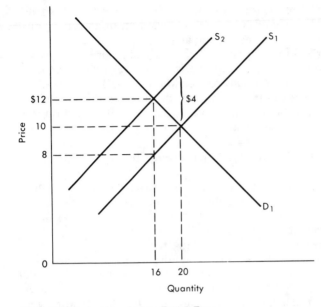

Figure 12-1   Incidence of an Excise Tax

A $4 excise tax on each unit of output shifts the supply curve from S_1 to S_2 and increases the equilibrium price by $2 ($12 − $10). Sellers gain an extra $2 of revenue per unit but must pay $4 per unit in tax. They therefore bear $2 of the tax burden. The remaining $2 of burden falls on the consumers of the product.

SCENE 2: PROGRESSIVITY FLATTENED?

> **Tax principle 2:** Statutory versus effective tax rates
> **Myth 2:** "Statutory marginal tax rates are the effective average tax rates that people pay."

"The sweeping tax reform of 1986 must be undone," stated candidate Mitchell Brooks. "That act reduced the 14 marginal tax brackets that ranged from 11 to 50 percent to just two basic brackets—15 and 28 percent. This law greatly reduced the progressive character of the personal income tax. The tax legislation of 1990 has not rectified this loss of progressivity under the tax code. Marginal tax rates are now 15, 28, and 31 percent and the top rate is far below the 50 percent rate that existed before 1986."

"My opponent not only supported the 1986 legislation but has hinted that she prefers a single tax rate. A flat-rate tax and progressivity are mutually exclusive!"

Analysis

Candidate Mitchell Brooks is confusing statutory tax rates—the marginal tax rates set in the law—with effective average tax rates. A progressive tax is one for which the tax payment rises as a proportion of income as income increases. Restated, it is a tax for which the *average effective tax rate* rises with income. *The average effective tax rate is determined by dividing the family's actual tax payment by the amount of its total income.* For example, if a household paid $3,000 of income tax on total earnings of $30,000, then the average effective rate is 10 percent ($3,000/$30,000). Actual tax payments depend not only on the tax rates, but also on such things as personal exemptions, tax deductions, and tax credits, which reduce the actual tax owed. The notion of the average effective tax rate differs from that of the *marginal tax rate,* which is *the tax owed on an additional dollar of income earned.* For example, the family in our example may have paid a 28 percent marginal tax rate on the last few dollars that it earned, even though its average effective tax was 10 percent.

The sweeping tax reform act of 1986 retained considerable progressivity in the tax code, even though it reduced the top marginal tax rate. This progressivity was accomplished in two ways. First, many of the previous tax deductions and ways of avoiding taxes were disallowed. Hence, the lower top marginal rate of 28 percent—now 31 percent—applied to larger amounts of taxable income. Second, personal exemptions were raised and the standard deduction was increased. Many families therefore no longer owed *any* income tax. Their effective average tax rate fell to zero, thus maintaining the progressivity of the personal income tax structure.

Candidate Mitchell Brooks also was wrong when he stated that flat-rate taxes and progressivity are mutually exclusive. A hypothetical example of a flat-rate tax plan will help demonstrate this point.

Notice from Table 12-1 that the personal exemptions and standard deduction total $10,000 for each family and that a single 20 percent marginal tax rate is applied to all taxable income. Taxable income is found by subtracting the $10,000 from the family's total income. The tax paid is found by multiplying the taxable income by the 20 percent marginal tax rate. Of particular importance, the average effective tax rate, which is found by dividing the family's total income (far lefthand column) by the actual tax paid, rises as income rises. Observe from the far righthand column that this particular flat-rate tax plan *is* progressive. The point is that flat rates (or three flat rates, as in the federal income tax) produce progressive average effective tax rates when coupled with generous personal exemptions and standard deductions.

Table 12-1   Statutory Marginal Tax Rates Versus Average Effective Tax Rates: Progressivity with a Flat Tax Rate

Exemption and Standard Deduction: $10,000 per Family
Statutory Marginal Tax Rate: 20%

Income	Taxable Income	Taxes Paid	Effective Average Rate
$ 10,000 or less	$ 0	$ 0	0.0%
15,000	5,000	1,000	6.7
20,000	10,000	2,000	10.0
25,000	15,000	3,000	12.0
30,000	20,000	4,000	13.3
50,000	40,000	8,000	16.0
100,000	90,000	18,000	18.0
500,000	490,000	98,000	19.6

SCENE 3: TAX THE ECONOMISTS!

Tax principle 3: Tax trade-offs
Myth 3: "Since tax experts disagree on proposals to change the tax law, they necessarily disagree on all matters relating to taxes."

Susan Archer is preparing an article for her syndicated column, which appears in numerous newspapers nationwide. She just returned from a hearing held by the House Ways and Means Committee, where three prominent economists who specialize in taxation presented their ideas on the federal tax code.

Ms. Archer began to type on her word processor. The following column resulted:

Surprise, surprise! Economists cannot agree. This time the disagreement is over whether the changes in the income tax law over the past decade have resulted in an improved tax code. Appearing before the House Ways and Means Committee, three prominent economists sharply disagreed on matters such as the fairness of the tax, whether or not existing deductions should be removed, and whether or not the income tax should be replaced by a national sales tax.

Dr. Raymond Kaufman of the University of New England contended that the federal income tax law fails miserably on the criterion of tax fairness. He pointed out that equals are not treated equally under the new law, nor do people with higher incomes necessarily pay more tax than those with lower incomes. He showed that two families, each making $50,000 annually, can owe extremely large differences in taxes, depending on their circumstances. One of his hypothetical families received much of its income from interest from tax-exempt state and local bonds, had high mortgage interest payments on first and second homes, lived in a state having a high income tax (deductible), and contributed large amounts to charities. This family paid an effective average tax rate of less than 5 percent.

Meanwhile, the other hypothetical family received all of its income as wages and salaries, rented its home, lived in a state having a high sales tax (nondeductible) and no state income tax, and contributed little to charity. This family paid an average effective tax rate of over 20 percent.

To achieve greater tax fairness, Dr. Kaufman recommended taxing all income regardless of source, eliminating all deductions, increasing the number of marginal tax brackets, and returning to a more progressive structure of marginal tax brackets.

Dr. Edward Borsk of the Institute of Tax Analysis diverged from his prepared remarks to challenge Kaufman's earlier remarks. Borsk stated that the effects of the proposal would be extremely costly to society. He testified that the tax code is a legitimate instrument for promoting broad economic and social goals. The special tax-exempt status of interest on state and local bonds permits state and local governments to borrow money for worthwhile civic projects at lower costs than otherwise would be the case. Financial investors are willing to accept lower interest rates for the use of their money because the interest will not be taxed. The tax-exempt bonds, therefore, enhance the quality of life in our cities and states by allowing them to provide more services at a reduced tax expense. The preservation of strong state and local governments is an important social goal in our society, said Borsk.

Similarly, the deduction for mortgage interest, which contributes to the quality of the nation's housing, and charitable contributions, which aid a vast array of religious, educational, and cultural organizations, are essential to promoting important social goals, said Borsk.

Finally, Dr. Robert Carver of Dandford University pointed out that the original reason for the tax reform of 1986 was to simplify the tax code. Here it has failed miserably. The code remains a tangled mess of exclusions, exemptions, deductions, tax credits, and special provisions that together add up to a complex, ambiguous method of raising revenue for the operation of the government. Carver offered an interesting quotation from Elihu Root, U.S. secretary of state, who, in writing a friend, addressed the issue of tax complexity decades ago:

> I guess you will have to go to jail. If that is the result of not understanding the Income Tax law, I shall meet you there. We will have a merry, merry time, for all of our friends will be there. It will be an intellectual center, for no one understands the Income Tax law except persons who have not sufficient intelligence to understand the questions that arise under it.*

Carver's solution was to replace the federal personal and corporate income tax code with a value-added tax of the type used in several European nations. This tax is paid by manufacturers and merchants on the value contributed to a product at each stage of its production and distribution. According to Carver, such a tax would greatly simplify the overall tax system at the federal level.

What can we conclude from all this contradictory testimony? My conclusion, offered in jest, is *to tax the tax economists*, with tax rates rising progressively daily until these people can prove beyond a reasonable doubt that they agree on something. Anything! Until then, let's not invite them before Congress to confuse us further.

Analysis

Susan Archer makes a common mistake: she jumps from an observation of disagreement by economists on questions of public policy to a conclusion that tax experts cannot agree on anything.

Economists *do* agree on core aspects of the basic theory of taxation and tax incidence. Additionally, they agree there are at least three criteria for a "good" tax:

1. The tax should be fair.
2. The tax should be easily understood and inexpensive to collect.
3. The tax should distort private decisions as little as possible unless it is thought to be an appropriate instrument for promoting desirable social goals.

Each of the three witnesses referred to by Ms. Archer would no doubt agree to these criteria. Yet these three tax experts, and millions of Americans, strongly disagree on various proposals to change the tax law. Isn't this a contradiction?

At least three distinct but interrelated reasons for the paradox may be gleaned from Susan Archer's column. First, *some of the tax criteria are hard to define specifically*. What is "tax fairness," for example? Fairness cannot be measured in dollars, inches, or centimeters. It is a concept, like utility, that is subject to the interpretation of each individual. Dr. Kaufman argued that deductions should be eliminated to achieve *fairness*. Dr. Borsk, on the other hand, seemed to be arguing that removing the deductions for charitable giving would be *unfair* to the millions of people who benefit from educational, social, and cultural giving. Sim-

*Elihu Root, quoted in Ray M. Sommerfeld, et al., *An Introduction to Taxation*, 2nd ed. (New York: Harcourt Brace Jovanovich, 1972), p. 57.

ilarly, those who benefit from special provisions often sincerely view them as completely "fair and reasonable," while others call the same provisions "loopholes." Disagreement over tax matters will exist as long as there is no generally accepted definition of fairness.

A second reason why economists can agree on broad criteria of a good tax and yet disagree on specific tax proposals is that *individuals weigh the things they value differently*. Recall that this is an important element of the economic perspective introduced in Chapter 1. Dr. Kaufman placed a high weight on tax fairness, as he defined it. He was concerned that exemptions, exclusions, and deductions produced tax inequities. Kaufman appeared to place little weight on the criterion of using the tax to promote social goals. Dr. Borsk, on the other hand, vigorously defended special exemptions (state and a local bond interest) and deductions (mortgage interest, charitable contributions) because he placed a high weight on the proposition that a good tax ought to distort private decisions in socially desirable ways. Dr. Borsk apparently does not value tax simplicity very highly because the deductions he favors add complexity to the tax code.

Dr. Carver's testimony indicated that he gave top priority to tax simplicity. He wished to achieve greater simplicity by substituting a value-added tax for the personal and corporate income tax. The implication is that he places little weight on using taxes to promote such social goals as improved housing, better educational programs, and greater charitable giving.

A final reason that people can disagree so completely on tax matters is that *trade-offs among the criteria exist*. Because there are often basic conflicts in achieving goals, achieving several highly valued things simultaneously is not always possible. As evidenced by the reported testimony of Dr. Kaufman and Dr. Borsk, there may be a trade-off between use of the income tax to promote social goals and tax fairness. Use of the tax to promote home ownership, charitable giving, and strong local government carries with it the opportunity cost of reduced tax fairness. Likewise, simplifying the tax through consolidation of tax brackets or use of an alternative revenue source such as the value-added tax may reduce tax fairness. For example, the value-added tax would result in lower-income people spending a higher fraction of their income on taxes than higher-income people; the wealthy save part of their income, and such savings escape the tax. No wonder intelligent people — economists included — disagree on tax matters! Conflicting goals, differing priorities on things people value, and difficulty in defining such vague ideas as fairness guarantee considerable disagreement on tax issues.

SUMMARY

The art of taxation requires a good understanding of the economy and of the economic perspective. Plucking the goose is bound to promote "hissing" and to affect the economy in numerous ways. Awareness of the ideas of tax incidence, statutory versus effective tax rates, and trade-offs among tax goals enhances public understanding of why the hissing occurs. This awareness also helps policymakers to design tax laws that minimize tax hissing and detrimental secondary effects.

A continuing examination of all taxes, an ongoing process of reform, and public tolerance for debate and controversy are required to ensure that the tax system in the United States remains as fair and purposeful as possible.

STUDY QUESTIONS

1. In what central way is paying taxes different from buying a product produced in the private sector?
2. Suppose that the supply curve S_1 in Figure 12-1 was more elastic than that shown. Would the market price rise by a greater or a smaller amount when the excise tax of $4 was imposed? What can be concluded about the elasticity of supply and the incidence of an excise tax?
3. Suppose that the government shifted the entire social security tax to the *employee*, rather than requiring the employer to pay half of it. What could be expected to happen to the market wage rate in the long run? Explain.
4. What is the difference between a statutory marginal tax rate and an average effective tax rate?
5. Use the accompanying tax schedule for a hypothetical economy to answer the questions that follow:

Taxable Income	Taxes Paid
$ 0	$ 0
100	0
200	10
300	20
400	50
500	80
600	110

   a. What are the two positive marginal tax rates in this tax schedule (assume no deductions or exemptions)? For which income brackets do these two marginal tax rates apply?
   b. Compute the effective tax rate for each of the earning levels in the table. Is this tax schedule regressive, or is it progressive?
6. Under what circumstances is a flat-rate marginal tax rate consistent with a progressive average effective rate?
7. Suppose that the government decided to eliminate all tax deductions as a way to reduce marginal rates. Speculate on how each of the following might view the proposal:
   a. American universities
   b. Workers in the home-construction industry
   c. Churches
   d. States having income taxes
8. How would a value-added tax that replaced the personal and corporate income tax reduce overall tax complexity?
9. Suppose there are two taxes and each brings in the same amount of tax revenue. Explain how one might be considered superior to the other on the fairness criterion, while the other might be considered superior on the "promotion of social goals" criterion.

13

HOLEY BUCKETS

The Economics of Poverty, Income Inequality, and Redistribution Policies

Concepts and Terms Examined in This Chapter

1. Poverty
2. Noncash Benefits
3. Personal Income Distribution
4. Income Mobility
5. Equity-Efficiency Trade-off
6. Contributions Standard
7. Needs Standard
8. Equality Standard
9. Income Supplement Scheme
10. Investment in Human Capital

How equal should incomes be? What is the right distribution of income? All economies face these questions, but public debate on the "correct" answers is particularly acute in market economies. These systems reward participants according to their contributions to producing goods and services. Because economic contributions vary extensively, income differences arise. This inequality conflicts with ideas about fairness that are rooted in egalitarianism. Economics cannot answer these questions, but it can help to define the problems and identify the costs and benefits of income redistribution. For that purpose, a panel of three economists, a moderator, and an audience were assembled to analyze this important subject.

PANEL DISCUSSION: POVERTY, INCOME INEQUALITY, AND PUBLIC POLICY

Moderator: My name is Hector Cruz. The three panelists today are distinguished economists who have agreed to (1) provide and interpret facts about poverty and income inequality in the United States, (2) discuss areas of agreement and disagreement among economic experts on the issue, (3) identify economic principles essential to understanding these issues, and (4) propose alternative public policies to remedy the situation.

On my far right is Professor Albert Lenstein; on my near right, Professor Everett Milligan; and on my left, Professor Anne Cromly.

Poverty: Definition and Trends

Professor Milligan, please begin by providing some background information on the extent of poverty in this country.

Mr. Milligan: Well, first poverty must be defined. In 1963 the federal government established an official poverty line that reflected minimum food requirements and other needs. For example, in 1963 a typical nonfarm family of four was considered poor if it earned less than $3,130 of annual personal income. Since 1963, the poverty line has been increased to reflect changes in the consumer price index. In 1989, the poverty line for the typical family of four was $12,675.

Please notice the following graph, labeled Figure 13-1, which I will show on the screen via the overhead projector.

The solid line shows the total number of poor persons (measured on the left vertical axis) who lived in poverty in the United States during each year since 1960. The broken line depicts the percentage of total population who were poor (measured on the right vertical axis) during each year. One can see from the figure that the poverty trend was clearly downward during the 1960s. In 1960, 39.9 million Americans, 22.2 percent of the total population, lived in poverty. By 1970, the number of poor people fell to 25.4 million, and the percentage of population in poverty declined to 12.6 percent.

Notice, however, what happened to the trend lines during the 1970s. The number of poor in 1970 and 1980 were about the same, and the percentage of total population in poverty declined only slightly, ranging between 12 and 13 percent throughout the decade.

A severe economic recession in the early 1980s largely explains the steep rise in poverty during that period. A secondary factor was the attempt by govern-

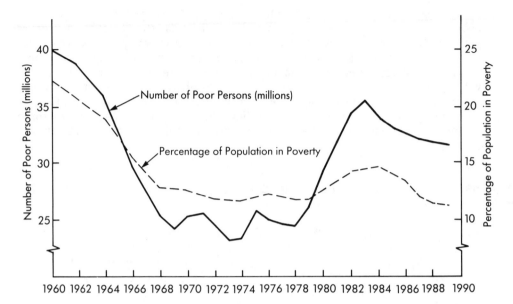

Figure 13-1 Progress Against Poverty, 1960–1989

The solid line shows the number of poor persons (measured in millions on the left-hand axis) who were in poverty in the United States for selected years between 1960 and 1989. The broken line indicates the percentage of the total population in poverty (measured on the right-hand axis) for those same years. The progress made against poverty in the 1960s did not continue during the 1970s and 1980s. In particular, poverty increased dramatically in the early 1980s and, although declining from 1983 through 1989, remained at relatively high levels during these years.

ment to hold down the rising costs of welfare programs. In 1983, 35.3 million Americans, or 15.2 percent of the population, were living in poverty.

Both the number of people in poverty and the rate of poverty declined between 1983 and 1989, a period of expanding national income and falling unemployment rates. Nevertheless, 31.5 million Americans—12.8 percent of the population—still lived in poverty in 1989. Moreover, poverty rates remained extremely high for several groups. In 1989 the poverty rate for black families was 30.7 percent; for Hispanic families, 26.2 percent; for children under 18, 22.5 percent; and for families headed by females, 42.8 percent.

Mr. Lenstein: Mr. Milligan's chart, I might add, is measuring "absolute" poverty, not "relative" poverty—a very important distinction. For instance, the federal government defines poverty by a specific dollar figure that represents some minimum level of goods and services essential to a family's economic well-being. A more appropriate definition of poverty might include people whose incomes fall a certain percentage below the national average. This definition measures "relative" poverty.

I'm reminded of a quotation by George Crabbe (*The Village*, 1783):

Where Plenty smiles, alas! she smiles for few,
And those who taste not, yet behold her store,
Are as the slaves that dig the golden ore,
The wealth around them makes them doubly poor.

Ms. Cromly: I don't think that a relative standard of poverty is of much help, here, Mr. Lenstein. *Relative* to the standard of living in many less-developed nations of the world, our poverty population is rich! Twenty-two thousand poor households in the United States own heated swimming pools or Jacuzzis. Nearly half of our poverty households have air conditioning, 62 percent own cars, and 31 percent have microwave ovens.*

Mr. Lenstein: Ms. Cromly makes a valid point. Nevertheless, I prefer to define the poverty line as families earning less than 50 percent of the median national income. This definition indicates that more poverty exists than the level measured in the Census Bureau data. But this preference is simply a value judgment on my part; all definitions of poverty are necessarily arbitrary. I appreciate the need to select a definition and stay with it so that society can judge the extent of progress made from year to year and decade to decade.

Ms. Cromly: The definitional difficulties go beyond the issue of absolute versus relative poverty and complicate this problem enormously. For example, during the 1970s the federal government dramatically increased its spending on noncash transfers. Noncash benefits include food stamps, Medicare, Medicaid, housing assistance, and school lunch programs, all of which serve a function similar to that of income: they allow people to obtain needed commodities. Yet, if you improve people's lives with additional food, medical care, housing, and education, it's hard to argue that they are just as poor as before.

Recognizing this problem, the Census Bureau recently began estimating alternative poverty rates that include the value of noncash benefits. This alternative approach reduced the number of people in poverty by about one-fourth. For 1989 the alternative measure indicated that the percentage of the population in poverty was 9.0 percent.

Moderator: Mr. Milligan and Mr. Lenstein, do you agree with Ms. Cromly that noncash benefits should be included as income for measuring poverty?

Mr. Milligan: Yes, but the traditional Census Bureau data are normally used and constitute the most complete data available. Therefore, I chose to use it in Figure 13-1.

Mr. Lenstein: There is a danger here. I have no objection to making proper adjustments in how we define income, as long as the purpose is to increase the accuracy of the data and not to engage in "now-you-see-it, now-you-don't" chicanery. Poverty cannot be eliminated by defining it away.

Ms. Cromly: I agree that definitions can be used to understate a problem. There is an equal danger that data are used to overstate the problem. Some groups in society, for example, those who train people to serve the poor or those who favor alternative economic systems, have a vested interest in exaggerating the problem.

Moderator: Okay, so the definitional issue remains unresolved. But is it fair to conclude that much progress was made to reduce poverty in the 1960s; that the progress continued at a slower pace, via noncash transfers, during the 1970s; and that the 1981–1982 recession caused poverty to rise? (affirmative nods)

---

*Data cited by Robert Rector, "Poverty in U.S. Is Exaggerated by Census," *Wall Street Journal*, September 25, 1990, p.18.

Income Inequality

Moderator: Are income inequality and poverty the same thing?

Ms. Cromly: No. Poverty, defined in absolute terms, presupposes that a minimum income level is required to buy the basic life necessities. A society could have no poverty but still have considerable income inequality. Income inequality is measured by the degree of dispersion around the average income. Any society has income inequality if some people are richer than others.

Mr. Lenstein: I've prepared a table that shows the distribution of income in the United States. I'll project it on the screen (Table 13-1).

This table shows the distribution of family income by quintiles in the United States for 1989. Quintiles are units of one-fifth, so each quintile includes 20 percent of all families. If the income distribution were perfectly equal, each quintile would account for 20 percent of the total income. Note that the actual distribution is very unequal. Those families in the lowest 20 percent of the families accounted for 4.6 percent of the total income in 1989. The highest 20 percent accounted for 44.6 percent.

Moderator: Does this information include welfare payments, unemployment compensation benefits, social security income, and the like?

Mr. Lenstein: Yes, it does. If we excluded those transfers the distribution would be even more unequal. For example, the lowest quintile of families would account for only about one percent of the total family income. On the other hand, these figures represent before-tax income. The distribution would be somewhat less unequal than that shown in the table if we used after-tax income. Overall, the tax system in the United States is slightly progressive.

Table 13-1 also provides information on the income *level* at the upper limit of each quintile. Families having incomes below $16,003 in 1989 were in the lowest quintile, and those who received more than $59,550 were in the top quintile. Normally, these numbers increase annually at a pace similar to the rate of inflation.

Moderator: Did you wish to comment on the table, Ms. Cromly?

Ms. Cromly: We must remember that important information is not included in the figures. First, noncash transfers are not included as income. Included, the noncash transfers would tighten the distribution. Second, income mobility is not considered. Most people change income quintiles during their lives. They have low incomes when they are young; later, during their prime earning years, their income increases substantially; and finally, in retirement, their income

Table 13-1 Distribution of Family Income in the United States, 1989

Quintile (Fifth)	Income Share	Income at Upper Limit of Each Fifth
Lowest 20%	4.6%	$16,003
Second 20%	10.6	28,000
Third 20%	16.5	40,800
Fourth 20%	23.7	59,550
Highest 20%	44.6	

Source: U.S. Bureau of the Census, *Current Population Reports,* Series P-60, No. 154.

falls. Even if every family in the nation had the same lifetime income, one would still observe an unequal distribution of income in any given year! Third, the U.S. income distribution is much the same as the distribution in other industrial nations, including countries with extensive welfare programs. Finally, one's judgment on whether or not the income distribution is too unequal depends on what standard one uses to make the judgment.

Moderator: What are you referring to?

Ms. Cromly: Three standards are used to judge fairness. The first is a *contributions standard*. Under this standard, a "fair" distribution is one that closely reflects the degree to which a person contributes to the production of goods and services. A competitive market system distributes income in this manner. The second possibility is a *needs standard*. To what extent does the distribution of income enable all to meet their basic needs? The third measure is an *equality standard*. This standard suggests that a fair distribution of income is a perfectly equal one.

Mr. Milligan: Ms. Cromly makes a good point. It's difficult to find agreement on what constitutes a "fair" distribution of income. Fairness is defined differently by each individual, and economists are no exception.

Moderator: Mr. Lenstein?

Mr. Lenstein: I agree that these are difficult judgments, yet people make them daily and implement them through public policy. Economists have an important task to clarify the existing information on income distribution and explain the opportunity costs created by each policy choice.

Mr. Milligan: I agree. (affirmative nod from Ms. Cromly)

Moderator: Mr. Lenstein mentioned the term opportunity cost. What opportunity costs are involved when taxes and transfer payments are used to redistribute income?

Equity-Efficiency Trade-off

Mr. Milligan: Economists generally agree that a trade-off exists between "equity" and "efficiency." The term *equity*, as employed in this context, refers to a more equal distribution of income, presumably an income distribution conforming more closely to society's collective sense of fairness and justice.

Just what is this sense of economic equity? In the United States, it seems to mean (1) a fair economic race, with an equal start, equal access to advantage, and equal protection from disadvantage along the course and (2) a modified system of rewards through private charity and public policy so that absolute poverty does not exist and the distribution of income is more, but not totally, equal.

Moderator: How can government justify using tax and transfer programs to achieve equity?

Mr. Milligan: One justification is that if society values something, and the private sector does not provide it, public provision is warranted so long as benefits exceed costs. If people value a reduction in poverty and a more equal distribution of income, government should provide them in the same manner that it provides national defense, court systems, and other "public goods."

Ms. Cromly: But to say that society values equity is not to say that it values it at any cost. Dividing the pie up more equally through tax and transfer policies may reduce the size of the economic pie. In other words, important opportunity costs in the form of lost output and national income are involved here.

Moderator: Are you referring to the efficiency portion of the equity-efficiency trade-off?

Mr. Lenstein: Yes. In this context, the term efficiency is used in a dynamic sense to encompass what might be termed the "employment, productivity, and economic growth" goal. The great majority of people in the United States place a high value on employment, productivity, and expansion of real income.

Mr. Milligan: Particularly their own! The point is that people value both equity and efficiency, but they may have to give up some equity to achieve more economic growth, and vice versa. Figure 13-2 shows this idea graphically. Note the graph on the screen.

Mr. Lenstein: Right side up, please! (laughter)

Mr. Milligan: Mr. Lenstein, I must remind you that you are coming up for tenure soon.

Mr. Lenstein: Technology has passed you by. I recommend that you take Overhead Projection 101.

Mr. Milligan: I teach that course. (laughter)

Please note that the graph is intended only as a conceptual aid. The actual shape of the curve in Figure 13-2 had not been determined empirically. The vertical axis in the figure measures efficiency (size of national income), and the horizontal axis measures equity (the degree of equality in the distribution of income). The curve represents the best trade-off between efficiency and equity. Assume that the economy is initially at point C and that there is a desire to increase national income. Policies that promote the expansion of national income may reduce the degree of income equality. At position B, national income is higher

Figure 13-2   The Equity-Efficiency Trade-off

A trade-off may exist between equity (a more equal distribution of income) and efficiency (more goods and services). Assuming that the economy is initially at point C, it may discover that to get more equality, it must sacrifice some national income (point D). Society must choose where to locate on curve ABCDE.

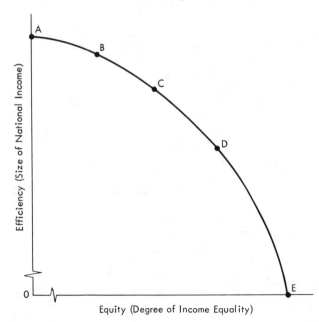

than at C, but equality is lower. To accomplish the extra growth of national income, society must give up some equality (a notion that resembles the recent policy of the Soviet Union).

Next, observe the opposite situation—a desire to increase equality. Policies that increase equality (a move from C to D) may reduce national income. Point D clearly represents more equality than C, but it just as clearly comes at the expense of less national income (a situation possibly reflected in U.S. transfer payment policies during the 1970s).

Moderator: Permit me to summarize at this point. (1) People value both greater equality and greater national income. (2) Achieving greater equality may cost society by reducing national income. (3) Because equality comes at a price, society must choose how much equality to purchase.

Mr. Lenstein: Might I add a fourth point? Society should search for and implement policies that shift the entire curve in Figure 13-2 outward. For example, policies that reduce discrimination enable us to expand national income *and* generate greater income equality.

Moderator: Assuming that all such policies have been exhausted, what point on the curve should society select?

Mr. Milligan: That is not for economists to decide! People and society must individually and collectively choose the location. They do this through their consumption, saving, investment, and work decisions and through private donations and political participation.

The Leaky Bucket Analogy

Ms. Cromly: Arthur Okun proposed an interesting experiment to test public attitudes toward the efficiency-equity trade-off.* The experiment involves transferring income from the wealthiest 5 percent of families to the poorest 20 percent. The top 5 percent would be taxed an added $4,000 each and the proceeds redistributed to the lowest 20 percent. The poor group contains four times as many families; therefore, each family would receive $1,000 of extra income. The program, however, has an unsolved technological problem: the money must be carried from the rich to the poor in a leaky bucket. *The leak represents the lost national income that results from the disincentives to work, save, invest, and produce caused by the tax and transfer plan.* As a result, the amount of money received by the poor will be less than the potential amount poured into the bucket.

Suppose that 10 percent of the money leaks out, leaving $900 for each poor family and a national income loss of $100 for society at large. Should society still make the switch? What if 50 percent leaks out? What is 75 percent leaks out, or even 99 percent? Would one still favor the redistribution?

No *best* economic answer exists because the choice depends on personal valuations of equality versus efficiency.

Mr. Lenstein: And I thought that Leakey's bucket was something used to carry bones away from archaeological excavations. (boos)

Moderator: Can you be more specific in stating the sources of leakage from the tax transfer bucket?

Ms. Cromly: Essentially, there are three sources of leakage: reduced work

---

*Arthur M. Okun, *Equality and Efficiency: The Big Tradeoff* (Washington, D.C.: The Brookings Institution, 1975).

incentives for taxpayers; disincentives to save, invest, and take risks; and disincentives for transfer recipients to work and acquire skills.

Moderator: Would you please explain these leakages in greater detail? I'm still unclear how these constitute lost income to a society. How can a transfer from one person to another reduce national income or slow its growth?

Ms. Cromly: Higher marginal taxes contribute to the leakage of lost national income. Increased funding for transfer payments necessitates higher taxes. Some economists contend that Americans respond to higher real taxes by reducing their work time and increasing their leisure.

Mr. Milligan: The spillover effects are quite far-reaching. Increased taxes make work more expensive and leisure relatively cheap. Some workers exchange their full-time jobs for part-time ones; refuse overtime work; demand longer vacations, holidays, and special leaves; increase their absenteeism; reduce personal investment in the acquisition of education and skills; demand shorter workweeks; and abandon the motivational influence of trying to get ahead. The higher real tax rates needed to finance larger income transfers may reduce incentives to work and, therefore, reduce national income.

Mr. Lenstein: Wait a minute! To date, most studies lend little support to this "supply-side" theory. Sure, it's true that increased tax rates reduce people's after-tax return from an hour of work and, therefore, make leisure less expensive, but this is only one of two possible effects. If people desire to maintain their previous level of after-tax income, they will need to work more.

Ms. Cromly: But, Mr. Lenstein, you wouldn't deny that there exists some tax rate above which the work reduction impact would dominate and the total size of the leak from the tax transfer bucket would become substantial.

Mr. Lenstein: That's true. One or two European countries *may* have tax rates in that range.

Mr. Milligan: A second area of leakage is the reduction in saving, investing, and risk taking caused by high marginal tax rates. Several economists contend that tax-transfer programs, especially the social security program, retard saving. Workers believe that their social security taxes represent an amount of current income set aside for retirement. But social security is not a pension fund, and the tax payments generate no added savings or loanable funds for society. The revenue is just moved from the person taxed to the person receiving the social security check. These economists suggest that people save considerably less than they would in the absence of the social security program. This choice reduces loanable funds, causing an increase in the interest rate, which produces declines in investment, capital formation, and growth of national income.

Moderator: That brings us to the third leakage: disincentives for transfer recipients to work and acquire skills. That is a complex topic. I hope that we can be brief.

Ms. Cromly: This is a substantial leak in the tax-transfer bucket. People receiving cash or in-kind transfers face a marginal tax rate, just as do those in higher income brackets. For the transfer recipients, the marginal tax rate involves no taxes at all, but rather losses of welfare or noncash benefits when work income rises. For example, in many states a recipient of Aid to Dependent Children benefits loses 67 cents of welfare for each extra $1 of income earned. That represents a 67 percent marginal tax rate on work income. (The highest marginal tax bracket for work income under the federal income tax law is 31 percent.) When transportation, food, child care, and clothing costs are considered, the effective marginal tax rate may even approach or exceed 100 percent, that is, to earn a dollar of income, one incurs costs and loses transfers that equal or exceed $1. Such a system discourages recipients from finding work and becoming financially independent.

Moderator: Are you suggesting that we do away with these programs?

Ms. Cromly: No! The purpose is to reinforce my earlier point that the tax transfer bucket leaks. People must recognize that reality so as to make a rational decision on how much leakage to accept to accomplish income redistribution goals.

Moderator: May I summarize here? Do we agree that taxes and transfers reduced poverty and income inequality but that they also reduced labor supply, savings, and national income? (affirmative nods)

Mr. Milligan: A study done several years ago made a "ballpark" estimate that the *transfer* portion of the tax-transfer programs in the United States reduced poverty by 75 percent and income inequality by 19 percent. But the programs also caused labor supply to fall by nearly 5 percent and produced as much as a 20 percent decline in savings. The leak from the Okun bucket was 23 cents for each dollar transferred, *excluding* the impacts of the taxes used to finance the transfers.

Ms. Cromly: These leaks must be recognized if we are to make wise judgments on how much redistribution to support.

Strategies to Reduce Poverty and Income Inequality

Moderator: I want to end this discussion by posing the same question to each of you. Perhaps your answers will serve as springboards for future discussion and thought. My question is, What general approach for solving the problem of poverty and income inequality would you favor?

Ms. Cromly: I prefer a complete reduction of absolute poverty in the United States. I'm not particularly concerned about the present extent of income inequality. Historically, the greatest progress in reducing poverty occurred during periods of vigorous economic growth and high levels of employment. I'm willing to "buy" more economic growth, at the expense of greater income inequality, because I think that the growth of national income will reduce absolute poverty. This is not a "trickle down" strategy; it is a "rising tide raises all boats" philosophy. The poor in the United States fare best when the economic "game" is a "positive-sum" one, that is, when the gains to the poor come from added national income and not from a redistribution of income. In a "zero-sum" game—where gains for the poor come only from losses to the nonpoor—the progress in reducing absolute poverty diminishes appreciably.

Moderator: How do you propose to accomplish this "growth strategy?"

Ms. Cromly: I favor tax cuts, reduced government spending, reduced regulation, incentives to stimulate savings and investment, and stable monetary policy. I also favor changing the emphasis of social welfare programs from cash and noncash transfers, which promote consumption, to private-sector job creation, which increases production.

Moderator: Won't cutbacks in government spending and transfer programs increase poverty?

Ms. Cromly: Unfortunately, yes, in the short run. But I firmly believe that, in the long run, the interests of low-income families, taken as a group, would be best served by a "growth and jobs strategy."

Moderator: Thank you, Professor Cromly. Mr. Lenstein, what approach do you favor?

Mr. Lenstein: I think that this society is wealthy enough to continue its efforts to reduce poverty and to "buy" added income equality. Just because something has a price, even a high one, does not mean that we should not buy it. I place a high value on reducing poverty and income equality. I'm also skeptical of proposals that *promise* long-term gains for the poor at the expense of short-term losses. So often, the promised gains fail to get delivered.

I'm also critical of many current social programs that are wasteful. As an alternative, I support an "income supplement" approach to poverty and inequality. Such an approach would establish a guaranteed base income level reflecting family size and composition. Permit me to project such a plan on the screen. Table 13-2 illustrates a hypothetical income supplement plan for a family of four.

Please note in Table 13-2 that as income is earned, the base income supplement of $8,000 declines by 50 percent of the family's earned income. For example, as earned income increased from $4,000 to $6,000, the income transfer declines from $6,000 to $5,000. As the "break-even" level of income ($16,000) is approached via earned income, the supplement diminishes and then disappears. Such a program has many attractive features. It would establish a minimum income for all, guarantee uniformity of benefits throughout the nation, maintain anonymity for recipients, reduce administrative expense, and provide work incentives greater than those under the existing programs. In addition, the plan could contain a work requirement for able-bodied recipients and be coordinated with training and job creation programs.

Moderator: Mr. Milligan. Our time is running short, but I do want to hear your view.

Mr. Milligan: Perhaps a combination of approaches would be optimal. For example, one might be able to combine successfully the ideas of Ms. Cromly and Mr. Lenstein. But, given the spirit of your question, permit me to discuss a third general strategy: an investment in human capital approach.

Human capital consists of the aptitudes, abilities, skills, and know-how that are embodied within individuals that enable them to be productive and thereby generate income. People enhance their human capital when they obtain education and learn skills on the job.

I prefer this approach because it attacks a cause, not a symptom, of poverty. The causes of poverty are numerous and complex. Lack of income is just a

Table 13-2 Typical Income Supplement Plan
(Family of Four)

Earned Income	Income Supplement	Total Income
$ 0	$8,000	$ 8,000
2,000	7,000	9,000
4,000	6,000	10,000
6,000	5,000	11,000
8,000	4,000	12,000
10,000	3,000	13,000
12,000	2,000	14,000
14,000	1,000	15,000
16,000	0	16,000

"symptom" of poverty. It's important to ask why those in poverty can't earn sufficient income. One very important reason is lack of education and job skills.

This strategy of promoting greater human capital appeals to me because it can shift the equity-efficiency curve outward. Perhaps it is appropriate to put additional resources into programs that educate and train the disadvantaged as a long-term strategy for economic growth. One program that I would like to see developed more fully is government-subsidized employment and job training in the private sector. It makes more sense to pay corporations to hire and train heads of poverty families than to make direct cash and in-kind transfers to poor people. I'm reminded of the old Chinese proverb: "Give a person a fish and he shall eat today. Teach a person to fish and he shall eat forever."

Moderator: Aren't those programs notoriously costly?

Mr. Milligan: That is a problem. But costs are everywhere, as we saw earlier in our leaky bucket analogy. The relevant decision rule is not to eliminate costs (that's impossible) but to maximize net benefits (benefits *minus* costs).

Moderator: I wish to thank each of you for your contributions here today. Someone once said that if you ask three economists the same question, you will get four different answers. That is not the case today. There was much agreement on basic principles. The disagreements were over interpreting facts, weighing competing values, and recommending policies. I learned much from your remarks, and I suspect that the audience did as well.

Thank you.

APPENDIX: "HOLEY BUCKETS"

(Folk Song Style)

This is the author's version of an old folk song:

My bucket has a hole in it, Mr. Lenstein, Mr. Lenstein.
My bucket has a hole in it, Mr. Lenstein, a hole.

Well fix it, Ms. Cromly, Ms. Cromly.
Well fix it!

With what should I fix it, Mr. Lenstein, Mr. Lenstein?
With what should I fix it, Mr. Lenstein, with what?

With a plug, Ms. Cromly, Ms. Cromly
Fix it with a plug!

With what should I cut it, Mr. Lenstein, Mr. Lenstein?
With what should I cut it, Mr. Lenstein, with what?

With an axe, Ms. Cromly, Ms. Cromly.
Cut it with an axe!

With what should I hone it, Mr. Lenstein, Mr. Lenstein?
With what should I hone it, Mr. Lenstein, with what?

With a whetstone, Ms. Cromly, Ms. Cromly.
Hone it with a whetstone!

With what should I wet it, Mr. Lenstein, Mr. Lenstein?
With what should I wet it, Mr. Lenstein, with what?

With water, Ms. Cromly, Ms. Cromly.
Wet it with water!

With what should I fetch it, Mr. Lenstein, Mr. Lenstein?
With what should I fetch it, Mr. Lenstein, with what?

With a bucket, Ms. Cromly, Ms. Cromly.
Fetch it with a bucket!

My bucket has a hole in it, Mr. Lenstein, Mr. Lenstein.
My bucket has a hole in it, Mr. Lenstein, a hole.

Morals:

1. A bucket is worthless unless society has something to put in it.
2. Leaky buckets present problems.
3. Solutions for fixing leaky buckets aren't always as simple as they seem.
4. A hole in a bucket doesn't prevent the use of the bucket.
5. A holey bucket may simply be an excuse for not doing something you don't want to do in the first place.

STUDY QUESTIONS

1. Explain the difference between *absolute* and *relative* poverty. How could relative poverty decline while absolute poverty was increasing?
2. What is the role of noncash benefits in reducing *official* poverty? Do you think that those transfers should be counted as income for purposes of defining poverty?
3. Explain how a specific distribution of income could be considered fair based on a *contributions standard* yet be judged unfair if a *needs* or *equality* standard were employed.
4. Do you value equity, that is, a more equal distribution of income? Do you value it at any and all costs? Explain.
5. Transfer payments themselves do not reduce total personal income in a society; they simply transfer income from one person to another. So how can transfer payments reduce national income? How is national income lost from the leaky tax-transfer bucket?
6. Explain how the social security tax-transfer program might reduce national savings.
7. Assuming a desire on your part to eliminate absolute poverty in the United States over the next 10 years, explain how you think it could be accomplished at the least opportunity cost.
8. Explain, using the ideas discussed in this chapter, each of the morals listed at the end of the appendix.

14

SHOULD WE LAUGH OR CRY?

The Economics of Inflation
and Unemployment

Concepts and Terms Examined in This Chapter

1. Inflation (Demand-Pull and Cost-Push)
2. Consumer Price Index (CPI)
3. Unemployment (Frictional, Structural, Demand-Deficient)
4. Natural Rate of Unemployment
5. Underemployment
6. Full Employment
7. Hidden Unemployment
8. Unemployment-Inflation Trade-off
9. Stagflation

Abraham Lincoln reputedly remarked, during the dark days of the Civil War, that he laughed because otherwise he would have to cry. Political cartoons, more than any other form of social commentary, embody this same spirit. They often evoke dual emotional responses from viewers—amusement and concern. In this chapter, we use them to introduce concepts that relate to the persistent problems of inflation (Figure 14-1) and unemployment (Figure 14-2). Please find and refer to each cartoon as it is mentioned. This cross-referencing will reinforce your understanding of the points being made.

INFLATION

Definition

Inflation is an upward movement of the general price level in the economy. Do not confuse this with price changes of a single item. A rise in the price of a single product or service, say, medical care, is not inflation. Prices on other goods or services, such as computer equipment, conceivably could be falling at the same time the price of medical care was rising. These declines in the prices of other products may fully offset the rise in the price of medical care, leaving the overall

Figure 14-1

THE CHRISTIAN SCIENCE MONITOR

"It droppeth as the gentle rain from heaven"

"That's Right, Chief — We're Looking This One
Straight In The Eye, But He's Not Blinking"

Figure 14-2
From *Straight Herblock* (Simon & Schuster, 1964)

price level in the economy unchanged. It is only when price increases are wide-spread in the economy, and the overall average level of prices is rising, that inflation is occurring. The inflation record in the United States, 1967–1990, as measured by changes in the consumer price index (CPI), is shown in Table 14-1. *The CPI is an index that compares the prices of a market basket of products and services in a current year with the prices of similar goods in a different (base) year*. Changes in the CPI, then, measure the rate of inflation from one year to the next.

The general price level in the economy and the purchasing power of the dollar are inversely related. When inflation occurs, each dollar of monetary income commands fewer real goods and services. Another way of saying this is that inflation reduces the purchasing power of a person's paycheck (Figure 14-3).

Causes

There is considerable disagreement on the cause of inflation. Economic theories exist for two general types of inflation: demand inflation and supply inflation. *Demand inflation* (demand-pull) is a rise in the price level caused by an increase in total spending in the economy. In its pure form, demand-pull inflation occurs when total spending in the economy exceeds the capacity of the economy

Table 14-1 **Inflation in the United States 1967–1990**
(Percentage Changes in Average Annual
Consumer Price Index)

Year	Annual Rate of Inflation	Year	Annual Rate of Inflation
1967	2.9%	1979	11.3%
1968	4.2	1980	13.5
1969	5.4	1981	10.4
1970	5.9	1982	6.1
1971	4.3	1983	3.2
1972	3.3	1984	4.3
1973	6.2	1985	3.6
1974	11.0	1986	1.9
1975	9.1	1987	3.6
1976	5.8	1988	4.1
1977	6.5	1989	4.8
1978	7.7	1990	5.4

Source: Bureau of Labor Statistics, U.S. Department of Labor.

Figure 14-3

In the valley of the jolly . . . ho ho ho . . . green giant

to produce goods and services. The box in Figure 14-4 is akin to the *productive capacity of the economy*. In other words, the box represents all the potential output from the land, factories, machines, and workers in the country. This capacity is fixed at any point in time, because these resources are limited. Imagine the creature in the box to be the *total spending* of consumers, businesses, and government. This total spending can exceed the economy's productive capacity because all three groups are able to spend beyond their current incomes. They may do this by spending past savings or by borrowing. When aggregate demand grows faster than the capacity to satisfy it, something must give way. And what gives way is the price of the available goods and services. The overspending in the economy bids or *pulls* prices upward, creating demand-pull inflation.

Nailing the lid of the box is a losing battle when the creature inside is excess total spending. It has the same effect as freezing one price in the economy by law. The demand-pull inflationary pressures simply cause higher prices somewhere else. An example would be freezing the price of beef below its equilibrium level. In a short time, consumers would buy all the available beef at the "frozen" price. When the beef was gone, the remaining consumers would turn to fish or poultry. This new demand for fish and poultry would pull up the price of these two commodities. The creature would simply break out where the prices were not frozen.

Demand-pull inflation usually occurs when the economy is growing and expanding. Unemployment and unused plant capacity are normally very low in this situation. So long as demand-pull inflation remains in the 1 to 3 percent range, most economists are not alarmed. But one danger of mild demand-pull inflation, in an otherwise healthy economy, is that it can contribute to *inflationary expectations*, which can contribute to *rapid* inflation. Most people learn quickly. As they see

Figure 14-4

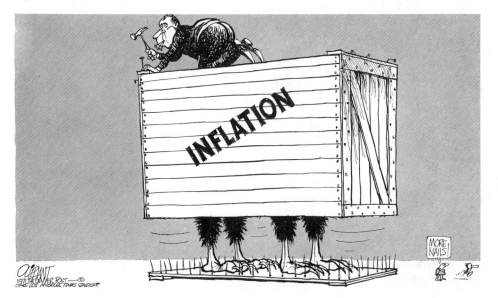

prices rise, they realize that they should buy their dreams immediately, rather than wait and save for the future. The new house or car will cost more next year than it does today. Consumers begin to reduce their saving, increase their purchases, and further aggravate the problem of demand inflation—too many dollars chasing too few products. They anticipate inflation and adjust their behavior in ways that contribute to the severity of the problem (Figure 14-5).

Thus, in the long run, the general health of the economy may be threatened by mild inflation even though initially it may seem to be a small price to pay for full employment and prosperity (Figure 14-6).

A second general type of inflation is termed *supply inflation* (cost-push). Just as excessive demand can *pull* prices upward, rapidly increasing costs can *push* them in a similar direction. When labor costs are the cause of the price pressures, the inflation is referred to as *wage-push*. Strong labor unions contribute to inflationary pressures in the economy when they negotiate wage increases that increase per-unit labor costs. This kind of inflation occurs when the increases in the wage rates exceed increases in productivity—output per person-hour. Part, or all, of these increased labor costs are passed on to the consumer in the form of higher product prices (Figure 14-7).

Wage-price spirals occur when wage increases cause prices to rise and, in turn, those higher prices cause even greater wage demands, "to stay ahead of inflation." The higher wage demands cause a second round of price rises, and the spiral is off and running.

Figure 14-5

THE CHRISTIAN SCIENCE MONITOR

'It's beginning to dawn on me . . . the more I feed you, the more you come back'

"Pay No Attention To Rover. He Just Likes To Join In"

Figure 14-6
From *Herblock's Special for Today* (Simon & Schuster, 1958)

'DON'T ANSWER THAT! IT'S MA BELL, TELLING US THE PHONE RATES JUST WENT UP THIRTY SIX PERCENT!'

Figure 14-7

No matter how fast the worker in Figure 14-8 runs, he will never make headway on the cost of living, because his running is pushing the rapidly moving prices. So it is with wage-push inflation. Of course, wage increases need not start the wage-price spiral. Inflation may begin as demand-pull. In labor's attempt to stay even with or ahead of the cost of living, however, inflation may *become* wage-push inflation. That is, wage increases may exceed gains in productivity and cause unit costs and prices to rise, even after excess demand is removed.

Corporations can indirectly contribute to wage-push inflation by passively agreeing to the demands of labor unions. Some corporations agree to large wage settlements with their unions because, in an inflationary environment, they know that they are able to pass on some of these increased labor costs to consumers in the form of higher prices. The union members get higher wages, the corporation maintains its profit margin, and the consumer gets "hammered" (Figure 14-9).

Finally, it should be noted that, although wage-push inflation was a concern in the 1960s and 1970s, it was not an important factor in the 1980s. During the past decade, union power in the United States has been on the decline. Intense competition from imported manufacturing goods has reduced union employment and greatly inhibited the ability of U.S. unions to gain inflationary wage increases. In 1990 less than 14 percent of the nation's labor force belonged to unions.

A second type of cost-push inflation is caused by sudden *supply shocks*. These supply shocks involve rapid and unexpected increases in the price of

Figure 14-8

Still Racing His Shadow

important resources used in the production process. Two such supply shocks occurred in the 1970s. The first resulted from the Arab-Israeli war of 1973, and the second occurred at the end of the 1970s when Iraq invaded Iran. In each case, oil supplies were disrupted, enabling OPEC to raise the price of oil.

Whether of the wage-push or supply shock variety, cost-push inflation differs from demand-pull inflation in an important aspect. Demand-pull inflation can continue so long as total spending continues to rise. On the other hand, cost-push inflation is self-limiting. Price level increases resulting from cost-push forces are accompanied by declines in purchases of national output. Quite simply, people find that they cannot buy as many goods and services at higher price levels. This circumstance leads to lower production levels, more unemployment, and reduced demand for raw materials. Wages and raw material prices therefore eventually stabilize or even decline, ending the inflationary episode.

Not all economists accept the idea of supply inflation. Following chapters discuss the monetarist view, for example, that all inflation is caused by excessive growth of the money supply and is therefore demand-caused. According to the monetarist view, attempts by unions, corporations, or foreign suppliers to increase wages or prices may cause specific prices to rise, but not the general price level, unless the Federal Reserve "ratifies" the actions by increasing the money supply. If the Federal Reserve refrains from providing new money to the economy, consumers who pay the higher specific prices will discover that they lack sufficient money to continue to buy other things they were purchasing. The demand for those latter items will fall and their prices will decline, offsetting the higher prices caused by unions, corporations, or foreign suppliers.

Figure 14-9

"GEE, WHAT A FUN GAME"

Costs

Having described the general types of inflation, we can now address our inquiry to the costs of inflation. These costs are misunderstood. As a whole, mild inflation does not directly make an economy more or less productive. For every loss from high prices, there is a gain, and vice versa. Every time a price increases, someone must receive the proceeds from that price as increased income. Either workers receive higher wages, resource suppliers higher revenues, landlords higher rents, lenders higher interest income, or common stockholders higher dividends. At the same time, however, whenever a price increases, buyers are worse off than before because their money income will not buy as much of the product as previously. The main effect of mild inflation is to redistribute the current income and wealth of the economy among the citizens.

If everyone fully anticipated inflation and all incomes automatically rose by an amount equal to the rate of inflation, rising prices would be a minor concern. The problem is that inflation rarely is fully anticipated by all and not everyone shares equally in the proceeds from the higher prices. Some individuals and groups bear more than their share of the losses, while others receive a disproportionate share of the benefits. Hence, one major cost of inflation is the inequity that it creates by changing the income distribution.

Who gains from unanticipated inflation, and who loses? The person who belongs to a union that negotiates a wage increase sufficient to offset the rise in prices does not lose. Another worker who gets no raise, even though the CPI rose by, say, 10 percent, experiences a wrenching decline in his or her standard of living. Likewise, if inflation leads to higher profits for a particular seller, then that person gains relative to the purchasers of the seller's products.

People who borrow money benefit from unanticipated inflation at the expense of those who lend it. Borrowers repay loans with dollars that are not worth as much as they were when they took out the loan. Creditors, on the other hand, are hurt by unanticipated inflation for the same reason that debtors benefit. For this reason, lenders boost interest rates when they expect inflation to occur.

One group particularly hurt by inflation are people with fixed incomes. Pensioners and people living on past savings watch helplessly as inflation erodes their standard of living. Because some fixed-income families are also low-income families, inflation can cause devastating effects on human lives.

Rapid inflation is a particularly perplexing problem. Groups and individuals expend resources to protect their wealth from erosion and to fight over shares of the redistributed gains. Strikes and their attendant costs rise. People begin to view saving as something to be avoided. Less saving reduces the pool of funds available to finance investment, and real interest rates (adjusted for inflation) rise, causing slowdowns in investment and long-term economic growth. Normal business practices get suspended. For example, suppliers break long-term contracts with their industrial customers because rising costs mean that these suppliers will suffer large losses if they are forced to sell at the contracted-for price. These disruptive effects of rapid inflation tear apart the social fabric and produce social and political stresses that make it difficult to find solutions to the problem (Figure 14-10).

Once inflation becomes rapid, stopping it without incurring a major recession, or worse, becomes difficult. During past episodes of rapid inflation, numerous suggestions were offered. Some economists said, "Reduce the money

'THE MOST OBVIOUS INFLATION SOLUTION IS TO FIRE US . . . I HOPE NOBODY THINKS OF IT!'

Figure 14-10

supply"; others, "Raise taxes"; still others advised, "Enact stiff wage and price controls." And then there were those who recommended breaking up labor unions and large corporations, or encouraging investment and expansion of total supply. Some suggested that we pretend inflation wasn't happening by using *indexing*, the practice of tying all agreements involving prices and income to the cost of living so that when inflation occurs, wages, rents, interest income, profits, and government transfer payments increase automatically and proportionately. Although proponents of each of those positions still can be found among economists, a growing consensus has emerged that over the long run, the best way of controlling inflation is to contain the growth of the money supply. Chapters 15 through 19 discuss inflation (and other macroeconomic topics) in considerable detail (Figure 14-11).

UNEMPLOYMENT

A problem of equal, and sometimes greater, magnitude than inflation is *unemployment*. Unemployed persons, officially defined, include all those civilians 16 years of age or older who had no employment during a particular week, were available for work, and (1) had engaged in specific job-seeking activity within the past four weeks, (2) were waiting to be called back to a job from which they had been laid off, or (3) were waiting to report to a new job scheduled to start within the following 30 days.

For reasons we will soon discuss, 100 percent employment is neither achievable nor desirable. Economists agree that some *natural rate of unemployment* exists in a market economy. Attempts to reduce unemployment below this natural rate produce accelerating inflation. Traditionally, the economy was said to be fully employed when 96 percent of the labor force was working, or alternatively,

The Christian Science Monitor

What you do is, you grab the bull by the horns . . .

Figure 14-11

when 4 percent were unemployed. Today, nearly all economists agree that the 4-percent figure is too low and that the natural rate of unemployment lies in the 5.0 to 5.5 percent range. The rapid inflow into the labor force of young adults and people seeking part-time work has made the older full employment target obsolete. Therefore, unemployment rates of today and those of two decades ago must be compared cautiously. Keep this fact in mind when examining Table 14-2. It shows the annual unemployment rates in the United States, 1967–1990.

Types

FRICTIONAL
STRUCTURAL
DEMAND-DEFICIENT

Unemployment is usually categorized as one of three types: frictional, structural, or demand-deficient unemployment.

Frictional unemployment is the unemployment that occurs because of the normal operation of the labor market. Unlike wheat exchanges or other "auction" markets, the labor market never fully clears. People are continuously quitting their present jobs in search for new ones, entering the labor force to seek work for the first time, reentering the labor force after a period of absence, or awaiting the start of a new job that will begin within 30 days. All of these people are temporarily unemployed. As they find jobs or withdraw from the labor force, other people take their place in the pool of those searching for work or waiting for their new jobs to

Table 14-2   Unemployment in the United States 1967–1990

Year	Annual Rate of Unemployment	Year	Annual Rate of Unemployment
1967	3.7%	1979	5.8%
1968	3.5	1980	7.0
1969	3.4	1981	7.5
1970	4.8	1982	9.5
1971	5.8	1983	9.5
1972	5.5	1984	7.4
1973	4.8	1985	7.1
1974	5.5	1986	6.9
1975	8.3	1987	6.1
1976	8.6	1988	5.4
1977	6.9	1989	5.2
1978	6.0	1990	5.4

Source: Bureau of Labor Statistics, U.S. Department of Labor.

begin. Therefore, a pool of frictionally unemployed people always is present, even though the specific individuals in the pool change. Because this type of unemployment is a natural part of the working of the labor market, it is not of great concern to economists.

Structural unemployment is a type of unemployment that occurs when the job skills or locations of job seekers are not the same as those described in the job vacancy notices. During prosperous economic periods, for example, there may be numerous job openings for accountants, computer programmers, engineers, and business managers. Unfortunately, the people looking for work may be housewives, teachers, actors, and bricklayers who do not possess the skills required for the available jobs. Similarly, job openings may be located in, say, Los Angeles, but job seekers may be residing in New Orleans or Pittsburgh. Thus, structural unemployment—round pegs and square holes—can and does exist even when the total demand for labor is strong.

Many structurally unemployed people have low levels of education and training. This lack of skill hinders their attempts to find jobs even when many job vacancies exist. Some of these people are unemployed because their former work was made obsolete by automation and advanced technology; they are termed "technologically unemployed." Others are unemployed because of shutdowns of plants; they are said to be "displaced workers."

Low-skilled workers are not the only people who find their services obsolete, however. The highly skilled can also become structurally unemployed when sudden changes in consumer demand occur or when government-sponsored projects abruptly end. These people may discover that it is impossible to find work commensurate with their skills. In some instances, they may be forced to accept jobs that require very little skill. Although they are working and thus not *unemployed*, they are *underemployed*; they are working at jobs below their capacities (Figure 14-12).

Demand-deficient unemployment, also called cyclical unemployment, is associated with recessions, or business downturns. Such recessions result from declines in overall spending (aggregate demand) in the economy. Government economists and officials attempt to foresee recessions and head them off with

"I'm an unemployed electronic nuclear digital data computer micro systems engineer and if I say that hot dog is done, lady — it's done!"

Figure 14-12

appropriate policies, but their foresight is less than perfect. Sometimes the "leading indicators," a series of economic variables that give a clue to the future state of the economy, fall so suddenly and rapidly that they do not provide enough time to implement corrective actions. The economy nosedives (Figure 14-13).

As spending declines, businesses discover that they cannot sell all their output. Because their inventories (unsold goods) are rising, they see no need to continue their present rate of production. Consequently, they lay off workers and operate their plants at less than capacity.

Unemployment associated with recessions is the major unemployment problem in the economy; when it occurs, it may involve millions of people. The unemployment rate reached 24.8 percent of the work force during the Great Depression of the 1930s, 8.6 percent during the recession of 1975, and nearly 11 percent in the depth of the 1981–1982 downturn (Figure 14-14).

As unemployment problems increase during recessions, some people become disillusioned with their chances of finding a job and give up their search. When this occurs, these people are no longer officially unemployed members of the labor force. In effect, they become the "hidden" unemployed. Studies indicate that during recessions the official statistics understate the actual level of unemployment because of the existence of this *hidden unemployment*.

Ironically, policies designed to reduce inflation also sometimes contribute to cyclical unemployment. Recall that demand-pull inflation is caused by excessive

'OUR LEADING INDICATORS ARE DROPPING TOO, CAPTAIN ... IF THAT'S ANY CONSOLATION....'

Figure 14-13

spending in the economy. Policies that reduce total spending or demand may reduce demand-pull inflation, but they may also temporarily increase unemployment. For example, the federal government may decide to reduce its spending on the construction of new highways, irrigation projects, and federal buildings across the nation. Such actions might help alleviate inflation, but they could also create an unemployment problem among construction workers.

In fact, most economists perceive *a short-run trade-off between unemployment and inflation* under usual economic circumstances. When plotted graphically, this relationship is termed the *Phillips curve,* named after the economist who first noted it. Policies that reduce inflation may increase unemployment (Figure 14-15). Likewise, policies designed to reduce unemployment—such as increasing government spending, or reducing taxes on consumers and business, or increasing the money supply—may create demand inflation. The Phillips curve and its relationship to *stagflation,* which is simultaneous unemployment and inflation, are discussed in Chapter 19.

Costs

The individual and social costs of unemployment and underemployment are a major concern to economists. These problems relate directly to the core issue in economics: the use of limited resources relative to the virtually unlimited wants

Figure 14-14

of people in society. Society does not possess sufficient amounts of resources—land, labor, and capital—to fulfill the many needs and wants of its members. Given this realization, it is tragic to discover that millions of human resources are unused, even though these people seek work and are capable of contributing to the fulfillment of individual and collective wants. From an economic perspective, the major cost of unemployment is the lost income and output that society forgoes because of the failure to utilize all its valuable human resources. This loss diminishes the quality of life of everyone in the economy.

The consequences of chronic unemployment are especially costly to the people directly affected. They lose income and also may become emotionally depressed, suffer loss of prestige and status, lose valuable job skills, and experience family problems. The job loss not only affects the unemployed person, but it disrupts the lives of everyone in the family. The children may have to forgo benefits such as proper health care, higher education, and future financial security.

A final problem with unemployment is that the individual costs are not evenly distributed in society. Nonwhites and teenagers bear a disproportionate share of unemployment as compared with other groups. In 1990, the level of unemployment for all civilian workers was 5.5 percent, but among blacks it was 11.3 percent, and for teenagers, 15.5 percent. All economic actions that increase overall unemployment produce consequences that are most heavily borne by people in these groups. Also, unemployment hits industries with differing force. In 1990, the unemployment rate in construction was 10.0 percent, for example, while the rate in professional services was 3.0 percent.

In conclusion, both inflation and unemployment are serious problems that occasionally burden the economy. Their costs are great; their solutions are often difficult. Long periods of simultaneous full employment and price stability have been rare in this century, although the record of the last decade has been promis-

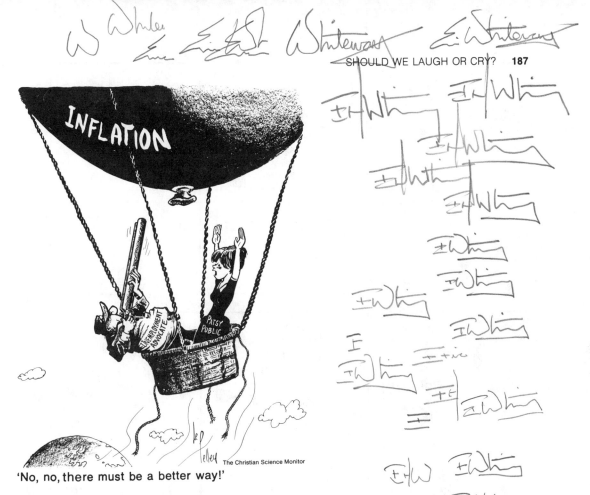

'No, no, there must be a better way!'

Figure 14-15

ing. Subsequent chapters explore these problems and other macroeconomic issues in detail.

Fortunately, most economists are far more optimistic about the prospects for achieving economic stability under capitalism than are Professors Croughton and Atherton (Figure 14-16).

STUDY QUESTIONS

1. Explain how a person's purchasing power (real income) could decline in a particular year even though he or she received a salary increase. Explain how someone's real income could rise in a specific period even though rapid inflation occurred.
2. How does demand (demand-pull) inflation differ from supply (cost-push) inflation? Explain the following statement: "Inflation can be caused by demand factors and then sustained by cost-push forces."
3. "If everyone expects inflation to occur, people may behave in a manner that *causes* the anticipated price rises." Explain this statement.
4. Update Tables 14-1 and 14-2. A good source is the most recent *Economic Report of the President*.

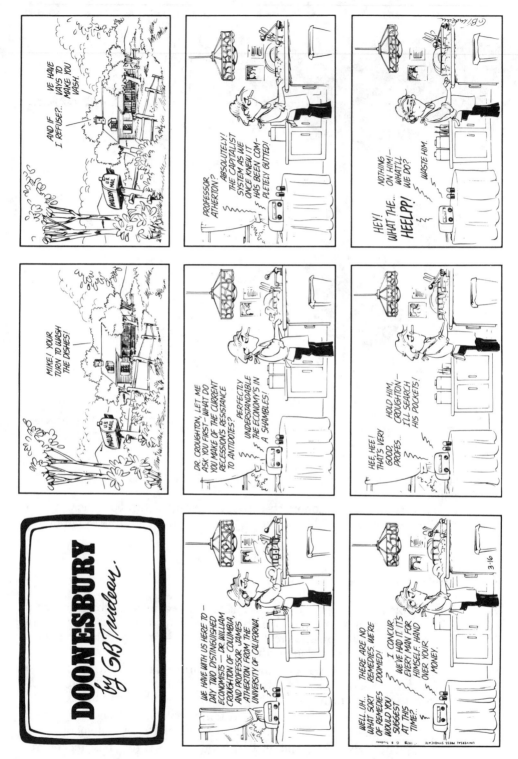

Figure 14-16

5. In what respect is frictional unemployment inevitable in an economy characterized by imperfect job information and considerable movement into and out of the labor force and specific jobs?
6. Why are recessions and increased unemployment closely linked?
7. How does structural unemployment differ from unemployment caused by deficient aggregate demand?
8. Why should society, in general, be concerned about unemployment? What are the costs of unemployment to society?
9. Speculate as to why teenage unemployment rates far exceed those for the overall labor force.

15

RUB A DUB DUB, THE ECONOMY AS A TUB

The Economics of Spending, Saving, and National Income

Concepts and Terms Examined in This Chapter

1. Consumption
2. Saving
3. Investment
4. Marginal Propensity to Consume (MPC)
5. Marginal Propensity to Save (MPS)
6. Equilibrium Income, Output, and Employment
7. Changes in Equilibrium Income
8. Multiplier
9. Classical Economics
10. Keynesian Economics

The performance of the nation's economy touches the lives and livelihood of each member of the society. Economists therefore are keenly interested in the factors that determine the levels of national income, output, and employment. These factors provide the insight to determine the causes of fluctuations in the economy. This chapter will examine two important theoretical viewpoints that attempt to explain these matters.

The simplest approach to these topics is the use of an analogy. Think of the economy as a glass tub similar to the one shown in Figure 15-1. At any moment, the capacity of the economy to produce real output and income is fixed. So it is with the glass tub; it can contain only a finite level of water. The top of the tub in the figure represents the capacity of the economy, or its *potential* level of output and income. The level of water in the tub may be likened to the *actual* output and income in the economy. That level may be far below the economy's capacity, near it, or exactly equal to it. The level of water (income-output) cannot exceed the tub's ability to hold it.

Notice that the level of water in the tub is comparable to both total income, Y, and total output, Q. The reason is that these two measures are different sides of the same coin. Output is the dollar value of all finished goods and services produced in some period. The value of this output must equal the amount of income generated in producing it. Assume, for instance, that an automobile is produced and sold for $10,000. That means *output is $10,000.* The price also measures the revenue received from the sale of the automobile. This revenue becomes income for people in the form of profits, interest, rent, and salaries and wages. So *income is also $10,000.* Every time a price is paid for a newly produced product or service, it is measured as output on one indicator and income on another.

The production of goods and services, and the national income that results, are directly related to the level of *employment* in the economy. To produce more products, additional workers are usually required. In terms of the water-tub analogy, a full tub represents a level of income and output at which there is full

Figure 15-1 The Economy as a Tub

The tub economy has two spending faucets—consumption and investment—and two drains—consumption and savings. The faucets create income and the drains temporarily withdraw income from the economy.

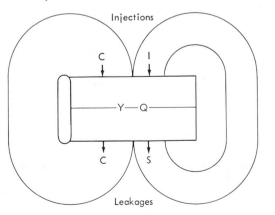

employment. Lower levels of income and employment correspond to situations in which demand-deficient unemployment exists (Chapter 14).

Notice that the two sources of inflow, or injections, in Figure 15-1 are labeled C and I. These symbols represent consumption and investment, which are the two types of spending in the private sector of the economy. *Consumption is the spending on products and services that are used up by the buyers in a short period of time.* Examples would be the purchase of hamburgers, gasoline, magazines, legal services, typing services, groceries, and the like. *Investment is the purchase of capital goods.* Businesses purchase capital goods such as plant and equipment because such items are useful in producing other goods. A bakery buys a new computerized oven to increase its production of bread. A farmer invests in a tractor to produce wheat. These expenditures on capital are examples of investment spending.*

Consumption and investment spending flow into the economy to stimulate production, create income, and increase employment. Thus the inflows can be thought of as faucets from which water flows into the tub in Figure 15-1. One person's spending is someone else's income.

The next important aspect of Figure 15-1 to note is the drains through which the water escapes. These drains represent the leakages—consumption (C) and saving (S). Do not be confused by the fact that consumption is both a leakage and an injection. This consumption leakage always matches the consumption injection. The consumption transaction is simply being split into two parts. Consumption creates income for one party (injection) when a sale is made, but the purchaser experiences a decline in available income by the same amount. The continuous consumption injection from the faucet is always equal to the continuous consumption leakage from the drain.

Saving, the second leakage in the figure, *is that part of income that is not spent on goods and services.* In this case, it is income minus consumption. The unspent income can be placed in a savings account, used to buy stock, or placed in a drawer—so long as it's not spent, it represents saving in economic analysis. Saving is an important leak in the economy because unspent income directly reduces demand for goods and services. These funds must be borrowed and spent by others, or the level of national income and output will decline. Ideally, all saving will be borrowed and spent by businesses on new plant and equipment. This investment not only will stabilize the level of national income and output in the tub, but also will expand the capacity of the tub over the long run (generate economic growth).

It is clear, then, that water is continuously flowing into the tub in Figure 15-1, creating income, and just as continuously is draining. A stable equilibrium level of water (national income and output) will occur when the rate of inflow into the tub (C + I) just matches the rate of outflow (C + S). Because the consumption flows are equal, I and S become crucial variables to study. In the absence of

---

*In addition to the purchase of capital goods, economic investment includes all new construction and net changes in business inventories. Note the distinction between *economic investment*, as defined here, and *financial investment*, such as the purchase of stocks and bonds. Economists do not consider the latter type of spending as investment because it does not represent purchases of capital goods. It is only *when* and *if* the proceeds from the sale of stocks and bonds are used to buy new plant and equipment that investment occurs.

government, equilibrium national income and output occur when investment equals saving $(I = S)$.*

THE CLASSICAL VIEW

Adam Smith (1723–1790), David Ricardo (1772–1823), and Jean Baptiste Say (1767–1832) developed a theory that viewed the market economy as self-regulating and self-adjusting. According to their analysis, if left free to operate without government interference, the economy would automatically generate and maintain a full-employment level of income and output. Recessions, depressions, and inflation would not normally occur, and if they did, they would last only briefly.

These classical economists perceived the economy as depicted in the water-tub analogy illustrated in Figure 15-2. There the tub is completely full. According to Say, "Supply creates its own demand." Any production of products is accompanied by the payment of income to the owners of the resources used to produce the products. Workers receive wages; landlords receive rent; and capitalists, who provided capital and management, receive interest and profit. The income received by these three groups is sufficient to buy all the products produced in the economy. The production of products creates income that converts into demand for these products. *All this earned income is spent.*

At first glance, this theory seems to ignore the saving leakage. But the classical economists had an explanation for that problem too. Notice that the saving drain and the investment faucet are *directly connected.* All water (saving) escaping from the tub automatically returns to it as investment spending. The tub remains full, and full employment and maximum income prevail.

The classical economists believed that investment would equal saving

Figure 15-2   The Classical View

According to the classical economists, consumption (C) is always equal to itself, and investment (I) just equals saving (S), at a full-employment level of income (Y) and output (Q).

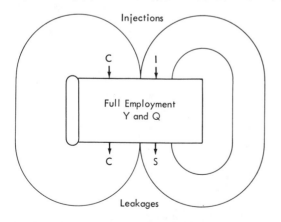

*For simplicity, we are assuming that exports (a spending injection) and imports (a leakage) are equal and therefore of no net consequence to the level of national income. This assumption is relaxed in Chapter 16.

automatically; the market for saving and investment funds was the mechanism ensuring that equality. The classicalists theorized that people saved to earn an interest return. Interest was a price paid to savers for not consuming. If the interest rate increased, people would save more; if it declined, they would reduce their saving. On the other side of the process, businesses would borrow the saving (a leakage) and purchase capital goods (an injection). Firms would borrow and invest more at low interest rates than at higher ones. This classical view of the behavior of savers and investors is shown in modern supply and demand terms in Figure 15-3.

The predicted behavior of savers is shown by the supply curve; that of investors by the demand curve. As in all supply and demand situations, the price (interest rate) settles where the curves intersect. At that equilibrium interest rate, *the quantity of saving equals the quantity of investment spending.* The interest rate fluctuates to reflect the relative strengths of demand and supply and ensures that I = S.

This analysis led the classical economists to conclude that C + I (income-creating injections) would always equal C + S (leakages) and that income would remain at the full-employment level. The self-regulating characteristics of the private sector ruled out the possibility of severe unemployment and recession.

Now we can introduce government into the tub economy. What should its role be to keep the economy operating efficiently at full employment?

For the classical economists, the policy prescription was obvious. The government should maintain a neutral position by balancing its budget. Government spending is an additional injection that creates income, and government tax collections are an added leakage. Since the private economy automatically balances itself at full employment, the government should offset all government spending by an equal amount of tax revenues.

The balanced-budget policy is depicted in the water-tub illustration in

Figure 15-3 Classical Interest Rate Mechanism in Modern Supply and Demand Terms

The classical economists believed that both saving and investment were determined by the interest rate. An equilibrium interest rate equated the quantity of saving and quantity of investment.

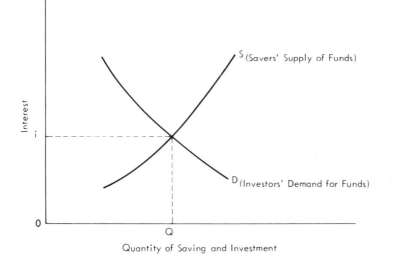

Quantity of Saving and Investment

Figure 15-4. Government spending (G) puts water into the tub. Taxes, a third drain through which water escapes, represent a part of income that is not spent by households or businesses. But if G = T, then the level of income achieves its full potential. *Full employment is assured if government balances its budget.*

THE KEYNESIAN VIEW

Proponents of the classical view were not so naïve to believe that the economy would always remain *exactly* at full employment. They recognized that shifts in the spending habits of consumers and the supplying behavior of producers could cause temporary unemployment difficulties, but they felt that *over the long run*, the economy would adjust to the full-employment equilibrium position. That belief was severely strained by the Great Depression, which lasted from 1930 to 1941 in the United States and produced unemployment rates that at one time reached 25 percent of the work force. After the first two or three years of the depression, people began to wonder, "How long is the long run—the time necessary for the economy to rebound, as classical theory guaranteed it would?" The English economist, John Maynard Keynes, aptly put it this way: "In the long run we are all dead."

The time was ripe for a new theory of spending, saving, and national income. In 1936, Keynes provided that new perspective. He constructed a model of the market economy that described how economic events such as the Great Depression could occur. Although modified and extended, his theory remains the core for much of contemporary macroeconomic analysis.

The Keynesian theory views the investment injection into the economy as *disconnected* from the saving leakage. Investment and saving actions are separate and distinct. Investment spending, the purchase of capital goods, is undertaken mainly by businesses, whereas households are the primary savers. Savers and investors are *different groups* making *different economic decisions* based on *different motives*. The saving plans of households need not equal the investment plans of businesses.

Figure 15-4   The Classical Policy Prescription: Balanced Budgets

According to classical economists, because the private economy tended toward an equality of consumption plus investment spending (C + I) and consumption plus saving (C + S) at a full employment level of national income and output, government should balance its expenditures (G) and its tax revenues (T).

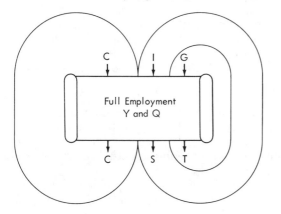

The Keynesian theory agrees with the classical one that businesses make investment decisions on the basis of their interest costs of borrowing and their expectations for a profit return. A bicycle manufacturer will not build a new factory if it must pay 15 percent interest on the borrowed funds and expects the new capital to yield only a 10 percent return. But if the return is projected to be more than 15 percent, then it will find it profitable to borrow and invest.

Savers operate from a different set of motives. They save as a precaution against uncertainty (loss of job, large medical expenses), to purchase expensive items for cash, and just from general habit. According to Keynesian economists, savers in the aggregate do not respond in a predictable way to changes in interest rates. The volume of saving in the United States does not rise automatically when interest rates increase, nor does it fall when rates decline. When interest rates rise, people may put more saving in fixed-return assets such as savings and loan certificates, but the amount is usually simply transferred from some other form of saving, say, common stock. The total *volume* of saving is insensitive to changes in interest rates even though the *form* of saving may change when rates change.

Keynesian macroanalysis holds that saving is mainly determined by *the level of income in the economy.* Saving increases when national income rises, and it falls when national income declines. Check your individual behavior. As your income rises, you probably save more, and as it falls, you save less. You may even find yourself using past saving (negative saving) to purchase things if your income falls far enough. This relationship between saving and income, the *marginal propensity to save*, is central to Keynesian income and employment theory.

In economic analysis, *marginal* means "extra" or "additional," and *propensity* means "the tendency for an action to occur." Therefore, the marginal propensity to save (MPS) is a measure of the tendency of the nation's population to save a portion of each additional dollar of after-tax income. It is the amount that saving increases when national after-tax income increases by one dollar.

Once the economy's MPS is known, the *marginal propensity to consume* (MPC) is easily determined. All after-tax income is either spent or saved by people in the economy. Therefore, for example, if the MPS in the economy is .2, then the marginal propensity to consume is .8. This means that when income rises by a dollar in the economy, people will spend 80 cents and save 20 cents. The MPC plus the MPS always equals 1.

These are the main conceptual tools necessary to understand the Keynesian theory of income, output, and employment determination. The Keynesian tub economy is shown in Figure 15-5. Notice that the investment faucet and saving drain are not linked. This lack of connection reinforces the idea that investors make their decisions independent of savers. Investment can and does fluctuate greatly from one year to the next. On the underside, the saving drain is rather stable; it changes only when the level of national income in the economy rises or falls.

Now the potential for problems becomes apparent. Suppose that the tub is full and that investors plan to inject more water (investment spending) into the tub than households plan to save. The capacity of the tub is insufficient to hold the growing volume of total spending. This situation is analogous to demand-pull inflation. Product prices rise as people try to outspend each other for the limited supply of products.

Demand-pull inflation is but one of the potential problems once the investment and saving faucets are unlinked. If less water is placed into the tub

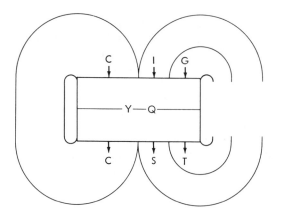

Figure 15-5 The Keynesian View

According to Keynesian economists, the economy's investment faucet and saving drain are not automatically equated by way of the interest rate mechanism. Saving and investment plans can and do diverge, creating changes in the level of national income and output in the economy. Government can reduce the severity of these recessions and inflationary expansions by managing the government spending faucet and tax revenue drain.

through the investment faucet than flows out through the saving drain, the level of water in the tub will recede. Investment plans may decline below the level of planned saving because of high interest rates, poor sales, or general pessimism in the business community. As investment plans decline below saving plans, the levels of income, output, and employment decline in the economy. This decline is called a recession. If the downward trend continues, the economy faces a full-scale depression.

The classical tub tended to produce full employment. The Keynesian tub tends to establish equilibrium at levels either above or below the full-employment level of income, and to move from one condition to another. Booms and busts, and inflation and unemployment occur; and *instability*, not stability, characterizes the economic system.

THE MULTIPLIER: A KEYNESIAN COMPLICATION

How can the economy maintain full employment when investment is unstable? Before discussing the answer, a complication must be added to the analysis. The instability of the economy is increased because a change in investment spending creates *more than an equal change in income*. Not only is the flow from the investment faucet unstable, but any changes in the rate cause magnified changes in the national income.

A dollar of additional new investment spending creates $1 of new income to the person receiving it, but the process does not stop there. Whoever receives that extra dollar usually spends a portion of it and saves the remainder. The recipient of that fraction of the dollar spent will again spend most of it and save a portion. This process continues for some time. The impact on the economy—the amount of new income created—depends on the economy's marginal propensity to consume and the marginal propensity to save.

For example, assume that the MPC in the economy is .8, the MPS is .2, and $1 of new investment occurs.* The person receiving the first dollar of additional income created by the new investment spends 80 cents of new income. From the perspective of the total economy, income at this stage has increased by $1.80 (first person $1 and second person $.80). The process continues. The second recipient spends part of the 80 cents of new income and saves part of it. Because the MPC is .8, spending increases by 64 cents, and the person receiving the money from the sale has an income increase of a like amount. Total income in the economy has increased by $1.00 + $.80 + $.64, or $2.44. This process continues once more. This is the *multiplier* concept in action. An increase in new investment spending increases income by a multiple of the initial spending increase, and a decline in investment reduces income by a multiple of the decrease. Changes in investment spending generate larger fluctuations in income, output, and employment:

$$\text{Multiplier} = \frac{\text{Ultimate change in income}}{\text{Original change in spending}}$$

The multiplier process raises some logical questions. *How much* will income ultimately change when investment spending changes? Will this process continue indefinitely and run out of control? The answer to these questions relates to the idea of equilibrium income itself—the beginning concept in the chapter.

Back to the tub analogy. Equilibrium income occurs when I = S, or when injections equal leakages. When this condition is reached, the level of income does not change. As each new investment dollar, over and above the amount already going in, is put into the tub, the level of income begins to expand. But this expansion also enlarges the saving leak and allows more saving outflow. This occurs automatically because the level of saving is determined by the volume of income. Income expands *until the new saving outflow matches the original change in investment inflow*. At that new, higher level of income, a new equilibrium is produced. The key variable in this process is the marginal propensity to save (MPS) because it determined the size of the income multiplier:

$$\text{Multiplier} = \frac{1}{\text{MPS}}$$

For instance, if investment originally increased by $10 billion and the economy's MPS were .2, then total income in the economy would have to expand by $50 billion to restore equilibrium. This $50 billion of additional income would produce $10 billion of new saving (.2 × $50 billion = $10 billion). When investment increases, income increases and the increase in income stops when the new saving offsets the initial change in investment. This process restores equilibrium at a higher level of national income. In the classical theory, the interest rate fluctuated to ensure that S = I and that equilibrium income occurred. But in the Keynesian economy, when investment plans and saving plans diverge, *income itself* fluctuates until a new equilibrium level of income is achieved. The resulting equilibrium may be at any level of national income, not just the full-employment level.

*We are also assuming that each of the people in the example spends and saves in a fashion identical to the population in the aggregate.

The multiplier effect is a key outcome produced by any change in injections. The multiplier works with new investment, government spending, and consumer spending. It converts modest changes in spending into larger changes in income, thus adding to the possibilities of an inflationary, overflowing tub, on the one hand, or unemployment and a receding level of water, on the other.

KEYNESIAN POLICY: CONTROL THE FAUCETS AND DRAINS

How can the unstable private sector of the economy be guided so that it performs consistently and equitably to meet the goals of the society? The Keynesian answer to this question suggests a policy that is contrary to the one expounded by the classical economists. The classicalists recommended that government balance its budget; that government expenditures should equal taxes in all years. The Keynesian analysis suggests that the government should use its spending and taxing powers to *balance the economy*, not the federal budget. It should adjust government spending (G) and its tax revenues (T) to offset any imbalances that may exist between investment and saving in the private sector of the economy.

The key to maintaining a fully filled tub (full-employment economy) is demonstrated in Figure 15-5, referred to previously. The pumps must be maintained to ensure that I + G = S + T at a desirable level of income. If the faucets and drains in the private sector do not work at a balanced rate, inflation, unemployment, and other economic problems will occur. What should be done, for example, if investment injections exceed saving leakages and demand-pull inflation occurs? This problem could be offset by reducing government injections (G) or increasing tax leakages (T). The use of these policies could reduce the spending in the economy to a level consistent with the ability of the economy to match it with products and services.

What if investment injections were less than saving leakages and the economy were moving toward recession or depression? In this case, the government should offset these conditions by increasing its own spending injections or reducing tax leakages.

In short, government policy should, according to Keynesian economists, maintain I + G = S + T at the full-employment level of income, output, and employment in the economy. If the private sector faucets and drains are not in balance, then the government faucet and drain should be unbalanced in the opposite direction. This prescription is referred to as "countercyclical fiscal policy." Fiscal policy is the major topic of the following chapter.

STUDY QUESTIONS

1. Briefly define *investment* and *saving* as the terms are used by economists. Which of the following are investments?
   a. The purchase of a crane
   b. The purchase of common stock
   c. The purchase of an airline ticket
2. How are national income, output, and total employment all related to one another? Why do they usually vary in the same direction?

3. The classical economists felt that the amounts of saving and investment would always equal each other. Why? What would ensure this equality?

4. According to economic studies, the total volume of saving in the economy is not related to the interest rate. Can you cite a reason why one person might save less when the interest rate increased, whereas another might save more?

5. Answer the questions that follow on the basis of the accompanying data for a hypothetical economy in which there is no government and no foreign sector:

National Income	Consumption	Saving
$500	$400	$100
400	325	75
300	250	50
200	175	25
100	100	0

a. Determine the marginal propensity to consume.
b. Determine the marginal propensity to save.
c. If investment is $50 in this economy, what is the equilibrium level of national income?
d. By how much will national income fall if investment declines by $25 billion? Use your answer to determine the size of the multiplier.

6. If the multiplier in an economy is 10, what are the sizes of the marginal propensities to consume and save?

7. If government increased its spending by $20 billion and the marginal propensity to save in the economy was .4, how great an increase in total income would the economy experience? Explain.

8. In reality, federal tax revenues increase automatically as income increases, just as saving does. Why is this the case?

9. Since it is the S and T leaks that allow the tub economy to recede, why doesn't government simply plug these drains permanently?

10. The following diagram is one commonly employed to show the concept of equilibrium income (output, employment). Using the knowledge gained from this chapter, determine

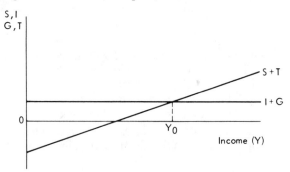

a. why the S + T curve slopes upward and to the right.
b. why Y_0 is the equilibrium level of income.
c. how an increase in investment spending would be depicted in this graph.
d. how one could graphically determine the multiplier effect of this increase in investment.

16

A CONVERSATION WITH A WIZARD

Aggregate Demand, Aggregate Supply, and Fiscal Policy

Concepts and Terms Examined in This Chapter

1. Price Index
2. Gross National Product
3. Aggregate Demand and Aggregate Supply
4. Interest Rate, Wealth, and Foreign Purchases Effects
5. Fiscal Policy
6. Recession
7. Lags
8. Supply-Side Fiscal Policy
9. Automatic Stabilizers
10. Budget Deficit and Surplus
11. National Debt
12. Crowding Out
13. Monetarism and New Classical Economics

Interviews with economists are published periodically in business magazines, magazines of economic affairs, and supplemental readers for economic courses. Usually the interviewer seeks information to help readers understand a particular issue or facet of economic analysis. In the interview that follows, we present the eminent Dr. George N. Post, a fictitious specialist in macroeconomic policy. The topics are macroeconomic analysis and fiscal policy.

Economic News: What led you to specialize in macroeconomic analysis, professor?

Dr. George N. Post: I decided that, given my initials, I had a comparative advantage in this area. Seriously, as a graduate student, I found macroeconomics to be of great relevance to the policy issues of the day. It still is.

AGGREGATE DEMAND AND AGGREGATE SUPPLY

EN: What sort of tools do macroeconomists use to analyze the economy?

Post: Although the models we employ are highly elaborate, they boil down to simple demand and supply analysis using aggregate data. Rather than measuring the price of, say, mascara on the vertical axis of our graphical model, we measure the price of all the goods in the economy—the price level. Rather than measuring the quantity of mascara on the horizontal axis, we measure the quantity of real national output—real GNP. Here is the way the model looks graphically. It will be useful to include this graph in the printed interview (Figure 16-1).

EN: Please define your terms. What do you mean by "price level" and "real national output"?

Figure 16-1 Aggregate Demand and Aggregate Supply

Aggregate demand and aggregate supply interact to establish the equilibrium price level and level of real gross national product (GNP) in the economy.

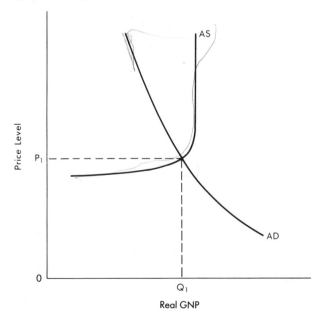

Post: You are forcing me to get a bit technical here. Perhaps we will lose our audience?

EN: Our audience is interested in economics; they'll hang in there. From what you have indicated, this is an important economic model.

Post: Yes, it is. The price level is an index number that relates the prices of the goods and services constituting the national output to the prices of these same items in a base year. For example, suppose the goods and services produced in 1990 were priced at $4 billion that year, but that these same items were priced at $3 billion in 1982, the base year. If we arbitrarily set the base year price index at 100, then the price index—that is, the price level—for 1990 is 133 ($4 billion/$3 billion). Stated differently, the price level in this example is 33 percent higher in 1990 than in 1982. In Figure 16-1, the vertical axis measures price index numbers such as those we have just described.

EN: And how are you defining "real GNP," your variable on the horizontal axis?

Post: First, the "real" means that the data have been adjusted for inflation. That way we can compare GNP from one period to another, as if inflation had not occurred. *Gross national product (GNP)* consists of the total market value of all final goods and services produced in the United States in a particular period. *Final goods and services* are things like pizzas, exercise bikes, legal services, industrial robots, and tanks that are bought by consumers, businesses, and government and do not become part of yet another consumer or capital good. These final goods and services are distinguished from *intermediate goods and services* such as hamburger buns used for fast-food hamburgers and accounting services used by the auto industry. If we counted the value of the hamburger buns *and* the hamburger or the accounting services *and* the new car, we would be double-counting the nation's GNP. The value of the buns and accounting services, after all, are included in the final value of the hamburgers and autos, respectively.

EN: The downsloping curve in your diagram is labeled AD. Tell us about it.

Post: "Aggregate" means "total," or the sum of all individual, business, and government demand. *Aggregate demand* demonstrates the relationship between various possible price levels and levels of real GNP that will be purchased by consumers, businesses, and government. Notice that the curve shows an inverse, or negative, relationship between the price level and spending on real GNP. If all else is equal, higher price levels are associated with lower total amounts of goods and services demanded.

EN: Why so?

Post: There are three reasons. First, when the price level rises, the demand for money increases because people require more dollars to purchase the same quantity of goods and services. This increase in money demand will cause the interest rate to rise. The rise in the interest rate will reduce investment spending and therefore decrease total spending and real GNP. Economists refer to this effect as the *interest rate effect*. Second, the increase in the price level will reduce the *real* value of people's savings. That $5,000 in the savings account will no longer buy as many goods as before. Therefore, people will increase their saving—that is, reduce their consumption spending—to restore the real purchasing power of their saving. Again, the quantity of goods and services demanded will be reduced. We might call this effect the *wealth effect*.

Finally, a *foreign purchases effect* also helps explain the inverse relationship between the price level and real output. As our price level rises relative to price levels in other nations, we buy more goods produced abroad and sell fewer goods to foreign buyers. A higher U.S. price level reduces our exports, resulting in a smaller domestic level of real GNP.

EN: What determines where the aggregate demand curve is located? It seems to me that you have just arbitrarily positioned it.

Post: The location of the AD curve will depend on factors *other than the price level* that affect the desires of consumers, businesses, and government to purchase real output. These are the things we hold constant when a particular AD curve is constructed. When these things change, the entire AD curve shifts either rightward or leftward.

EN: This is terribly abstract. Can you give me some examples of why the AD curve might shift?

Post: Sure. Suppose that stock prices fall and that consumers, feeling less wealthy, decide to reduce their spending as a way to increase their saving. The result will be less real output demanded at each price level—a leftward shift of AD. Or suppose that businesses reduce their purchases of capital goods because interest rates have gone up, or that government decides to reduce its spending, independently of any change in the price level. These actions by businesses and government also would shift the AD curve to the left. Finally, the AD curve would shift leftward if our exports fell relative to our imports. That shift would mean that people abroad are buying fewer U.S. products and we are buying more products produced abroad.

Of course, all this analysis gets reversed if we are speaking of an *increase* in aggregate demand—a rightward shift of the AD curve in Figure 16-1.

Also, it is worth noting that the AD curve shifts rightward or leftward by a horizontal distance greater than an initial change in spending. Initial changes in consumption, investment, government, and net export spending (exports minus imports) get magnified into greater changes in spending and aggregate demand through the multiplier effect [recall Chapter 15].

EN: Tell us quickly about aggregate supply. I want to make sure we have plenty of time to discuss fiscal policy.

Post: Okay, but let me first say that I have drawn a very simple aggregate supply curve in Figure 16-1. There is much controversy about the shape of this curve. *Aggregate supply* tells us the amount of real GNP that producers are jointly willing to produce and sell at each price level. The general shape of the curve is upsloping, indicating a direct, or positive, relationship between the price level and real GNP supplied. The reason for this general shape is that higher product prices provide a profit incentive for firms to produce more output, particularly when increases in wage and other input costs lag behind price increases. If you can get $5 a unit for your produce, rather than $3, you will have an incentive to produce more units of it.

Observe that the AS curve is quite flat until the full employment level of real GNP is reached and then it becomes vertical. There is an important implication here. If excess capacity exists in the economy (flat section of the AS curve), aggregate demand and output can increase without causing much of a rise in the price level. To understand this, imagine an AD curve shifting slowly to the right over this range. But, when all the resources are being used, further rightward shifts in AD cause the price level to rise, while real output changes little.

EN: What factors might shift the aggregate supply curve?

Post: Well, the aggregate supply curve is a cost curve, of sorts. Anything changes the per-unit cost of production in the economy, independent of changes in real GNP, will shift the AS curve one direction or the other. For example, if the price of oil rises, it is likely that per-unit production costs will rise. Thus the AS curve will shift upward and to the left. Alternatively, suppose that new technology permits firms to get more output for each unit of input used. Per-unit production cost will fall, and the AS curve will shift downward and to the right.

EN: Is there anything else you would like to say about the AD-AS model?

Post: No, other than to stress that the equilibrium price level and equilibrium level of real GNP are P_1 and Q_1, as shown by the intersection of AD and AS in Figure 16-1.

FISCAL POLICY

EN: Lets turn to the topic of fiscal policy. What is it? How does it relate to the AD-AS model?

Post: *Fiscal policy* is the deliberate use of federal taxation and spending actions to change aggregate demand in the economy and thereby influence the price level and level of real GNP. Our AD-AS model is very useful for forecasting the consequences of alternative fiscal policies. The purpose of fiscal policy is to shift the AD curve either to the right or the left. In other words, it is a policy of "demand management."

EN: Suppose the economy is in recession. What policies would you advocate?

Post: Well, let's first be certain we know what that term means. A recession is defined as *a situation in which real output declines during two or more successive quarters*, a quarter being a three-month period. As output declines, profits fall, unemployment rises, and real national income recedes. This change would be shown by a leftward shift in AD in Figure 16-1.

What can the government do to counteract the decline in aggregate demand? First, the federal government could cut tax rates or end certain taxes altogether. This action would increase people's after-tax income, leading eventually to increased consumption spending. An increase in consumption spending is depicted by a rightward shift of the aggregate demand curve. Sales will rise, inventories will fall, and firms will rehire laid-off workers to produce more goods. As economic activity increases, the economy will begin to climb out of its slump (Q will rise).

A second option is to leave taxes alone and just increase government spending. That action would directly increase aggregate demand. Finally, government could encourage investment spending, perhaps by offering tax concessions to businesses. Of these three methods, tax cuts have been the most popular.

EN: You make fiscal policy sound very easy. What if people save their tax reduction rather than increase their consumption?

Post: A lot of people spend their entire take-home pay each month. When their take-home income rises because of the tax cut, they increase their spending. Saving will rise to some degree, but historical experience indicates that tax cuts result in an increase in consumption spending. There are other complications, of course.

EN: Could you elaborate on what you mean by "complications"? That word usually contains some hidden messages.

Post: Timing is a major problem. Two *time lags* are present between the identification of the need for a tax cut and the actual impact of the cut on the recession. The first lag is the time necessary to formulate the tax proposal and have it passed by Congress. Officials must prepare the tax proposal, convince the president of its desirability, and present it to the House Ways and Means Committee. The committee reviews the legislation, consults economic experts, discusses the package, and sends it to the full House. The house then debates the bill, votes on it, and sends it to the Senate, where the entire process is repeated.

This all takes time, sometimes nearly six months, and the process makes it extremely difficult to take swift, prudent economic action.

EN: It sounds as though you prefer Congress to act as a rubber stamp for administration tax proposals. Isn't the careful review of tax matters an important task of Congress?

Post: I neither expect nor want Congress to rubber-stamp decisions. I am simply identifying a bottleneck that impedes the timely exercise of economic policy. Long congressional delays make the job very difficult. Economic advisers are notoriously better at analyzing the present than prophesying the future. The farther into the future they are forced to plan because of the congressional lag, the more they must become involved in prophecy.

EN: You mentioned that there were *two* time lags.

Post: Yes, a second lag involves the time between the signing of the tax reduction into law and its final total impact on the economy. People must collect their additional after-tax income and decide how to spend it. The multiplying effects of the initial increases in spending also take time. All in all, the tax cut may require six to nine months to generate its full effect on the economy.

These time lags place the government economic officials in a difficult position. They must identify a recession at its very early stages and initiate proper policy immediately, so that the effects of the policy will not be too late. Timing is crucial. Forecasting must be reasonably accurate and sensitive to signs of early trouble.

EN: Past economic forecasts have been uneven; they have been off the mark as often as they have been accurate. Am I wrong?

Post: No. But we are able to identify a recession when it is happening, or at least after it has continued for a while. No forecasting is required there. Furthermore, many forecasts *have* been accurate.

EN: How do you respond to the charge that past attempts to fine-tune the economy through fiscal policy produced the double-digit inflation of the late 1970s and early 1980s?

Post: That charge is a gross oversimplification. That was a period of extreme supply shocks from oil price hikes. These shocks shifted the aggregate supply curve to the left because higher costs of production and transportation meant that producers were not willing to offer as much for sale at the existing price level. You will note from Figure 16-1 that a leftward shift of AS causes the price level to rise.

EN: That interpretation is subject to dispute.

Post: I realize that. My point here is that I do not believe that fiscal policy *causes* the fluctuations in the economy. It may not eliminate them, but it often reverses the direction of the economy in a positive way.

To those who think that the economy will automatically operate at a full-employment, noninflationary level if only the government balanced its budget, all I can say is that everyone is entitled to an opinion—even an erroneous one.

EN: Spoken like a true "fiscal activist." I did not think there were any of you left.

Post: I'm not talking about fine-tuning the economy. That idea has been discredited. Rather, I'm simply saying that fiscal policy is a useful tool to avoid the extremes of severe recession and rapid inflation. Once we begin to see either happening, we ought to take fiscal actions.

EN: The Reagan administration cut taxes by 5 percent in 1980, 10 percent in 1982, and 10 percent in 1983. Were these examples of fiscal policy?

Post: Yes, clearly, they were fiscal policy actions. They were changes in the federal budget designed to increase employment and economic growth, and that is fiscal policy. But the rationale for those tax cuts differed from the traditional "demand expansion" one. Instead, the rationale was that the cuts in marginal tax rates (the rates on the last dollars earned) would stimulate work effort, increase saving and investing, and generally expand aggregate *supply* in the economy. A glance back at Figure 16-1 will remind us that a rightward shift in AS will increase real output and lower the price level.

EN: Thus the term "supply-side tax cuts"?

Post: Yes, I'm a skeptic on this idea, however. My view is that tax cuts expand aggregate demand and the increased demand brings forth greater output and national income. In that respect one could argue that the Reagan policies were Keynesian, even though that administration openly disavowed Keynesian ideas.

EN: Before we began discussing tax cuts, you indicated that increased government spending and policies that encourage investment spending are also antirecessionary. Would you care to elaborate briefly on these?

Post: Yes. Tax cuts, especially reductions in the personal income tax, operate mainly to increase consumption spending. This is only one of the three parts of total demand. Government spending is a second component. The government can build mass-transit systems, develop new energy sources, establish educational programs, hire public employees, make grants to state and local governments, and spend funds on a multitude of other projects. When they involve new spending, these programs stimulate the economy. This type of fiscal policy has a rather direct impact on national income, employment, and production.

Finally, the government can encourage increased business spending on new capital items. In the past, the *investment tax credit* was a key tool here. This tax provision allowed companies to use a percentage of their expenditures on *new* plant and equipment as a credit to reduce the corporate income tax that they had to pay. For example, if the credit was 10 percent, then every $100 a firm spent on new investment reduced its income tax by $10. The idea was to make investment less costly and encourage firms to undertake more of it. The credit added to tax complexity, however, and was not a very effective fiscal policy tool. The provision was repealed in the tax reform of 1986.

EN: In summary, then, you contend that the government should reduce taxes on consumers, increase its own spending, and provide tax breaks to stimulate private investment during a recession. Wouldn't those actions—

Post: Pardon me, but that isn't quite what I said. Those are three options that are available to combat a recession, but that doesn't mean that I support using all three at the same time. The correct combination of policies would depend on the severity of the unemployment and recession problem.

EN: Thanks for the clarification. What I was getting to was that any one of these policies or a combination of them increases the national debt. Isn't this irresponsible economic policy? Shouldn't we balance the federal budget?

Post: It would be *irresponsible to try to balance the budget* during a recession. If government attempted to balance the budget during such a period, it could make the problem worse and the budget would still end up in a deficit. Think this through. Assume that unemployment increases to 10 percent and general business activity declines. People earn less income in the aggregate and spend less. This general decline reduces tax revenues on two fronts — personal income tax receipts decline, and corporate tax revenues fall. To balance the budget, government would have to reduce its spending or increase tax *rates*. Either action would reduce spending even more and compound the unemployment and falling income problem. As incomes dropped even further, tax revenues would decline still more. The government would end up with the deficit it tried to avoid, and the economy would be in worse shape than previously.

Responsible fiscal policy during a recession is to increase spending and reduce taxes. The resulting larger national debt is of minor concern to me.

EN: Why isn't the debt of concern?

Post: The reason a recession occurs in the first place is that there *is not enough* borrowing in the economy. The saving (nonspending) of households and businesses is not sufficiently being borrowed by consumers and firms and being respent. Thus government must borrow a portion of this saving and spend it to keep income from falling.

In return for their voluntary loans to the government, businesses and individuals receive assets that provide interest income. These assets — the public debt — are in the form of U.S. savings bonds and Treasury bills and notes. Remember that for every dollar of debt (liability), a dollar of assets exists. These assets are voluntarily held and are relatively risk-free devices through which people can earn a return. We should change the name of the accumulated budget deficits that we now call "the national debt" to "the national assets." This title would be just as accurate and much less threatening to people.

EN: Do you completely reject the idea that the federal government should balance its budget?

Post: No. The federal government should balance its budget only when full employment and steady growth exist in the economy. We might even need an actual budget *surplus* when the economy is booming and producing rapid inflation.

EN: Wouldn't the economy extract itself from a recession — balance itself — if it were given enough time?

Post: Maybe. Many economists thought so in the early 1930s, but it took a decade and a world war to end that "slump." In the meantime, the economy lost income and output that can never be regained, and millions of people suffered tremendous hardship.

EN: It is your position, then, that government must take action or recessions will get progressively worse?

Post: Not quite. Some features of the economy help slow the growth of a recession. These features are called *automatic stabilizers*. They are programs or laws, already in place, that tend to promote a budget deficit during a recession and a surplus during rapid inflation.

EN: Can you provide an example of an automatic stabilizer?

Post: Several exist, but the income tax is the best example. A large percentage of all federal revenues comes from this source. As a recession occurs, people are laid off from their jobs and national income declines. This causes an automatic reduction in federal tax revenues and enables consumption spending to remain higher than would otherwise be the case. This cushions the recession and keeps it from becoming more severe.

Other automatic stabilizers include unemployment compensation, food stamps — anything that maintains or increases purchasing power in the economy as a recession occurs.

EN: Most of this discussion has dealt with recessions. What about inflation? Does fiscal policy have a role in solving this problem?

Post: The same tool — taxes, spending, and control of investment incentives — can be used to combat demand-pull inflation.

Demand-pull inflation is caused by excessive spending in the economy. Total demand at the existing price level is too large relative to the economy's capacity to produce goods and sources. Prices are *pulled* upward as people compete with one another to buy the limited products and resources. The best way to see this is to return to Figure 16-1 and draw in a substantial rightward movement of the aggregate demand curve. At the existing price level P_1 the quantity demanded will now exceed the quantity supplied. Hence, the price level will rise. Put differently, prices will be pulled upward as people compete with one another to buy the limited goods and services. An interesting twist on this analysis is that fiscal policy also can be used to fight inflation.

EN: Can you be more specific?

Post: The government can use the reverse of the policies used to counteract recession. Government could *reduce* its own expenditures, *increase* taxes to reduce consumption spending, or *eliminate* the special provisions that encourage investment spending. The budget should be balanced, or even moved into surplus, to withdraw spending from the economy.

EN: Wouldn't these actions cause unemployment?

Post: That is a definite possibility, at least in the short run. Ideally, the brakes could be applied gently, so as to slow the economy and price rises without causing a major recession. Too often in the past the government hit the brakes so hard the driver went flying through the windshield.

EN: Sounds to me that you are talking about fine-tuning again.

Post: Well, let's call it "smooth braking." That sounds better to me. The best course is to keep inflation low in the first place. That way we won't have to worry about how much pressure to apply to the brakes. Don't let the vehicle get moving faster than it can be safely driven.

EN: You mentioned supply shocks as causing cost-push inflation. Fiscal policy can't do much to prevent that type of inflation, can it?

Post: Remember, inflation normally is not a one-time rise in the price level; it is a continuous month-to-month, year-to-year phenomenon. A supply shock might cause the price level to rise, but inflation can continue for a long period only under conditions of rising aggregate demand. Thus fiscal policy has a role to play in ensuring that a supply shock does not set off continuing inflation. Monetary policy is also a key element here, but you asked me to confine my remarks to fiscal policy.

ALTERNATIVE VIEWS

EN: Isn't it true that many economists believe that fiscal policy has little direct impact on the economy? They feel that the money supply action of the Federal Reserve Board, not fiscal policy, is the major influence on the economy.

Post: Yes, these economists are known as monetarists. They have made significant contributions to our understanding of the economy. They theorize that changes in the rate of growth of the money supply cause recessions and expansions in the economy and that a too rapid increase in the money supply causes inflation. They conclude that fiscal policy fails to affect the economy unless it forces changes in the rate of monetary growth. It's the change in monetary growth, then, not fiscal policy, that has an effect on the national economy.

EN: You don't subscribe to that view?

Post: No, not fully. I agree that excessive growth of the money supply will cause inflation, but I don't agree that this is the only cause of inflation. Nor do I agree that fiscal policy is totally ineffective. Fiscal policy can change the amount of *spending* in the economy, independent of changes in the money supply, by increasing the rate at which a given money supply is spent.

Monetary policy is a useful tool in aiding fiscal policy. Both are needed to achieve a healthy, stable economy. That means setting government expenditure and taxing policies to bring total demand in equilibrium with the economy's capacity to supply goods and services. It also means avoiding wide swings in the growth of the stock of money.

EN: What is meant by the term *crowding out,* as it relates to fiscal policy?

Post: When the economy is in a recession and government reduces taxes to stimulate spending, its tax revenues fall and it needs to borrow funds to finance the budget deficit. Some economists contend that the increased government borrowing competes with private borrowing and drives interest rates up. The higher interest rates reduce private borrowing and spending. Thus the intended impact of the fiscal policy tax cut is thwarted to some degree: consumption and investment spending do not increase to the extent envisioned.

EN: Isn't there also a tendency for the value of the dollar to rise?

Post: Yes, there is also a crowding out effect that works through the international economy. The higher U.S. interest rate is attractive to foreigners, who desire to increase their holdings of American stocks and bonds. To get these securities, foreigners exchange their currencies for U.S. dollars. The demand for U.S. dollars therefore rises, increasing the international value of the dollar. This dollar appreciation means that foreigners see our goods as costing them more than previously. They need to use more units of their currencies to buy our exports. Conversely, American consumers need fewer dollars to buy imported goods. In short, American exports fall and American imports rise, each contributing to a decline in real output produced in the United States. This crowding out of so-called *net exports* (exports *minus* imports) partially offsets the positive impact of the fiscal policy.

EN: Aren't these fatal flaws of fiscal policy?

Post: They need not be if the monetary authorities help out by increasing the supply of money. The increase in money supply will keep interest rates from rising.

EN: But if the monetary authorities "help out" by increasing the supply of money, won't that just cause inflation in the long run?

Post: That's the monetarist view, but I'm not convinced that, under all circumstances, an increase in the rate of growth of the money supply is inflationary. Increased money growth can reduce interest rates and cause aggregate demand to rise. If the economy is operating far below its capacity, the increased aggregate demand will increase production and employment, not prices.

EN: New classical economists also criticize active fiscal policy, don't they? Would you enlighten us?

Post: Like the classical economists of old, these economists believe that the economy will not stray for long from price stability and full employment. *Price level surprises*—unexpected changes in the price level—*will* alter the level of real GNP, but the economy has self-correcting mechanisms that will return it to full employment and price level stability in the long run.

For instance, suppose that AD shifts leftward in Figure 16-1 because of an unexpected decline in foreign purchases of American exports. Real output will temporarily decline, but this decline in output will cause input prices such as wages to fall. When input prices fall, the AS curve will shift rightward, the price level will fall, and the equilibrium level of national output will return to its full employment level.

Economists disagree on how quickly such an adjustment will occur in the absence of fiscal policy. The new classical economists believe that the AS adjustment will be relatively swift; Keynesian economists believe that it may take years. I fit in the Keynesian camp. In my judgment, wages and other input prices tend to be inflexible downward, except under conditions of very severe recession. In general, we just don't see quick cuts in wages when national output falls. Therefore, when a recession occurs, fiscal and monetary policy may be needed to move the economy back toward full employment.

EN: Your colleagues refer to you as "the wizard of macroeconomics." That is obviously meant as a compliment. There is a problem with that description, though. The dictionary lists two definitions for *wizard.* They are (1) a person especially gifted at a particular activity and (2) a person who engages in deception, magic, and witchcraft. Which definition applies?

Post: It depends on what you want to believe, I suppose. A little skepticism is always healthy. Our knowledge about macroeconomic aspects of the economy is still developing.

STUDY QUESTIONS

1. Suppose that GNP is $5 billion in a hypothetical economy in 1990, whereas the same goods would have cost $2 billion in the base year, 1982. What is the price index in 1990? By what percent did the price level rise between 1982 and 1990 in this example?

2. Define the term *GNP*. Which of the following are final goods or services, as opposed to intermediate goods or services, in measuring GNP?
   a. A new automobile bought by an individual
   b. The shoelaces used in new shoes

   c. The oil used to refine gasoline
   d. A haircut purchased from a barber
3. Why does the aggregate demand curve slope downward and to the right? Cite a factor that would shift the AD curve to the right. Cite a different factor that would shift the AD curve to the left.
4. Why does the aggregate supply curve, in general, slope upward? Why does the AS curve have a segment that is vertical? Cite a factor that would shift the AS curve downward and to the right. Cite a different factor that would shift the AS curve upward and to the left.
5. What is fiscal policy? Is a decline in tax revenues resulting from a recession a fiscal policy action? Explain.
6. Suppose the marginal propensity to consume for the economy is .8. By how much will consumption spending increase if taxes are reduced by $20 billion?
7. Use the aggregate demand and supply model to show
   a. demand-pull inflation
   b. cost-push inflation
   c. supply-side economics
   d. expansionary fiscal policy
   e. contractionary fiscal policy
8. Explain: "Our grandchildren inherit 'national assets' in the form of Treasury bills, notes, and U.S. savings bonds that equal the amount of national debt inherited."
9. What is meant by the term "crowding out" and how might this problem reduce the effectiveness of fiscal policy?
10. List and discuss two time lags involved in undertaking fiscal policy.
11. How does the multiplier concept examined in Chapter 15 relate to fiscal policy?
12. Explain the differences between monetarist and Keynesian views on the causes of economic instability.
13. In what respect are the views held by the monetarists and the new classical theorists the same?

17

MONEY: IT GROWS ON T'S

The Economics of Money and Its Creation

Concepts and Terms Examined in This Chapter

1. Money
2. Demand Deposits
3. M1, M2
4. Near-money
5. Liquidity
6. Federal Reserve System
7. Reserve Requirement
8. Excess Reserves
9. Adverse Clearing Balance
10. Fractional Reserve System
11. Money Supply
12. Banking Multiplier

"The computer is doing some weird things today," stated Bill Williams to his fellow computer operator. "It's slow and sluggish."

"Maybe we should get the maintenance people to look at it," Dave Grey responded.

"Let's run a program and see if we can identify the problem ourselves," Williams suggested. Then he quipped, "It's spring, and it probably has its mind on something else."

"Probably has its mind on something else"—very funny. Williams thinks he's a real comedian. If he only realized that his diagnosis is partially accurate. I *do* have my mind on something else. I would like to go on the lecture circuit and tell my story about the supply of money. Say, maybe *you* would be willing to hear my story.

Oh, first I should tell you who I am. I'm a computer. I might add (or subtract, multiply, divide) that I'm one of the best in the business. I work for the Federal Reserve System in Washington, D.C., and keep track of the nation's money supply. The work is boring, routine, and repetitious, but the Fed is a decent employer. My only real concern is that everyone here seems to be preoccupied with money.

My employer, the Federal Reserve System, is a powerful institution, but most people know little about it. The Fed was established in 1913 to oversee the monetary and banking system of the United States. It supplies the economy with currency (Federal Reserve notes) and regulates the overall supply of money. I'll tell you about that in a bit. (Computer students, please pardon the pun.)

COMPONENTS OF THE FEDERAL RESERVE SYSTEM

The Federal Reserve System consists of three basic components. The major policymaking body is the Board of Governors, which is composed of seven people, each appointed by the president of the United States to a 14-year term. The terms are staggered, so that every two years a new appointment is necessary. The Board of Governors gets advice from the Open Market Committee and a group called the Federal Advisory Council, but ultimately the board itself is responsible for making the important decisions affecting the availability of credit in the banking system and the supply of money in the economy.

The board's decisions are administered through the second component of the system. That component comprises the 12 regional Federal Reserve banks and their 12 branches throughout the nation. The country is divided into 12 regions, and each region has a Federal Reserve bank. These are bankers' banks that serve commercial banks; they do not directly serve private individuals.

BAD COMMAND OR FILENAME

Excuse me. That wasn't intended for you. Williams just inserted a misspelled command. They put garbage in and I flash them an error message. Makes them mad, but I'm a stickler on punctuation and grammar. . . . Oh, same to you, Williams!

The third part of the system consists of the thousands of banks and thrift institutions that provide accounts on which depositors can write checks. Included are commercial banks, savings and loans, and credit unions. By law, these depository institutions are required to maintain cash deposits (reserves) in Federal Reserve banks. They also are permitted to borrow from the Federal Reserve banks, just as individuals borrow from banks, savings and loans, and credit unions.

Additionally, the Fed's 12 regional banks clear checks for the bank and thrift institutions located in different areas of the country. For example, say that you live in Enid, Oklahoma, and write a $30 check on your account held at the First National Bank of Enid. Say that the check is made out and sent to *Newsleak Magazine* in New York City, and Chase Manhattan sends it to the Federal Reserve Bank of New York, which "clears" it. That means that the Fed channels the check back to the Enid bank and transfers the $30 from your account to the *Newsleak* account in New York.

I will summarize the three layers of the Federal Reserve System in a diagram (Figure 17-1). Notice that I am at the top of the heap, because I work for the Board of Governors. I keep track of the money supply in the country; without me, they would have to make monetary policy without any reliable information. In all due modesty, that means that I am probably the most important part of this system. That's why I'm itching to tell my story.

DEFINING MONEY

I'm sure you realize that money is an elusive commodity. People want it only to get rid of it; they spend it once they have it. It burns holes in their pockets, or it slips through their fingers.

Actually, money has only three functional uses. First, it serves as a *medium of exchange*. It is the means by which things having economic value can be bought and sold without resorting to direct barter (actual physical exchange of the products, such as cattle for bread). People don't really want money for its own sake. They want it so that they can exchange it for things they do want.

Money also serves as a *standard of value*; it is a common denominator in the exchange process. If a textbook costs $30, then you know that its value in trade

Figure 17-1   Components of the Federal Reserve System

The Federal Reserve System consists of three parts: the Board of Governors, 12 Federal Reserve banks, and thousands of commercial banks and thrift institutions. The chair of the Board of Governors serves as the chief spokesperson for the Fed.

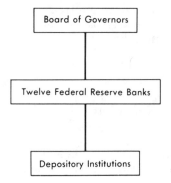

is twice that of a $15 concert ticket. Placing values in monetary terms allows quick comparisons between the relative trading values of commodities.

Finally, money acts as a *store of value*; it holds value over time. Money earned last summer stored value until you spent it this school year. The fact that people are willing to maintain money in checking accounts and billfolds for periods of weeks or months attests to their recognition that money is a way to store value.

Remember anything that acts as a medium of exchange, standard of value, and store of value is actually money.

FILE CREATION ERROR

Well, they're all only human; it's just that Williams is more human than others.

Historically, many items have been used as money. Some North American Indians used beads, some African tribes used stones, early Europeans utilized cattle, later shifting to gold and silver. French trappers employed the first "folding money"—furs. Money is anything that performs the functions of money and is solely accepted as such. It's as simple as that.

What is money in the United States? I should know, I'm measuring its volume daily. Money is all currency, defined as coins and Federal Reserve notes in circulation, plus all bank accounts on which checks can be written. These *checkable deposits* include conventional checking accounts (demand deposits), negotiable orders of withdrawal (NOW accounts), automatic transfer service (ATS accounts), travelers' checks, and share drafts. Economists term this definition of money M1.

$$M1 = \text{Currency in circulation} + \text{Checkable deposits}$$

A broader definition of money, M2, adds noncheckable savings deposits, money market certificates, money market mutual fund shares, and other similar financial assets to the M1 definition. For some purposes, M2 is a preferred measure of the money supply, but because M1 remains the most often cited money supply statistic, I will use it in my discussion.

The decision on what to include and exclude in defining money is quite arbitrary. Several items possess some attributes of money. We have already mentioned saving account deposits. *Near-monies* include government securities, the cash value of life insurance policies, and common stock. The distinction between money, officially defined as M1, and near-monies is the degree of liquidity. *Liquidity is the ability of an item to be consistently and quickly exchanged for products and services.* You can spend cash or write a check and directly get products in exchange. But you cannot take a U.S. savings bond to a store and use it for payment. You must first convert the bond to money (currency or a checking deposit) and then go to the store. Money is highly liquid; near-monies are less liquid than money but more liquid than typical goods.

MONEY CREATION: AN INDIVIDUAL BANK

Next, I'll tell you something that only the insiders know about money—a real exposé. *Commercial banks create money out of thin air!* That's right! In fact, I've been recording such actions while I've been speaking to you. It happens all the time. Here—I'll print out and explain a portion of two transactions that just occurred. This is the first change in the T-account (balance sheet) for the 18th National Bank of Biloxi, Mississippi:

The 18th National Bank of Biloxi Balance Sheet Changes

Assets (Things Owned)		Liabilities (Claims against Things Owned)	
Cash	+$1,000	Checkable Deposits	+$1,000

The bank's assets increased by $1,000 because a Biloxi businessman, I. D. Posit, put $1,000 of currency into his checking account. (He received the $1,000 by selling a U.S. bond to the Federal Reserve, but don't worry about that yet.) The deposit increased the bank's assets (things owned) by $1,000, but also increased its liabilities (claims against things owned) by $1,000. The bank must pay $1,000 on demand when the businessman writes a check on his account for that amount. Balance sheets must always be balanced, and this is no exception. Assets increased by $1,000 in the T-account, and liabilities increased by the same sum.

Excuse me, Williams, bless his heart, just fed in a monster program. I'll have to pause, because it requires all my capacity ....
....
....
....

As I was saying, the Biloxi bank found that it had $1,000 of new cash and demand deposits. Banks realize that most people do not withdraw all their demand deposits by requesting coins or currency. They hold only a fraction of their money in the form of currency. That means that banks don't have to keep a dollar of currency in their vaults for every dollar that depositors have in checking accounts. Because banks know that not everyone is going to want cash at once, the $1,000 of new cash in the Biloxi bank could support *more* than $1,000 of checkable deposits. The Biloxi bank could earn additional profits if it could determine some way to increase demand deposits further and make an interest return in the process. It can. It does.

Shortly after the new $1,000 of cash was deposited, a second transaction occurred in a separate part of the bank. Ima Debtor entered the establishment and requested an $800 loan. She had excellent credit references, and, after checking the bank's financial situation, the loan officer granted her the loan. But the loan was not in the form of currency. Rather, the $800 was deposited directly into Ima Debtor's checking account at the bank. The transactions appeared as follows on the bank's T-account:

The 18th National Bank of Biloxi Balance Sheet Changes

Assets		Liabilities	
Loans	+$800	Checkable Deposits	+$800

The bank increased both its assets (loans) and liabilities (checkable deposits) by $800. And, because checkable deposits are money, *the bank increased the money supply by $800. The 18th National Bank of Biloxi created $800 of money out of thin air*! The total amount of cash on hand did not increase. The bank simply *monetized* Ima Debtor's debt; it turned her promise to pay into $800 of money. The transaction was wise banking policy, perfectly legal, and fully *expected* by the Federal Reserve money managers. Money creation by commercial banks is a proper economic function in this economy. *Banks make loans, and in the process, create money in the form of new checkable deposits.* As they say in the computer business, store that in your memory bank!

Now look at the Biloxi bank's balance sheet. It shows both the original currency deposit of $1,000 (transaction 1) and the $800 loan (transaction 2):

The 18th National Bank of Biloxi Balance Sheet Changes

Assets		Liabilities	
1. Cash	+$1,000	1. Checkable Deposits	+$1,000
2. Loans	+ 800	2. Checkable Deposits	+ 800
Total	+$1,800	Total	+$1,800

The total money supply is $1,800, even though originally the bank received only $1,000 of new currency. *Note:* Currency held within the bank is not considered to be money, so the money supply in this example is $1,800, not $2,800. This example is just one of millions that I have accounted for during the telling of my story. The fact is that debt monetization, or bank money creation, occurs daily and is the major source of money in the economy. It is banks that create most of the money supply, not the people in the mints and printing offices who coin nickels and dimes and print currency.

Now, in all fairness to accuracy, I must divulge that banks destroy money, too. The money is not burned or mutilated beyond recognition but is destroyed when bank loans are repaid. It's just the reverse process of what I described before. When Ima Debtor pays her $800 loan, the bank's balance sheet will show − $800 in the loan account on the asset side, and − $800 in checkable deposits (money) on the liability side. Eight hundred dollars of money vanishes into thin air. But you can bet that if the 18th National feels it still has enough cash reserves to meet the cash requirements of its customers, it will reloan the $800 to someone else, thus recreating the money.

This whole process raises an important question. If commercial banks can create money, how can the Federal Reserve System control the size of the money supply? The answer is that the Fed has placed limits on the amount of this money-creating activity. A *reserve requirement* mandated by law requires banks to have cash reserves, either in the bank or in their Federal Reserve Bank account, equal to or greater than a fixed percentage of their total checkable deposits. This legal reserve requirement varies according to the size of the bank. I could handle the exact percentages, but, for your convenience, permit me to assume that the requirement is 20 percent. That figure is higher than the actual existing reserve requirement but is a nice round number to work with throughout my discussion.

A commercial bank must have *actual cash reserves* equal to or greater than the *required reserves*. If a bank has $100,000 in cash, then theoretically, it could have loans and checkable deposits equal to $500,000 ($100,000 ÷ $500,000 = 20 percent).

It is easy to see why the United States banking system is called a *fractional reserve system*. Banks do not legally have to back up each dollar of demand deposit with a dollar of actual currency. If all the people in the society tried to exchange their checking account deposits for cash at once, the banks would be able to pay only a fraction of the total deposits.

Such "bank panics" occurred occasionally in the old days. The worst bank run took place during the first stage of the Great Depression of the 1930s. Banks went under, depositors lost their money, and debtors had their loans recalled. Today, the threat of a general bank panic is a minor one. The government, through the Federal Deposit Insurance Corporation (FDIC), insures that accounts will be paid in full up to $100,000. This insurance alleviates people's concern for the safety of their checking account deposits. If a bank run began in spite if FDIC insurance, the Fed would simply supply the banks with as much currency as they needed to meet the demand. My bosses don't really care in what form people want their money—it can be cash or checking accounts. They are concerned about only the total amount of the money supply in the economy. If people want more of their money in the form of currency and less in checking account balances, the Fed is willing to oblige.

To summarize, then, the American banking system is a fractional reserve system. Depositors' accounts are given protection by special laws and procedures, not by the reserve requirement. *The major reason for the reserve requirement is that it allows the Fed to control the total volume of bank credit and the supply of money in the economy.*

> *A McDonald's hamburger weighs 1.6 ounces, is 0.221 inches thick and 3.1875 inches in diameter, and is placed on a 4.25-inch bun. . . . Now what does that have to do with the money supply? Nothing—and I apologize for the interruption. Williams just told Grey that he was going out for a McDonald's hamburger and I momentarily let my mind wander. Sorry. Back to the money supply.*

An important distinction exists between the extent to which an individual commercial bank can increase the money supply and the extent to which the banking system as a whole can do so. An individual bank can safely increase loans and create new money when it has *excess reserves*. It has *excess reserves* when its currency plus deposits held by the Fed are more than 20 percent of its checkable deposits (excess reserves = actual reserves − required reserves). That was the situation at the Biloxi bank when I. D. Posit entered $1,000 of currency into his bank account. That action increased checkable deposits by $1,000, but the bank was required by law to have only $200 of cash reserves for the $1,000 of new checkable deposits (20 percent of $1,000). Consequently, excess reserves of $800 remained (actual reserves of $1,000 minus required reserves of $200).

A bank can safely lend out its excess reserves, and that was exactly what the Biloxi bank did when it made an $800 loan to Ima Debtor. To repeat, *individual banks can safely expand the money supply by an amount equal to their preloan excess reserves.* But why couldn't the Biloxi bank continue to make loans? Its $1,000 of new cash reserves could theoretically support $4,000 of new loans, not just $800.

This is true in theory, but in reality, expansion of loans beyond $800 by the bank would be extremely risky. The reasons: *adverse clearing balances*. When Ima Debtor received her loan of $800, it was in the form of an $800 addition to her checking account. But I have recorded another transaction involving that $800. After receiving the loan, Ima stopped at the business office at Louisiana State University and wrote an $800 check for tuition, books, and some living costs. The university then deposited the check into its account at the Baton Rouge Bank of Commerce.

Now the idea of *adverse clearing balances* is demonstrated. The 18th National Bank of Biloxi, Ima Debtor's bank, had to pay the Baton Rouge Bank of Commerce $800 of cash reserves. This net loss of reserves from one bank to another caused by the clearing of a check is an adverse clearing balance. The 18th National's balance sheet change is now shown in the third set of entries.

The 18th National Bank of Biloxi Changes in Balance Sheet

Assets		Liabilities	
1. Cash	+ $1,000	1. Checkable Deposits	+ $1,000
2. Loans	+ 800	2. Checkable Deposits	+ 800
3. Cash	– 800	3. Checkable Deposits	– 800

The 18th National lost $800 of reserves and witnessed an $800 decline in checkable deposits because of the adverse clearing balance, *but note that it still remains safely within the 20 percent reserve requirement*. Cash reserves are $200 ($1,000 – $800). Deposits are $1,000. The bank is still meeting the 20 percent reserve requirement. If the bank had lent Ima Debtor more than its excess reserves of $800, then the adverse clearing balance would have left the bank in a position in which it did not have adequate reserves. But because the 18th National limited its expansion of loans and the money supply to $800, the amount of its *excess* reserves, the adverse clearing balance did not present a problem.

THE BANKING SYSTEM AND MONEY CREATION

I shall now make another revelation that only money insiders realize. *That which is true for an individual bank is not true for the banking system as a whole.* Although each individual bank can safely create new deposits only to the extent that it has excess reserves, all the commercial banks, taken together, expand the money supply *by a multiple of excess reserves*.

It took me some time to comprehend this when I first went to work here at the Fed. I noticed how carefully individual banks seemed to adhere to the maxim, "Lend out any excess reserves, but don't lend beyond that." But I also noticed that when new cash reserves were injected into the banking system by Federal Reserve polices, the money supply increased far beyond the amount of new excess reserves. This was a real puzzle. However, I must proudly say that I had the capacity to sort out this apparent contradiction. I'd like to share this insight with you.

Individual banks can have adverse clearing balances, *but the banking system as a whole cannot experience this feature*. For instance, the 18th National Bank of Biloxi lost $800 of cash reserves to the Baton Rouge Bank of Commerce when Ima Debtor wrote out a check to the university. But the 18th National's loss of $800 of reserves was the Baton Rouge Bank of Commerce's gain of the same amount. *The total cash reserves* in the *total banking system* did not change as a result of the transaction. The $800 of new money originally created by the 18th National when it made its loan to Ima Debtor was still alive and well. The Bank of Commerce now had $800 of new cash reserves and $800 of new checkable deposits. The Bank of Commerce, however, did not need $800 reserves to back up the $800 of new checking account money in the university account. It needed only 20 percent of $800 ($160) as reserves. The remainder, $640, was *excess reserves.* And even though I haven't yet recorded the next transaction by the Bank of Commerce, I can tell you what will happen. They will lend out their excess reserve of $640 and create $640 of new deposits—still more new money. The money supply will move from $800 of newly created money to $800 + $640 = $1,440 of newly created money. Here, I'll print out the Baton Rouge Bank of Commerce T-account situation:

Baton Rouge Bank of Commerce Changes in Balance Sheet

Assets		Liabilities	
Cash	+$800	Checkable Deposits	+$800
Loans	+ 640	Checkable Deposits	+ 640

Now, as seen in the balance sheet, the $800 of new reserves for the Baton Rouge bank allows it to increase its loans by $640, because it has that amount of excess reserves. The process continues throughout the banking system as reserves flow from bank to bank. The original increase in cash of $1,000 placed in the bank by I. D. Posit caused initial excess reserves of $800 and ends up increasing the money supply by $4,000. Carefully follow the process shown in Table 17-1 as I print it.

If you understand this diagram, you have my money secrets completely understood. The $1,000 of new currency deposited originally produced excess

Table 17-1 Expansion of the Money Supply by the Banking System

	Bank	New Deposits	Total Reserves	Required Reserves	Excess Reserves	New Loans (Money)
Bank 1	18th National	$1,000	$1,000	$ 200	$ 800	$ 800
	Payment to university ← Loan to Ima Debtor ←					
Bank 2	Baton Rouge Bank of Commerce	$ 800	$ 800	$ 160	$ 640	$ 640
	Seller deposits ← Purchase ← Loan ←					
Bank 3	First Seattle	$ 640	$ 640	$ 128	$ 512	$ 512
	Process continues until new ← Loan ← loan becomes insignificantly small					
	Final outcome	$5,000	$5,000	$1,000	$4,000	$4,000

reserves of $800. This excess of $800 provided the base through which the total U.S. banking system expanded the money supply by 5 × $800, or $4,000. This is new money: money created out of thin air by the commercial bankers. Each bank lent out only its excess reserves, but the composite result of that behavior was a multiple expansion of the money supply. The money expansion formula is 1/reserve requirement. In this case, the banking multiplier is 1/.20 = 5. This means that an increase in *excess reserves* in the system of $1 will cause an increase in the money supply of $5 if the banks can find willing loan customers.

I should add a few qualifications to make sure I'm providing completely accurate information. No one likes a simplistic computer. The expansion process may be short-circuited. A borrower may insist on taking all loan funds in currency rather than establishing a checking account in that bank. Or a bank may not be able to find a worthy loan customer. In either situation, the banker is not able to monetize debt and create a new checking account.

Another important thing to remember is that the expansion process takes time. My example took minutes to explain, seconds for me to compute, but in the economy, three or four rounds of money expansion may take months. Finally, I must emphasize that the process operates in both directions. Reductions in reserves in the system may mean that banks will have to limit their new loans below those being paid off. This will reduce their checkable deposits to a level that is consistent with the available reserves. Otherwise the banks will discover that they are not meeting the legal reserve requirement. Multiple contraction of the money supply—money vanishing into thin air—is simply the money creation process working in reverse and occurs when loan payoffs exceed new loans.

Excuse me. The Fed just fed in some information about their latest decisions on monetary policy. Let me store this information and I'll get back to you. . . .

MONETARY POLICY: A PREVIEW

Say, that was interesting. Let me tell you about it. But, first, I should explain the term *monetary policy*. The Fed is responsible for maintaining proper growth of the money supply, and the policies it uses are called monetary policy. If the money supply is increased too quickly, too much money will chase too few goods and prices will rise. Excessive growth of the money supply is the cause of inflation. On the other hand, if the money supply grows too slowly, economic expansion may be choked off, and the economy may be thrust into a recession and unemployment. The Fed is continually undertaking actions to see that neither extreme occurs. But, if either inflation or unemployment does occur, the Fed usually tries to counter the problem. For example, if the economy is in a recession and experiencing high rates of unemployment, the Fed usually moves to an *easy-money policy*— one that increases the money supply. If rapid inflation is occurring, the Fed moves to restrict the growth of the money supply.

The Fed can determine the rate of growth of the money supply because it has the power to change the amount of reserves and excess reserves in the system. We've just seen how increased or decreased reserves have a multiple effect on the amount of money in the economy.

Well, the Fed policy statement that I just stored stated that the Fed desires to increase the growth rate of the money supply at this time. It recommends increased purchases of U.S. government securities to accomplish this. Such purchases are directed by the Fed's Open Market Committee and are naturally called open-market operations. I didn't intend to get into this, but because it fits in with the Biloxi example we have been using, I couldn't resist.

Do you recall how that entire money creation process started? I told you not to worry about it at the time, so perhaps you don't remember. If my memory serves me right, I. D. Posit of Biloxi *sold a U.S. bond to the Fed for $1,000 of currency.* This action placed $1,000 of new cash reserves into the system. Well, when I. D. cashed in that bond, he was doing exactly what the Fed wants people to do when it tries to expand the money supply. It "buys" bonds from banks and individuals and pays cash for them. The bonds were *not* money and could not be used as reserves by banks. But the cash the Fed pays for them *is* money and provides new reserves that support a multiple expansion of the money supply. That's the open-market operation portion of monetary policy in action. It works in both directions, of course. (Chapter 18 discusses open-market operations and other tools of monetary policy in some detail.)

FILE CAN NOT BE COPIED ONTO ITSELF

My error message was itself in error. I see now that William's command was, in fact, correct. That will cause trouble. Oh well, I can use a good checkup and some rest. Moonlighting as an economist is creating diminishing marginal returns. To tell you the truth, I'm Fed up to here!

"The computer errored again," declared Dave Grey.

"What's the problem now?" asked Williams.

"I just got an error statement, but when I ran the command again, the computer accepted it and completed the task. The thing has also been spewing out extraneous printouts every now and then that seem to be totally unrelated to any of our programs."

"That can't happen."

"I know it can't, but it does," Grey stated. "The printouts seem to be about money supply expansion."

"You're kidding!" exclaimed Williams.

"No!"

"Do they make any sense?"

"In fact, they do," Grey responded. "It's a decent description of how banks create checking deposit money."

"It must be something from some past program that it failed to properly delete," said Williams. "That does it! I'll call the maintenance people and have them get out here immediately."

Perhaps I should sign off. Ah . . . R&R! And then on to the lecture circuit. I wonder if Williams would be willing to be my operator and straight man?

STUDY QUESTIONS

1. What is the composition of the money supply, M1, in the United States? Based on this definition, which of the following are officially money? Officially *not* money?

a. A $5 Federal Reserve note
b. A U.S. savings bond
c. A deposit in a credit union on which a share draft can be written
d. A gold bar
e. A copper penny
f. A checking account entry (demand deposit)
g. Currency held within a bank

2. "Money is what money does." What does money do?

3. How can a commercial bank create money (other than illegally counterfeiting currency)? How can a bank destroy money (other than burning currency)?

4. Assume the following T-account and a 20 percent reserve requirement:

Bank A

Assets		Liabilities	
Cash	$ 200	Checkable Deposits	$1,000
Loans	800		
	$1,000		$1,000

a. Is this bank legally meeting the reserve requirement?
b. If someone deposited $2,000 of new cash in the bank (cash increased by $2,000 and checkable deposits by $2,000), how much *excess* reserves would the bank have?
c. By how much could this bank safely expand its loans under the circumstances? Explain.
d. By how much would the money supply increase in the banking system as a whole as a result of the $2,000 of new cash?

5. Banks and thrift institutions possess only about one-fifth of our checking account deposits in the form of cash. What features of the American banking system prevent bank panics (runs on the banks)?

6. Suppose that the Bank of Boston has excess reserves of $5,000 and checkable deposits of $200,000. Assuming a reserve requirement of 25 percent, what are the firm's actual reserves?

7. Suppose that Congress passed a law changing the present fractional reserve system (approximately 12 percent) to one that required 100 percent reserves for all checkable deposits. If this were the only change in the law, what do you think would happen to the money supply as a result of the change? Explain.

8. Rework the expansion of the money supply shown in Table 17-1 on the assumption that the reserve requirement is 10 percent, rather than 20 percent. How are you able to determine the values listed in the "Final outcome" row without continuing the expansion process to its end? Hint: What is the new banking multiplier?

9. If you deposit a $20 bill into your checking account at a commercial bank that has a 12 percent reserve requirement, by how much will the bank's excess reserves rise?

10. Suppose that a person holding an account in the Bank of Bunco writes a check on that account and the recipient of the check deposits it in another bank. What impact will these transactions have on the Bank of Bunco's (a) checkable deposits and (b) total amount of required reserves?

18

IT'S A SOBERING EXPERIENCE WHEN MONEY GETS TIGHT

The Economics of Monetary Policy

Concepts and Terms Examined in This Chapter

1. Federal Reserve Board
2. Open-Market Operations
3. Monetary Policy
4. Money Supply
5. Prime Interest Rate
6. Reserve Requirement
7. Discount Rate
8. Federal Funds Interest Rate
9. Monetarists
10. Nominal versus Real Interest Rate
11. Monetary Rule
12. Exchange Rates

Monetary policy consists of the deliberate actions taken by the Federal Reserve Board to change the rate of growth of the money supply. Such changes influence economic activity and therefore national income, national output, employment, and the price level. Monetary policy can be either restrictive (tight), expansionary (loose), or something in between. In the scenes that follow, a tight monetary policy is studied, but bear in mind that the principles discussed apply equally to situations in which the Federal Reserve is following an expansionary monetary policy.

The year 1981 is the setting for the scenes that follow. That year was chosen because it was a time of rapid inflation and tight monetary policy. The tight monetary policy eventually reduced inflation dramatically. How was the reduction accomplished? As you read the stories, look for the interrelationships that exist. The final scene integrates the material presented in the earlier scenes.

SCENE I: BUY OR WAIT?

Ronald Nielsen, a 35-year-old bricklayer, and his wife, Mary, a novelist, faced a difficult decision. The Nielsens had purchased a building site three years previously in suburban Denver, Colorado, with the expectation that eventually they would begin construction of a three-bedroom, split-level home. During those three years, the Nielsens had saved their money and had planned their house design. They were now ready to build. However, two factors complicated their plans. Mortgage loan money to finance construction was in short supply, and home-mortgage interest rates were extremely high.

The Nielsens had recently consulted a loan officer at Rocky Mountain Savings and Loan in Denver. There they discovered that conventional mortgage loan money, although in short supply, was available to those with superior credit ratings. The Nielsens qualified for a mortgage loan because of their above-average income, job security, and credit references. The terms of the proposed loan, however, came as a real shock. The savings and loan was willing to finance the $100,000 house if the Nielsens would pay $20,000 as a down payment (over and above the value of the lot). This would leave a loan of $80,000. The interest on the mortgage would be 17 percent annually. The Nielsens were amazed, disappointed, and disgruntled.

Just three years before, Ron and Mary had inquired about a mortgage loan at the same institution. At that time, the savings and loan was willing to accept a down payment of $10,000 to grant a 30-year mortgage at 10 percent. The difference between a 17 percent and 10 percent mortgage interest rate represents a substantial sum of money. An $80,000, 30-year loan at 17 percent would require a monthly payment in principal and interest of $1,140.80. At 10 percent, the payment would have been $702.06.

"The current mortgage rate and down payment terms suggest a 'let's wait' decision," stated Ron Nielsen. "However, there's another factor, and that's what makes the decision tough." The additional factor was the rising costs of constructing a house. Housing costs were increasing by over 10 percent annually, and most observers were forecasting similar increases in the near future. The Nielsens were concerned that their $100,000 house might cost them much more if they waited a year or more to build.

The Nielsens' dilemma was, "Should we build today at 17 percent, or should we wait for mortgage rates to fall, even though construction costs might be higher?" "It's a difficult decision," lamented Mary Nielsen, "and ironically, it must be made on the basis of factors we don't fully understand. Why has the mortgage rate increased by seven percentage points in just three years? What will be the situation one year from now? It's these unanswered questions that make things difficult."

SCENE II: INVESTING IN TREASURY BILLS

Fifty-seven-year-old Martha Wheeler, a newspaper copy editor in Baton Rouge, Louisiana, was also confronted with a problem. Ms. Wheeler's quandary was not how to spend money but, rather, how best to invest it. She had inherited $25,000 as a portion of her father's estate and wished to save those funds so that they would be available to supplement her pension when she retired in three years.

Ms. Wheeler had originally placed her $25,000 in a passbook savings account at a local savings and loan association. The risk-free account earned 7 percent interest and her money was relatively liquid; that is, she could withdraw her savings at any time without paying a penalty.

Martha was rightfully concerned that inflation was eating away at the real value of her savings. "You don't have to be a mathematical wizard to realize that, at a rate of inflation of 12 percent, I am actually losing purchasing power on my savings. I need to find a financial investment that pays more than the 7 percent being paid on my passbook account."

A close friend recommended that she use her $25,000 to purchase either land or common stock, on the premise that either might serve as a hedge against inflation. Ms. Wheeler rejected that advice because she felt that both were too risky. The value of common stock and land, she reasoned, can decline as well as increase, and land is not always easy to sell. "What if I need the money quickly and cannot find an immediate buyer?" she questioned.

Rejecting common stock or land, Martha decided to withdraw her $25,000 from the passbook account and place it in a money market mutual fund. She chose a fund that purchased large-denomination U.S. Treasury bills (short-term marketable certificates originally issued by the U.S. Treasury to finance the federal debt). Martha's $25,000 would buy shares in the fund and that way she could receive the high interest return available on those securities.

"There are many things I don't understand about Treasury bills—such as why they are yielding a substantially greater return now than they were one year ago," Ms. Wheeler admitted. "But a money market fund that buys those instruments appears to be the best place to put my savings."

SCENE III: POSTPONING CONSTRUCTION

Stephen B. Sutton, age 48, an executive for a Chicago-based manufacturer of fire extinguishers, was perplexed. Sutton had been given the final authority to make a recommendation on a proposed plant expansion. He and his associates were strongly convinced that the long-term demand for fire extinguishers would outstrip the capacity of the existing 40-year-old manufacturing plant.

Mr. Sutton had requested that an elaborate study of the proposal be undertaken, and it recently had been completed. The study had reached three important conclusions: (1) The existing production facilities would be inadequate to meet product demand in the decade ahead; (2) construction of a new plant would allow for the incorporation of the latest production techniques and would reduce per-unit production costs; and (3) the additional revenues resulting from expanded sales of extinguishers and the lower per-unit costs would ensure an adequate return on the massive investment that would be required. Still, Mr. Sutton was undecided. Interest rates had skyrocketed since the completion of the study.

The firm had planned to finance the new construction partly from internal funds (retained corporate profits) and partly from a commercial loan tentatively approved by a large national bank. The prime interest rate—the rate charged by banks to their best customers—had increased from 15 percent to 20 percent in less than a year.

"Our corporate projections indicated that we could expected an excellent rate of return on the investment," declared Mr. Sutton, "but that estimate was based upon a 15 percent cost of borrowing. At 20 percent, it's a different story."

Sutton admitted that the decision was complex. He and his fellow corporate officers were particularly concerned that double-digit inflation might continue and make it extremely costly to construct the plant in the future. The logic of the motto "Buy now, it will cost more tomorrow" seemed persuasive. "But on the other hand," reasoned Sutton, "if tight money and high interest rates continue, the construction of new office buildings and high-rise apartments will suffer dramatically. More than 70 percent of our extinguishers are purchased for use in new complexes of this type."

After numerous consultations with staff and managers, Sutton reached a conclusion: postpone construction. Sutton commented, "Hundreds of other firms in the country are reaching similar conclusions." He then quipped, "Can you imagine how many executives are having ulcer flare-ups and are forced to forgo their Friday afternoon happy hours? It's a sobering experience when money gets tight."

SCENE IV: WATCHING THE DOLLAR RISE

Todd Craig, import buyer for Ragtag, Inc., put down the *Wall Street Journal* and exclaimed, "Jackpot!" A year earlier, Mr. Craig had negotiated import agreements to buy assorted apparel over a two-year period from various companies located in a number of nations. These agreements established prices in terms of the currencies of the export nations. For example, the stipulated price of T-shirts from India was 35 rupees for each shirt; the price of rain jackets from South Korea, 7,000 won apiece; and so forth.

Mr. Craig's company regularly bought foreign currencies through large U.S. banks to make the payments required by the contracts. That is, Ragtag, Inc., used U.S. dollars to buy foreign currencies at current market exchange rates. As is true of other market prices, however, exchange rates can fluctuate over time. The *Wall Street Journal* article bore out this fact; its headline read, "Dollar Up Sharply."

Commenting to his assistant, Mr. Craig said, "In the past nine months, the value of the U.S. dollar has risen about 20 percent against the value of the currencies we buy to obtain Ragtag products. That, my friend, is very good news for us!"

The assistant nodded in agreement, knowing full well that the appreciation of the American dollar meant that Ragtag now needed fewer dollars to obtain units of foreign currencies such as yen, rupees, or pounds. Because each American dollar now could command more Indian rupees, Ragtag could buy each T-shirt from India with fewer dollars. Similarly, Ragtag could now purchase each raincoat from South Korea at less dollar expense because the dollar had appreciated in value. From Ragtag's perspective, the rise in the international value of the dollar had reduced the company's costs of obtaining imported apparel. Thus the dollar's appreciation had enhanced the firm's potential for profit.

"But why is the dollar appreciating so rapidly?" wondered the assistant. "I suppose I should know, so I had better not ask," he thought to himself.

SCENE V: CONTINUING THE BATTLE

The chair of the Federal Reserve Board, the economy's money managers, faced a monumental problem. The economy was experiencing two-digit inflation.

The Federal Reserve moved quickly into a restrictive monetary policy. Soon, tight money faced decision makers in the private economy. The restrictive monetary actions were designed to reduce the rate of growth of the money supply and purge the economy of excessive spending along with the inflation it fostered.

"The Federal Reserve will continue to follow a policy of restraining the growth of money and credit. We think that's absolutely fundamental to dealing with the inflation problem." Admittedly, the Fed's task of reducing the inflationary pressures without propelling the economy into a recession was a delicate one.

The Fed was not without its critics. Many observers were concerned that interest rates were already high and that a tight money policy would increase them further, causing further woes for interest-sensitive industries such as housing and autos. The chairman replied, "Let me say as strongly as I can that the way we're going to get those interest rates down is by persisting in policies that will indeed continue to bring the inflation rate down." He further indicated that the economy was still experiencing a veritable explosion of business loans, even at the high interest rates, and that restrictive monetary policy would be necessary until borrowing and spending were reduced to a noninflationary level. The Federal Reserve Board chairman was clearly prepared to continue the inflation battle with the monetary tools at his command.

SCENE VI: MAKING SENSE OF IT ALL

Dr. Michael Alston wished he did not have to cancel his tennis match that June day in 1981. "If only I didn't have that interview," he mumbled to himself as he entertained thoughts of a perfect forehand smash. In a short time, a gentleman carrying a tape recorder entered Alston's office. After the two exchanged pleasantries, the recorder was activated and the interview began. It was to be printed in full in *Economic News*.

Economic News: I appreciate that you were willing to cancel a tennis match to talk with us today, Professor.

Alston: Well, I appreciate this opportunity to visit with you and your readers.

EN: As you know, our topic is monetary policy. What exactly is it?

Alston: Monetary policy consists of actions taken by the Federal Reserve that either increase or decrease the rate of growth of the money supply. The purpose of the actions is to influence the level of national income, the rate of economic growth, and the rate of inflation in the economy.

EN: How are you defining *money supply*?

Alston: I'm using the M1 definition, all currency in circulation plus checkable deposits.

EN: The Fed is currently engaging in a *tight*-money policy. It is restricting the rate of growth of the money supply. How is the Fed able to accomplish this?

Alston: That's a somewhat complex area—do you want me to be specific?

EN: Sure, I'll interrupt if your answer gets too confusing.

Alston: OK. The Fed can reduce the money supply, or for that matter increase it, because it is able to change or influence the amount of "cash reserves" in the commercial banking system. We have a fractional reserve system that allows banks to make loans and, in the process, create checking account money. The banks take promises to pay—which aren't money—and convert them into currency or checkable deposits, which are the real thing. Of course, the banks can't create money in an unlimited fashion, since they are required by law to have a certain level of actual reserves for each dollar of checking account money. The smaller the amount of reserves in the system, the smaller the money supply, and vice versa.

EN: Are you saying that the Fed reduces the money supply by restricting the ability of the commercial banks to create money by making loans?

Alston: Exactly. When banks have made all the loans they are allowed, given their level of reserves, any action that reduces these reserves will force the banks to restrict the granting of new loans as previous ones are paid off. That reduces M1.

EN: But how does the Fed reduce reserves in the system?

Alston: Mainly through "open-market operations" undertaken by the Fed's Open Market Committee. When the Fed desires to restrict the money supply, it sells some of its U.S. security holdings in the open market to banks, corporations, or individuals.

EN: You mean Treasury bills and notes?

Alston: Precisely. These are securities issued by the Treasury when it borrows to finance budget deficits incurred by the federal government. The Federal Reserve System is a major holder of these securities because it is a major lender to the federal government.

When the Fed sells some of its U.S. securities holdings to the public or commercial lending institutions, the buyers exchange "money" (cash or checkable deposits) for pieces of paper (Treasury bills and notes) that are not money. The reserves in the banking system are therefore reduced and the growth of the money supply is restricted. In fact, this causes a multiple contraction of the money supply. (Recall our discussion of the banking multiplier in the previous chapter.)

EN: But how can the Fed be sure that people will purchase the securities they wish to sell?

Alston: The Fed floods the financial market with the securities. The increase in supply drives down the price of the securities and increases the interest yield. The price of a government security and its effective interest yield are inversely related. An example may help explain this relationship. A $100,000 Treasury bill is simply a promise by the government to pay $100,000 to the person who redeems the bill at a specific date, usually three months after the date of issue. The bill sells for less than $100,000, that is, at a discount, to allow the holder to earn an "interest" return. If it sells for $98,000, the holder gains $2,000, which is about a 2 percent return ($2,000/$98,000) for the three months (8 percent annually). So what happens when the Fed floods the financial markets trying to sell these government securities? The market price of the $100,000 bill falls to, say, $96,000 and the bill yields $4,000, or about 4 percent ($4,000/$98,000) over the three months (16 percent annually). As you can see, the price of these government securities and their interest yields are inversely related.

Remember now, the Fed's goal is to influence the money supply, not to sell U.S. securities at high prices. To attract buyers the Fed offers prices low enough—and therefore the yield high enough—to make the purchase of these securities a "good deal" for individuals, corporations, and pension funds. These buyers pay for these securities with checks. As the checks clear to the Fed from the banks and thrifts, reserves get withdrawn from the system. U.S. securities are now (1981) very attractive because they are returning an interest rate of approximately 14 percent.

EN: Which explains why funds are flowing out of traditional saving accounts that pay only 7 percent interest.

Alston: Yes. In the future, the thrift institutions will be able to counter this outflow by offering competitive market interest rates on their accounts. The Depository Institutions Deregulation and Monetary Control Act of 1980 phases out restrictions on the interest rates that institutions may pay to their customers.

EN: Are there methods other than open-market operations that the Fed can use to reduce the money supply?

Alston: Open-market operations are the device that the Fed most often uses. Another option is for the Fed to change the legal reserve requirement, or ratio. The Fed uses this powerful tool sparingly. To reduce the money supply, all the Fed has to do is increase the reserve requirement. The existing level of reserves in banks would then be inadequate relative to the amount of checkable deposits. Hampered by inadequate reserves, lending institutions could not issue new loans. By refusing new loans, they could reduce their demand deposits to a level that was supportable by their cash reserves, that is, to a level that would meet the higher reserve requirement. The curtailment of lending would reduce the money supply in the economy.

EN: The Fed recently increased its discount rate. What is the purpose of that?

Alston: The discount rate is the interest rate the Fed charges on loans to financial institutions. Banks and thrifts occasionally borrow from the Fed's regional banks in order to meet the legal reserve requirement. Normally, they first try to borrow excess reserves from other banks, but sometimes they need to borrow from the Fed itself. When the Fed increases its discount rate, financial institutions find that it is costlier to borrow from the Fed. At a higher discount rate, the amount of reserves that banks borrow from the Fed declines. The fewer the reserves in the system, the lower the total money supply. Thus a change in the discount rate influences the money supply.

I should add here that changes in the discount rate make the news and attract attention, but the buying and selling of U.S. securities is a far more important action by the Fed. Often, the Fed will change the discount rate simply because interest rates in general have changed. In other cases, a discount rate change is a signal by the Fed indicating its intent to change the growth of the money supply by buying and selling U.S. securities.

EN: What is the federal funds interest rate? Is that just another term used for the money market mutual fund rate?

Alston: No. Federal funds are excess reserves that banks make available to each other as overnight loans. During the normal course of banking, some banks find that they have temporary excess reserves beyond those required by law, while others discover they are somewhat short of reserves. The federal funds interest rate is the rate that banks charge on these overnight loans. The rate rises when excess reserves in the system are small and falls when excessive reserves are relatively plentiful.

EN: Okay, now we know how the Fed conducts monetary policy. The next question is, Why is the Fed in a tight-money stance at this time?

Alston: Inflation. The Fed thinks that the major cause of the present inflation is excess growth of the money supply, which increases aggregate demand. At the existing price level, the amount of goods and services demanded exceeds the amount supplied. Hence, prices rise.

EN: Demand inflation?

Alston: Right. One way to reduce spending is to reduce the growth of the money supply. There are two views as to how this works. Keynesians contend that reductions in the growth of the money supply work by increasing interest rates and reducing the availability of credit. Take an example. Say that a manufacturing firm is attempting to decide whether to build a new plant. It might decide to wait now that the prime interest rate is 17 percent. This represents a reduction in spending relative to the level that would otherwise exist. Investment decisions are made daily in the economy. The restricted credit and high interest rates affect each of these decisions, and many firms opt to delay their plans. Declines in investment spending cause a decline in aggregate demand and inflation.

Monetarist economists explain the public's response differently. They suggest that a decline in the money supply leaves people with less cash and lower checking account balances relative to their other assets. The natural reaction is to restore this balance of money to other assets. The other assets include such items as bonds, stocks, houses, cars, and mundane things like food in freezers and clothes in closets. The usual method of restoring a cash balance is to reduce spending on a full range of these items. Such restoration may work for some individuals, but the community as a whole *cannot* increase its cash balances; one person's reduction in spending leaves less cash in someone else's billfold or checkbook. The attempt by individuals to restore their cash balances eventually leads to a reduction in aggregate demand for the entire range of goods and services produced in the economy. This reduction in aggregate demand causes the price level to fall; that is, goods and services become less expensive. As the price level falls, people do not need as much money to buy the lower-priced goods and services. The amount of money demanded will therefore match the new, lower stock of money supplied. In this manner, the lower stock of money has produced a lower price level. The time lag between the reduction in the money supply and the change in the price level may be a year or more, however.

EN: That was not easy for me to follow. A restatement or summary would be helpful.

Alston: I'll give it a try. Keynesians see restrictive monetary policy as a process that works as follows: as the money supply declines, interest rates rise, investment spending declines, aggregate demand falls, and the rate of inflation slows. Monetarists argue that restrictive monetary policy is more direct in its consequences. As M1 declines, people spend less on an entire range of goods and services. After a period of time, aggregate demand declines, and inflation subsides.

EN: Both groups see monetary policy as working through aggregate demand. I don't see that the distinction is all that important.

Alston: In many respects it is not. But there are some subtleties here. For example, Keynesians tend to look at the level of interest rates—say, the federal funds rate or the prime lending rate—as an indicator of the tightness or looseness of monetary policy. According to some Keynesians, the job of the Fed is to set proper interest rates through changes in the money supply. Monetarists claim that one cannot be certain what will happen to interest rates when the Fed changes the money supply. When inflation is expected over the life of a loan, lenders increase the *monetary* (or nominal) interest rate to ensure that they earn an adequate *real* interest rate. A decrease in the money supply that is expected to reduce inflation will *reduce* interest rates in monetary terms. Therefore, strict monetarists view the money supply itself, not interest rates, to be the "controllable" variable.

EN: What do you mean by your term *real interest rate*?

Alston: The real interest rate is the stated rate (nominal rate) minus the expected rate of inflation over a period of the loan. If lenders are charging 3 percent nominal interest and expect inflation to be zero, the real rate is 3 percent. The same is true for 17 percent interest minus 14 percent expected inflation. Lenders wish to get some real return—real purchasing power increase—from their loan.

EN: Are there other differences between Keynesians and monetarists?

Alston: Yes. Keynesians view the economy as being inherently unstable and in need of active management. Otherwise, it produces inflation in some periods and recessions and unemployment in others. Therefore, the Fed must take an active role and set interest rates that are appropriate for balancing the economy. In times of rapid inflation, the money supply should be restricted to increase interest rates and reduce aggregate demand. These actions should also be accompanied by appropriate fiscal policy actions.

Monetarists have more of a "classical" perspective on the economy. They believe that the economy is reasonably stable if left unmanaged. Fed policy changes most often create the observed problems of inflation or recession. For example, one prominent monetarist—Milton Friedman—has stated that the Fed has been the major source of instability in the economy. The policy implication is that the Fed ought to use its monetary tools to create a stable economic environment. It can do that by adhering to a *monetary rule* that would force it to increase the money supply annually at a set 3–5 percent rate. This supposedly would accommodate the long-term growth of output in the economy and hold inflation in the 1–2 percent annual range.

EN: The Fed chairman recently said that the way to get interest rates down is to get inflation down. Do you agree?

Alston: Yes. "Credibility" is the key word here. The Fed must convince lenders and borrowers that it will stick with a noninflationary monetary policy. Once inflation falls, nominal interest rates will fall.

EN: In the meanwhile, interest rates are high and rising. What is the implication for the international value of the dollar?

Alston: Many factors influence the international value of the dollar. Our domestic interest rate is indeed one of them. When our real interest rate rises relative to rates abroad, people desire to buy U.S. securities to get a higher rate of return on their financial investments. But they cannot buy U.S. securities with rupees, yen, pesos, or won. They must exchange their own currencies for American dollars. Hence, the demand for dollars increases in the international exchange market, and the dollar appreciates in value. That is what is happening in foreign exchange markets now: The dollar is appreciating.

EN: What are the implications for the effectiveness of monetary policy?

Alston: The rising value of the dollar reinforces our tight money policy. Our exports *fall* because foreigners find that our goods are more expensive in terms of their currencies. Each yen, for instance, will buy fewer dollars than before. Conversely, our imports *rise*; each dollar can buy more yen, and therefore the dollar price of imports falls.

When our exports decline and our imports rise, total spending on *U.S.-produced* goods falls, helping to dampen domestic inflation.

EN: But, *at the expense of* a worsening trade deficit!

Alston: No question about that. When exports rise and imports fall, an existing *trade deficit* worsens. Of course, our import firms won't mind—they will profit from the higher-valued dollar, which makes for cheaper foreign goods.

EN: We have discussed many things—inflation, interest rates, Treasury bills, investment, exchange rates. Aren't you overemphasizing the extent to which these are related to monetary policy?

Alston: Not at all! These issues and events are *interrelated*; all are related to monetary policy. Changes in one factor in the economic system influence many other factors in the economy. Current monetary policy is restrictive, and this policy works its way out by influencing individual decisions in the economy. In fact, monetary policy *must* affect individual decisions if it is going to succeed. That's the point!

EN: Do you think the present tight-money policy will accomplish its objective of reducing inflation?

Alston: I think that the Fed's policy will succeed in reducing inflation, but we likely will experience a recession and unemployment in the process. Perhaps that is the price we must pay for a policy of increasing the money supply too rapidly in the past. Monetarists think so. A recession is one way of reducing inflation. It is a very costly method, though, because many people are thrown out of work, and the economy suffers a loss of income and output.

EN: Our time is nearly gone, Dr. Alston. Is there any final comment you wish to make?

Alston: One important point should be made. We have been discussing restrictive monetary policy because that is the present situation. But monetary policy works in both directions. During past recessions, the Fed initiated *expansionary* monetary policies. It bought bonds, reduced the reserve requirement, and lowered the discount rate to create more excess reserves in the banking system. These actions enabled banks to expand the money supply by a multiple of the excess reserves. Monetary policy has been used as a tool in aiding expansionary fiscal policy, as well as a tool in fighting inflation.

EN: Thank you for your analysis, professor.

Alston: The pleasure has been mine. (It was either this or tennis.)

POSTSCRIPT

The tight monetary policy of 1981 did indeed contribute to a major economic recession. However, it also dramatically reduced inflation. In 1980 the inflation rate was 13.5 percent, and in 1981 it was 12.4 percent. By 1983 the rate had fallen to 3.2 percent, and it remained relatively low throughout the 1980s. Monetary policy shifted from tight to relatively loose, or easy, in 1986, as the Fed successfully spurred the economy toward recovery and expansion. Most economists gave the Fed high marks for conducting a monetary policy that promoted growth between 1982 and 1990, while holding inflation in check.

STUDY QUESTIONS

1. Why is a checking account entry "money," whereas a Treasury security is not?
2. If you read in the newspaper that the Fed had increased the reserve requirement, what might you conclude about its intentions?
3. If the Federal Reserve entered the open market and *purchased* large quantities of securities, what would happen to (a) the interest yield on outstanding government securities, (b) commercial bank reserves, and (c) the money supply?
4. Explain why the market price of a U.S. security and its interest yield are inversely related.
5. Define each of the following terms: prime interest rate, discount rate, federal funds interest rate, nominal interest rate, real interest rate, mortgage interest rate.
6. Why might a prolonged tight-money policy produce a recession?
7. Using your knowledge from the preceding chapter, explain what Dr. Alston meant when he stated that the Fed's sale of a Treasury bill to the public will cause a "*multiple* contraction of the money supply." Why a *multiple* contraction?
8. Discuss the differences in the Keynesian and monetarist views on how an excessive increase in the money supply causes inflation.
9. Explain how a tight money policy might lead to a decline in American exports and an increase in our imports.
10. What basic economic concept was involved in Dr. Alston's final thought, "It was either this [the interview] or tennis"?

19

HERE'S LOOKING AT YOU, KID

Perspectives on the Phillips Curve

Concepts and Terms Examined in This Chapter

1. Phillips Curve   *WHAT IT IS / WHY NO LONGER VALID.*
2. Aggregate Supply Shock   *INCREASED COST OF PROD.*
3. Natural Rate of Unemployment   *LOWEST POSS. SUSTAINED LEVEL*
4. Long-Run Vertical Phillips Curve
5. Rational Expectations Theory
6. Incomes Policy
7. Wage and Price Controls and Standards
8. Monetary Rule

At one time or another, every student is haunted by the idea that she or he didn't study enough for the test to be taken the next morning. The following dialogue capitalizes on that common situation to explain the theories of the inflation-unemployment relationship. The "spirited" format provides a step-by-step, pro-grammed-learning approach to Keynesian, monetarist, and rational expectations perspectives on the Phillips curve.

Hey, you in room 304. Got a minute?
Who is that? Who is talking? Where are you?
Can you spare me half an hour to answer a few questions?
Who are you? Am I going crazy? I hear a voice.
I'm the Spirit of Economics 101. I taught at this school before I passed away.
Before you passed away?
Yes.
Oh!
Say, do you have a few minutes?
I suppose that I do.
I'd like to ask several questions; you might call it a poll.
I see.
Have you read the chapter on the Phillips curve that you were assigned in Economics 101?
Yes.
Tell the truth, kid.
Well, I skimmed it.
The reason that I asked is because my poll is over material in that chapter. Actually, my poll is a test.
A test!
Don't get excited. After all, this is a test, only a test. In the event of an actual emergency . . .
This is unreal!
My first multiple-choice question is . . .
Multiple choice? I hate multiple-choice tests.
Tough, kid, tough. That's what you are getting.

THE PHILLIPS DATA POINTS: 1956–1990

Do you have your Brue and Wentworth textbook handy? Look at Figure 19-1.
Is that book any good?
Terrific! You should try reading it.
Question 1 is, "The curve labeled PC_1 in Figure 19-1 (a) was first discovered by an economist working for the Phillips Petroleum Company, (b) indicates an apparent trade-off between inflation and unemployment, (c) both (a) and (b), (d) neither (a) nor (b)."
This test is a breeze. The answer is (b).
You are right. But don't get cocky, kid. The first multiple-choice question is always a confidence builder. Wait until you get to the questions over the graphs. Response (b) is correct, though. The graph shows points that indicate the rates of inflation and unemployment for each specific year. A. W. Phillips first plotted such points for the British economy. Economists in the United States discerned the same

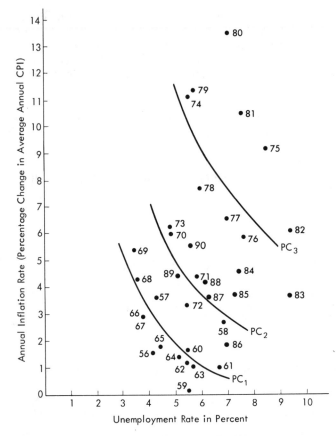

Figure 19-1 The Phillips Data Points: 1956–1990

Between 1956 and 1969, the Phillips data points seemed to be grouped around Phillips curve PC$_1$. During the 1970–1982 period, the points tended to lie above and to the right of PC$_1$. Had the Phillips curve shifted outward to PC$_2$ and PC$_3$, or was the original idea of a Phillips relationship erroneous?

pattern for our economy. High rates of unemployment, for example, the 6.7 percent rate in 1961, appeared to be associated with low rates of inflation—1 percent in 1961. On the other hand, low rates of unemployment, such as the 3.5 percent rate in 1969, seemed to be accompanied by high rates of inflation—5.4 percent for that year. The Phillips curve led economists to conclude that there was a trade-off between inflation and unemployment. To get less unemployment, society had to accept higher inflation; to get lower inflation, it had to accept higher unemployment.

Are you ready for question 2?

Sure.

Okay. Here it is: "The policy implication that economists drew from observing the Phillips curve shown as PC$_1$ in Figure 19-1 was that (a) policymakers needed to decide where to locate on the curve and then use Keynesian macroeconomic policies to achieve that location, (b) unemployment could not be reduced below a 6 percent natural rate, (c) inflation could be controlled by increasing employment in the economy, (d) all of the above."

That's a tough one. I know (c) is wrong so (d) must also be wrong. It must be (a).

Why?

The curve shows that lower levels of unemployment were associated with higher rates of inflation and vice versa. I can see why that would lead policymakers to argue about where to locate on the curve. They might ask, "Is more inflation acceptable if it means less unemployment?"

Good. Many economists perceived the historical Phillips curve to be a stable relationship between unemployment and inflation. Naturally, they focused policy discussions on how much inflation or unemployment to accept. Also, they began to suggest policies that would shift the Phillips curve inward.

Such as?

Such as training and retraining programs to reduce structural unemployment and passage of antidiscrimination legislation. These programs, if successful, would lower structural unemployment at each level of inflation, thereby pushing the curve inward. Consequently, fiscal and monetary policy could be more expansionary without producing as high a rate of inflation as in previous experiences. Did you know that?

Can't say that I did.

You do now.

Yes, I suppose that I do.

Question 3 is, "During the 1970s, Phillips data points were located (a) on or near the right-hand portion of the 1950s, and 1960s curve, (b) on or near the left-hand portion of the 1950s and 1960s curve, (c) to the left and below the 1950s and 1960s curve, (d) above and to the right of the 1950s and 1960s curve."

Could I leave that question and come back to it later?

No.

I'll guess (b) then.

Wrong! The correct answer is (d). As you can see in Figure 19-1, the Phillips data points for the 1970s fell above and to the right of those in the 1956–1969 period. Notice the point for 1979, for example. The unemployment rate was 5.8 percent, and the inflation rate was 11.3 percent. Compare that with the point for 1963 where the unemployment rate was similar but the rate of inflation was only 1.2 percent.

Very interesting!

The 1970s and first few years of the 1980s were a period of stagflation — high unemployment and rapid inflation. Beginning with 1983, the data points fell back toward PC_1, but still remained to the right of it.

The Keynesian Perspective

Question 4: "Which of the following is an explanation given by Keynesians for the apparent outward shifts of the Phillips curve? (a) OPEC oil price increases caused a large 'aggregate supply shock' that worsened the unemployment-inflation trade-off, (b) unions caused cost-push inflation, (c) inflationary expectations arose and caused further inflation, (d) a changed composition of the labor force increased unemployment levels, (e) all of the above."

I'll say (a).

You are just guessing again. See, I told you the questions got harder. The answer is (e) "all of the above." Keynesians argued that supply shocks, such as the

1,000 percent increase in oil prices over the decade of the 1970s, caused supply, or cost-push, inflation. They contended that inflation can be caused by either rising aggregate demand or by declining aggregate supply and that the increases in resource prices — costs to producers — shifted the aggregate supply curve for the economy to the left. You might recall from the micro portion of your economics course that one of the things that determines the location of a supply curve in a market is resource costs. The same is true for the aggregate supply curve for the economy. Higher costs of resources result in leftward shifts of aggregate supply.

Unions, which demanded and received wage increases that exceeded productivity increases, also contributed to inflation, according to this view. When wages rise faster than productivity, the latter defined as output per worker-hour, then average and marginal costs to the firm rise, supply curves shift left, and product prices increase. Figure 19-2 in your book shows the aggregate outcome of these changes.

What page?

I don't recall; it is somewhere in Chapter 19.

OK. I found it.

The graph in Figure 19-2 measures the economy's general price level (P) on the vertical axis, and the level of real output (Q) on the horizontal one. Initially, assume that aggregate demand is AD and that aggregate supply is AS_1. The price level would be P_1 and the level of real output Q_1. Next, suppose that an aggregate supply shock in the form of higher oil prices occurs and that unions force wages upward to keep up with inflation, but that those wage increases exceed productivity gains. As a result, the aggregate supply curve shifts backward from AS_1 to AS_2 to AS_3 and the general price level increases from P_1 to P_2 to P_3. Notice also that the level of real national output falls from Q_1 to Q_2 to Q_3. That is, a recession and increased

Figure 19-2   Supply (Cost-Push) Inflation

Assuming a stable, downward-sloping aggregate demand curve (AD), reductions in aggregate supply from AS_1 to AS_2 to AS_3 will cause inflation and reduce the nation's level of real output.

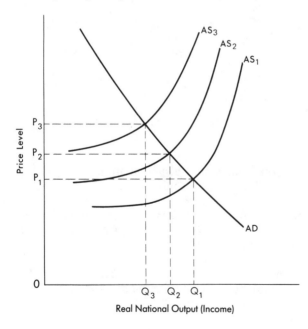

Real National Output (Income)

unemployment occur at the same time inflation takes place. The rising price level and higher levels of unemployment in Figure 19-2 correspond to an outward shift of the Phillips curve (Figure 19-1).

How do inflationary expectations enter into the picture? That was choice (c), which was also correct.

I suppose that once inflation begins, people expect it to continue or even worsen.

And so? Go on.

They decide to buy products immediately rather than wait, because they think that the prices will be even higher in the future.

Yes, and that behavior shifts the aggregate demand curve in Figure 19-2 rightward, which drives up the price level even further. Also, workers begin to build expectations of inflation into their wage demands. Hence, expectations can produce both demand and supply inflation and cause the Phillips data points to be located above the previous ones. In effect, the Phillips curve shifts rightward, as shown by PC_2 and PC_3 in Figure 19-1 earlier.

Do you recall anything from your lecture about choice (d), "a changed composition of the labor force caused higher levels of unemployment?" How does that help to explain the outward shift of the Phillips curve?

Are you asking me?

Who else? Let's make it question 5: "The changed composition of the labor force—more women and teenagers—helped to shift the Phillips curve outward, according to Keynesians, because (a) women and teenagers had higher unemployment rates than the average and as the labor force composition became more heavily weighted toward them, the average went up, (b) women and teenaged workers added extra income to families, they spent more, and that caused inflation, (c) both (a) and (b), (d) neither (a) nor (b)."

Choice (a) is correct.

Yes. The change in the weighting caused by the rapid influx of women and teenagers into the labor force in the 1970s meant that the unemployment rate increased statistically and was higher at each level of inflation than in the 1955–1969 period. As a result, Phillips data points fell to the right of those along the earlier curve.

The Monetarist Perspective

Are you still listening to me?

Yes. This is really exciting.

Don't be sarcastic, kid. You need this review. Answer questions 6 through 9 on the basis of Figure 19-3.

That graph looks complicated.

It is. No one said Economics 101 is easy. You'll have to study Figure 19-3 carefully. Question 6: "Figure 19-3 illustrates the view that (a) the long-run Phillips curve is perfectly horizontal, (b) the long-run Phillips curve is vertical at the natural rate of unemployment, (c) the short-run Phillips curve shifted outward due to supply shocks, (d) none of the above."

Beats me. I'll try (d).

Poor guess. The answer is (b), "the long-run Phillips curve is vertical at the natural rate of unemployment." The natural rate of unemployment is the rate to which the economy tends when all parties to contracts correctly anticipate the rate of inflation. This view suggests that no trade-off exists between inflation and unemploy-

ment in the long run. The only trade-off is between less unemployment than the natural rate today versus more than that rate tomorrow. Stating this another way, if the Federal Reserve uses an easy-money policy to stimulate the economy, it can reduce unemployment below the natural rate temporarily, but this will cause inflation and eventually an above-normal unemployment rate later.

I'm confused.

Look closely at the curve labeled $SRPC_1$ in Figure 19-3. The movement from point A to B on that short-run Phillips curve is explained by monetarists as follows. Policymakers, erroneously perceiving that $SRPC_1$ was a stable, long-run Phillips curve, engaged in expansionary fiscal and monetary policies to reduce unemployment from 6 percent to 4 percent. The increase in the money supply caused the price level to rise and unemployment to fall below the natural rate of 6 percent. The decline in unemployment occurred because workers were fooled. Expecting inflation to remain at the 2 percent rate, they agreed to wage increases that reflected that expectation. But inflation turned out to be 4 percent. The firms received the higher prices for their products, but they had to pay only the wages that were established in the labor contracts. Hence, labor became cheaper both relative to capital and to the prices firms were receiving for their products. The firms responded by hiring more workers, and

Figure 19-3 The Vertical Long-Run Phillips Curve

According to monetarists, the long-run Phillips curve is vertical at a natural rate of unemployment. Expansionary monetary policies temporarily reduce unemployment, but once workers adjust fully to the inflation that results, unemployment moves back toward a natural rate. The idea of a stable Phillips curve is an illusion.

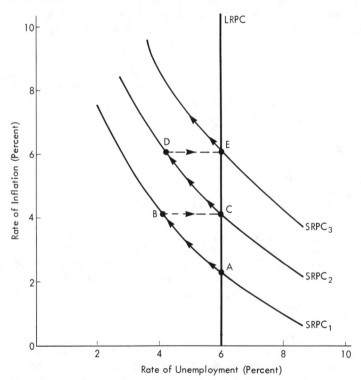

unemployment temporarily fell below the natural rate, as shown in Figure 19-3. According to this view, a given short-run Phillips curve such as SRPC₁ exists only so long as the expected rate of inflation remains unchanged.

Question 7: "The movement from point B to C in Figure 19-3 occurred because (a) the Federal Reserve further increased the money supply, (b) the federal government increased its spending and cut taxes, (c) supply shocks from outside the economy occurred, (d) workers demanded and received wage increases on their new contracts that reflected the new, higher 4 percent rate of inflation."

I'm beginning to recall this graph from the lecture. The answer is (d).

Yes. Can you explain why?

Once the long-term labor contracts expired, workers demanded and received higher wages. They desired to restore their real purchasing power that had been reduced by unanticipated inflation, and they adjusted their expectations about future inflation, incorporating the present rate of 4 percent rather than the previous rate of 2 percent. The new short-run Phillips curve becomes SRPC₂. It exists because the rate of inflation is now 4 percent and workers expect that rate to continue.

So why did unemployment return to 6 percent (point C)?

I suppose corporations laid off workers once they found that labor had become more expensive relative to capital and to their product prices.

Correct!

Question 8: "The movement from point C to D in Figure 19-3 is explained by (a) a decrease in the money supply, (b) a reduction in government spending, (c) an increase in the money supply, (d) a decrease in savings."

I imagine that it is (c) "an increase in the money supply." That is what explained the initial move from A to B.

I'm impressed, kid. According to this view, the federal government still was erroneously thinking about the economy in terms of the traditional Phillips curve. It assumed the supply shocks had caused the Phillips curve to shift outward (recall the Keynesian perspective). Policymakers, targeting 4 percent unemployment as full employment, began the scenario once again by expanding the money supply to move leftward along SRPC₂ in Figure 19-3. That created even more rapid inflation.

And the temporary gains in employment were eliminated once workers readjusted to the higher inflation and the Fed slowed the growth of the money supply.

Exactly! The economy moved from D to E.

Look at Figure 19-4 where the Phillips data points are connected year to year. See the spiraling effect. Monetarists contend that the points roughly correspond to the model that we just discussed.

Question 9: "According to the monetarists, the high rates of inflation shown in Figures 19-3 and 19-4 were caused by (a) increased government regulations, (b) reductions in government spending, (c) inappropriate monetary policy, (d) greedy labor unions."

Response (c).

Yes, the monetarists placed the blame for inflation squarely on the Federal Reserve's improper monetary policies. Those policies were based on the erroneous notion that it could permanently reduce unemployment by expanding the money supply. According to the monetarists, the short-run Phillips curves exist only because the actual rate of inflation can be either greater than or less than the expected rate of

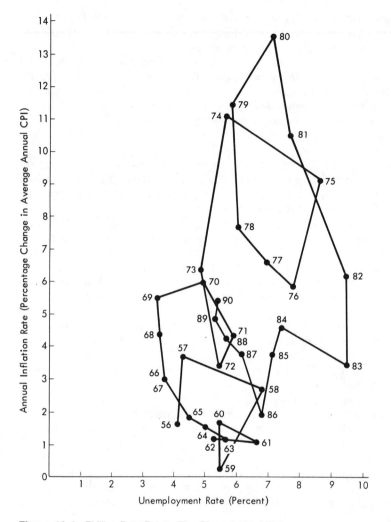

Figure 19-4 Phillips Data Points: The Chronological Pattern

Connecting the Phillips data points chronologically produces a spiraling pattern. Prior to 1982, periods of falling unemployment seemed to be associated with rising rates of inflation, followed by periods in which unemployment rates increased to previous levels, but inflation rates failed to decline to their old levels. Monetarists claim this general pattern is consistent with their view that, in the long run, excessive growth of the money supply increases prices, but does not permanently reduce unemployment below its natural rate.

inflation. If the actual rate is greater than the expected rate, unemployment temporarily falls; if the actual rate is less than the expected rate, unemployment temporarily rises. In the long run, however, people adjust their expectations of inflation to the existing rate, the short-run Phillips curve shifts upward or downward, and unemployment returns to the natural rate. Therefore, there is no long-run trade-off between inflation and unemployment.

The Rational Expectations Perspective

Question 10: "The theory of rational expectations holds that (a) people use all available information in forming expectations about the future rate of inflation, as opposed to just assuming that present rates will continue, (b) there is a long-run trade-off between inflation and unemployment, but not a short-run one, (c) people always get what they expect, (d) people generally behave irrationally.

Well, based on what I see in music videos, I'll say (d).

That's not funny, kid.

Who's laughing?

The answer is (a). They contend that people use all available information to form rational expectations on future inflation. People reflect on any past errors they may have made and eliminate any regularity of errors in subsequent anticipations. Notice that this fits nicely within the economic perspective. Thus policymakers cannot count on fooling workers and others into thinking the inflation rate will remain at the present level when the Fed is, in fact, undertaking policies that will produce a higher rate.

The implication is that policymakers cannot systematically reduce unemployment below the natural rate, even in the short run. Workers and others respond to announced changes in the activities of the government by changing their own expectations about inflation. The new behavior renders the planned policy ineffective. For example, workers demand higher wages because they anticipate higher future rates of inflation. Firms are willing to grant these increases because they anticipate increased product demand and higher product prices. Output in the economy remains stable while prices and wages simultaneously rise.

In terms of Figure 19-3, expansionary actions by the Fed move the economy rather directly from A to C to E. No one is systematically fooled into thinking the existing rate of inflation will continue. In both the short run and the long run, no trade-off between inflation and unemployment will be observed. This theory implies that inflation can quickly rise or fall along curve LRPC, depending upon the government's fiscal and monetary policy.

The rational expectations theory also is demonstrated in Figure 19-5 in the book. Here is a question on it.

Question 11: "The rational expectation theory as it relates to expansionary government policy is shown by (a) the rightward shift of aggregate demand from AD_1 to AD_2, (b) the leftward shift of aggregate supply from AS_1 to AS_2, (c) the shift of aggregate demand from AD_1 to AD_2, followed immediately by a shift of aggregate supply from AS_1 to AS_2, (d) none of the above."

The answer must be (c). The shift from AD_1 to AD_2 represents the increase in aggregate demand resulting from the government expansionary policy. The shift in aggregate supply from AS_1 to AS_2 comes about because costs go up immediately because of the expectation of higher prices.

Very good! Notice that the level of output remains at Q_1, but the price level rises to P_2. The economists who adhere to the rational expectations theory are called "new classicists." Just like the old classicists, these economists tend to think that the economy is self-regulating, and they reject the Keynesian view that government can effectively "manage" the economy. Output will automatically tend toward Q_1 in Figure 19-5.

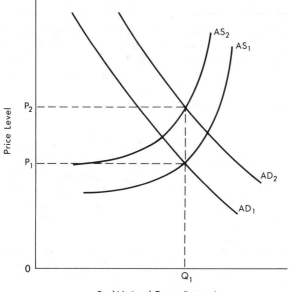

Figure 19-5   Rational Expectations Perspective

The theory of rational expectations suggests that an increase in aggregate demand (AD_1 to AD_2) caused by expansionary monetary policy will immediately produce higher costs of production and therefore an offsetting decline in aggregate supply (AS_1 to AS_2). The price level will rise (P_1 to P_2), but real output will remain the same (Q_1).

> *And by the way, kid, the people in the music videos are acting rationally. Do you think they can make more money doing something else?*

POLICY IMPLICATIONS

> *Because economists disagree on the matters relating to the causes of inflation, unemployment, and stagflation, they also disagree on the proper stabilization role for government in the economy. The next set of questions are on the policy implications of the different views.*
>
> *Question 12: "Most Keynesians believe that (a) the economy tends toward periodic episodes of inflation, unemployment, or both and that government should use fiscal and monetary policies to prevent the extremes of each, (b) rational expectations render fiscal and monetary policies ineffective, (c) the Fed should increase the money supply at a fixed annual rate, (d) none of the above."*

The answer is (a).

There's hope.

> *In addition, some Keynesians in the past supported one of several types of incomes policy. An incomes policy is governmental actions that limit monetary wage, rent, interest, and profit increases and thereby reduce cost-push inflation. The idea is to push the Phillips curve inward by controlling cost increases and breaking inflationary expectations. Examples of income policies are legal wage and price controls and voluntary wage and price standards, both of which were used in the 1970s. These*

incomes policies proved to be ineffective, and therefore few economists now support them.

Aren't you getting a little wordy?

I didn't hear that, kid. Question 13:

Question 13: "Monetarists, viewing the cause of stagflation as inept government monetary policy, contend that the best way to achieve economic stability is to (a) balance the federal budget, (b) increase the money supply at an announced, steady, 3 to 5 percent annual rate, (c) vigorously enforce the antitrust laws, (d) establish an incomes policy."

Answer (b) is correct. According to my professor, monetarists argue that we would not have had serious stagflation if the Federal Reserve had not misinterpreted the Phillips curve and engaged in inappropriate monetary policies.

True. Strict monetarists favor a monetary "rule" that would legislate the Federal Reserve out of the business of countercyclical monetary policy. The Fed's task under the "rule" would be to increase the nation's money supply annually at a set rate, for example, 3 to 5 percent.

Question 14: The rational expectations theorists (a) favor fine-tuning the economy through fiscal and monetary policy, (b) advocate permanent wage and price controls, (c) agree with the monetarists that the best policy for the Federal Reserve is to increase the money supply at a known, stable rate, (d) favor enacting high tariffs on imported products.

That's easy. It is (c).

True, rational expectation theorists, or new classical economists, agree with the strict monetarists that the Federal Reserve should increase the nation's money supply at a set, known, noninflationary rate. Shifts in monetary policy will only change the price level, not the nation's level of real national output. Because any level of inflation is consistent with full employment, we may as well choose a zero rate of inflation!

Which of these three positions—Keynesian, monetarist, and rational expectations—is correct?

I can't say; the evidence is mixed. The quick end to the double-digit inflation of the early 1980s lent some credence to the rational expectations theory. On the other hand, this rapid decline in inflation was accompanied by a severe recession; that is, real national output did not remain at its natural level. This decline in output is more consistent with the Keynesian and monetarist views. During the mid-1980s, the Federal Reserve expanded the money supply quite rapidly. National output rose rather rapidly, unemployment fell, and inflation remained relatively low. These outcomes fit more with the Keynesian perspective. Look around; take note of the news; you will hear a mixture of Keynesian, monetarist, and rational expectationist voices. Ultimately, evidence—and not debating skills or novelty of views—will determine which voices are correct.

Speaking of hearing voices. What am I doing talking to you?

*　　*　　*

Sound of an alarm clock. An hour later the following conversation occurs:

"Are you ready for your Economics 101 exam?" asked Martha Nohr, as she and Nate Arnold walked toward their class.

"I hope so!" replied Nate. "I studied my notes for several hours. How about you?"

"I think I'll do okay," replied Martha. "Did you read the book?"

"I skimmed it! That's where I'm a little bit vulnerable," said Nate laughingly. "It's funny that you should ask. I had this weird dream last night. I heard this voice—it claimed it was the Spirit of Economics 101, asked me if I had read the book, and proceeded to give me a multiple-choice exam over the Phillips curve chapter."

"That's funny, chuckled Martha. "It's all these graphs—they blow your mind."

Here's looking at you, kid (and wishing you well).

STUDY QUESTIONS

1. What information is provided by a single Phillips data point? What information is provided by a Phillips curve?

2. Where did the Phillips data points for the 1970s fall relative to the 1955–1969 Phillips curve? Explain the Keynesian explanation for these points.

3. Why, according to monetarists, does unemployment temporarily fall when the actual rate of inflation is greater than the expected rate? What happens to the Phillips curve when people adjust their expectations to the higher actual rate of inflation?

4. What is implied by a long-run Phillips curve that is perfectly vertical?

5. In what respect does the rational expectation perspective of the Phillips curve differ from the monetarist view?

6. What is meant by the term *incomes policy*? Who would be more likely to support such a policy, a Keynesian or a monetarist? Explain, drawing on information in this and previous chapters.

7. Use *Economic Indicators,* found in most college libraries, to update Figure 19-4 for the years since the publication of this edition of the text. Does the clockwise progression of data points continue?

8. What will happen to real national output if government decides to reduce the cost-push inflation shown in Figure 19-2 by *reducing* aggregate demand? On the other hand, what will happen to the price level if government instead decides to combat the decline in real national output by *increasing* AD? In view of your answer, explain the following statement: "Cost-push inflation presents the government with a policy dilemma."

20

MR. MALTHUS

The Economics of Growth

Concepts and Terms Examined in This Chapter

1. Population Growth
2. Economic Growth
3. Diminishing Marginal Returns
4. Production Function
5. Gross National Product (Real, Per Capita)
6. Capital Formation
7. Technological Innovation
8. Sources of Economic Growth
9. Productivity

WINTER 1805, HAILEYBURY, ENGLAND

The winter was not a pleasant time to be a student at the college of the East India Company. The cold, frequent rains created a depressing atmosphere in which to study. Students and instructors turned moody and devoted much of their energy to trying to stay warm in their poorly lighted, drafty classrooms.

It had been considerably brighter in the spring. The pleasant weather and occasional sun warmed the body and encouraged the mind to consider how good it was to be alive. That was a great time to be young, to be at peace with the world, and to be interested in political economy. Thirty years before, political economy had been a field known to only a handful of scholars. In 1776, however, Adam Smith had changed all that. His pathbreaking book, *An Inquiry into the Nature and Causes of the Wealth of Nations*, established the new field of economics. Ah, spring was a time to learn about Adam Smith.

Smith saw the economy as a grand and harmonious concert in which private self-interest was transformed into maximum social well-being and progress. The actions of buying and selling, specializing and trading, saving and investing, and making profits or losses were all controlled by competition in the marketplace. If these natural actions were left free to operate without government interference, they would produce a glorious outcome—economic growth and progress. The division of labor and the use of machinery would produce an expanded volume of products and income. As income increased, people would be able to increase their saving, which, in turn, would be used by businesses to purchase even more machinery. The benefit of this continual process would be economic growth that improved the quality of life of everyone in the economy.

But that was in the spring! Winter is a more appropriate season for taking a class from *this* instructor. His pessimism stands in stark contrast to Adam Smith's glorious vision. Professor Malthus is a controversial and puzzling person, and students and faculty at the East India Company's college often speculate about his background, personality, and ideas.

No one really understands where or why he developed his deep pessimism about the world. He was born in 1766, the son of Daniel Malthus, an intellectual, who had close rapport with the leading thinkers of his day. The older Malthus regularly discussed philosophy with people such as Rousseau and Hume. He was a supreme optimist. In this regard, he was very much a man of his times, for this was the Age of Enlightenment. He and his contemporaries strongly believed in people's ability to reason and to use that faculty to perfect individuals and society. According to these thinkers, the future would be one of boundless human and social progress.

Thomas Malthus never displayed his father's optimism. He studied at Cambridge as a young man and became an Anglican minister. In 1798, one year after he had assumed his first parish assignment, he published *An Essay on the Principle of Population*. That essay transformed Malthus from an obscure parish minister into an internationally famous intellectual, and led scholars to label the discipline of political economy the "dismal science." Malthus sought to deal the prevailing prophets of progress a staggering intellectual blow.

It is a depressing experience to read and listen to Malthus, but that is the only way to complete the course of study at the college of the East India Company. The hand and the pen begin to take notes while the mind and the ear listen to Professor Malthus present his grim scenario for the future.

Throughout the animal and vegetable kingdom Nature has scattered the seeds of life abroad with the most profuse and liberal hand; but has been comparatively sparing in the room and the nourishment necessary to rear them. . . .

Taking the whole earth . . . and supposing the present population equal to a thousand millions, the human species would increase as the numbers 1, 2, 4, 8, 16, 32, 64, 128, 256 [a geometric progression], and subsistence as 1, 2, 3, 4, 5, 6, 7, 8, 9 [arithmetic rate]. In two centuries the population would be to the means of subsistence as 256 to 9; in three centuries as 4096 to 13, and in two thousand years the difference would be almost incalculable. . . . The necessary effects of these two different rates of increase, when brought together [are] very striking.*

Very striking! This man drops catastrophes right in front of you with total dependence on understatement. Why, if population tends to grow faster than the availability of food, the human species is destined for misery and poverty! We will all live like the beggar families in the shanty row on the east side of town. The last time we passed through that area, it was difficult to keep from becoming nauseated, observing people digging through ox dung for undigested seeds and grains.

It is evident truth that, whatever increase in the means of subsistence, the increase in population must be limited by it, at least after the food has once been divided into the smallest shares that will support life. All the children born, beyond what would be required to keep up the population to this level, must necessarily perish. . . .

This is difficult to believe. The professor is stating that the standard of living in the world will be reduced to a subsistence level at which the population has just enough food to stay alive and everyone lives with continual hunger. The limited food supply will create starvation and disease, which will continue until the population is reduced to the number that can be supported by the available food. Not even increasing the food supply will raise the standard of living above the subsistence level, since more people will survive and population will grow until, once again, a point is reached where each person has only enough food to exist. Economic growth will cease completely.

It all seems too unreasonable—too unjust. Is this to be humanity's fate? Why could not the food supply increase at a rate even faster than the geometric rate of population growth?

Man is necessarily confined in room. When acre has been added to acre till all the fertile land is occupied, the yearly increase of food must depend upon the melioration [improvement] of the land already in possession. This is a fund which, from the nature of all soils, instead of increasing, must be gradually diminishing.

It may be fairly pronounced, therefore, that . . . the means of subsistence could not possibly be made to increase faster than in an arithmetical ratio.

The law of diminishing returns! Malthus often employed this idea to explain economic events. If all the fertile land is being used, then the only way to get more food is to add more and more tillers, sowers, and reapers to the growing process and to add more manure to the soil. The problem is, however, that each

---

*All quotations of Malthus are excerpted from various editions of *An Essay on the Principle of Population*.

addition of these resources yields less of an increase in food output than did the preceding one.

It would be nice if the law of diminishing returns did not exist, for then the world's food supply could be grown in the flowerpot of the ledge outside this classroom window. But that is ridiculous! No matter how much time, work, seed, and manure one added to that amount of earth, one could never raise more than a handful of grain. Maybe Malthus has arrived at the same conclusion on a larger scale. In a sense, the earth is just a giant pot, and we are using its fertile area fully at this time. Society cannot produce more land.

Outside the weather is still wet and cold. Walking along the streets of Haileybury late in the evening does not help one escape the depression of Malthus's lecture. Children returning from their factory jobs wander by with blank eyes. Most of them will have to rise at 5:00 in the morning to begin another 14-hour day in the factory. Maybe Malthus is right. Why should one expect life to get better? The misery around this area seems to support Malthus's gloomy forecast for the future. Yes, maybe he is right.

AUTUMN 1990, MADISON, WISCONSIN

Autumn is a pleasant time to be a student at the University of Wisconsin. The air is crisp and comfortable, and the foliage around the campus forms a collage of every imaginable shade of red, orange, yellow, and brown. It is especially good to be back for the second year on campus, since the freshman year is so difficult and confusing. Teachers' expectations are so much greater than they were in high school that it takes a full year to learn the system. Now there is even time to get ahead on assignments once in a while, instead of always being behind.

My term paper on Malthus is a good example. It isn't due for another two weeks, but it is finished. That old pessimist was really an interesting person to research. It is amazing how a man could have had such a dramatic effect on economics and yet have been so wrong in his conclusions.

Today's lecture in my Principles of Economics course is on economic growth. Maybe it would be a good idea to reread my Malthus paper before going to class.

ECONOMICS TERM PAPER: WAS MALTHUS RIGHT?

Population growth is a major problem in some less-developed nations of the world. Just as Thomas Malthus predicted, famine, starvation, infant mortality, and disease are common to these areas. The available quantities of food have not increased as fast as the rate of growth of population.

With the exception of the less-developed countries, however, the past 193 years *do not support the Malthusian predictions.* Population has increased in each of the industrialized nations of the world, but the quantity of food and other economic production has risen even faster. The result has been a positive rate of economic growth as measured by real gross national product (real GNP) and GNP per capita. *Gross national product* is the dollar value of all final products and services produced in a specific year. *Real* GNP is GNP adjusted to exclude the impact of inflation on the value of the output. GNP *per capita* is GNP per person, or GNP/population.

From 1870 to 1970, for instance, real GNP grew at annual average rates of 3.6

percent in the United States, 8.9 percent in Japan, 6.0 percent in Germany, 2.8 percent in the United Kingdom, and 5.0 percent in Canada. Over the same 100-year period, real GNP per capita grew annually at rates of between 1.3 percent and 2.0 percent in these countries. These growth rates contradict Malthus's gloomy predictions of economic stagnation and subsistence wages.

Thomas Malthus was even wrong in his forecasts concerning population growth. Instead of experiencing geometric population growth, some nations, such as the United States, England, and Japan, have discovered that their population growth rates have declined in the last two decades.

Why did Malthus miscalculate so badly? For the most part, events occurred for which he had no foreknowledge, and these events changed the data with which he worked and that supported his conclusions. First, millions of acres of new fertile land came into production after 1798. Most of this land was concentrated in the United States, Canada, and Australia. Suddenly, more agricultural output existed, because additional units of land (Malthus's critical resource) were added to the production process.

The discovery and cultivation of new land is not the only reason for the growth of food supplies and other products over the past two centuries. The quantity and productivity of other factors of production increased, also. *Capital formation* has been particularly important. This is the buildup of new factories, tools, and machines that increases worker productivity and enables greater output of products and services. In agriculture, the increased use of tractors, cultivators, harvesters, and other implements has increased food production *per unit of land*—in other words, has produced a greater yield from each acre.

Technological innovation, defined as improvements in the techniques of combining resources to produce products and services, has also increased economic growth. In agriculture, farmers now use hybrid seeds, improved fertilizer, irrigation, and more efficient farming methods. This technological change is a major reason why the Malthus forecasts were incorrect.

The impact of capital formation and technological advance can be shown as a shift in the agricultural *production function*. A production function is a relationship between resource inputs and the output that results. The concept is depicted in Figure 20-1.

The variable resource in Figure 20-1 is labor, measured along the horizontal axis; the output—food—is shown on the vertical axis. For each production alternative shown, land and capital, together with the level of technology, are assumed to be constant.

First, focus attention exclusively on curve PF_1. Note that food production rises as more laborers are added to agricultural production. Each added worker, however, contributes less and less to increases in food output. Another way of stating this is that the production function increases, but at a diminishing rate. For example, adding the fourth worker increases output from Q_3 to Q_4, but the fifth worker would only expand output from Q_4 to Q_5. This is an example of Malthus's principle of diminishing marginal returns. Because land and capital are assumed to be fixed, added workers increase the output of food, but they do so at a diminishing rate.

Next, study the PF_2 curve. It has the same properties as PF_1, *but*, at each level of employment, output is higher than shown by PF_1. The upward shift of the production function from PF_1 to PF_2 is caused by the use of *more* land, *more* capital, and *improved* technology. This shift illustrates that farmers can grow much more food when they have more land and capital and improved technology. For instance, five workers can produce Q_* units of food at PF_2 but only Q_5 units at PF_1.

Figure 20-1 summarizes four methods by which society can increase food

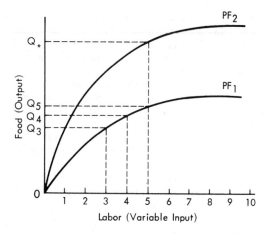

Figure 20-1   Diminishing Returns and Shifts in the Production Function

Curve PF₁ illustrates Malthus's notion of diminishing marginal returns. The addition of the fourth worker adds the distance Q_3 to Q_4 to food output, whereas the addition of the fifth worker only adds Q_4 to Q_5. The shift in the production function to PF_2 is caused by adding more land, capital, and technology; it enables greater output from any level of employment. For instance, five workers produce Q_5 units of food at PF_1 and Q_* units at PF_2.

supplies: use more labor (movements along the production function), cultivate and plant more land, employ more capital, and improve technology. The last three methods are depicted by upward shifts of the production function.

The rapid capital formation in agriculture also had the effect of aiding the growth of other parts of the economy. It allowed machines to do the work of people, thus enabling fewer and fewer farmers to produce the needed food supply for growing populations. *Factor substitution* occurred as capital (tractors, combines, bailers) replaced labor (planters, hoers, hand harvesters). In 1820, each farm worker in the United States grew enough food to support 4 additional people. Today each farm worker grows enough food to sustain nearly 100 other people. This increased productivity has allowed people to become involved in alternative economic activities—making steel, training managers, singing songs, designing computers, healing wounds. The result has been faster growth in the economy's capacity to produce nonagricultural goods and services.

Well, so much for my term paper on Malthus; it is time to go to class. This lecture should be easy to comprehend, since it deals with Malthus and economic growth.

Class Lecture

Today, I wish to discuss the general topic of economic growth. My discussion will proceed as follows. First, the sources of economic growth will be discussed. Second, the important role of economic incentives in producing growth will be emphasized. Finally, I will discuss the slowdown in economic growth experienced by the United States over the last 15 years.

Between 1900 and the present, U.S. output in real terms has risen at a compounded average rate of about 3 percent annually. While this rate may not seem spectacular, keep in mind that it implies a doubling of the nation's output about every 23 years. We shall see, however that growth in the United States has slowed during the past two decades.

There are several sources of economic growth, and they merit listing on the blackboard. The first is "increased labor inputs," which have come about because of increased population and a larger percentage of the population in the labor force. Second is "improved labor inputs." People are more educated and healthier than they were in the past. As a result, the nation's stock of human capital has risen, contributing to greater productivity and economic growth. Third is "increased physical capital." For a nation to increase its stock of physical capital, it must save, that is, it must forgo some present consumption to produce capital goods that allow for greater future consumption. Additions to the stock of physical capital enable individuals to produce more in an hour of work, or in other words, improve their productivity.

A fourth source of economic growth is "economies of scale." As the size of firms and markets rise, the society experiences increases in output that exceed the additions in inputs. Recall that economies of scale were discussed earlier in the course.

A final source of economic growth is "improved technology." One prominent researcher recently estimated that "advances in knowledge" contributed 28 percent of the total growth of output in the United States over the years 1929–1982.* New knowledge, when applied to the production process, is capable of reducing the quantity of resources necessary to produce products. It also provides new products. In addition, it often transforms nonresources that seem useless into valuable productive resources. For example, a piece of ore containing uranium was considered useless before the discovery of nuclear reactions. Now it is used as fuel in nuclear power plants. The abundant resource silicon has found extensive new use in the electronics industry.

It is important to emphasize that incentives play a vital role in the growth process. Population growth is not the sole reason for the "additional labor inputs." Individuals have entered the workforce because of a desire to better themselves and their families economically. Likewise, employers have expanded employment because they have had a profit incentive to increase their production.

The "improvements in labor inputs" owe to the incentive to become better educated and more skillful. Individuals invest in human capital (attend college, undertake training) because they believe that future gains in income will more than offset present sacrifices. Firms undergo the expense of training workers on the job because they recognize that selling the added output produced by the more skillful workers will more than recoup the costs of training.

"Increases in the stock of capital" also occur because of economic incentives. Individuals have an incentive to save as a way to earn interest and dividends that increase their future ability to consume. This saving is borrowed by those who have an incentive to purchase and employ new capital as a way to expand production and profits. Even "economies of scale" are related to incentives. Competition provides an incentive for firms to become large enough to realize production, transportation, and marketing costs that, on a per unit basis, are as low as possible. Those firms that achieve economies of scale will increase their profits and their ability to compete with other domestic and international firms.

Finally, improved technology or "advances in knowledge" relate to incentives in that research and development activities occur because individuals and corporations see opportunity to gain from new production techniques and product innovations.

To repeat: *economic growth occurs in those economies where there are individual*

---

*Edward F. Denison, *Trends in American Economic Growth, 1929–1982* (Washington, D.C.: The Brookings Institution, 1985).

incentives to increase production. These incentives are important in socialist as well as capitalist economies. The economic perspective tells us that people compare costs and benefits in making their decisions and undertaking actions. The United States has experienced economic growth because its economic system rewards actions that increase output.

So much for the sources of economic growth and the role of incentives. Let us next turn to a closely related topic: the recent slowdown of economic growth in the United States. The pessimists—let's call them neo-Malthusians—believe this slowdown may be permanent.

"Pessimists! Slowdown! Neo-Malthusians! This sounds relevant to my paper. Where did I put my pencil?"

The long-term trend of economic growth masks the fact that economic growth has slowed in the United States during the past two decades. For example, between 1950 and 1970, real gross national product rose by 100 percent. Between 1970 and 1990—the same number of years—it increased by 72 percent.

We have seen that growth of output can occur either because more resources are used or because the productivity of resources rises. Slower growth can also be traced to these factors. Productivity growth has slowed during the past few decades in the United States, thus slowing the growth of output. Between 1948 and 1966, productivity—defined as output per hour of work—rose at an annual rate of 3.3 percent. It fell to 2.1 percent annually between 1966 and 1973, 1.1 percent over the 1972–1978 period, and about 0.2 percent annually between 1978 and 1982. Since 1982, productivity growth has risen to more normal levels, but the rate of annual growth remains disappointing when judged by the 1948–1966 standard.

Productivity growth is of great importance to economic growth. The society cannot increase its *real earnings* per hour of work unless it increases its *real output* per hour of work. Recall the economic perspective: Income derives from production and exchange.

There is common agreement that the United States needs to increase its productivity growth to achieve growth rates of output closer to those experienced during earlier periods. This change can be accomplished through devoting more resources to research and development, providing incentives for firms to acquire more capital, implementing new labor relations systems that emphasize cooperation and profit sharing, keeping the economy at levels that maintain high utilization rates of production facilities, and reemphasizing the importance of education and training to achieving economic growth. But this will not be an easy task; rather, it will be a real challenge.

I see that time exists to answer a question or two. Are there any questions?

"Yes. I am doing my paper on Malthus and wondered how his prediction that population growth would overwhelm economic growth fits into all of this. You have not mentioned it."

It fits in two ways. First, for some purposes it is better to look at the growth of *per-capita* output or income, rather than just output or income, to determine how an economy is doing from year to year. An economy can experience real growth and declining per-capita output if the population grows faster than the economy. In the case of the United States, the generalizations of which I just spoke still hold: the growth of output per person has slowed during the past 20 years.

The second way that it fits has to do with growth on a worldwide basis. Malthus's pessimism appears warranted if one looks at several parts of the world. Rapid population growth remains unchecked in some nations. Seventy percent of the earth's total inhabitants live in less-developed countries. Famine, malnutrition, and disease are consistent characteristics of life in parts of Asia, Africa, and South America. Worldwide there are roughly 7 million more people each month! So, yes, population growth is a concern.

Keep in mind, however, that people have *hands* and *minds* that are useful in producing things as well as *mouths* through which they consume. The problem may not be population growth, but rather the inability of particular economic systems to find productive uses for their labor resources. Researchers find that countries having higher standards of living tend to experience lower birth rates. When potential hourly earnings rise for males and females, the "price" (opportunity cost) of children increases because considerable time is required to raise children. This higher "price," in a sense, provides an incentive to have fewer children. Recall the economic perspective in this regard. Apparently, this "price" (opportunity cost) effect outweighs the fact that children become "more affordable" as earnings rise. So perhaps economic growth rather than just reductions in population should be emphasized. Then slower population growth might follow.

One final point: in some cases, the hunger problem results from the lack of incentives to produce food. Many poor countries actually fix the price of food *artificially* low, presumably as a way to reduce starvation. But this only worsens matters because the price does not reflect the true demand and supply conditions. The price therefore fails to provide the proper incentives for people to grow food for themselves, to produce other goods and services to gain sufficient income to buy food, or to produce food for sale to others.

Well, the period is over; we must stop.

Maybe I was too harsh on Malthus in my paper. Sounds as if economic growth is not something that can be taken for granted. It is starting to snow slightly. Winter can be awfully cold in Madison.

STUDY QUESTIONS

1. Explain Malthus's reasoning for his conclusion that wages would fall to a subsistence level and would tend to remain at that position.

2. "If the law of diminishing returns did not exist, the entire food supply of the world could be grown in a flowerpot." Is this statement accurate? Explain.

3. Briefly define *technological advance*, and cite an example of it. How is it possible for new technology to overcome or postpone the tendency for the increasing use of a resource to result in diminishing returns?

4. Define *GNP*, *real GNP*, and *GNP per capita*. Explain the circumstances under which real GNP might rise in a country while real GNP per capita fell.

5. "Some of our present resources were not resources a century ago. Likewise, many things that are not resources today may become valuable resources sometime in the future." Explain this statement from the perspective of an economist, and cite examples to illustrate your explanation.

6. List the sources of economic growth. Which of the sources would be depicted by a movement along a production function like the one in Figure 20-1? Which would be depicted by an upward shift of the curve?

7. Explain the role of economic incentives in contributing to economic growth.

8. Explain: "Increases in real hourly wages economy-wide are closely re-lated in the long run to increases in productivity."

9. Birth rates tend to fall as a nation's standard of living rises. Doesn't this fact contradict the economic perspective that people "buy" more of things when their income rises?

APPENDIX: PRICE RISES TO THE OCCASION

(This is the authors' updated version of a very old fable involving a poor gypsy who saved the life of a king.)

Once upon a time there was a young economist named Fiscal Optimal, who taught economics at Large State University. One day, Fiscal was attempting to explain to his Principles class the best known concept in economics — the marginal propensity to assume (MPA). Three times Fiscal covered the concept; three times he received puzzled looks of despair. "How can I teach them a complex concept such as this," he thought to himself, "when most of them cannot remember if a demand curve slopes upward or downward?"

Fiscal was frustrated and suddenly he exclaimed, "I quit, I quit!" He left the classroom, never to return to Large State University again. Instead, Fiscal and his wife, Scarcity, became beach bums. Each day, they spent hours on the beach sunning, surfing, and playing chess with friends. If fact, Fiscal became the chess champion of the beach.

One day, Fiscal was on the beach when he heard a desperate cry for help. A man was drowning in the surf. Fiscal to the rescue! The man was pulled to the shore, given mouth-to-mouth resuscitation, and saved. He turned out to be a very important and wealthy businessman, and he offered Fiscal and Scarcity a $25,000 reward as a token of his appreciation!

Fiscal glanced at his chessboard, then refused the offer. "I am a simple man," he stated to the businessman. "All I wish is that you cover this chessboard with silver dollars — one dollar on the first square, two on the second, four on the third, eight on the fourth, 16 on the fifth, and so on."

The business man was puzzled. "It's obvious that this fellow is economically illiterate," he thought. "I offer him $25,000, and all he wants is some silver dollars on a chessboard. These young people are weird."

However, he agreed to the deal and shook hands. Fiscal looked at Scarcity, and both broke out in wide grins.

Note: Get out your electronic calculator. The fourth square gets eight silver dollars, the fifth square get $16. What does the fortieth square get? Would you believe *one trillion dollars*? And that leaves 24 more squares to go!

By the tenth square, the businessman began to realize the consequences of his agreement. He signaled to his 6'8", 280-pound bodyguard, Ray Price, who was standing helplessly nearby because he could neither swim nor think. "Ray, tear up the chessboard and stick this guy's head in the sand."

With a tug, a hug, and a push, Price tore up the chessboard, grabbed Fiscal, and stuck his head in the sand. Then the businessman wrote out a check for $25,000, handed it to Scarcity, and walked to his limousine.

Morals:

1. Exponential, or geometric, growth adds up quickly.
2. Price can prevent exponential growth.
3. Living with Scarcity may not be the same as living in poverty.

21

A YEN FOR SOLITUDE

The Economics of International Trade

Concepts and Terms Examined in This Chapter

1. Mutual Gains from Trade
2. Exports and Imports
3. U.S.-Canadian Free Trade Agreement of 1989
4. Absolute Advantage
5. Comparative Advantage
6. Tariff
7. Import Quota
8. Nontariff Trade Barriers
9. Strategic Trade Policy
10. Comprehensive Trade Act of 1988

LEAVING THE WORLD BEHIND

"Excuse me, Adam, I'm going to leave this warm fire and slip into something a little more comfortable," stated Jennifer. She walked away from the fire, crawled into one of the two small backpacking tents, removed her hiking boots, and slipped into her goosedown sleeping bag.

Jennifer and Adam Moore and their close friends from college days, Bob and Nancy Loeb, had planned this backpacking excursion for nearly a year. Today they had completed the second 6-mile segment of a rigorous hike that would take them over 25 miles into the heart of the Olympic National Park wilderness area in northwestern Washington State. The trek began at the Whiskey Bend trailhead and followed the Elwha River upstream as it descended through Douglas fir, silver fir, and western hemlock forests. Eventually, the river would become a stream, and the trail would parallel and crisscross it as it wandered through mountain meadows circled by vistas of rugged snowcapped peaks.

"We'd better call it a day, too," said Nancy Loeb.

"I suppose you are right," replied her husband, Bob.

Bob and Adam gathered together the miscellaneous items of camping gear that had to be stowed, including the small aluminum cookstove, the nesting pots and pans, the fuel flask, the eating utensils, the matches, and the instant coffee, and placed them in a nylon stuffing bag. Adam tied a cord to the bag, tossed the cord over the limb of a nearby fir, and hoisted the bag upward to hang beside the four backpacks, well out of reach of black bears that might visit during the night. (Providing that the bears did not possess capital goods such as minitrampolines or ladders.)

Morning arrived with a glorious dawn. Bob and Nancy Loeb, trout-fishing aficionados, scurried to the nearby Elwha River, fishing rods in hand, entertaining visions of catching a couple of the rainbow trout. After numerous casts into the clear, deep pools that formed between the boulders and ripples of the fast-moving water, Nancy's spinning rod arched over like a production function, and she exclaimed, "I have a nice one on, Bob!" The trout broke the surface and rippled off line from the ultralight reel.

"Don't lose him, I'm hungry," said Bob, as he watched Nancy reel in the fish. After a short struggle, Nancy had the 14-inch rainbow on the shore and began casting again. Bob, too, finally caught a fish, and Nancy, yet another.

Back at the campsite, Jennifer was busily involved with a hobby of her own. The forest filtered the emerging sunrays into a kaleidoscope of shadows and brightness, and Jennifer sought to capture that mood through the lens of her camera.

Breakfast was delicious. Along with the three trout, the group ate dehydrated apricots and banana bread while sipping coffee. What a change of pace from just a few days before! Adam Moore left the hustle and bustle of his job as a manager of the men's clothing department of a department store located in a major mall. Pin-striped suits, designer sweaters, and men's cologne seemed light-years removed from this spot in the wilderness.

"Imagine what an incongruity it would be to see someone coming down one of the switchbacks on the trail wearing a suit and carrying an umbrella," thought Adam.

Just four days earlier, Jennifer Moore was busy working as an executive for the Boeing Corporation. Now she was deep in the wilderness. She left on a positive note—her division had just concluded the sale of seven 747s to Japan Airline.

Nancy Loeb was a homemaker with two small children. The peacefulness of this campsite—the only noises being the gurgling sound of the nearby river and the occasional chattering of some friendly chipmunks—certainly contrasted to the noise, commotion, and general disarray that often characterize a household containing two pint-sized, happy, and slightly mischievous youngsters.

Bob Loeb drew lines prior to this trip. His skill as an architect had little transferability to the skills needed to survive several days of hiking carrying 40 pounds of equipment on one's back. As Bob sat silently, his mind wandered to the parallel outlines of firs stretching as straight as a plumb line upward.

Finishing his coffee, Bob glanced at the others, sensed the common bond and mood, and stated, "This is a beautiful spot; I hate to leave it."

"There is such a sense of simplicity here," reflected Nancy. "The feeling of solitude, of self-sufficiency, of independence, is almost overwhelming."

"That's exactly what I enjoy most about backpacking," said Adam. "Here we are, 12 miles from nowhere. In a sense, we've left a world of interdependence, high technology, and complexity for one of simplicity and self-reliance."

"We've left the world behind," stated Nancy. All nodded in agreement.

Postscript: Jennifer, Adam, Nancy, and Bob, although packing lightly, had brought several personal items and much equipment along. Just a few items of particular interest are the following:

1. Hiking boots (Adam): made in Italy: leather for the boots imported from Argentina; rubber soles imported from France.
2. Ragg brand socks (Jennifer): made in Norway.
3. Swiss army knives (all): made in Switzerland; stainless steel imported from Sweden.
4. Raingear: manufactured in South Korea.
5. Fuel flasks: made in West Germany.
6. White gasoline: refined in the United States; oil imported from Saudi Arabia.
7. Minolta SLR 35mm camera (Jennifer): made in Japan.
8. Engagement rings (Nancy and Jennifer): made in the United States; stones cut in Israel; diamonds originated in South Africa.
9. Sleeping bags: made in the United States; goosedown imported from Canada and the People's Republic of China.
10. Mepp spinner (fishing lure): made in France; Rapala fishing lure: made in Finland; balsa wood imported from Ecuador.
11. Garcia fishing reel: made in Sweden; Maxima fishing line: made in West Germany.
12. Vuarnet sunglasses (Nancy): made in France.
13. Tin cans: tin imported from Bolivia.
14. Backpack frames: made in the United States; aluminum alloy includes materials imported from South Africa.
15. Nikon SLR 35mm camera (Bob): made in West Germany.
16. Instant coffee: made in the United States; coffee beans imported from Brazil.
17. Silva compass: manufactured in Finland.
18. Aluminum nesting pots and pans: made in England.
19. Nylon stuffing bags: made in the United States; nylon produced from oil imported from Nigeria.

20. Seiko watch (Adam): made in Japan.
21. Banana bread: made in Nancy's kitchen; bananas imported from Honduras.
22. Hershey chocolate bars: cocoa imported from Ghana.

THE SCOPE OF INTERNATIONAL TRADE

"We've left the world behind," stated Nancy.

This statement is more a reflection of Nancy's lack of awareness of international trade than of reality. It is impossible to leave the world behind, even on a wilderness backpacking trip! Much like Atlas, the mythical Greek god, the Moores and Loebs carry part of the world on their shoulders. The hiking boots, Swiss army knives, cameras, fishing lures, compasses, raingear, and fuel flasks mentioned in the scene were all exports from abroad and imports to the United States. *Imports are goods and services sold in a different country from the one in which they are produced. Exports are goods and services produced in a specific nation and sold to customers in other nations.*

Consumers in the United States spend more on imported goods than people in any other nation. Likewise, U.S. producers export more goods, measured in dollars, than exporters in any other single country. International trade constitutes about 12 percent of U.S. GNP. Yet many other nations are more dependent on international trade than is the United States. Their *absolute* amounts of trade are lower than the United States, but their *relative* involvement in trade is higher. For example, exports constitute about 45 percent of the GNP of the Netherlands and between 20 and 30 percent of the GNPs of the United Kingdom, Canada, New Zealand, and Germany.

In the early 1990s the best customers for U.S. exports, in descending order of the dollar volume of sales, were Canada, Japan, Mexico, the United Kingdom, Germany, Taiwan, and South Korea. These same nations, again in descending order, were the major suppliers of imported goods to the United States. The strong trade relationship between the United States and Canada will be further bolstered by the U.S.-Canadian Free Trade Agreement of 1989. This agreement will eventually end all tariffs and other trade barriers between the two countries.

Over the long term, U.S. exports and imports tend to balance out. However, between 1982 and 1987 the United States suffered a serious deterioration in its trade balance. In 1982 net exports (exports minus imports) were $26.3 billion; by 1987 imports *exceeded* exports by a record $112.6 billion! Although annual trade deficits—imports in excess of exports—declined between 1987 and 1990, they remained at high levels during this period.

One cause of the trade deficits during the 1980s was a faster rate of economic growth in the United States than in many other nations. As national income in the United States rose, the demand for imported goods increased. Meanwhile, the foreign demand for U.S. exports did not keep pace. Another factor at work was a large U.S. federal budget deficit, which reached $220 billion in 1986. Some of this budget deficit was financed by foreigners who lent money to the U.S. government by buying newly issued U.S. Treasury securities. The upshot was that U.S. consumers had more after-tax, after-lending income available for buying imported goods.

WHY DO NATIONS SPECIALIZE AND TRADE?

Nations specialize and trade for the same reason that people do—it is in their best interest. In other words, they expect to gain through exchange. Recall from the discussion of the economic perspective that production and exchange are the sources of income and wealth in society. For example, Bob Loeb was an architect who chose to specialize in an area of employment for which he had special interest and aptitude. By specializing, he was more productive and earned more income than if he were a "jack-of-all-trades, and master of none." Bob implicitly recognized that it was in his best interest to work in an occupation where, relative to others, he was most productive. The income he earns from his work is then available to buy other goods and services that he desires. In the same manner, other people specialize to produce items Bob desires; and some people spend part of their income to contract for Bob's architectural specialization and trade. The total production of goods and services is greater with the division of labor than without it.

People in different nations recognize this same potential for mutual gain. By specializing in areas of production in which they have relative advantages, corporations or government-owned enterprises sell goods to foreign customers in exchange for money. The income generated from export sales allows people to import products that either they cannot produce or could produce only at opportunity costs higher than the price of the imported goods.

THE LAW OF COMPARATIVE ADVANTAGE

The law of comparative advantage is the paramount explanation for why nations gain from trade. Originally conceived by David Ricardo, a British economist, the law states that *the total output of a nation will be greatest when each product is produced by the nation that has the lowest opportunity cost.*

Two examples of this somewhat complex law are provided in the pages that follow. The first example explains a special subset of comparative advantage—one that economists refer to as absolute advantage.

Absolute Advantage

Absolute advantage is a situation in which each trading partner can produce one product more efficiently than the other partner.

Recall that the backpackers ate a breakfast of trout, freeze-dried apricots, banana bread, and coffee. The last two items involve imported products. We'll go bananas in this example. Assume that the world's economy consists of two nations—the United States and Honduras—and two products—wheat and bananas. Also, suppose that both countries can produce either product. The United States' capabilities for producing wheat are generally known, but could it produce bananas? The answer is "Yes, if it so desired." It could construct domelike structures (à la Detroit's Silverdome), haul in the appropriate soil, and use high technology to produce just the right climatic conditions necessary to grow a crop of picture-perfect bananas. The opportunity costs of producing bananas would be extremely

Table 21-1 Illustration of Absolute Advantage (Hypothetical Output per Unit of Resource Employed)

	Wheat	Bananas
United States	7 units	1 unit
Honduras	1 unit	4 units
Total	8 units	5 units

high, though, because the United States does not have resources well suited for that task. On the other hand, it does possess climate, soil conditions, labor force, and technology conducive to growing wheat.

Likewise, Honduras can produce low-cost bananas because of its particular mix of resources, but those resources are poorly suited to growing wheat. Thus, in this simple two-nation world, Honduras has the advantage in producing bananas and the United States has the advantage in growing wheat.

Tables 21-1 and 21-2 formalize this concept and show how specialization according to absolute advantage can increase total world output. Table 21-1 shows that the United States has an absolute advantage in producing wheat, because each unit of resource employed can produce 7 units of wheat, compared to only 1 unit in Honduras. Honduras has an absolute advantage in growing bananas; each unit of resource employed produces 4 units of bananas, contrasted to only 1 unit in the United States.

Specialization will increase the output from each unit of resource used. This is illustrated in Table 21-1. The prespecialization outputs are shown in parentheses.

To check your understanding of the gains from specialization that are indicated in Table 21-2, ask yourself these questions:

1. If the United States shifted 1 resource unit from the prespecialization production of bananas (shown in parentheses), how much would wheat production in the United States rise? (Answer: 7 units)
2. If Honduras shifted 1 resource unit from the prespecialization production of wheat, how much would banana output rise? (Answer: 4 units)
3. What would be the total output of wheat and bananas after the specialization? (Answer: 14 units of wheat and 8 units of bananas)
4. What are the gains from specialization? (Answer: $14 - 8 = 6$ units of wheat; $8 - 5 = 3$ units of bananas)

Table 21-2 Illustration of the Gains from Specialization (Hypothetical Output per Unit of Resource Employed)

	Wheat	Bananas
United States	14(7)	0(1)
Honduras	0(1)	8(4)
Total	14	8
Gain	$14 - 8 = 6$	$8 - 5 = 3$

Law of

Comparative Advantage

The previous example illustrated the principle that nations should specialize in producing products for which they have an absolute advantage. Absolute advantage explains some trade flows in the world, but it does not explain why two-thirds of world trade takes place among nations with very similar resource endowments. Do specialization and trade among such nations provide potential for mutual gain? The answer, perhaps surprisingly, is "Yes."

Adam Moore wore Italian-made hiking boots into the Olympic wilderness. Those boots provide a starting point for a discussion of comparative advantage. Italy is well known for its shoe and boot industry; several brands are the world's leading sellers (for example, Kastinger hiking boots and Nordica ski boots).

For purposes of illustration, once again assume that only two nations exist in the world, the United States and Italy, and each can produce two products, computer chips and boots. But in this case also assume that the United States has an absolute advantage in the manufacture of *both* products. This situation is shown in Table 21-3.

According to the information in Table 21-3, the United States has an absolute advantage in producing both computer chips and boots. From each unit of resource employed, the United States can produce 3 units of electronic chips; Italy can only produce 1 unit. Likewise, the United States has an absolute advantage in producing boots (6 units versus 5 units from each unit of resource). Would the United States be better off not trading with Italy? The answer is "No." The principle of comparative advantage declares that each nation should produce the product involving the lowest opportunity cost. The following analysis helps to clarify this concept.

The opportunity cost of producing 1 unit of computer chips in the United States is 2 units of boots ($6/3 = 2$). Italy's opportunity cost of producing 1 unit of computer chips is 5 units of boots ($5/1 = 5$). Because the United States' opportunity costs are less (2 compared with 5 units of boots), the United States has a comparative advantage in producing computer chips and should specialize in that production. Italy's opportunity costs of producing boots (1/5 unit of computer chips) is less than the United States' (1/2 unit of computer chips), so it should specialize in its area of comparative advantage—boot production.

The general principle that nations should specialize where they have low opportunity costs relative to trading partners can be tested by examining the impact that specialization has on total world production. Based on the information in Table 21-3, if the United States transferred just 1 resource unit from boot manufacturer to computer chips, computer chip output would rise by 3 units and

Table 21-3   Illustration of Comparative Advantage (Hypothetical Output per Unit of Resource Employed)

	Computer Chips	Boots
United States	3 units	6 units
Italy	1 unit	5 units
Total	4 units	11 units

Table 21-4 Illustration of Gains from Specialization (Hypothetical Output per Unit of Resource Employed)

	Computer Chips	Boots
United States	6* (3)	0(6)
Italy	−1**(1)	15(5)
Total	5 − 4 = 1	15 − 11 = 4

*Transfer of 1 resource unit from boots to computer chips.

**Transfer of 2 resource units from computer chips to boots.

boot output would fall by 6 units. If Italy transferred 2 resource units (1 isn't sufficient to demonstrate the gain) to boot production, the output would rise by 10 units and computer chip production would decline by 2 units. The postspecialization situation is shown in Table 21-4. The amounts shown in the parentheses represent the prespecialization situation.

The net outcome of this specialization may be summarized as follows:

1. Change in computer chip output: in the United States (+3); in Italy (−2); net increase: (+1).
2. Change in boot output: in the United States (−6); in Italy (+10); net increase: (+4).

Specialization creates greater total output of both computer chips and boots! Both nations can experience an increase in their standard of living by specializing in producing goods and services where opportunity costs are less than those of the other nation and engaging in trade.

FACILITATING TRADE: THE USE OF MONEY

It should now be clear why nations specialize and trade, but most world trade does not involve direct barter (the direct exchange of Italian boots for U.S. computer chips, for example). Instead, money is used as a medium of exchange.

International trade, like domestic trade, is greatly facilitated by the use of money. Firms or people specializing in the production of specific goods or services exchange those products for money and then use the money to buy other goods and services. Within an economy—for example, the United States—prices are stated in dollar amounts and buyers use dollars to purchase the products. The buyers possess dollars, and that is exactly the currency that the seller desires.

The situation is much different in the international market. How many dollars does it take to buy a German-made auto priced at 10,000 marks or a Japanese camera selling for 20,000 yen? That question must be answered because *domestic producers want payment in their own currency* so that they can pay wages, rent, interest, dividends, and taxes. To meet this need and to facilitate international trade, a market for foreign currency, or foreign exchange, developed. In this market, currencies of one nation are exchanged for currencies of another nation. Chapter 22 discusses the market for foreign exchange in detail. There it will be discovered that, as in all markets, the key elements of the foreign exchange market are demand, supply, equilibrium price, and equilibrium quantity.

A FINAL QUESTION: WHY ARE THERE TRADE BARRIERS?

It is well known that many nations restrict the free flow of imports to the consumers in their nations. These trade restrictions are of three basic types:

1. *Tariffs:* taxes or duties placed on imports.
2. *Quotas:* limits on the quantity or total value of an imported item.
3. *Nontariff barriers:* unnecessary regulations which make it costly for importers to get their goods approved for sale.

Trade barriers raise an important question: If people and nations benefit from specialization and international trade, why do so many governments impose tariffs, quotas, and nontrade barriers? There are three broad reasons, discussed in the following paragraphs.

Strategic Trade Policy

Some governments, notably Japan, allegedly use trade barriers strategically to reduce the risk of product development borne by domestic firms and to permit them to obtain economies of scale (Chapter 7). Protected from foreign competition, these firms grow more rapidly than competing firms abroad that do not have protected home markets. This rapid growth of output reduces the average costs of production for these firms, and the reduced costs then permit them to charge lower prices than international competitors abroad. As a result, the "protected" firms come to dominate world markets (because of lower costs), as well as their domestic market (because of trade protection). Dominance in world markets supposedly enables these firms to return economic profits to the citizens of the home nation in excess of the sacrifices that result from reduced import competition caused by the trade barriers.

The theory of strategic trade policy suggests that comparative advantage can be fostered in specific industries through public policy. Comparative advantage in high-technology industries allegedly is beneficial because new technology advances often are transferable to other industries in the domestic economy. The fatal flaw of strategic trade policy is that it invites retaliation by trade partners. Nations hurt by strategic trade policies invariably counter with such strategies of their own. The end result is that trade diminishes worldwide, and consumers in the affected nations lose the previous gains from that trade.

Misunderstanding of the Gains from Trade

A second broad reason for trade barriers rests upon a commonly accepted myth that the gain from international trade is the increased domestic employment in the export sector. This myth suggests that exports are "good" because they increase domestic employment, whereas imports are "bad" because they deprive people of jobs at home. In reality, the real benefit from trade is the overall increase in output obtained through specialization and exchange. A nation can fully employ its resources — including labor — with or without international trade. International trade, however, permits these resources to be used in ways that increase society's total output and therefore its overall well-being.

Thought of differently, international trade is not needed for a nation to locate *on* its production possibilities curve (Chapter 2). Instead, world trade permits an economy to reach a point *beyond* its domestic production possibilities curve. The gain from trade is this extra output — the *imports* obtained at less cost than goods that would have had to be produced domestically. The only valid reason for exporting part of our national output is to obtain imports of greater value to us. Specialization and exchange enable individuals and nations to achieve this highly desirable outcome.

Political Considerations

The third general reason for trade restrictions is purely political. Changes in trade patterns *do* redistribute income among people and areas, even as overall output and income are rising. Corporations, unions, and communities hurt by exports naturally attempt to gain relief through government action, and they frequently are successful. But studies clearly show that the gains some people get from restricting trade come at the expense of far greater losses to consumers across the nation. One relatively recent estimate is that trade restrictions cost Americans more than $80 billion a year. Consequently, saving particular jobs through trade restrictions is extremely costly. For example, the estimated annual cost of trade restrictions per job saved is $750,000 in the carbon steel industry and $220,000 in the dairy industry.

The long-run trend, beginning with the Reciprocal Trade Act of 1934 and more recently involving Tokyo Round agreements, has been for lower tariffs worldwide. But, in the late 1980s, renewed clamor for tariffs and quotas occurred in the United States in response to large U.S. trade deficits and the perceived strategic trade policies implemented by Japan and others. The Comprehensive Trade Act of 1988 contained procedures for initiating unfair-trade investigations against nations engaged in persistent patterns of unfair trade. This law has resulted in direct negotiations between Japan and the United States to eliminate strategic and political trade restrictions.

Meanwhile, world trade has continued to expand. It increasingly touches all of our lives, even when we occasionally have a yen for solitude and seek to leave the world temporarily behind. This thought returns us to our hikers.

*　　*　　*

"It's been a great experience," concluded Adam Moore as he, Jennifer, Nancy, and Bob reached the parking lot from whence they had begun. Ten days seemed like a month to the now weary, ragged foursome. The weather had been beautiful, the scenery spectacular, the fishing good, and the sense of solitude overwhelming.

The Loebs loaded their gear in their Toyota van, said one last "Goodbye" to the Moores, and started down the road that led back to the world of work and commerce. The Moores followed in their Volvo.

STUDY QUESTIONS

1. Explain why a nation that has an *absolute* advantage in producing products A and B might decide to specialize in A and trade for B.

2. Lobbyists from the automobile industry have proposed that the United States limit the number of foreign imports. Which of the following groups would gain from such an action? Which would lose?
   a. Ford automobile dealers
   b. Toyota automobile dealers
   c. Consumers purchasing new cars
   d. Sellers of used cars
   e. Wholesale auto-importing firms
   f. Mechanics who specialize in foreign cars
   g. U.S. auto workers

3. Assume that the United States can use a specific amount of its resources to produce either 20 sewing machines or 800 dresses and South Korea can employ the same amount of its resources to produce either 10 sewing machines or 600 dresses. In which of the two products should the United States specialize? Why?

4. Answer the accompanying questions on the basis of the following information about the cost ratios of two products — hair dryers and radios — in the countries of Alpha and Beta:

   Alpha: one hair dryer = 2 radios
   Beta: one hair dryer = 4 radios

   a. What is the domestic opportunity cost of producing each radio in Alpha?
   b. What is domestic opportunity cost of producing each radio in Beta?
   c. In which product should each of these nations specialize? Explain why.

5. In what respect is international specialization and trade similar to specialization and trade among regions in the United States? In what respect is it different?

6. Distinguish between a tariff, an import quota, and nontariff trade barriers. What is the purpose of these trade restrictions? Why do most economists oppose them?

7. The U.S. textile and apparel industry has pushed for legislation that would impose quotas on imports of foreign textile and apparel goods. This same industry imports one-half of its machinery. In what way are these two behaviors consistent? Which of the two behaviors is inconsistent with society's goal of gaining as much output from its limited resources as possible?

8. Explain, referring to the economic perspective: "Nations do not trade; people trade."

22

WHO STOLE LIZZY'S PROFITS?

The Economics of International Finance

Concepts and Terms Examined in This Chapter

1. Foreign Exchange Market
2. Exchange Rates
3. Determinants of Exchange Rates
4. Currency Appreciation and Depreciation
5. Exchange Rate Intervention

International trade is on the rise. Improvements in transportation and telecommunication have reduced the cost of conducting long-distance economic transactions. As a result, more businesses have chosen to expand their activities beyond the borders of their own countries. These improvements in transportation and communication have brought new opportunities for economic success and new risks for business failure. This chapter focuses on one small business and its adventure into international trade to explain the market for foreign exchange. The scenes that follow also illustrate how international currency markets and national economic policies can influence the success of enterprises engaging in world trade.

DAY ONE: THE INTRODUCTION

Harvey Cornwell is just getting comfortable in his new office chair. At age 31, he decided to sell his caramel corn factory and travel around the world. After all, Pop had sold his share of the business three years before and had retired to live in Australia, where he spent his time diving along the Great Barrier Reef and sampling different Australian brews. Harvey missed Pop. It just wasn't the same making caramel corn without his old mentor around.

After traveling around the world for a year, Harvey decided that he needed to work; he had too many good ideas and too much energy just to play at this stage in his life. So Harvey decided to start his own business as an international business consultant. After all, he had an MBA degree, had run a successful business for 14 years, and had traveled around the world. What other qualifications does an international business consultant need? All of this explains why Harvey was sitting in his chair, surveying his newly furnished office when Lizzy entered.

Lizzy was the energetic owner of the business across the street. Its freshly painted sign read, "Lizzy's Place: Cuckoo Clocks R Us." Struck by the original title, Harvey had browsed through the store on two occasions inspecting the wide variety of merchandise. The store specialized in genuine German Black Forest cuckoo clocks and accessories. It contained not only large, small, and medium-size clocks, but also wristwatches with miniature cuckoos, posters of clocks, T-shirts that said "I love my cuckoo," books about cuckoo clocks, dusters, covers, and even sweaters for cuckoos to wear during the winter months. Lizzy's Place was a truly amazing store!

"So you are an international business consultant?" Lizzy asked as she walked briskly into Harvey's office.

"At your service, ma'am," replied Harvey.

"Don't give me any of that ma'am business; I'm old enough to be your younger sister," Lizzy stated as she sat down in the guest chair opposite Harvey's desk.

"I am not a big fan of consultants. My father once defined a consultant as a person who can describe 100 different ways to make love, but has never had a date."

Harvey decided to keep quiet. He wasn't going to touch that comment with a ten-foot pole, not in this day and age. Besides, this was one of the rare times he couldn't think of anything witty to say.

Lizzy continued, "I need someone to investigate my business and find out why the profits have declined so badly in the last year. Unfortunately, I don't have enough time to look around for better help. Are you interested in the job? I am willing to pay you $500 a day plus expenses, but you have to get the job done in five days."

"Certainly," Harvey replied, "I'll take the job. How could I refuse such a warm invitation? This job sounds interesting. Nevertheless, let me ask you a few questions. First, why don't you look into this problem yourself?"

"Well, the truth of the matter is that I have better things to do. I just bought the store from my father one year ago. He wanted to retire to the Florida Keys and work with environmental groups to preserve the offshore reefs from damage done by careless divers. I'm looking for an alternative to my current job and thought this business might help me make the transition."

"What do you do now?" Harvey asked.

"I'm a professional sports agent, and I represent several starting quarterbacks in the National Football League. Johnny Longbomb is my current problem. I'm attempting to renegotiate his contract with the Indianapolis Colts. He signed a terrible contract for $800,000 a year, and I am aiming to get him a $4 million two-year contract. I make 10 percent of his contract, so I need to direct my energies toward that task. Mr. Cornwell, I'm hiring you for the same reason I hired my typist. I'm a heck of a lot better typist than he is, but my comparative advantage is to negotiate sports contracts."

"So why don't you just sell Lizzy's Place?"

"The clock shop," said Lizzy, "is just the first component of what eventually will be a corporate structure consisting of several interlocking import enterprises. So get to work! Keep me informed of your progress each day."

DAY TWO: THE BUSINESS AND ITS SUPPLIERS

Bright and early the next day, Harvey began looking at the accounting books of Lizzy's Imports. He was pleased to see she understood the MR = MC management principle he struggled to learn years ago. When costs rose in her business, she laid off part-time staff, identified products that were not selling and sold them at a deep discount, and refused employee requests to restock products that cost more than the discounted prices. For instance, the clock with a model of the pop singer Madonna as the bird seemed like a good idea when it came out in 1990, but the public had quickly lost interest in the clocks when Madonna's popularity waned shortly thereafter.

Moreover, Harvey found that Lizzy's Place was losing less money than would be the case if it shut down. That is, Lizzy's fixed costs were more than her operating losses.

Harvey stopped in to report on his progress to Lizzy.

"Well, Lizzy, I've got good news and bad news. The good news is that you are following sound management practices. It was not an obvious financing, management, or administrative mistake that drove down your profits. The bad news is I still have not solved the case."

"Thanks for the vote of confidence on my management ability, but frankly I already knew that was not the problem. Please get back to work and find out something I don't already know," replied Lizzy.

"Don't have a cow!" thought Harvey. "This is only day two."

He then stated, "I need some information about your suppliers. Have they increased the price of their goods to you?"

"No, my contract with the German suppliers is good for two more years. They will not increase their prices in that time, and we have not renegotiated that contract. I refuse to renegotiate contracts other than those for my football clients."

Harvey, momentarily stumped by the slide in Lizzy's profits, decided to invite his former college economics professor to lunch to see if she could give him some leads to pursue.

"Harvey," Dr. Tandy inquired after listening to his description of the problem, "do you remember our discussion of exchange rates in our economics class?"

"Not really," Harvey admitted, "I was very busy with the caramel corn business then. We had no foreign customers, so I cut classes during the last part of the course."

"Yes, you were always a busy young man with a good mind and a short attention span. Let me review with you how foreign exchange markets work. Maybe looking in that direction will help you find a solution to Lizzy's falling profits."

"I'm listening."

Foreign Exchange Markets

"Foreign exchange markets are widely dispersed, highly organized systems of exchange in which the currencies of participating countries are bought and sold. Banking institutions and brokerage companies usually participate in this market. The market exists to facilitate exchanges between citizens of different countries. If a U.S. buyer like Lizzy wants to purchase a product (clocks) from a seller in another country (Germany), the buyer must exchange dollars for the currency of the seller's country, (deutsche marks, or DM). Most sales between companies in different countries are made in the seller's currency. In this case, Lizzy must purchase deutsche marks in the foreign currency market and use those deutsche marks to pay for the merchandise her suppliers provide. To obtain these deutsche marks she must pay the exchange rate.

Exchange Rates

"An exchange rate is the domestic price of one unit of foreign currency. For example, if Lizzy must pay $0.50 to buy one German deutsche mark, then the $/DM exchange rate is $0.50.

"Exchange rates enable consumers in one country to translate the prices of foreign goods into units of their own currency by multiplying the exchange rate times the foreign price. For example, if the Black Forest cuckoo clocks were priced at DM 1,000, then the cost of those clocks to Lizzy would be $500 (DM 1,000 × $0.50 = $500).

"These exchange rates change from day to day, hour to hour, minute to minute—maybe Lizzy's profits are being eaten up by changes in exchange rates."

"How so? What is the consequence of a change in the exchange rate?" Harvey asked.

"When the exchange rate changes, the dollar is said to *appreciate* or to *depreciate*. If the exchange rate changes so that a dollar buys more deutsche marks than it did previously, then the dollar has appreciated, or become stronger. For example, if the exchange rate changes so that $0.40 buys one deutsche mark, then Lizzy's costs will *fall* in dollar terms. Lizzy will now need only $400 (DM 1,000 × $0.40), rather then $500, to buy a DM 1,000 clock.

"On the other hand, if the dollar price of deutsche marks rises, more dollars will be required to buy them. For example, if it takes $0.60 to buy one deutsche mark, then Lizzy's cost will *increase* in dollar terms. She will have to pay $600 (DM 1,000 × $0.60), not $500 or $400, for a clock priced at DM 1,000 in Germany. In this case, the dollar has become weaker; it has depreciated against the German deutsche mark in international exchange markets.

"It seems to me that you should determine what exchange rate existed a year ago when Lizzy took over her business and compare it to the current exchange rate."

"Thanks, Dr. Tandy. You have been a great help. I now have some good leads. I will let you know how all this turns out."

With those comments, Harvey left the restaurant and headed for the library to do his research.

DAY THREE: THE GREAT DISCOVERY

"Lizzy, I presume," stated Harvey as he entered Lizzy's office.

"I have discovered what has happened to your profits. Your suppliers didn't change their prices, but depreciation of the international value of the dollar has increased your dollar expense of purchasing deutsche marks to pay your suppliers. I should have caught this fact when I first looked at your accounting records!"

"Good morning, Harvey, and, yes, it is good to see you, too. Now slow down and tell me what you are talking about." Lizzy turned in her chair and hung up the telephone. "I was just leaving a message for the general manager of the Indianapolis Colts, but I think I'll just let him wait for a while. Now tell me about your discovery."

"The $/DM exchange rate changed after you took over the company and increased your costs. That is why your profits plunged."

"Excuse me, Harvey, but I don't know what exchange rates are or how they can affect my business. Back up and start from the beginning.

"Okay, the exchange rate is the amount of U.S. money you must pay to buy the German currency necessary to pay for your store merchandise. Because both the United States and Germany have flexible exchange rates, that rate is determined in the currency market. Both countries normally allow the market for foreign exchange to determine the value of each currency. This foreign exchange market operates just like any other market. The price of currency (the exchange rate) is determined by the supply and demand for the two currencies.

"There is a *supply of deutsche marks* on the market because Germans want to buy American products, but they need to exchange deutsche marks for dollars to purchase U.S. products. They use the dollars they obtain to buy American products, financial assets, or properties.

"Meanwhile, the *demand for deutsche marks* arises because U.S. citizens, as well as firms like yours, want to buy German products—in your case, clocks and all the supporting merchandise. American importers use dollars to buy deutsche marks.

"This demand and supply relationship for deutsche marks is illustrated in my Figure 22-1."

"Well," remarked Lizzy, "It looks like something I saw in my old textbook *Economic Scenes*."

"Hey," Harvey said, "I had that same book. Great book, wasn't it!"

"It was clear that the authors thought so. Just get on with it, Harvey. What does this graph have to do with Lizzy's Place?"

"As shown by the intersection of D_1 and S_1, the market-clearing price for a deutsche mark on the international exchange market was $0.50 a year ago. That was the price you had to pay to buy German currency to pay your suppliers for their merchandise. Now look at the current equilibrium price—note the intersection of D_2 and S_1."

"Hey, I'm paying $0.80 for every deutsche mark now. Why did the dollar price of deutsche mark go up?" asked Lizzy.

Harvey replied, "Something has increased the demand for deutsche marks. I need to find out what caused this shift in the demand curve and therefore what depreciated the dollar."

"You're right," agreed Lizzy. "It's nice to know why my costs jumped so dramatically when I thought I had them well under control because of the two-year contract with suppliers. I did have the deutsche mark price of the clocks locked in, but not the dollar price. Why did the dollar depreciate? I don't want to get blindsided by an event like this in the future. Good work, Harvey, but now get me *the rest of the story*."

Figure 22-1   The Market for Foreign Exchange: An Increase in the Demand for Deutsche Marks

American imports from Germany create a demand for German deutsche marks, and U.S. exports to Germany generate a supply of deutsche marks. The dollar price of deutsche marks, or the exchange rate, is determined at the intersection of the supply and demand curves. An increase in the demand for deutsche marks raises their dollar price, that is, causes the dollar to depreciate in value.

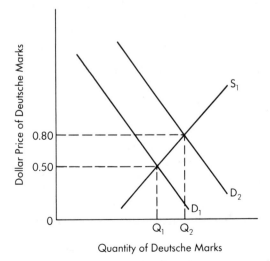

DAY FOUR: THE INTERNATIONAL BANKING CONSPIRACY

Harvey spent most of the morning reading old issues of the *Wall Street Journal* and other financial newspapers. A pattern of events was unfolding that he couldn't believe. But he remembered the advice of his economics professor, who said, "Eliminate all the impossible explanations, and you are left with the correct explanation, no matter how improbable it seems." With a mind full of apprehension, he persuaded Dr. Tandy to eat lunch with him again and discuss this situation.

"Dr. Tandy," Harvey began, "I have discovered that the dollar has depreciated in value. I am still puzzled over the factors that caused the exchange rate to change. Can you give me some help?"

"Well, Harvey, I assume you are still talking about the exchange rate between the United States dollar and the German deutsche mark, so I will use it as an example. Three types of events could cause the U.S. dollar to *depreciate* relative to the deutsche mark: (1) The American economy could grow more rapidly than the German economy; (2) the U.S. inflation rate could be higher than Germany's; and (3) our interest rates could be lower than those in Germany. To simplify, I am going to explain all of these factors in terms of changes in the demand for deutsche marks. In reality, the supply of deutsche marks may also be affected.

"A nation's imports rise as its national income grows. Thus, in the first case, our rapid growth would mean that our demand for imports would rise more rapidly than Germany's demand for U.S. exports. The result would be an increase in the demand for deutsche marks to finance the greater American imports."

Dr. Tandy drew a graph (identical to Figure 22-1) on the table napkin. The graph showed a rightward shift of the demand curve for deutsche marks—from D_1 to D_2—and a rise in the dollar price of deutsche marks (depreciation of the dollar).

"A higher U.S. inflation rate would have the same effect. American consumers would discover that German products were becoming less expensive than American products. To obtain these German products Americans need to buy deutsche marks. Thus the demand for deutsche marks would rise, as from D_1 to D_2, and the dollar price of deutsche marks would increase (dollar depreciation).

"Finally, if our interest rates were lower than those in Germany, U.S. financial investors would have an incentive to buy deutsche marks to purchase German bonds and other debt instruments. But to get the German bonds, Americans must buy deutsche marks. In the market for deutsche marks, the demand curve would shift to the right, again as shown by the shift from D_1 to D_2. Note that the dollar price of deutsche marks rises, and the dollar depreciates."

"Does the process work in reverse?" Harvey asked. "Would a lower relative U.S. growth rate, a lower rate of inflation in the United States, or higher American interest rates contribute to a rightward shift of the *supply* curve for German money and cause the dollar price of deutsche marks to fall (appreciation of the dollar)?"

"Yes, the process works in reverse," replied Dr. Tandy, drawing a new graph (Figure 22-2). "You *do* learn quickly. Germans will supply more deutsche marks in the currency markets in order to buy dollars. The supply curve of deutsche marks will shift from S_1 to S_2, and the dollar price of deutsche marks will decline. Because each dollar can buy more deutsche marks, the dollar has appreciated in this case."

"Well, then I have discovered a tragic conspiracy," boasted Harvey. "There have *not* been any major changes in the relative growth rates, inflation rates, and

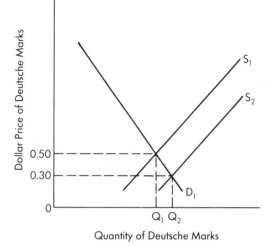

Figure 22-2   The Market for Foreign Exchange: An Increase in the Supply of Deutsche Marks
An increase in the supply of deutsche marks will reduce their dollar price and appreciate the value of the dollar; each dollar will now buy more deutsche marks than before.

interest rates between the United States and Germany during the past year. Instead, there has been major activity by the U.S. Federal Reserve Bank and other central banks to sell large amounts of dollars on the exchange market. Bank leaders even met openly in Geneva a year ago and announced they thought that the price of the dollar was too high (the dollar price of deutsche marks was too low). Since then these banks have been selling dollars in greater than normal amounts. That is, they have been buying currencies like deutsche marks with their dollars. Moreover, the president of the United States, the secretary of commerce, and the treasury secretary are in on this conspiracy. In several news conferences, they encouraged the central banks to sell dollars. Now, you and I both know these central banks are not attempting to make money by selling dollars. Central banks are government agencies, and they are not in business to make profits on their transactions. I conclude that they must be conspiring to drive Lizzy out of business. What do they have against Lizzy? Do you think she is an international spy?"

"Oh, Harvey," groaned Dr. Tandy. "You are a quick learner, but you leap to some wild conclusions. There is one more thing I have to tell you. Then you can put this mystery to rest."

DAY FIVE: THE SOLUTION

"Hello, Harvey, have you solved the 'Great Mystery'?" asked Lizzy as she noticed him standing in the waiting room to her office.

"Yes, I have, but you won't like the answer. It still doesn't solve your problem."

"Well, tell me about it anyway. I can take a little bad news," Lizzy said, as Harvey sat down near her desk.

"The problem had little to do with you when it all started. A year ago the

Board of Governors of the Federal Reserve System and other governmental central banks decided to do something to help the United States reduce the severe trade deficit that existed between United States and Germany and between the United States and Japan. American citizens were spending far more on German and Japanese products than German and Japanese were spending on U.S. exports. This deficit was creating pressures in the United States to enact restrictive tariffs and quotas. It also was causing German and Japanese banks to hold large numbers of U.S. dollars in their vaults.

"The central banks decided to sell millions of dollars on the exchange market. Thought of another way, the central banks bought vast quantities of deutsche marks and yen, using dollars. Our focus, of course, is on the deutsche mark. The increase in the demand for deutsche marks in the foreign exchange market increased the dollar price of deutsche marks. That is, the value of the U.S. dollar depreciated relative to the deutsche mark. The idea was to increase American exports and decrease American imports. American exports would rise because people abroad could get more dollars with each unit of their own currencies. Meanwhile, because Americans could get fewer units of foreign currencies with each dollar, they would reduce their imports."

"Harvey drew a graph (review Figure 22-1) on Lizzy's desk calendar to illustrate the impact of the policy on the exchange rate.

"The increased selling of dollars (buying of deutsche marks) increased the demand for deutsche marks and led to a higher price for the deutsche mark, or a lower valued dollar."

"Well, did the policy work?" Lizzy asked.

"So far is seems to be working. Exports from the United States to Germany have increased, and imports from Germany have declined since last year. The trade deficit still exists, but it is smaller than before the policy change."

"So I get hurt because the central banks are trying to correct a trade imbalance—that doesn't seem right. Why hurt businesses like mine? I give people jobs. My profits help contribute taxes to the federal coffers. Why don't they solve the trade deficit some other way?" Lizzy asked.

"Now don't take this result personally, Lizzy. It has nothing to do with you. It's impossible for governments to intervene in markets for foreign exchange without touching some people's lives in a negative way. You will need to take the lead of other importers and adjust your business to the reality of the new exchange rate. Also, you can hope that this depreciation of the dollar is temporary."

"Well, that's no solution: wait around until the dollar appreciates some time in the future. By that time, I'll be broke!" Lizzy sputtered.

"No, no," Harvey replied, "That's not my only recommendation. But you may still not like it."

"Oh, yeah? So what do you propose?" she asked.

"Continue to retain me as your consultant. I have some great ideas to enhance your business. You could switch to a Swiss supply source and buy the clocks cheaper than from Germany. I also have found several producers in the United States that make clones of German cuckoo clocks. They look just like the originals and cost one-third the amount you pay for the German clocks. It's time to turn to some substitute products. Act as everyone else does when the price of something rises; seek out substitutes."

"I see your point, Harvey, but why should I hire you? I can do the research myself and make these changes in my business."

"You can, but you shouldn't, Lizzy. Remember what you said five days ago. You have better things to do. You did then, and you still do. Unless you are willing to give up your income from being a sports agent, you are better off hiring me to find the best alternative products to sell and to monitor changes in the exchange rates of these products. Remember the notion of opportunity costs and the law of comparative advantage!"

"You are right, Harvey. I'll retain your services, but only as long as you raise more revenue than you add to my costs. Fair enough?"

"Fair enough," replied Harvey. "Meanwhile you should call the Indianapolis Colts general manager and work out an agreement for Johnny Longbomb. Neither you nor Johnny is making any money while he is unsigned and not playing."

"Watch your step, Cornwall. I hired you to consult with my cuckoo clock business. I do not need your help as a sports agent. Remember, free advice is usually worth as much as you pay for it."

STUDY QUESTIONS

1. If the dollar declines in value (depreciates) in the foreign exchange market, will it be easier or more difficult to sell U.S. products in other countries?

2. Suppose that before leaving on a trip to Canada, you read the following headline: "Value of U.S. dollar rises strongly against Canadian dollar." How will that increase alter the cost of your trip?

3. Explain how American exports create a supply of foreign currencies and our imports produce a demand for foreign currencies.

4. Predict the impact of each of the following occurrences on the value of the dollar:
   a. Interest rates soar in the United States, but remain constant elsewhere around the world.
   b. Economic growth expands rapidly in the United States, while recessions occur in the economies of our major trading partners.
   c. Deflation (a decline in the price level) occurs in the United States, while inflation is occurring in most other nations.
   d. Several central banks decide to buy large amounts of dollars in the foreign exchange market.

5. Explain how a rapid appreciation of the dollar would affect the profitability of U.S. import firms such as Lizzy's Place?

6. Explain why the following statement is true: "A rising American dollar price of British pounds implies a falling British pound price of American dollars."

7. One solution to Lizzy's drop in profits might be to increase the prices of the imported goods in her store. Under what elasticity of demand circumstances (Chapter 5) would this strategy work best? Under what elasticity conditions would price hikes most likely fail to restore her profits?

8. Discuss: "There would be much less international specialization—and thus lower gains from international trade—in the absence of a foreign exchange market."

GLOSSARY OF ECONOMIC TERMS

Ability-to-pay principle Theory of taxation that holds that people should be taxed according to their financial means, regardless of the direct benefits they receive from government.

Absolute advantage, law of Principle that trade will be beneficial to parties when each of them can provide a good or service that the other wants at a lower cost than if each provided for itself.

Aggregate demand A relationship expressing the total real output that consumers, business, and government will purchase at each general price level.

Aggregate supply A relationship expressing the total real output that producers will offer for sale at each general price level.

Appreciation of the dollar An increase in the international value of the dollar relative to the currency of some other nation; a dollar now buys more of another currency.

Automatic stabilizers Built-in features of the economy that automatically cushion recessions and retard expansions by injecting new spending or withdrawing spending power from the economy. Examples: unemployment benefits, income tax revenues.

Average revenue Total revenue divided by the number of units sold. Also referred to as per-unit revenue. AR = TR/Q.

Average total cost Total cost divided by output. Also termed per-unit cost. AC = TC/Q.

Balanced budget A budget in which government expenditures equal tax collections.

BUSINESS CYCLE · TROUGH · PEAK

DIFF. BTW. COMPAR.

VS. DEPRECIATION

282

& NATIONAL DEBT

Budget deficit The amount by which government expenditures exceed tax revenues.

Budget surplus The amount by which government tax revenues exceed expenditures.

REAL $ INVESTMENT

Capital Human-made items used to produce and deliver goods and services. Examples: machines, tools, transportation equipment.

Capital formation The production, accumulation, and use of human-made resources (plant, equipment, etc.) in an industry or economy. This improves productivity and enables economic growth.

Capital gains Increases in the value of an asset. *Realized* capital gains occur when the asset is sold. This income is taxed at special rates.

Capitalism An economic system characterized by private ownership and use of the means of production and distribution.

VS MONOPOLY

Cartel A group of producers or nations that act jointly in their production and pricing decisions. Example: OPEC.

Circular flow model A diagram illustrating the movement of money, products, services, and resources in the economic system. It shows the interdependence of all economic activity in the economy.

Collective bargaining The process of negotiation between management and a union to determine wage rates and working conditions.

Comparative advantage, law of Principle that trade will be beneficial to parties when each of them can provide a good or service that the other wants at lower opportunity cost than the trading partner.

Competition The effort of two or more parties, acting independently, to secure the business of a third party by offering the most favorable terms.

Complements Products or services that are used in conjunction, or jointly, with each other. If an increase in the price of A reduces the demand for B, then A and B are complements. Examples: tuition and textbooks, skis and ski-lift tickets.

Comprehensive Trade Act of 1988 U.S. legislation that sets up procedures for initiating unfair-trade investigations against nations charged with engaging in persistent patterns of unfair international trade.

Consumer Goods Items used to satisfy human wants. Products or services "used up" by buyers, as distinct from capital goods, which are used to produce other goods or services.

VS. CAPITAL GOODS

Consumer price index (CPI) A price index that compares the prices of a market basket of products and services in a current year with the prices of those same commodities in a different (base) year. Changes in the CPI are used to determine the rate of inflation in the economy.

& P.P.I.

Consumer sovereignty The idea that the consumer is the "ruler." The power of purchasers to determine, through their "dollar votes," what is to be produced in a market economy.

Consumption The using up of products and services in the satisfaction of human wants. Total consumption is the sum of all spending on products and services that are used by the purchaser.

Countervailing power The tendency for power on one side of a market to produce offsetting power on the opposite side. Example: monopsony hiring power versus union monopoly power.

Crowding out Theory that federal budget deficits increase interest rates, which then reduces private investment spending. According to this view, government spending "crowds out" investment spending.

CONNECTION: BUDGET DEFICIT

Demand A relationship expressing the quantities of a product or service that buyers are willing and able to

& LAW OF SUPPLY

purchase at various prices, all other things being constant.

Demand curve A graph of a demand relationship, showing the quantity of a commodity that buyers are willing to purchase at various prices. The usual demand curve slopes downward and to the right, indicating an inverse relationship between price and quantity demanded.

Demand deposit A promise by a bank to pay some amount of money to the owner of the deposit or to someone receiving a check from the owner. Checking account entry.

Deficient demand unemployment A situation in which people are out of work because of the general slowing of economic activity in the economy, that is, unemployment associated with recessions and depressions.

Demand determinants Factors that change the willingness and ability of consumers to buy commodities at each specific price. Examples: population, tastes, income, price and quality of related products, price expectations.

Demand inflation A condition of generally rising prices caused by levels of spending in the economy that exceed the ability of the economy to produce commodities and services. Also called demand-pull inflation.

Depository institution A financial institution that accepts deposits on which checks can be written.

Depreciation of the dollar A decrease in the international value of the dollar relative to the currency of some other nation; a dollar now buys less of another currency.

Depression A prolonged and severe recession characterized by major declines in real income and large increases in unemployment. Example: Great Depression of 1930s.

Derived demand Demand for a product or resource based on its contribution to the product for which it is used. Example: the demand for labor is derived from the demand for the products that labor helps produce.

Differentiated oligopolies Oligopolistic industries in which firms offer products or services that are distinct or different in some way from the products or services of rival firms. Examples: the automobile industry, the breakfast cereal industry.

Diminishing marginal returns A range of a production function over which added units of a resource input lead to successively smaller increases in output, or total product.

Diminishing marginal utility The principle that satisfaction (utility) declines with the consumption of successive units of a commodity.

Discount rate The interest rate that the Federal Reserve charges on loans it provides to commercial banks.

Diseconomies of scale Increases in minimum average cost produced by increased size of a firm.

Easy-money policy Federal Reserve actions that increase the rate of growth of the nation's money supply and reduce interest rates. This policy is used to push the economy out of a recession.

Economic growth The increase in the economy's real output or income over time. Growth rates are expressed in terms of real GNP and real GNP per capita.

Economic profit Total revenue minus total cost, where total cost includes a normal profit. Net revenue.

Economic resource A person or thing that possesses the ability to produce or aid in producing commodities and services that people value. Also, a factor of production. Classified into three groups: land, labor, and capital.

Economics The study of how society chooses to allocate scarce resources, produce products and services, and distribute the products and services to members of society.

Economies of scale Reductions in minimum average cost produced by increased size of a firm.

Effective tax rate The percentage of overall income paid in the form of a particular tax.

Efficiency Producing maximum output at minimum costs.

Elasticity coefficient (Midpoint formula)

$$\text{Elasticity} = \frac{Q_1 - Q_2}{(Q_1 + Q_2)/2} \div \frac{P_1 - P_2}{(P_1 + P_2)/2}$$

Elasticity of demand The degree to which consumers alter their purchases in response to a change in the price of a commodity or resource. If the percentage change in quantity demanded exceeds the percentage change in price, demand is *elastic*. If the percentage change in quantity demanded is less than the percentage change in price, demand is *inelastic*.

Elasticity of supply The degree to which sellers alter their offerings in response to the change in price of a commodity or resource. If the percentage change in quantity supplied exceeds the percentage change in price, supply is *elastic*. If the percentage change in quantity supplied is less than the percentage change in price, demand is *inelastic*.

Entrepreneur The person who takes the initiative in combining the other resources—land, labor, and capital—in producing goods and services; the innovator and risk taker who attempts to anticipate the wants of consumers.

Entry barriers Obstacles that prevent new firms from coming into an industry. Examples: patents, large economies of scale.

Equilibrium price The price that equates the quantities supplied and demanded in a market. A situation in which there is no tendency for the price to change, unless the factors held constant change.

Excess reserves All deposits held by banks that exceed the legal reserve requirement.

Explicit costs Money outlays that a firm makes to obtain resources; accounting costs such as wages and salaries, rent, interest, payments for equipment, and payments for raw materials. Compare "Implicit costs."

Exports Goods and services produced in a specific nation and sold to customers in other nations.

Externality Third-party effect. Positive or negative impact that is transferred to nonparticipants in a particular market. Examples: pollution (negative externality), inoculations against disease (positive externality).

Fallacy of composition The reasoning error of assuming that what is true for the part must necessarily be true for the whole.

Federal funds interest rate The interest rate charged on overnight loans between banks. Such loans are normally made for purposes of meeting the Federal Reserve's legal reserve requirement.

Federal Reserve System The central institution that oversees the monetary and banking system of the United States. It consists of the Board of Governors, 12 Federal Reserve banks, and member commercial banks. The Fed supplies the economy with currency and regulates the overall supply of money.

Final goods and services Goods and services that have been purchased by consumers, business, and government and do not become part of yet another consumer or capital good.

Fiscal policy The federal government's use of spending and taxing to influence the performance of the national economy. Examples: tax cuts, government spending changes.

Fixed costs Production costs that do not change as the level of output changes. Examples: insurance, cost of building and equipment.

Flat-rate income tax An income tax proposal that would levy a single tax rate on all taxable income.

Foreign exchange market The market in which the currency of one nation is exchanged for that of another nation.

Foreign exchange rate Price of one currency in terms of another.

Foreign purchases effect A decrease (increase) in aggregate real output that results from a decrease (increase) in foreign purchases brought about by a rise (fall) in the domestic price level.

Fractional reserve system A national banking system in which checking account entries exceed the actual cash reserves in the system. In the United States, banks have demand deposits that exceed the cash in the bank or cash deposited in the Federal Reserve bank. Yet, because of a reserve requirement, the Fed is able to control the total volume of bank credit and the supply of money in the economy.

Frictional unemployment Unemployment associated with the normal operation of the labor market. Unemployment arising from job quits, discharges, and job search by new and returning entrants to the labor force.

Full employment A condition in which the economy's resources are being fully used. Traditionally, a condition in which 96 percent of the labor force is employed, or 4 percent is unemployed. Many economists now use 94 percent and 6 percent to define full employment.

Gross national product (GNP) The total market value of all final goods and services produced by the economy during a specific year.

GNP per capita A measure of the average gross national product for each person in the country.

Homogeneous oligopolies Oligopolistic industries in which the firms produce generally standardized products. Examples: the crude oil industry, the steel industry.

Human capital The skills, knowledge, experience, and health embodied within people that enable them to be productive and earn income.

Implicit costs The money payments that self-owned resources could garner if they were employed in their best alternative employments. These costs are not part of a firm's accounting costs. Compare "Explicit costs."

Imports Goods and services sold in a nation different from the one in which they are produced.

Income effect Change in quantity of a good demanded by a buyer owing to a change in real income resulting from a price change.

Income mobility The degree to which a person or family moves from one level of income to another.

Incomes policy Government actions designed to control increases in the money income of people and institutions in the economy and thereby reduce inflation. Examples: mandatory wage-and-price controls, tax-based incomes plans (TIPs), jawboning.

Increasing marginal returns A range of production function over which added units of a resource input lead to successively larger increases in output, or total product.

Indexing The practice of tying all agreements involving prices and incomes to a cost-of-living index so that when inflation occurs, wages, rent, interest, profits, and transfer payments increase automatically and proportionally.

Inflation A general upward movement of the prices of most products and services in the economy. Usually measured by percentage changes in the consumer price index (CPI).

Interest rate effect A decrease (increase) in aggregate real output that results from an increase (decline) in the interest rate brought about by a rise (fall) in the price level.

Intermediate goods and services Goods and services used in the production process that eventually become part of final consumer or capital goods.

Inventory Stocks of goods that firms have on hand; unsold goods.

Investment Spending by business firms on capital (plant and equipment, etc.). Total investment is the sum of all spending on capital goods by business firms and other buyers.

Investment in human capital The purchase or acquisition of skills, knowledge, experience, and health that enable people to enhance their productivity and income. Examples: college education, on-the-job training.

Investment tax credit The tax provision that allows firms to subtract a specific percentage of their expenditures on new plant and equipment from the corporate income tax they owe.

Keynesians Economists who theorize that the economy is inherently unstable and that fiscal policy is the most influential means available to promote full employment, price stability, and economic growth.

Labor market The resource market in which labor services are bought (rented) and sold (rented out).

Liquidity The ease with which an asset can be quickly converted into products and services. Money is perfectly liquid; near-money is not.

Long run A period sufficiently long for firms to alter their basic capacity by changing the level of their plant and equipment. Also, a period sufficiently long for firms to enter or exit industries. In the long run, all costs are variable.

M1 A measure of the money supply that includes all currency in circulation plus checkable deposits.

M2 A measure of the money supply that includes all currency in circulation, plus checkable deposits, plus saving deposits.

Marginal analysis A comparison of added benefits and costs of an economic action.

Marginal cost The change in total cost associated with the production of one more unit of output. The added cost of producing one more unit. $MC = \triangle TC/\triangle Q$.

Marginal product The extra or additional number of units of a commodity that results from the employment of one more unit of a factor of production, when all other factors are held constant. When the factor is labor, the marginal product is the output added by hiring one more worker.

Marginal propensity to consume A measure of the tendency of the nation's population to consume a portion of each additional dollar of income. The change in consumption resulting from a dollar change in income. $MPC = \triangle C/\triangle Y$.

Marginal propensity to save A measure of the tendency of the nation's population to save a portion of each additional dollar of income. The change of saving resulting from a dollar change in income. $MPS = \triangle S/\triangle Y$.

Marginal revenue The added revenue gained by selling one additional unit of output. The change in total revenue associated with selling one more unit of output. $MR = \triangle TR/\triangle Q$.

Marginal revenue product The added revenue a firm obtains from hiring one more worker and selling the added output. The change in total revenue associated with hiring one more worker.

Marginal tax rate The percentage tax rate assessed on each additional dollar of income.

Marginal wage cost The extra, or added, cost to the employer of hiring one more worker. MWC = $\triangle$TWC/$\triangle$Q.

Market A grouping of buyers and sellers, exchanging products or services in some geographical area.

Market failure Areas of production or consumption where economic resources are not efficiently allocated by markets. Examples: monopoly, externalities, pure public goods.

Mixed economy An economic system characterized by an active market and government sector. The United States has this type of economic system.

Monetarists Economists who theorize that changes in the growth of the money supply cause inflation and recessions. These economists view fiscal policy as being ineffective.

Monetary policy Exercise of the Federal Reserve's power to increase or decrease the nation's money supply and thereby influence the economic condition of the economy. Tools of monetary policy include open-market operations, changes in the reserve requirement, changes in the discount rate.

Monetary "rule" The principle that the Federal Reserve should be given the charge to increase the nation's money supply at a legally set rate, irrespective of the temporary state of the economy.

Money Anything that is generally accepted as a medium of exchange, a store of value, and a standard of value.

Money multiplier Process by which the loaning of excess reserves by banks creates a multiple expansion of the money supply. Money multiplier = 1/reserve requirement.

Monopolistic competition A market situation characterized by numerous sellers, slightly differentiated products, and relative ease of entry. In the long run, only normal profits occur.

Monopoly A market in which there is a single seller, no close product substitutes, and blocked entry.

Monopoly profit A higher than competitive profit achieved by restricting production below the competitive level and charging a higher than competitive price.

Monopsony A market situation where there is a single buyer of a resource or product.

Multiplier The notion that a change in investment of government spending will increase income by some multiple. K = $\triangle$Y/$\triangle$I or $\triangle$G; K = 1/MPS.

National debt The amount of money that the government owes to lenders. Government borrows to finance expenditures that exceed tax revenues.

Natural Monopoly A situation in which the economies of scale are so extensive that only a single firm can successfully achieve the lowest possible costs of providing the product or service.

Natural rate of unemployment The unemployment rate to which the economy tends when all parties to contracts correctly anticipate inflation.

Near-money An asset that has many of the characteristics of money but is not as liquid as money. That is, people will not accept near-money as payment for products and services. Examples: corporate bonds, common stock, government securities.

Net exports Exports minus imports

New classical economics The theory that the economy is stable at the full-employment level of national output in the long run because of flexible product and resource prices.

Noncash benefit Government transfers in forms other than cash. Examples: food stamps, medical care, housing, subsidized lunches.

Nonprice competition The activities of firms designed to increase sales and market share without altering product prices.

Nontariff trade barriers Unnecessary regulations that make it costly for importers to get their goods approved for sale.

Normal profit The amount of profit necessary to keep capital and other factors of production in their present employments. This is compensation equal to the foregone gain of providing some other product or service.

Oligopoly An industry or market where a small number of firms accounts for most of the sales in an industry.

Open-market operations The Federal Reserve's main monetary policy tool, consisting of actions of buying and selling U.S. government securities in financial markets. Net buying of securities increases the money supply; net selling reduces it.

Opportunity cost The value of the benefit sacrificed by choosing one alternative rather than another. That which is forgone to pursue a first-choice of action.

Pegged exchange rate Foreign exchange rate (price for foreign currency) set by authorities.

Personal income distribution Shares of total income in the society received by persons or households. Often expressed in terms of percentages of total income received by each fifth of all income-receiving units.

Phillips curve A curve fitted to points that indicate the inflation and unemployment rates for each year in a set of years. According to many economists, the curve suggests a trade-off between inflation and unemployment.

Post hoc, ergo propter hoc fallacy "After this, therefore because of this." The reasoning error of concluding that event A caused event B, simply because event A preceded event B.

Poverty line An officially designated level of income below which an individual or family is considered to be poor. The poverty line in the United States is set at roughly three times the minimum food requirement.

Price-fixing An illegal agreement among sellers to charge the same prices for their products. A form of collusion.

Price leadership A pattern of behavior in an industry whereby one firm increases its price and, because of an "understanding," other firms respond by increasing theirs.

Price level The weighted average of the prices of the goods and services constituting national output. The price level is normally expressed as an index number that relates the prices of goods and services in a particular year to the prices of the same output when it was produced in a base, or reference, year.

Price level surprises Unexpected changes in the price level; changes in the price level that catch firms and workers off guard and therefore result in temporary changes in the level of national output.

Price rigidity A market situation where rivals are reluctant to change their prices, unless there is assurance that all rivals will match the change.

Prime interest rate The interest rate that commercial banks charge for loans granted to their best corporate customers.

Private property The basic institution of capitalism that gives people the

vs RECRESSIVE

right to buy, own, and sell economic resources and products. Private ownership and use of the factors of production, including capital, is an important feature of a market economy.

Producer sovereignty   The idea that the producer, not the consumer, controls the decision on what to produce in the U.S. economy. The view that large corporations, through product planning and massive advertising, shape consumers' demands for products and services.

Product differentiation   The activity of emphasizing attributes of a product that are actually or supposedly distinct from those of similar products of rivals. A form of nonprice rivalry.

Product market   Any place where buyers and sellers come into contact with each other for the purpose of buying or selling products and services for use in satisfying economic wants.

Production function   A concept, usually displayed graphically or algebraically, that shows the relationship between various levels of a resource (input) and the corresponding production outcomes (output).

Production possibilities curve   A curve showing the possible combinations of the output of two economic items, assuming that all existing resources are fully employed and technology is constant.

Productivity   Output per person-hour; output per unit of input.

Profit   The difference between a firm's total revenue and total cost. The residual after the payment of wages, rent, and interest to resource suppliers.

Profit motive   The incentive to produce products and services and sell them at prices that generate revenues that exceed costs. A major feature of a capitalist system.

Progressive tax   A tax where the rate increases as the tax base rises. Example: federal personal income tax, which has a higher tax rate at a higher income bracket.

Public sector   The segment of the total economy consisting of all government entities.

Pure competition   An industry or market characterized by many competitors, a standardized product, no control over price, and freedom of entry and exit. The long-run outcome of pure competition is an efficient allocation of resources. P = MC = AC.

Pure public goods   Commodities that have indivisible benefits and do not lend themselves to private sector production and sale. It is difficult to exclude people from receiving the benefits, even though they may not have paid for them. Examples: national defense, court system.

Quota   A legal limit on the quantity of a particular product or service that can be imported into a country.

Rational expectations theory   Hypothesis that people develop anticipations about government fiscal and monetary policies and then base their behavior on those anticipations. That behavior renders current fiscal and monetary policy useless as a tool to slow or stimulate the economy.

Real GNP   Gross national product adjusted to exclude the impact of inflation. Real GNP = monetary GNP/ price index.

Real income   The actual purchasing power of one's monetary income. Real income = monetary income/ price index.

Real interest rate   The rate of interest less the expected rate of inflation.

Recession   A period of at least two consecutive quarters of declining real GNP accompanied by lower real income and higher unemployment.

Regulation An economic function of government consisting of actions that set and enforce rules.

Reserve requirement The legal requirement that banks must maintain cash reserves equal to a specific percentage of their demand deposits.

Resource market Any place where buyers and sellers come into contact with each other for the purpose of buying or selling economic resources for use in the production process.

VS.
DISAVING

Saving Consumer after-tax income that is not spent on products and services.

Scarcity The concept that resources are limited. People desire more products and services than can be produced from the nation's limited resource pool. This is the central problem underlying all economic decisions.

Secondary effect The indirect consequence of an economic action or the effect of an effect. Example: raising the price of natural gas to reduce its consumption (primary effect) may increase the price of food (secondary effect) because fertilizer made from natural gas is used in the food production process.

Shortage A deficiency of quantity supplied relative to quantity demanded in a market. This occurs when price is lower than the equilibrium market price.

Short run A period in which a firm can vary its output through a more or less intensive use of its variable resources but cannot change the capacity of its plant and equipment. In the short run, some costs are fixed. Also, a period of time insufficient for firms to enter or leave an industry.

Socialism An economic system characterized by state or communal ownership and use of the means of production and distribution.

Stagflation A situation in which the economy experiences high levels of unemployment and rapid inflation simultaneously.

Strategic trade policy A set of policies such as tariffs and nontariff trade barriers undertaken by a nation to protect domestic industries from foreign competition. This protection permits the domestic firm to achieve economies of scale at home and therefore gain cost advantages in those international markets where there are no similar trade restrictions. Dominance in foreign markets eventually permits these firms to gain large economic profits.

Structural unemployment A situation in which people are out of work because they do not have skills that match those required for available jobs.

Substitutes Products or services that are interchangeable in satisfying consumer desires. If an increase in the price of A increases the demand for B, then A and B are substitutes. Examples: beef and pork, gin and vodka.

Substitution effect Change in the quantity of a good demanded by a buyer resulting from a change in the good's price, holding real income constant.

Supply A relationship expressing the quantities of a product or service that sellers are willing to offer for sale at various prices, all other things being constant.

Supply curve A graph of a supply relationship showing the quantity of a commodity that sellers are willing to sell at various possible prices. The usual supply curve slopes upward and to the right, indicating a direct relationship between price and quantity supplied.

Supply determinants Factors that change the willingness and ability of sellers to offer commodities for sale at each specific price. Examples:

MISERY INDEX

number of sellers, costs of production, price of other products, price expectations.

Supply inflation An increase in the general price level caused by increased costs of resources. Also referred to as cost-push inflation.

Supply shock A sudden, unanticipated rise in a price of a resource resulting in a reduction in aggregate supply. Often produces cost-push inflation.

Supply-side economics A set of proposals designed to increase aggregate supply in the economy, thereby reducing inflation and stimulating economic growth. Examples of such policies include tax rate reductions, regulatory reform, programs to increase saving and investment.

Surplus An excess of quantity supplied over quantity demanded in a market. This occurs when price is higher than the equilibrium market price.

Tariff A tax or duty on imported goods and services.

Tax deductions Allowances that taxpayers can legally subtract from their gross income to obtain their taxable income. Examples: charitable contributions, mortgage interest.

Tax equity Fairness of taxation. Principle that equals should be treated equally (horizontal equity) and unequals should be treated unequally (vertical equity).

Tax incidence Place of burden of a tax.

Tax shifting The partial or full transference of a tax from the party taxed to another party or group.

Technological innovation The introduction of new techniques for combining resources to produce products and services. This is a factor that promotes economic growth.

Tight-money policy Federal Reserve actions that reduce the rate of growth of the nation's money supply and in-

crease interest rates. This policy is used to reduce inflation.

Time lags The time between the enactment of an economic policy and its effect on the total economy.

Total cost The sum of a firm's fixed and variable costs. A firm's total payments to resource suppliers for use of land, labor, and capital in the production and distribution process. In economics, total cost also includes a normal profit.

Total product The total number of units of a commodity produced by a firm in a specific time period.

Total revenue A firm's total receipts from the sale of its product. Total revenue is equal to price per unit times the quantity of units sold.

Total revenue test A means of determining elasticity of demand. If total revenue and price move in the same direction, demand is inelastic. If total revenue and price move in opposite directions, demand is elastic.

Transfer payments Expenditures by government to people and firms for which there is no corresponding contribution to output. *Direct cash transfers* consist of money collected through taxes and delivered directly to recipients. *Noncash transfers* consist of transfers of products or services, such as food or health services, rather than cash.

Underemployment A situation that exists whenever workers are employed at jobs that have skill requirements far below their capabilities. Underemployment also occurs when people who desire to work full-time can only find part-time jobs.

Underground economy That portion of economic transactions in the economy that usually involve cash and escape taxation. Also referred to as the subterranean economy.

Unemployment The situation in which people 16 years of age or older are out of work and are either actively seeking jobs or are waiting to be called back to jobs from which they were laid off.

United States–Canadian Free Trade Agreement A 1989 accord that will eventually remove all trade barriers between the United States and Canada, that is, create a common free-trade zone.

U.S. government securities Treasury bills and notes issued by the federal government for the purpose of borrowing money.

Utility The amount of satisfaction a consumer receives from the use of a product or service. Want-satisfying ability.

Variable costs Production costs that change as the level of output changes. Examples: wages, fuel costs.

Wage-price controls (mandatory) Legal authority by government to set maximum wage-and-price limits and to prosecute violators. The most stringent form of incomes policy. Example: Nixon administration's mandatory controls in the early 1970s.

Wage-price standards (voluntary) A type of incomes policy that relies on voluntary compliance with wage-and-price guidelines established by government. Examples: wage-and-price guideposts established by the Kennedy, Johnson, and Carter administrations.

Wealth effect A decrease (increase) in aggregate real output that results from a decrease (increase) in real wealth brought about by a rise (fall) in the price level.

INDEX